EN SOUTHERN ILLINOIS:

A COMPLETE RECREATIONAL GUIDE

Lonnie D. Russell

Richard Goldstein

Les Winkeler

Cache
River
Press

Vienna, IL
Clearwater, FL

Library of Congress Catalogue Card Number 93-90943
ISBN 09627422-4-4

1st edition

Authors:
Lonnie D. Russell
Richard Goldstein
Les Winkeler

Publisher:
Cache River Press
Rt. 3, Box 239C
Vienna, IL 62595

Printed in the USA

Cover photographs courtesy of the Southern Illinoisan and the Carbondale
Convention & Tourism Bureau.

The authors are grateful to their wives and family members for support during the writing and production of this book. They are grateful to the many individuals who provided information and donated or consented to photographs. The authors thank the Southern Illinoisan Newspaper for providing photographs, Randy Tindall of Enterpise South for photographic work and Rick Linton for map composition while at the Southern Illinois Tourism Council. Thanks are also due to the tourism councils throughout Southern Illinois and the various tourism bureaus, especially the Carbondale Convention and Tourism Bureau.

Contents

•

•

•

Places to Go

•

Things To Do

●

Places to Eat

●

Places to Stay

Foreword

Lonnie Russell, Richard Goldstein and Les Winkeler paint a vivid portrait of the scenic beauty we call Southern Illinois. Their guide will be invaluable to visitors and residents alike as they explore the lush forests and clear lakes, enjoy the outdoor recreation and fascinating historical tradition, and revel in the cultural bonanza of festivals and celebrations. I encourage all to read this well-researched guide to the pleasures and riches of our region.

Paul Simon
United States Senator

Preface

Most people don't know it exists since, for too many people, Illinois and Chicago are synonymous. But, for those of us acquainted with the diverse beauty of the southern part of our state, that line of thinking is heresy. Southern Illinois in no way resembles the concrete maze of Chicago. And, Southern Illinois is a far cry from the prairie flatlands of the central portion of the state.

Southern Illinois is unique. The Ozark foothills take hold just south of Illinois 13. Hills are the essence of deep Southern Illinois. Southern Illinois has crystal clear lakes, pristine creeks and mighty rivers, but the hills define the region. Along the Mississippi River it is the bluffs which define the scenery, coming to a glorious climax at Pere Marquette State Park north of St. Louis.

On the other hand, there are portions of Southern Illinois that more closely resemble the bayous of Louisiana. Of these, the Cache River and LaRue Swamps are federally protected wetlands.

The people of the region are as diverse as the topography. The area was settled by immigrants from Europe who mined the coal and fluorspar and farmed the rocky hills. From the French Colonial settlements at Cahokia to the grand Victorian mansions of Cairo, Southern Illinois has a wealth of historic tradition waiting for inspection.

Amongst the natural beauty of the region are the cultural and educational centers, Carbondale and the Metro East, providing a complete recreational opportunity for Southern Illinois

Through it all, the area retained its natural beauty. It is a haven for people who enjoy seeing nature, not those who just want to see nature through the glow of neon signs or from the artificial grass of a miniature golf course.

Southern Illinois remains virtually unspoiled. **Take the time to enjoy it.**

Lonnie Russell
Richard Goldstein
Les Winkeler

Introduction

Southern Illinois is not just the lower part of the "Land of Lincoln"; it is significantly different from the rest of the Prairie State.

For instance, the southernmost tip of Illinois is some 70 miles farther south than Richmond, Va. The Shawnee National Forest, located entirely in Southern Illinois, is the only national forest in Illinois, and the Illinois Ozarks are among the few "mountain ranges" in the country that run east-west instead of north-south.

These are some of the reasons why newspapers in the area spell Southern Illinois with a capital "S"–to distinguish it from the flat, unforested region to the north.

This part of the state also is known as "Egypt," but trying to pin down just why it is called Egypt is a little like trying to figure out which came first, the chicken or the egg.

If you look at a map of Southern Illinois, you will see a number of towns with the same names as cities in the north African country of Egypt, names like Cairo, Thebes and Karnak.

But if you check back in the records, you will find that Cairo–which, by the way, is pronounced "care-oh," rather than "kie-ro," its counterpart in Africa–was founded in 1837, several years after Southern Illinois started to be called Egypt.

A more plausible story goes like this: The winter of 1830-31 in central and northern Illinois was the most severe the settlers could remember. Snow and ice stayed on the ground well into the normal planting season, preventing farmers from planting corn, their principal crop.

As a result, the harvest that year was meager and the farmers, fearful they would not have enough seed corn for the following year's crop, started to make trips to the southern end of the state, which had been spared the severe weather in the north, to buy seed corn.

On the way back home, when asked where they had been, they

said that, like Jacob in the Old Testament, they "saw there was corn in Egypt," and they went down into "Egypt" to buy corn. The name stuck.

Just how much of the state is Southern Illinois, or Egypt? There is no question that the region is bounded on the west by the Mississippi River, on the south by the Ohio River, and on the east by the Wabash River. There is less agreement about the northern boundary. Sometimes the region is considered to be the 34 southernmost counties of the state. Sometimes as many as 40 counties are included.

Traveling through Southern Illinois, you will occasionally hear it called "Little Egypt," a name sometimes applied to the whole area and sometimes just to the 11 southernmost counties.

However, purists, like the late Will Griffith, who published a magazine called the *Egyptian Key* in the early 1940s, have become quite incensed by the use of "Little Egypt" to describe their beloved Southern Illinois. "Little Egypt," Griffith moralized, was the name of a belly dancer featured at the Columbian Exposition in Chicago in 1893.

Culturally, Southern Illinois is a product of three civilizations–the Native Americans, who date back thousands of years; the Europeans who first explored and then settled the area, notably the French some 300 years ago–and then the English; and finally, the new Americans who moved west beginning after the Revolutionary War.

Names of locations in the area reflect these cultures, starting with Indian names like Kaskaskia, which became the first capital of the state of Illinois, and Cahokia, site of what was once the largest prehistoric community north of Mexico.

Father Jacques Marquette and Louis Joliet explored what is now Southern Illinois on a canoe trip down the Mississippi River in 1673. French traders and then settlers soon followed. The English were the next to occupy Southern Illinois. After winning the French and Indian War in 1763, Fort Kaskaskia was renamed Fort Gage. Then it was the Americans' turn, when George Rogers Clark and his "Long Knives" defeated the English in 1778.

However, the area still has a number of location names of French origin, such as Prairie du Rocher, meaning the "meadow by the rock", located beneath the imposing bluffs that overlook the American

Bottoms; and Beaucoup Creek, the creek "with plenty" (of water).

Over the years, French pronunciations have been lost in many cases. Du Rocher no longer is called "doo-roe-SHAY," but "doo-ROE-sher"; Beaucoup, pronounced in French "boe-COO," has become Americanized to "BUCK-up."

Many a Southern Illinois town has been named for a European capital, but its pronunciation has been Americanized or Mid-Westernized. So New Athens is pronounced with a long, rather than a short, "A". Contrary to popular belief, Vienna (pronounced VIE anna) was not named for the European capital, but was named after Vienna Reynolds, a daughter of a local building contractor.

Speaking of names, many Southern Illinois counties were named after Revolutionary War heroes. St. Clair County, for instance, which originally encompassed most of what is now Southern Illinois, was named for Gen. Arthur St. Clair, who was named commander-in-chief of the U.S. Army after the war and then governor of the Northwest Territory, part of which later became Illinois.

Randolph County, also one of the first Illinois counties, was named for Edmund Randolph, who fought in the Revolution and then served as secretary of state and attorney general under President George Washington. Washington County, of course, was named for the first president. Hamilton County was named for Alexander Hamilton, Revolutionary War soldier and later first secretary of the treasury. Jackson County was named for Gen. Andrew Jackson in 1816, when Illinois was still a territory (two years before statehood). In 1815, Jackson had won the Battle of New Orleans at the end of the War of 1812. He later went on to become the seventh president of the United States. Franklin and Jefferson counties were named for two other giants of American history–Benjamin Franklin and Thomas Jefferson.

Southern Illinois was the first section of Illinois to be settled, partly by Revolutionary War veterans who were given land grants by the federal government. Other pioneers streamed through Shawneetown on the Ohio River, where the land office was located in the early years of the 19th century. Land could be bought in those days for as little as $2 an acre.

The Bank of Illinois, the state's first bank, was established in

Shawneetown in 1816 at the home of its founder, John Marshall. The Shawneetown State Bank was established not long afterwards and the town became known as the financial capital of Illinois.

A favorite story in Shawneetown, even today, tells of a group of Chicago men who applied to the Shawneetown State Bank in the 1830s for a loan to help them develop what was then just a village on Lake Michigan. After due consideration, the story goes, bank officials turned down the loan application because "Chicago was just too far from Shawneetown ever to amount to anything."

Illinois achieved statehood in 1818. Kaskaskia became the first capital and Shadrach Bond was elected the first governor. But it is the home of the first lieutenant governor, Pierre Menard, that still stands. Overlooking the Mississippi River near Fort Kaskaskia State Historic Site, the home has been carefully restored and is open to the public as a museum.

Besides its man-made attractions, such as the Menard home, the Creole House in Prairie du Rocher (the oldest house in the region), the Crenshaw House (Old Slave House) at Equality, the early 19th century Rose Hotel in Elizabethtown, the antebellum Magnolia Manor in Cairo, and the 112-foot Cross of Peace at Alto Pass, Southern Illinois boasts a wealth of natural beauty.

Among the most scenic areas are the Pine Hills, with their 300-foot bluffs overlooking the Mississippi, the Garden of the Gods, and Giant City State Park, with its magnificent rock formations.

There are now a number of fine lakes in Southern Illinois–all man-made. When George Rogers Clark and his men traveled from Kentucky to engage the British at Fort Gage, they slogged their way through waist-deep water in seemingly endless swamps. Much of that water now has been contained in impoundments such as Lake of Egypt, Crab Orchard Lake, Little Grassy Lake, Devils Kitchen Lake, Cedar Lake, Lake Kaskaskia, and Rend Lake, to name a few.

For thousands of years, Southern Illinois has served as the winter home of huge flocks of Canada geese and other waterfowl. Crab Orchard National Wildlife Refuge near Carterville and the recently established Cypress Creek National Wildlife Refuge near Cache, the Rend Lake Conservation Area, and state conservation areas in Union and Alexander counties help maintain that waterfowl population, which annually attracts a multitude of hunters and bird watchers to the area. Southern Illinois' well-stocked lakes also are a big attraction to fishermen.

No description of Southern Illinois would be complete without mention of its institutions of higher education. Southern Illinois Normal University, or Southern Illinois State Teachers College, as it was sometimes called, was chartered in 1869. When the new school opened in July 1874, just 53 students enrolled for a four-week summer institute. Out of that small teachers college grew Southern Illinois University at Carbondale and Southern Illinois University at Edwardsville, plus a School of Medicine at Springfield, which together enroll some 35,000 students annually in a full range of under-graduate and graduate programs.

In addition to fulfilling its major roles of education, research and service to Southern Illinois, the SIU system, according to a recent study, pumps nearly a billion dollars annually into the region in direct and indirect benefits. This is an important contribution to the economy of the region, which depends largely on coal mining, light industry and service-related businesses for its livelihood.

Southern Illinois also is home to several excellent community colleges, including John A. Logan College at Carterville, Shawnee College at Ullin, Southeastern Illinois College at Harrisburg and Rend Lake College at Ina.

State, Federal, & Private Recreation Areas

Devils Kitchen Lake (Southern Illinoisan photo)

L ooking at a map of Illinois, notice the red designations for government (either state or federal) operations. Some of these represent colleges, some prisons, but most represent nature sites–state parks, conservation areas, state forests, nature preserves and federal recreation areas. As you look farther south you'll notice that the red designations get thicker and thicker. That's Southern Illinois.

The **Shawnee National Forest** accounts for most of the state south of Illinois 13. Within the forest are the sandstone-laden Shawnee Hills of which Giant City State Park is a prominent example. Slightly farther to the west are the older and less rocky, though still rugged, **Illinois Ozarks**. Better known for their presence in Missouri, the Ozark hills stretch into Illinois and their charm can be experienced, along with camping, picnicking, and hiking, in the Trail of Tears State Forest in Union County.

The Shawnee Hills and Illinois Ozarks are the deep Southern Illinois terrain with which people from the area are familiar. But also present are the amazing southern swamps centered around the **Cache River**. The only thing missing from these shallow green cypress and tupelo filled bodies of water are the alligators. On most other counts, including a plentiful supply of great blue herons, the shallow lakes, slow moving rivers and settled swamps would be mistaken for their cousins hundreds of miles to the south in Louisiana. Recreational areas that provide a taste of this swampy terrain include Horseshoe Lake in Alexander County at the border with Kentucky and Heron Pond and Little Black Slough in Johnson County only a few miles to the north.

North of the national forest you'll find that wilderness and accompanying recreational facilities are more dispersed. However, the **Mississippi**, **Ohio** and **Wabash Rivers** bounding the state provide some of the most beautiful vistas and most accessible recreation areas in Southern Illinois. Included among these sites are Pere Marquette State Park north of St. Louis on the confluence of the Illinois and Mississippi Rivers; and Beall Woods Conservation Area and Preserve south of Vincennes, Indiana, on the Wabash River.

Toward the interior of Illinois the typical recreational area north of Illinois 13 is a neatly manicured conservation area or state park (they look much the same) on a gently rolling, forested landscape with a lake planted in the center of it. Some of these areas provide the added bonus of a rich historical tradition like Red Hills State Park next to Lawrenceville. It was known as the crossroads for 19th century travel between Vincennes, Indiana, and all points west and south. Others have more prosaic beginnings like Pyramid State Park near Pinckneyville; it was born of extensive strip mining dating from the 1800s.

Southern Illinois is pockmarked by lakes and yet you would be hard-pressed to find one put there by Mother Nature. These lakes are the works of man, some built during the Depression by the Civilian Conservation Corps such as Crab Orchard Lake between Carbondale and Marion. The biggest lakes in Southern Illinois, Rend Lake near Benton and Carlyle Lake, were built for flood control in the 1960s and 1970s by the Army Corps of Engineers. Others like Lake of Egypt in Johnson County and Newton Lake, southeast of Effingham, cool the hot water from electric power plants.

Each lake has a unique combination of recreational facilities. Newton Lake is a secluded area with hiking and horse trails and a few boat ramps and picnic areas. It is better known for its fishing than for water sports. Rend Lake and Carlyle Lake, on the other hand, are recreational areas *par excellence*. Both provide abundant campsites along the banks and marinas to service the water sportsmen, while Rend Lake also has first class water-side lodging and fine dining.

The facilities from other recreational areas were built during the Depression by government works programs. The sandstone and oak lodges with dining facilities at Pere Marquette and Giant City State Parks are quite similar in appearance because they share the Civilian Conservation Corps (CCC) as builders. Likewise, the few remaining fire towers in the region, one at Trail of Tears State Forest and one buried deep within the Shawnee National Forest, were built by the CCC.

Interpretive centers like the Red Barn at Beall Woods are infrequent since they are expensive to maintain. But the Touch of Nature Environmental Center provides groups with a traveling guide to the natural riches of the region.

Map Key for State, Federal & Private Recreational Areas

1 ....Pere Marquette State Park
2 ....Frank Holten State Park
3 ....Horseshoe Lake State Park–Madison County
4...Carlyle Lake
5 ....Washington County State Conservation Area
6.....Kaskaskia River & Baldwin Lake Fish & Wildlife Area
7...Pyramid State Park
8...Rend Lake
9................................Randolph County Conservation Area
10...Kinkaid Lake
11 ....Lake Murphysboro State Park
12 ....Crab Orchard National Wildlife Refuge
13...........................Little Grassy and Devils Kitchen Lakes
14 ....Touch of Nature Environmental Center
15 ....Giant City State Park
16 ....Trail of Tears State Park
17 ....Union County Conservation Area
18 ....Horseshoe Lake Conservation Area
19 ....Ferne Clyffe State Park
20...Lake of Egypt Recreation Area
21 ....Sam Parr State Park
22...................................Newton Lake Fish & Wildlife Area
23...Red Hills State Park
24 ....Stephen A. Forbes State Park
25 ....Sam Dale Lake Conservation Area
26 ....Beall Woods Conservation Area & Preserve
27 ....Hamilton County Conservation Area
28...................................Saline County Conservation Area
29 ....Rim Rock/Pounds Hollow
30 ....Garden of the Gods

31	Bell Smith Springs
32	Dixon Springs State Park
33	Lake Glendale
34	Camp Ondessonk
35	Cave-In-Rock State Park
36	Mermet Lake Conservation Area

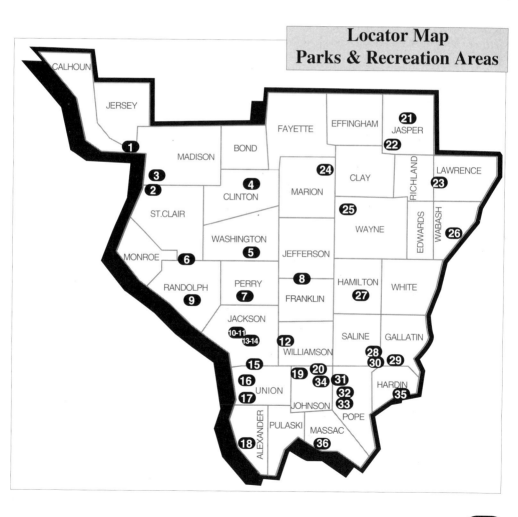

Locator Map
Parks & Recreation Areas

CALHOUN

JERSEY

FAYETTE   EFFINGHAM   JASPER **21**

22

1   MADISON   BOND

3   **24**   CLAY   RICHLAND   LAWRENCE **23**

2   CLINTON   MARION

25

ST.CLAIR   WAYNE   EDWARDS   WABASH **26**

4

WASHINGTON   **5**   JEFFERSON

MONROE   **6**

RANDOLPH   PERRY   **8**   HAMILTON   WHITE

9   **7**   FRANKLIN   **27**

JACKSON

10-11   SALINE   GALLATIN

13-14   **12**   **28**   **29**

WILLIAMSON   **30**

15   **20**

16   **19**   **34**   **31**   HARDIN

17   UNION   **32**   **35**

JOHNSON   **33**

ALEXANDER   PULASKI   MASSAC   POPE

18   **36**

11

① *Pere Marquette State Park*

There is no more ideally situated state park in Illinois than Pere Marquette. It lies across blufftops facing the Illinois River. The steep trails take visitors to spectacular vistas of the river and the government has taken advantage of the location by building an elegant lodge and conference center which provides dining, accommodations and a swimming pool. Other facilities are provided including a marina and stables.

The most outstanding of the two big lodges built in Southern

Park interpreter, Scott Isinghausen, at Lovers Leap

Illinois in the 1930s by the Civilian Conservation Corps is at Pere Marquette State Park; the other is at Giant City State Park. The main entrance of the lodge opens into a high-ceilinged lobby with a 700-ton fireplace dominating. The biggest chess set you're ever likely to see also graces the large windowed area. Beyond is the dining room which is well known for its fried chicken. Delicacies such as catfish from the nearby river are on the menu. A cocktail lounge is nearby.

Fifty luxury guest rooms are available. Cabins are provided for overnight accommodation as well, some of which provide scenic views of the Illinois River.

An extraordinary feature of the land bordering the Illinois and Mississippi Rivers in this area is an ancient, finely-granulated dust called loess. The loess has blown up from the river bed over the past million years and has become so tightly compacted that the 100 feet and more it has added to the blufftops does not erode. The result is such spectacular views as Lovers Leap and McAdam's Peak which towers 372 feet above the Illinois River.

McAdam's Peak looks down on a still portion of the Illinois River and the backwater called Stump Lake, a favorite of duck and goose hunters. It is a highlight of the park because in 1892 100 Mississippian Indian skeletons were discovered at the site. A plaque commemorates the find.

The park is named for the French priest-explorer Father Jacques Marquette. In 1673 the priest and his group, led by Louis Joliet, were the first Europeans to find the confluence of the Illinois and Mississippi Rivers, though the confluence is not visible from the park. A white cross commemorating their find is located just to the east of the park.

Modern day explorers and campers are well provided for at Pere Marquette. Both vehicular (class A with electricity) and tent **camping** (class B) are available. All campgrounds are equipped with toilets, showers, sanitary facilities, and picnic shelters. For would-be campers without the necessary equipment, park staff will build your campsite. On a wooden floor the staff will erect a wall tent with cots, a grill, a picnic table, a fire ring, fire extinguisher, broom, dust pan, trash barrel and camp light.

Only minutes from St. Louis, Pere Marquette is the most visited park in Southern Illinois. Reservations may be necessary for camping sites. Call (618) 786-3323, or for group camping write to the Pere Marquette Site Superintendent's Office, P.O. Box 158, Grafton, IL 62037.

Visitors with boats will find safe haven at the **Pere Marquette Marina**. Providing gasoline and overnight boat accommodation, the marina, (618)-786-3546, can be used as a base from which to explore the Illinois River or to see the confluence of the Illinois and Mississippi rivers only a few short miles to the east. The marina also features an outdoor cafe which serves light fare including sandwiches and ice cream. Some slips may be reserved. If anglers can escape the marina's lures for the river's currents they will find white and large-mouth bass, bluegill, carp, catfish, crappie and warmouth.

Horse enthusiasts are served by the **Pere Marquette Stables**. Two miles south of the lodge on Illinois 100, the stables offer hour-long guided rides for $10 and reductions for groups. The stables also provide boarding for horses that are privately owned. For more information call (618) 786-2156. The park has 12 miles of trails and a parking area for trailers.

Another reason for visiting Pere Marquette State Park is the **Raging Rivers Water Park** in Grafton (Jersey County) off Illinois 100. This is a giant water park with several flumes and waterslides as well as a wave pool. The park also features an area for small children to splash about. The park is open daily from Memorial Day to Labor Day, from 10:30 a.m. - 7 p.m. at the beginning and end of the summer and 8 p.m. in the middle. Prices are $12.95 for adults, $9.95 for children, free for children two and under and $4.95 for senior citizens over age 55. For more information call 1-800-548-7537.

To reach Pere Marquette, take I-270 to Illinois 3 heading north. From Alton, take Illinois 143/100 heading north along the scenic Mississippi. Stay on Illinois 100 until you come to the park entrance just west of Grafton.

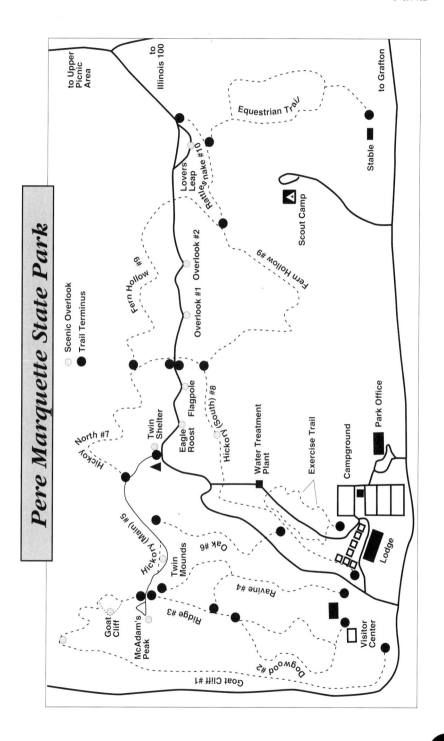

Pere Marquette State Park

Frank Holten State Park

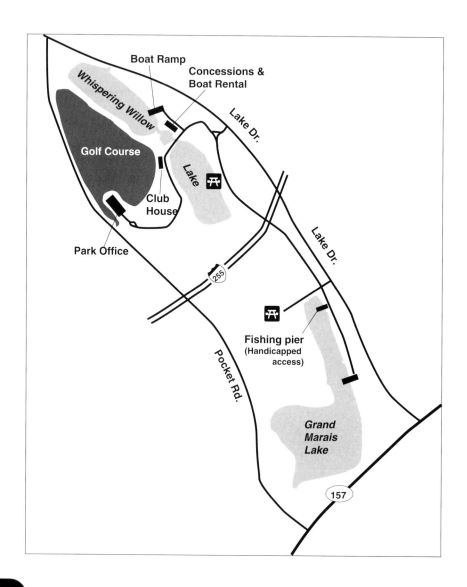

As you approach St. Louis the prairie lands and tree covered hills melt away in favor of concrete and clogged traffic. In short, Southern Illinois becomes urban. On the edge of St. Louis is one of America's most notorious cities, East St. Louis. Known for little more than poverty and violence, there is a state park at the center of this urban jungle whose green boundaries encompass an 18-hole golf course as well as lakes for fishing.

Formerly a city park, Frank Holten State Park has remained a show place for a city sorely in need of them. The radio controlled speed boat competition is a special event every September which draws competitors from across the country and an annual fishing derby each July gives children ages 14 and under a chance to show off their fishing prowess.

The 1,150-acre park features an open format with St. Louis' Gateway Arch clearly visible across the nearby Mississippi River. Grand Marais Lake on the southeastern end of the park has a fishing pier with handicapped access, and a boat ramp with the normal compliment of bluegill, catfish and a few largemouth bass.

Picnic areas are available in the center of the park near Grand Marais Lake and by Whispering Willow Lake on the opposite end. Nearly half of the picnic tables provide handicapped access as do the bathrooms. Concessions (there are no boat rentals) are on the northwestern side of the lake, as is the pro shop for the **golf course**. Rates are quite reasonable at no more than $12 for 18 holes on the weekend, a dollar less on weekdays.

Showing its roots as a city park, a soccer field, basketball court and softball field are all available for visitors. Hunting and camping are not allowed but a special treat is in store for bird lovers.

Frank Holten State Park is divided by I-255. To get to the park, turn off I-255 at the East St. Louis exit, turn right at the first stop sign then left and you will run into the park.

3 *Horseshoe Lake–Madison Co.*

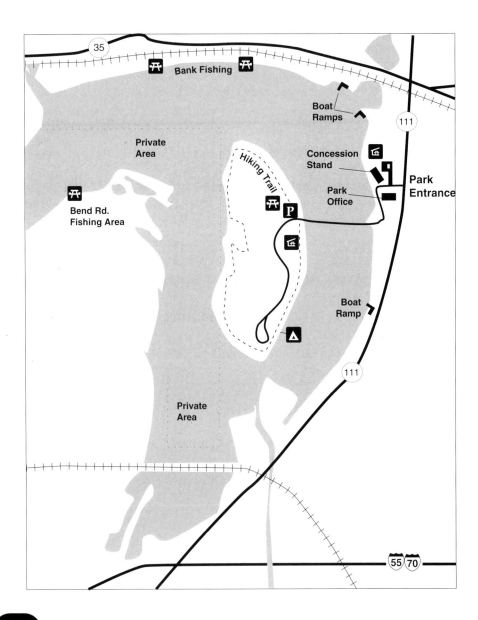

One of two prominent Horseshoe Lakes in Southern Illinois, the northern one is found in a very different environment than the lake at the base of the state near Cairo. Horseshoe Lake State Park in Madison County is in the midst of farm fields, but is only minutes from the urban centers of St. Louis and the surrounding Metro East area.

It lies on the outskirts of what was once the thriving Indian community of Cahokia. Although Indians lived in the area as far back as 8000 B.C., Cahokia was the first real civilization in North America and remains of a platform mound, that which Cahokia Indians are famous for, is still visible on the park grounds.

Indicative of its age, the lake is old and very shallow which means it is good for bluegill fishing. A road leading out to the island in the center of the lake provides many a fisherman with angling opportunities. Hikers can take a four-mile round trip tour of the island on the somewhat barren nature trail which circles it.

Picnic areas, shelters and a concession stand are available at the edge of the lake, and there is a camping area at the southern end of the island.

Horseshoe Lake is just off Illinois 111, north of Illinois I-55/70 near Granite City.

4

Carlyle Lake

The biggest lake in Southern Illinois and the biggest man-made lake in the state was built by the U.S. Army Corps of Engineers to control flooding along the Kaskaskia River. Since its completion in 1967 it has served this purpose in addition to providing outdoor recreation for millions each year. The wide open 26,000-acre lake is ideal for motor boating, sail boating and fishing, and the recreational areas surrounding the lake, including two state parks, provide camping sites, boat launches and swimming beaches for visitors. Hunters are served by the 11,000 acres of government land surrounding Carlyle Lake.

The recreational facilities at the lake are geared towards boaters and campers. Boat launches and camping sites are plentiful at each of the ten recreational areas surrounding the lake. In addition, three marinas and a sailboat harbor provide the necessities for boat owners and renters. There is no horsepower limit on the lake which makes skiing a popular activity. Sailors will find regattas in which they can match their skill with regional, national and international competition (see Sailing Section).

During the summer, interpretive programs are offered by rangers at the amphitheaters. Call for schedules. The fauna is a typical Southern Illinois mix of deer, squirrel, quail, rabbit, foxes and coyotes.

If your inclination is to eat the wildlife rather than learn about it, a controlled pheasant hunt is sponsored by the Illinois Department of Conservation at **Eldon Hazlet State Park**. Other Illinois regulated hunting is allowed on surrounding Army Corps of Engineers maintained land. Fishermen can cast for a wide variety of fish including carp, white and largemouth bass, channel cats, bullhead, drum as well as crappie and bluegill.

Eldon Hazlet was a Carlyle lawyer who had the idea that a lake was needed to control flooding in the Kaskaskia River basin. The park named for him is on the lake's southwest shore, and is packed with facilities. Most facilities are camping and camping related. Spaces for 336 camping trailers (class A), most of which provide handicapped access, and another 36 tent campers will fit into the main Illini camp-

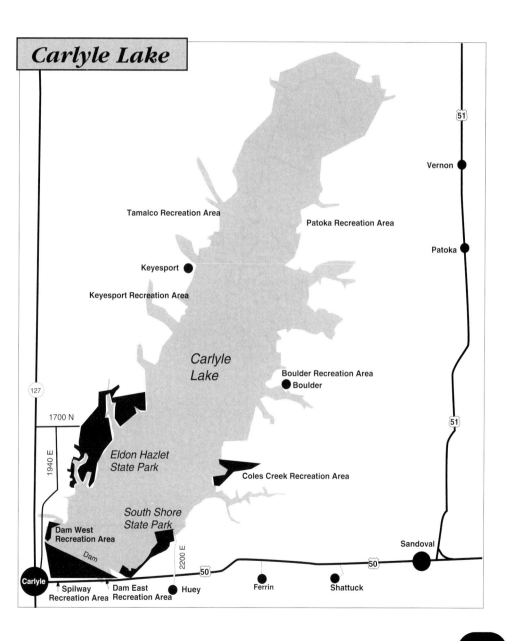

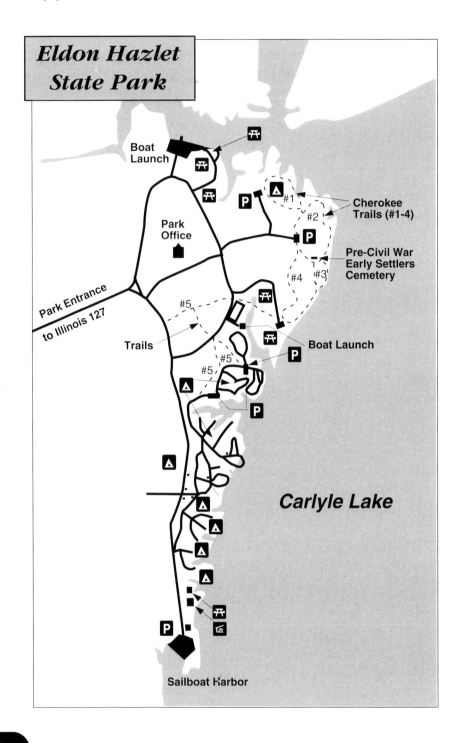

Eldon Hazlet State Park

Boat Launch

Park Office

Park Entrance to Illinois 127

Trails

#5

#5

#5

#1

#2

#4 #3

Cherokee Trails (#1-4)

Pre-Civil War Early Settlers Cemetery

Boat Launch

Carlyle Lake

Sailboat Harbor

ground alone. Illini occupies a narrow 1.5 mile strip along the lake, which means that many of the sites border the water. To assure a water-side site visitors may reserve one of 60 sites up to 14 days in advance. Both shower buildings have handicapped access. The concession area provides bait for fish and food for people, in addition to a laundry. Laundry detergent can be purchased from the concessionaire.

Boat ramps can be accessed on the northern and southern end of the park, and a **sailboat harbor** of the **Carlyle Sailing Association** is available for a fee to non members ($3 on weekdays and $5 on weekends). In addition to docking facilities the harbor provides parking, a playground area, showers and a large shelter with electricity. The complex has a boat launching ramp and electric hoists which can place boats as heavy as 2,000 pounds in the water. Overnight docking and open-water mooring is not permitted. Call (618) 594-3622 for more information.

The land around Carlyle Lake was flat farmland and is now simply flat. Hikers will have no difficulty walking the **trails** which are generally uneventful. An exception is the trail at the north end of the state park which leads to a small pre-Civil War cemetery.

To reach Eldon Hazlet State Park from St. Louis or the Metro East area, take U.S. 50 to Illinois 127 and go north. The lake and park are just east of Rt. 127. From the north or south, take Illinois 127 until you are about two miles north of Carlyle.

5 *Washington County*
Conservation Area

Entry sign at Washington County State Conservation Area

Washington County Conservation Area features a medium-sized lake and seasonal hunting to complement a plentiful supply of picnicking and camping areas.

The conservation area is rather flat but this makes for easy hiking along the seven-mile trail which circles the lake. Along the trail, the hiker will see stands of pines and fallow fields.

There are several picnic areas on the east and west sides of the elongated lake while all the camping areas and boat ramps are found on the west side. A concession stand is also located on the west side of the lake.

Class A and C camping are available and three camping pads with handicapped access are included within the A sites.

While hiking or enjoying a picnic, visitors will have the opportunity to spy some of the wildlife which call the conservation area home. These include rabbit, quail, dove, deer and woodcock.

Hunters, on the other hand, might take advantage of the game for shooting practice. Shotgun and archery hunting is allowed and a special "put and take" program brings quail and pheasants into the park.

The lake has an 11-mile shoreline with numerous fingers and contains largemouth bass, bluegill, crappie, catfish and carp for the fisherman's pleasure. Ten horsepower engines are allowed on the lake.

The conservation area is four miles south of Nashville just off Illinois 127. From I-64 take exit 50 then travel south for eight miles to the conservation area.

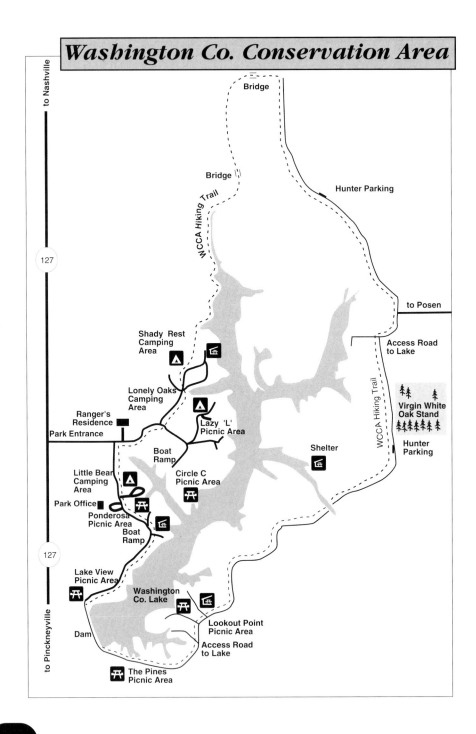

Washington Co. Conservation Area

6 *Kaskaskia River & Baldwin Lake Fish & Wildlife Area*

In the southwest corner of Illinois, about 70 miles south of St. Louis, the Kaskaskia River finishes its journey from the middle of the state at Champaign and empties into the Mississippi. At this end point for the Kaskaskia the nature preserve begins, following the river to Fayetteville in St. Clair County. Along the way visitors can take advantage of numerous oxbows for fishing, the mixed bottomland forest for hunting or trail use and the periodic boat ramps which give access to the river itself.

The preserve extends for 37 miles from the Mississippi. At mile 10 off Illinois 3 next to Evansville are boat ramps and parking. Further on at mile 20 off Illinois 154 is a boat ramp and marina and bait shop serving fishermen and boaters alike.

Just beyond this area is **Baldwin Lake**, a watery expanse which was built for cooling power plant discharge. On the west side of the lake is parking, a picnic shelter, a boat launch and a fishing levee with handicapped access. The lake is a good place to fish for largemouth bass, bluegill, catfish and hybrid striped bass thanks to its isolation and the hot water flow from the power plant. But Baldwin Lake rules do not allow water skiing, sail boating, or swimming, because the shallow flat land surrounding the lake make it prone to strong wind gusts. A 50 horsepower limit is imposed. Another popular activity at Baldwin Lake is viewing the thousands of geese and ducks which winter there.

Continuing along the Kaskaskia River, two more boat ramps give access to the river at mile 30 off Illinois 13 and at the end of the preserve area at Fayetteville off Illinois 15.

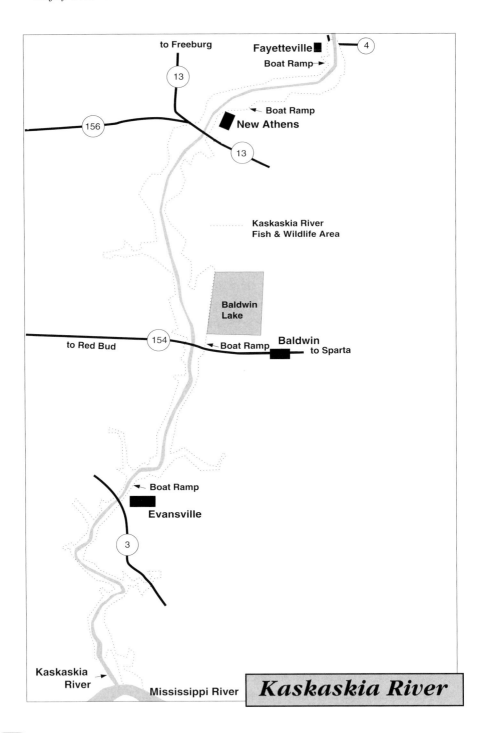

7 *Pyramid State Park*

Entry at Pyramid State Park

Driving through Perry County along Illinois 127 is not an exhilarating experience. To the right are corn fields and to the left are corn fields. Yet just off Illinois 127 west of Du Quoin, a veritable land of the lakes awaits you.

About 40 lakes, medium and small, have been dug out by strip mining and have filled with water. The lakes are scattered throughout the 2,500-acre park. Many are accessible only by hiking to them and make for secluded fishing for largemouth bass and bluegill. Some lakes also contain channel catfish and redear.

The lakes are the visible remains of the Pyramid Mining Company, one of America's early strip mining operations. The pits became "lakes" between 1932 and 1950 and vary in size from 24 acres to tiny 0.1 acre ponds, some of which are little more than pools. The water on the sizable lakes is very clean and 10 horsepower motors are allowed. Boat launches are provided at all of the larger lakes on the perimeter of the park and on lakes accessible by car.

Hike-in campsites are plentiful around the central horse trail including an equestrian campsite. Trails for hikers only are also available. The trails are very rugged owing to row after row of strip mining which has transformed the land. The campsites are class C and D and have no electricity. Water is only available on the south side of the park near the site office. A dump site is also provided nearby.

Firearm deer hunting is popular and the campsites may be filled with hunters, with trails closed to non-hunters during deer season.

To reach the park, turn off Illinois 127/13 (running north-south) where it meets Illinois 152. Go west about a mile on Illinois 152 to the south entrance of the park.

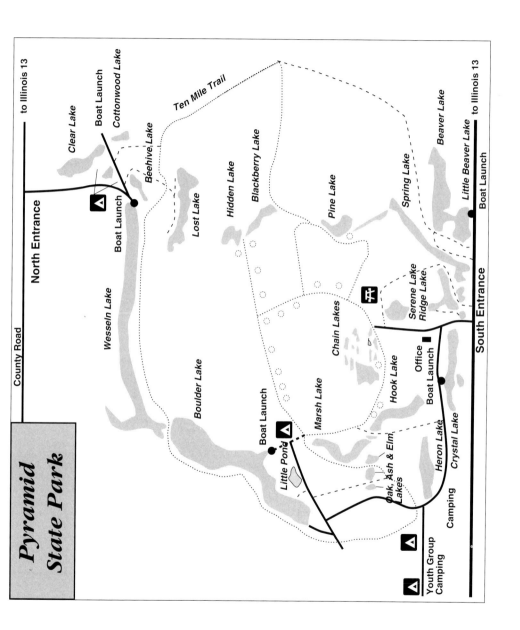

Pyramid State Park

to Illinois 13

County Road

North Entrance

Clear Lake

Boat Launch

Cottonwood Lake

Beehive Lake

Boat Launch

Ten Mile Trail

Lost Lake

Wesseln Lake

Hidden Lake

Blackberry Lake

Pine Lake

Boulder Lake

Chain Lakes

Marsh Lake

Boat Launch

Little Pond

Oak, Ash & Elm Lakes

Heron Lake

Crystal Lake

Hook Lake

Office

Boat Launch

Serene Lake

Ridge Lake

Spring Lake

Beaver Lake

Little Beaver Lake

to Illinois 13

Boat Launch

South Entrance

Youth Group Camping

Camping

Rend Lake

An Army Corps of Engineers project, Rend Lake was filled with water from the Big Muddy River in 1970. Today it is a water sportsman's paradise with recreational areas located at strategic points around the lake. Typical offerings at these areas include beaches, camping, hiking trails, picnic shelters and play areas and toilets.

View of a "Boatel" at Rend Lake Resort

Wayne Fitzgerrell State Park is on the east side of the lake and features the **Rend Lake Resort**, complete with fine dining, lodging, tennis courts, a swimming pool and a convenience store. The lodging includes cabins ($55/night) with a separate bedroom, pullout sleeper sofas, a television and a deck. Lodging also includes the lakeside "boatels," so named for their proximity to the water and boat slips in the dock. All of the boatel rooms feature a view of the lake from the back deck, and the second floor rooms have a bedroom with a good view of the lake.

Only yards from the accommodations, you'll find **Windows Restaurant**. It is a fine dining experience with a watery backdrop (see section on restaurants).

The rest of the park facilities are more conventional. Hiking and equestrian trails loop through the flat, forested topography. Boat ramps and a sailboat marina are found at the south of the park. There are numerous camping facilities, some with electricity for camping vehicles, others with only grills and picnic tables. Picnic tables with shelters provide a good view of the lake. The park also has a stable where horses can be kept overnight or longer. Arrangements for supervised horse riding are under negotiation.

The park has several popular special events for hunters and their dogs. One of these is a controlled pheasant hunt. Permits are $20 for each date. There are special package offers which include a night at the lodge and dinner in the restaurant for a single price. Another popular event is the regional and national dog trials. These trials test the speed and endurance of prime hunting dogs.

Another feature of the Rend Lake area is the golf course. A popular facility with locals and visitors alike, the course ranks among the best public courses in the Midwest.

Several Army Corps of Engineers recreational areas are found around the lake. These provide beaches, camping and picnicking, and special interpretive demonstrations.

Rend Lake is easily accessible from I-57 south of Mt. Vernon. Take exit #83 and go west on Illinois 154 to Wayne Fitzgerrell State Park.

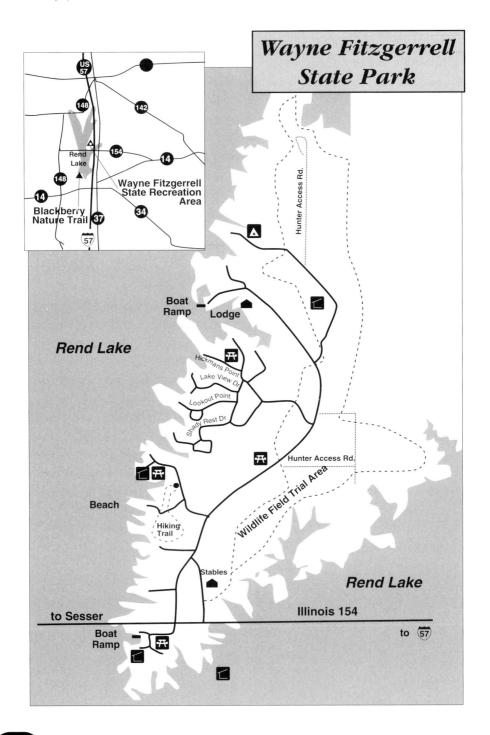

Wayne Fitzgerrell State Park

Wayne Fitzgerrell State Recreation Area

Rend Lake

Blackberry Nature Trail

Rend Lake

Boat Ramp

Lodge

Hickmans Point

Lake View Dr

Lookout Point

Shady Rest Dr

Beach

Hiking Trail

Hunter Access Rd.

Wildlife Field Trial Area

Stables

to Sesser

Illinois 154

to 57

Boat Ramp

Rend Lake

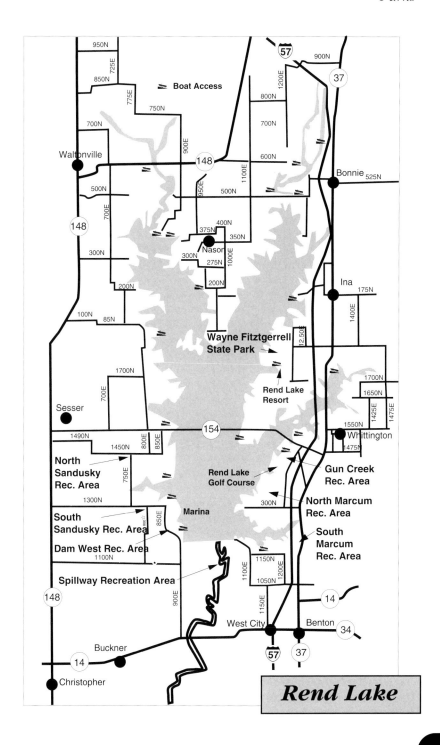

Rend Lake

Randolph Co. Conservation Area

Creek at Randolph County Conservation Area

"We are the start of Shawnee National Forest, at least to my mind anyway. We've got all the little hills and hollers." The Shawnee National Forest doesn't quite stretch to Randolph County, but the spirit of assistant site superintendent Jack Houghlan's statement holds. The gently rolling hills and sandstone bluffs in this fish and wildlife area are the geological foreshadowing of the land to its south.

The area has much more than fish and wildlife. Its facilities, picnic shelters, a lake with boat ramps and well maintained campgrounds, make it resemble a state park. The most popular sport is, however, hunting. Deer and squirrel (gray and red) are the most plentiful game, though dove, quail, woodcock and rabbit are all options for hunters. Fishermen can take boats with 10 horsepower motors onto the attractive lake to fish for smallmouth and largemouth bass, walleye, channel catfish and crappie. Rental boats are also available.

Equestrian activities are popular on the eight miles of horse trails which can also be toured on foot. The trails take the hiker or horseback rider through stands of mature oak-hickory woods as well as honeysuckle and multiflora rose. A stand of prairie grass maintained by conservation staff can be seen from the road.

The main area is much like a standard state park, but its satellite areas are far from it. The most beautiful of these is **Piney Creek Nature Preserve** (see Hiking Section). South of Steeleville, you will find the same land the settlers found and in which the Indians lived. It's an exquisite combination of sandstone bluffs and crystal clear streams and waterfalls. Through the preserve runs a trail that is rarely used. It is well worth the effort to find this out-of-the-way spot.

Randolph County Conservation Area is five miles north of Chester. From Chester, take New Palestine Road north until you come to County Road 1100 N which leads east directly to the conservation area entrance.

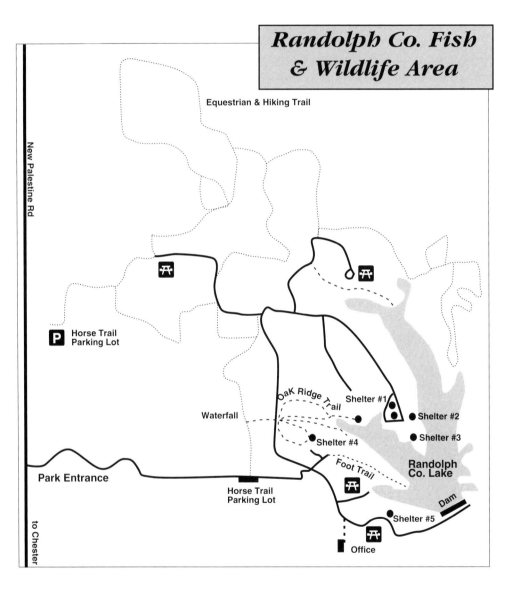

Randolph Co. Fish & Wildlife Area

Equestrian & Hiking Trail

New Palestine Rd

Horse Trail Parking Lot

Oak Ridge Trail

Shelter #1

Shelter #2

Shelter #3

Waterfall

Shelter #4

Randolph Co. Lake

Park Entrance

Foot Trail

Horse Trail Parking Lot

Dam

Shelter #5

to Chester

Office

10 *Kinkaid Lake*

Johnson Creek Recreation Area at Kinkaid Lake

At the northern tip of the Shawnee National Forest, Lake Kinkaid's 2,700 acres and 82 miles of shoreline with numerous fingers and coves are well served by private marinas and public recreational facilities. In the rugged terrain at the northwest end of the lake lies a Shawnee National Forest recreational site. Across the lake is a small private marina while a larger private marina and camping area can be found on the opposite end of the lake.

The marinas and boat ramps surrounding the lake serve the anglers and water sports enthusiasts who flock to the area. Water-skiing is permitted at the lake's widest point and anglers will find the lake brimming with bass, crappie, bluegill and some pike.

The federal recreation area called **Johnson Creek** is loaded with facilities, including several sheltered picnic areas with views of the lake, a boat ramp below the parking lot and a small beach with show-ers provided. Near the beach is a picnic table on top of a railed dock.

Continuing along the access road, visitors will find the camping areas high above the lake. The first of two areas is the equestrian campground, lying along the Kinkaid Lake horse trail. Beyond that is a campground for vehicles and tent camping. Toilets and water are available. Within the campground is Smokey Bear Lake. Actually a pond, Smokey Bear is reserved for fishing by children ages 12 and under. The camping area lies above the lake, but because of dense tree cover the lake is invisible. Only from site #27 and only when the leaves are off the trees does the lake come partially into view.

North of Johnson Creek along Illinois 151 and across the lake is the **Port of Ava Marina**, supplying slips, gasoline, rental pontoons and jon boats. On the opposite end of the lake off Illinois 149 is a larger private marina and camping area. **Kinkaid Village Marina** is a full service marina with a restaurant and lounge. Newly opened in 1993 is a boat shop. The marina building, shop area and some docks provide handicapped access, as do house boats.

Near the marina is a **private campground**. All the sites are on or near the water and come with or without electrical hook up. Prices are $8 and $5 per day. All of these private facilities are run by Southern Illinois Recreation Incorporated, call (618) 687-4914 for more infor-mation.

The southeastern end of the lake can be accessed from Illinois 149 about three miles west of Murphysboro. Take the road off Illinois 149 as directed by the signs. Johnson Creek Recreation Area is off Illinois 151 which runs north/south between Illinois 3 and Illinois 4.

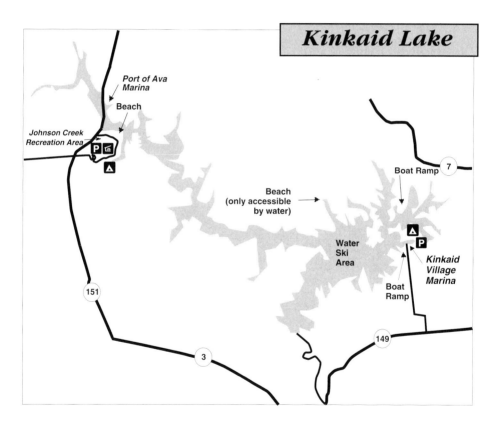

11 *Lake Murphysboro State Park*

Not far from the banks of the Mississippi River sits a medium size lake in a small state park with surprisingly beautiful vistas. Driving up on the south side of the lake at the concession, boat launch and sheltered picnic area, the visitor is met with one of those views that make you go "hmm."

Known as Lake Murphysboro, the wide expanse of water ends at an even wider expanse of deciduous and evergreen forest, making for an especially enjoyable picnicking and fishing location. There is a

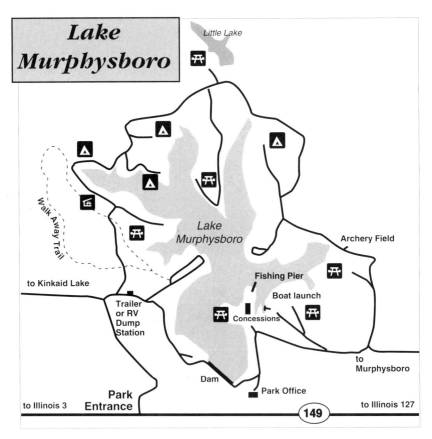

small bridge with handicapped access fishing over a cove at the same spot.

Other picnicking and camping areas dot the perimeter of the lake. The best of the camping locations is at the end of the vehicular camp-site where water surrounds three sides at #1, #2 and #3; and the tent camping #19 - #29 which are at the ends of a peninsula. Electricity is available and a sanitary dump site is provided on the lake's west side. There is a trail called Walk Away on the northwest side of the lake.

Fishermen can take advantage of the lake's stock of largemouth bass, bluegill, sunfish, channel catfish and crappie. Boating is allowed on the 145-acre lake, but with nothing more powerful than a 10 horse-power motor. The concession provides food and jon boats with oars.

Lake Murphysboro can be found two and-a-half miles west of Murphysboro off Illinois 149.

A good time awaits you at Lake Murphysboro

12

Crab Orchard Lake & National Wildlife Refuge

Canada geese at Crab Orchard National Wildlife Refuge

Though a wildlife refuge by name, 1.2 million human visitors took refuge from civilization at Crab Orchard in 1992. They came to take advantage of the array of recreational opportunities offered near the water and in the forests of this federal property.

A massive 43,000-acre tract of land, the wildlife refuge contains three lakes and a total of 23,500 acres available for public use. The biggest of the lakes, Crab Orchard, is equipped with two marinas, providing water sports enthusiasts and fishermen a base from which to explore the lake. The smaller lakes, Little Grassy and Devils Kitchen, also have their own marinas though there is a 10 horsepower limit on motors. Bass, bluegill, catfish and crappie are among the fish that will bite for the angler.

In the wilderness and along the banks of the lakes, visitors can use vehicular facilities with electricity as well as primitive tent camping. Though only a few hiking trails are available within the refuge, visitors in wheelchairs will be happy to know that two of them allow handicapped access. Likewise, fishing piers with handicapped access are common around the lakes. Animals that populate the wilderness areas range from the endangered bobcat to the common white tailed deer. Foxes, raccoons, mink, skunk, shrews, bats and rabbits also populate the refuge's forested areas.

The refuge is a major stopping point for Canada geese on the Mississippi Flyway and an observation area (also with handicapped access) is provided along Illinois 148 where these birds can be viewed. Where there are geese, **eagles** are not far behind. There are approximately 10 bald eagles during any given November to February season and these can also be viewed, although less reliably, from the observation area. Another place to view eagles is at the administrative headquarters off Illinois 148.

Hunting is an extremely popular activity at the refuge with goose and deer the primary targets. Firearm hunting is allowed in season. If the hunter is lucky he may be selected by random drawing to hunt within the more restricted sanctuary area forming the northeast section of the refuge. Programs to assist handicapped hunters are also conducted through this section.

Crab Orchard Lake encompasses 7,000 acres and is the most easily accessible recreation area in deep Southern Illinois. Lying next to and under Illinois 13, many of the lake's recreational areas are just an access road away from the busy east-west, four-lane highway. These include the lake's two marinas, Playport and Pirate's Cove II. Both are full service marinas offering boat rental, bait and repairs.

Pirate's Cove II is visible from Illinois 13. Driving beyond the marina, the visitor finds a campground at the edge of the lake. Some of the campsites have electricity available ($8); others are primitive ($6.50). The campground also provides a pier, picnic tables and grills as well as a concession with food and toilets with showers. Some of the best spots are at the tip of section "B" campground where the camper can look out on a beautiful lake vista.

A few yards beyond the turn to Playport Marina, Lookout Point Beach is found. This small beach is at an open grassy area with trees on the periphery. It offers grills, picnic tables and toilets but no concession for $1.

There is another beach due south of Carterville with little else but a toilet available for patrons.

On Illinois 148 south of Illinois 13 are two wildlife observation areas. Both have handicapped access and both enable the user to view geese, which are in abundance on the refuge from October to mid-winter.

Crab Orchard Lake is surprisingly short on nature trails. The one in existence is called the Chamness Town School Trail and is west of the administrative center off A-3 Road. A new trail right next to the Visitor Center at the intersection of Illinois 148 and Illinois 13 should be completed by the time this book is printed and will include a fishing pier with handicapped access. Both trails are accessible by wheelchairs.

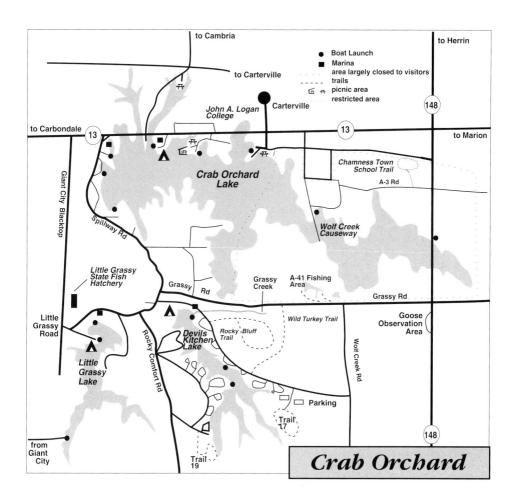

13

Little Grassy &
Devils Kitchen Lakes

The area surrounding Little Grassy and Devils Kitchen Lakes is more heavily wooded than around Crab Orchard Lake as well as more rugged. The wilderness atmosphere is decidedly stronger at these lakes. Also more secluded, this pair lie side-by-side to the south of their larger neighbor. Both have their main recreation areas on the north end of the lake centered around marinas with camping, boat ramps and concessions.

Marina at Devils Kitchen Lake at sunset

Devils Kitchen is surrounded by camping sites, with and without electricity; vehicular and tent camping are available. Little Grassy is also surrounded by campsites although these are group sites for scouts and other youth groups. At the extreme southern end of Little Grassy is a boat ramp and trail, which connect the refuge with Giant City State Park.

Both of these lakes can be reached from Giant City Road which leads south from Carbondale off Illinois 13 on the eastern edge of town. Turn west off Giant City Road seven miles south of Carbondale at the posted sign.

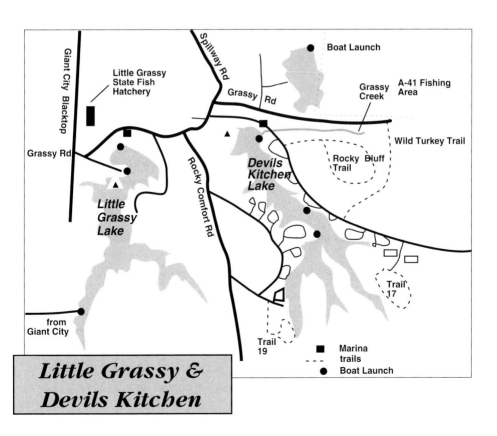

Touch of Nature Environmental Center

At Touch of Nature Environmental Center professional guides and interpretive programs unlock the mysteries of Southern Illinois' ecology and teach some of the almost-forgotten skills of early settlers as well as some up-to-date environmentally sound practices. An entity of Southern Illinois University, the center is geared toward use by groups, but is not picky about which group they serve. Scouts, the Elks, or a team from the office are all welcome to take advantage of the programs.

These programs range from an expedition down the Cache River in the summer to a demonstration of how to make maple syrup in the winter; a hike along the Big Muddy River to a workshop called, "Reduce, Reuse, Recycle: A way of life."

The facilities on site include a lodge, outdoor and indoor sports areas, cabins, a beach and numerous nature trails. The oldest and most innovative is Camp Little Grassy. Developed for children and adults with all manner of physical and mental disabilities, the program exposes people who might not otherwise experience them, the sights, sounds, trials and travails of nature. Arts, crafts, swimming, canoeing, camping and sports are conducted with the aid of professionals and volunteers.

Touch of Nature is renowned for accommodating persons with physical and mental disabilities, but less well known are the centers exclusively for the older population. Week long **Elderhostel** programs focus on topics relevant to the Southern Illinois flora or fauna and interweave lectures with nature walks and "extracurricular activities" like hayrides and wine tasting. An example of such programs is "Birds, Birds and More Birds in Southern Illinois," held at the end of April or beginning of May.

These are only a few of the services provided by Touch of Nature. To find out about the other programs and services, including conference facilities and a wilderness program for youth-at-risk, call (618) 453-1121.

Touch of Nature is located seven miles south of Carbondale. Turn south off Illinois 13 onto Giant City Road at the eastern edge of Carbondale (Pier 1 Imports is on the corner). Follow the signs from Illinois 13.

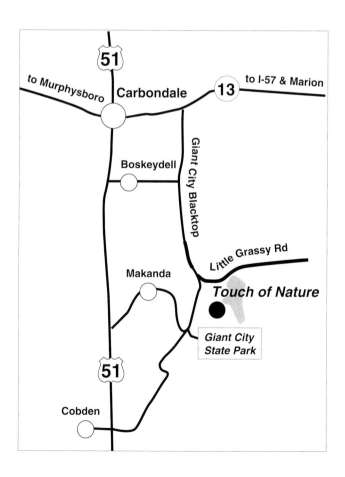

15

Giant City State Park

When deep Southern Illinoisans talk about "nature", Giant City State Park is probably what they mean. Numerous trails wind through forest, over plateaus and across sandstone bluffs which dominate the park. The bluffs are folded and creviced, pushed up by the termination of a recent ice age's glaciers. The effect has been called "streets" and "buildings", thus a "giant city." Actually, the streets are crevices and buildings fern and moss-covered rock formations. The wild flowers, trees and deer leave no doubt that Giant City is not an urban jungle.

The park combines the natural flavor of Southern Illinois with the modern conveniences of a resort. The most luxurious of these facilities is **Giant City Lodge**. The lodge is an impressive sandstone and white oak edifice built by the Depression-era Civilian Conservation Corps and used today as a restaurant and conference center. The lodge specialty is an all-you-can-eat Sunday dinner, consisting of fried chicken, mashed potatoes, green beans and more. After dining, visitors can admire the lodge's anteroom with its massive fireplace, columns and cathedral ceiling. The lodge also houses an indoor swimming pool and children's pool as well as a video game room.

The park's 34 guest cabins come in three varieties–good, better and best. The "Historic" cabins are one room with a queen-sized bed and a sofa-sleeper in the living room; the "Prairie" cabins are two room units with a queen-sized bed and a sofa sleeper in the living room; the "Bluff" cabins are the most luxurious with a deck, wet bar, fireplace and three beds including a sofa-sleeper.

There are four **camping** sites, one equipped with horse facilities, one for group camping and two for tent camping. Starting on the southwest side of the park and moving clockwise, the first is the equestrian camping site next to a horse trailhead. The group camp is on the southeast side by a softball diamond. Tent camping sites are near Little Grassy Lake.

The park's horse facilities include a stable which rents horses and guides. Fishermen can take advantage of Little Grassy Lake's boat launch and marina. An abundant supply of bluegill, crappie and bass are found in the lake. Hunting for upland game is also permitted.

The facilities at the park are impressive, but one of the park's biggest uses is **hiking**. Trails ascend the limestone bluffs to give a panoramic view of the forest canopy, then plunge into the lush vegetation to take the hiker into the cool shelter of forest and cliff faces. The trails include Post Oak Trail which provides handicapped access. The trail is covered with woodchips and includes a fishing pier with handicapped access. Another trail, Stone Fort, is so named for its skirting of a thousand-year-old, short stone wall. Built by the nomadic Lewis People in 800-900 A.D., the wall was possibly used as a defense against intruders.

The lodge at Giant City State Park

Giant City can be reached by going south on Giant City Road off Illinois 13 on Carbondale's eastern edge. The park is about nine miles down the road. You can also reach Giant City by heading south from Carbondale on U.S. 51. Take the Makanda turnoff at the yellow water tower (painted with the smiley face) and head east through Makanda and follow park signs.

Trail of Tears State Forest

Public use area at Trail of Tears

Deep within the rural countryside of western Union County, yet near easily accessible state routes, is the state forest and nature preserve known as Trail of Tears. This poetic name is taken from the forced 800-mile migration of the Cherokee, Creek and Chickasaw nations. In the winter of 1838-39, the Indians were moved from their homes to their present-day Oklahoma reservation. On the way, they camped in what is now the state forest.

The forest is an example of the Ozark Hills formation. Better known as a mountain range in Missouri, the Ozarks Hills are older than the Shawnee Hills adjoining them and are therefore worn by age. They lack the dramatic rocky cliff faces to be found in places like Giant City.

Nevertheless, the hills provide a steeply rolling terrain for the mature hardwood forest dominated by black and white oak and hickory as well as beech, maple, red oak and tulip trees. Also to be found in the forest are 620 species of flowering plants. The wildlife within the forest is extremely diverse. The normal array of deer, gray and red squirrel and raccoon is here, but so are more exotic timber rattlesnakes, fox, mink and the endangered bobcat.

The facilities offered in the forest are sparse but impressive. The picnic shelter and nature trail complex receives the majority of use and is a pleasant place to spend an afternoon. Within this area is one of the last standing **fire towers** in Southern Illinois. Built in the 1930s by the Civilian Conservation Corps (as were nearly all the forest's facilities), the tower has been saved from demolition by the site superintendent, Andy West. Unfortunately, the stairs leading up the tower are in disrepair and until the state provides the money it will not be possible to enter the tower.

An extensive network of **horse and fire trails** is available for use as is the half mile nature trail near the picnic shelter. The trail network will take the hiker or horseback rider to campsites for backpackers, while other campsites can be reached by vehicle. All camping is primitive tent camping (no electricity) though toilets and, at a few sites, log shelters are provided.

Hunters will find access to most of the state forest and the main game species are squirrel, deer, turkey and raccoon. Fishermen also can take advantage of a clear creek forming the western boundary of the forest. Catfish, perch, bluegill and crappie are the typical catch.

The Trail of Tears State Forest is bordered by Illinois 3 on its west and Illinois 127 on its east. Take the Trail of Tears Blacktop off either of these highways to reach the forest.

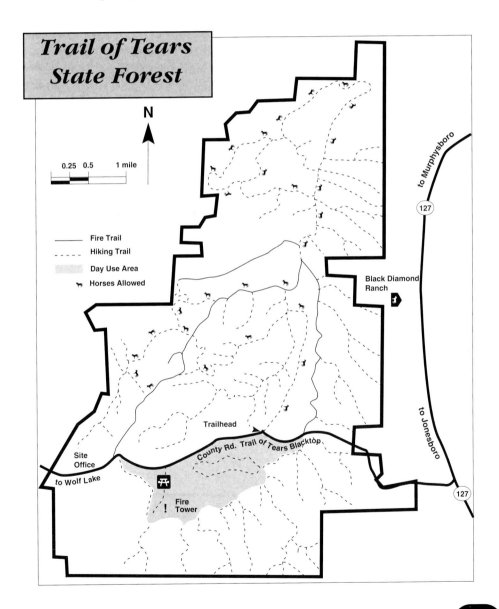

Union County Conservation Area

When goose populations declined in the 1940s Union County Conservation Area was established to increase the goose population. The sloughs and bottomland water areas of this 6,000-acre preserve are suited for waterfowl management. Eighty-five thousand geese, or about one-fourth of the goose population of Southern Illinois take advantage of the refuge and crops specifically planted for them. Bald eagles may be seen between mid-December and early February at this site.

The conservation area is off Illinois 146 at the western edge of the state, about eight miles northeast of Cape Girardeau, Missouri, and west of Anna. From I-57 take exit #30 at Illinois 146 and go west for 15 miles to a fork where Illinois 3 joins Illinois 146. Go south (left) on Illinois 146 to the conservation area entrance almost two miles away. From Cape Girardeau take Illinois 146 north.

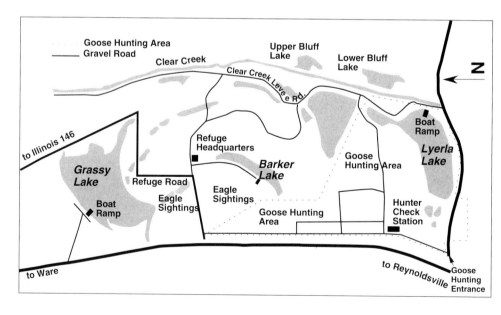

18 ## *Horseshoe Lake Conservation Area*

Boat dock among cypress trees at Horseshoe Lake

The shallow lake is obscured by massive trees whose roots are partially visible and which become wider at their base. But this is obvious only occasionally because most of the giant bald cypress and tupelo make no distinction between where the lake begins and where it ends. A far cry from the neatly manicured parks and recreation areas to the north, water and vegetation are a seamless continuum giving a distinctly swampy appearance. Yes, Dorothy, you're still in Southern Illinois, but you've wandered into one of its best kept secrets, Horseshoe Lake in Alexander County.

Apart from cypress and tupelo, the lake is surrounded by some man-made developments like tent and vehicular campgrounds with electricity. On the west side of the lake, showers are provided next to the vehicular campground. Water and picnic tables are also available at various points around the lake.

Boat launches are common, as are docks, though some on the east side of the lake appear precarious. At the southeast end of the lake just off Promised Land Road is a sheltered picnic area with a children's play area. The toilets at this site provide handicapped access. A dock on the west side of the lake is also accessible to the handicapped.

During the winter, geese crowd into the conservation area. The Department of Conservation estimates that 150,000 of them winter here each year. A happy result of this is that bald eagles are also common at the lake. Jim Melton, who runs a concession business at the park, reports that between 12 and 15 eagles live in the conservation area during the winter months. A visitor is most likely to see the eagles from mid-December through early February, Melton said.

The geese bring another kind of hunter to the banks of Horseshoe Lake–humans. Archery hunting for deer is permitted in addition to squirrel and dove hunting.

Fishing is a dream at Horseshoe Lake and anglers have even developed a new technique called bucktailing to cope with the four-foot deep lake. Bluegill, sunfish, crappie, largemouth bass and channel catfish are abundant.

Melton Fishing Camp and concession operation provides bait, tackle, boat rental and cabins and mobile homes for overnight visitors. Motor boats can be rented for $25 per day and a boat with paddles at

$4.50 per day. The shared bath cabins are $19.25 for double occupancy while the biggest mobile homes are $26.50.

Horseshoe Lake Conservation Area is in Alexander County off
Illinois 3 due south of Olive Branch. The conservation area can be
reached from I-57 by taking exit #1 at Illinois 3/127 and following
Illinois 3 north for ten miles.

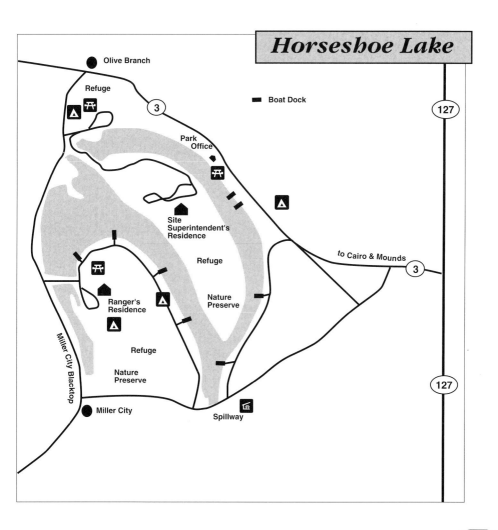

19   *Ferne Clyffe State Park*

This state park lives up to its name with ferns and cliffs aplenty. More properly called "bluffs," the rock formations in the park are crisscrossed with trails and one of the more scenic, Black Jack Oak (#5) in the center of the park, overlooks the small Ferne Clyffe Lake. The view from the bluffs is dazzling during fall as the leaves change from green to electric orange, red and yellow.

There is also a "waterfall" to be seen in the park. Various trails lead to a cliff face with rocky "streams" leading up to the bluff. The waterfall and streams are theoretical most of the time. Only after it rains will

Hawk's Cave at Ferne Clyffe State Park

water actually flow in the streams and fall from the 100-foot bluff.

A trail circles the lake from which bank fishing can be done for largemouth bass, channel catfish, redear and bluegill. Boating and swimming are not allowed in the lake. There are seven picnic areas, some with shelters and playground areas for children. All have parking, toilets and grills.

Numerous types of **campgrounds** are available to visitors. Deer Ridge Campground in the northeast corner of the park is a class A facility for camping vehicles with showers, toilets, a sanitary dump station as well as electricity, picnic tables and grills. The showers are seasonal, open from the end of April until late November.

A class D primitive site called Turkey Ridge is next to parking lots on the east side of the park. Individual camping spots, picnic tables and grills are provided at the site as well as drinking water and

Hikers at Ferne Clyffe State Park

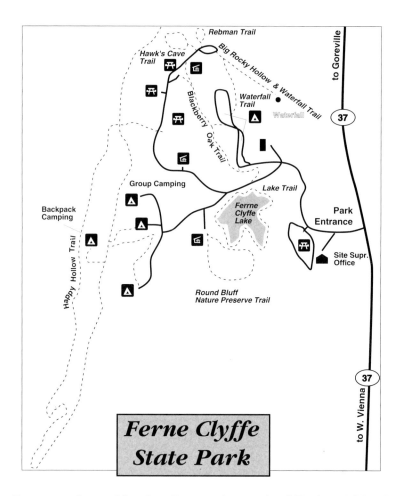

Ferne Clyffe State Park

toilets near the parking lot. Just to the north of Turkey Ridge is a group class D campsite with similar facilities. For more privacy there is a backpackers campsite. Located a half mile east of Turkey Ridge, this site provides toilets, although fresh water must be obtained from the parking lot.

Hunters will find deer and squirrel in abundance with quail and rabbits in lesser supply.

Ferne Clyffe State Park is between I-24 and I-57 in Johnson County just south of Goreville. From I-24 take exit #7 then west to Illinois 37 which leads to the park. From I-57 take exit #40 then east to Illinois 37. Go south about a mile to the park.

20 *Lake of Egypt Recreation Area*

On the southern banks of the Lake of Egypt is a secluded camping area. Looking out across the wooded shoreline, it is difficult to imagine that humans inhabit the area. It is all the more surprising then, that down the road to the picnic area several houses are visible. That is a truer picture of the lake–a beautifully wooded scenic landscape with houses owned by residents who appreciate lake scenery.

You don't have to worry about seeing houses from the isolated campground. The camping area extends from the shore into the forest. Only a few of the sites allow a view of the water (#33-#38).

The Wagonwheel picnicground offers a good view of the lake as

Picnic ground at Lake of Egypt

well as two shelters with a small grill for each. There are a few more picnic tables and grills filling out the remainder of the area.

A boat ramp is also provided nearby which offers anglers and boaters access to this power plant lake, renowned for fishing and water sports. Water skiing is permitted.

The recreation area is in the secluded southeastern corner of Lake of Egypt. To reach it, take exit #7 off I-24 then east for about five miles. A road branching off north (left) leads to Creal Springs. Take this road for two and-a-half miles north to the signs which point west (left) toward the recreation area.

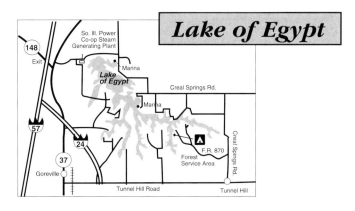

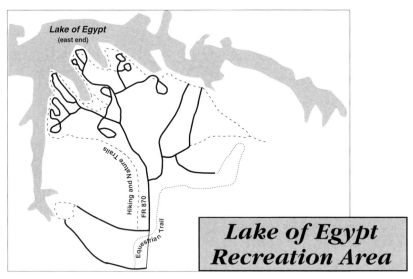

Sam Parr State Park

Lakeside view at Sam Parr State Park

Sam Parr was a Jasper County native who rose to the top of the Illinois Department of Conservation. After his death in 1966, the land that had been recently acquired as a conservation area in the county was renamed in honor of the expert on fisheries and became Sam Parr State Park.

As with many state nature areas north of Kinkaid Lake, the park is neatly manicured featuring a tree-lined impoundment at its center. Boat ramps and picnic areas are easily accessible from the park road and primitive class D camping is on the west side of the lake.

Picnic shelters occur at regular intervals on the west side of the lake and fishermen can take advantage of a boat ramp on the same side of the lake or a fishing access area on the east side. The horsepower limit for the narrow lake is 10. Fish to be caught are largemouth bass, bluegill, sunfish, crappie and catfish. Hunters can take advantage of small game and birds as well as hunt deer with bows.

The park is in the extreme northeastern corner of Southern Illinois in Jasper County. It is easily found at the intersection of Illinois 130 and Illinois 33, a few miles northeast of Newton.

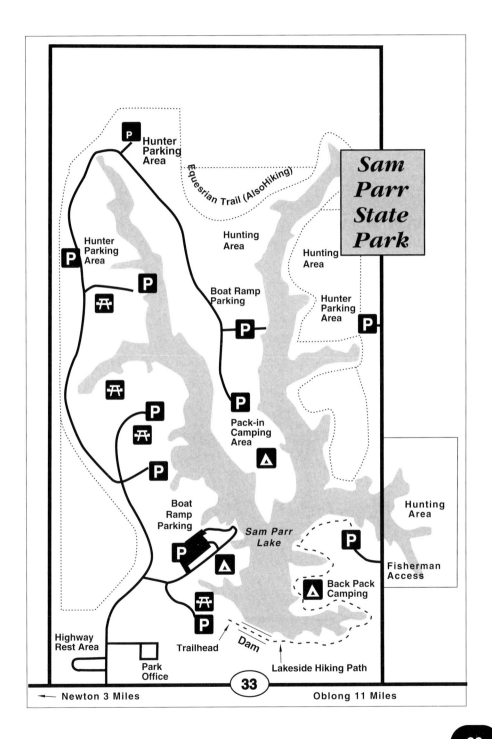

Sam Parr State Park

Hunter Parking Area

Equesrian Trail (AlsoHiking)

Hunter Parking Area

Hunting Area

Hunting Area

Boat Ramp Parking

Hunter Parking Area

Pack-in Camping Area

Boat Ramp Parking

Sam Parr Lake

Hunting Area

Fisherman Access

Back Pack Camping

Highway Rest Area

Trailhead

Dam

Lakeside Hiking Path

Park Office

33

Newton 3 Miles

Oblong 11 Miles

22 *Newton Lake Fish & Wildlife Area*

Created by a power company to cool its discharge, this lake features 22.5 miles of hiking and equestrian trails plus warm water that makes for a long fishing season for largemouth bass, walleye, crappie and channel catfish. A 25-horsepower limit is in effect for the lake. The trail is also used for cross country skiing.

Though camping is not provided at the lake, **Kuhl's Campground,** (618) 752-5473 is a commercial site with electrical hook-ups and dump stations south of the lake. Also to the south of the lake, but closer is **Rauch's Bait Shop**. Four miles to the west of the boat launch is **R & D Bait Shop** also for the angler in need of supplies. To reach the north access of Newton Lake from I-57 take any of the exits to Effingham

Entrance sign at Newton Lake

and proceed southeast on Illinois 33 for about eight miles to the town of Dieterich. Turn right (south) on the county road and proceed for about 10 miles until you see a bait shop. Turn east (left) and go about five miles to the park entrance. Many maps do not show the west-east road leading to the park entrance.

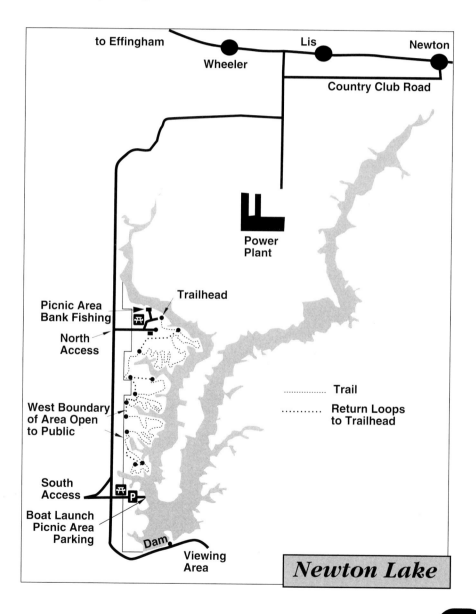

㉓ *Red Hills State Park*

View of the Lake at Red Hills State Park (Photo courtesy of Carl Aten)

This 948-acre park was born of a deal cut with the Piankashaw Indians. The park marks the western border of the Vincennes Tract, an area ceded to the United States in 1795 and the first bit of what would later become Illinois. Running through the park is the "Trace Road," the old frontier era route to the West.

The park lies on the border between Illinois and Indiana with a federal highway bisecting it. To the south of U.S. 50 is a 40-acre lake in which anglers can fish for bluegill, largemouth bass, channel catfish and sunfish. A boat launch is available although only electric trolling motors are permitted. A road circles the lake, making bank fishing a fairly simple proposition. Tame ducks also inhabit the lake and are happy to take food from visitors.

Surrounding the lake are picnic areas with grills. There is a shelter on the west side of the lake, a playground on the north side and to the east are several tent camping areas. The campsites include primitive camping as well as class A vehicular access pads (four of which allow handicapped access) with electricity, a sanitary dump station and showers. Circling the lake is a five-mile dual use hiking and horse trail.

The other half of the park, north of U.S. 50, is composed mostly of three miles of looped hiking trails. These trails take the hiker through deep ravines, around springs, through hardwood forests and over hills. Interspersed among the trees are more picnic areas where hikers can stop for a bite. The youth camping area is found on this side of the highway. In the north of this area at the far end topping Red Hill, for which the park is named, is a tower and cross built by community churches. The cross is used for religious services throughout the year. Easter 1993 marked the 50th anniversary of sunrise services at the cross.

Concessions at the park, which include boat rental, have been reintroduced with the establishment of a new restaurant. Despite the park brochure's reference to a "proposed visitor center," as of this writing its future is uncertain.

In keeping with the park's historical roots, **Old Settler Day** is held each year in late April. The weekend event includes traditional dance, food, children's games, plowing and disking and other displays and wares depicting life on the old frontier.

The state park is midway between Lawrenceville and Olney and is bisected by U.S. 50 in Lawrence County.

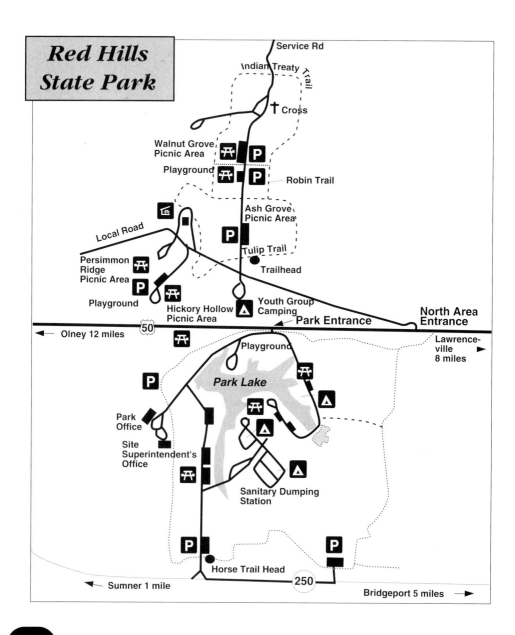

24 *Stephen A. Forbes State Park*

Stephen A. Forbes State Park is dominated by its 585-acre lake which can be used for fishing, swimming and water skiing. But it also contains some hidden treasures like a large secluded pond and a 19th century cemetery.

A rarity for state parks in the northern half of Southern Illinois, there is no horsepower limit for boats on the lake. Thus, water skiing is allowed on parts of the lake. Boat ramps are found at strategic spots. The main access is at the marina and concession area where boats can

Marina at Stephen A. Forbes State Park

be rented. There is also a floating walkway at this site which makes for easy walking between the tent campgrounds just across the water and the concession area.

Numerous boat slips are also available and may be rented on a yearly basis. A 200-foot beach gives more fun in the sun at the south end of the park.

Stephen A. Forbes was a biologist. You can experience some of his park's biology by walking the hiking trails or riding the horse trails. On the trails you'll see lots of hardwood oaks and hickory trees as well as creeks that wind throughout the park. All of the trails can be accessed from the road surrounding the lake. On the west side of the lake are the Henneman Cemetery and Marlow Pond trails, leading respectively to a century and one-half-old cemetery and a secluded fishing pond (see Hiking Section).

This conservation area has the facilities of a state park and the wildlife of a refuge. The mixed deciduous hardwood and pine forest is

Beach at Stephen A. Forbes State Park

the home for wild turkey, coyote and offers wide easy trails from which to see them. Hunters have the opportunity to bowshoot for deer and to use firearms to hunt for squirrel, doves, rabbit, quail and water-fowl.

The state park is northeast of Salem in Marion County. Go east down U.S. 50 to 1900 E which is eight miles from Salem. Turn north (left) at the sign which points to the park. The park is seven miles up the road.

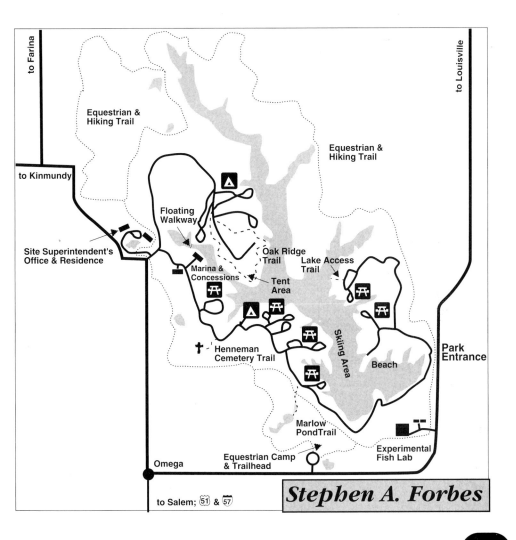

Sam Dale Lake
Conservation Area

A nature trail skirts Sam Dale Lake, a 194-acre lake with 8.5 miles of shoreline and a beach on the west side of the lake (no lifeguard on duty). Fishermen benefit from the lake's numerous finger-like projections which give lots of shelter for bluegill, largemouth bass, redear, crappie and channel catfish.

The nature trail on the north side, from which great blue herons and the telltale signs of beavers are often seen, provides a pleasant stroll along the lake before looping around back to the class B (camper vehicles only) campground.

Lake view at Sam Dale

The campsite is at the end of the park road and there is a class A camping site a few hundred yards back down the road. On the opposite side of the lake is the youth group campsite. The class B campsite contains two pads with handicapped access. There are plans for a solid fishing dock which will also encourage handicapped access by the summer of 1994. The toilets and drinking fountains provide handicapped access as does the beach.

Along the park road you'll meet the beach and stately oaks, spreading their branches in testimony to their age. On the south side of the lake is a playground and the concession area from which food can be bought and v-bottom boats rented. Also near the concession is the picnic area with the best view of the lake.

Nine hundred and thirty acres have been set aside for hunting. Firearm hunting is permitted although hunting for deer is permitted with bow and arrow only.

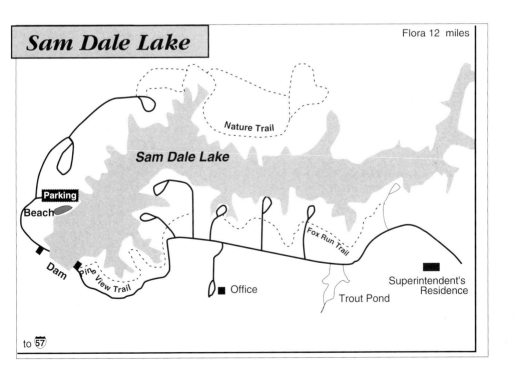

26 *Beall Woods Conservation Area & Preserve*

While cruising through the Southern Illinois countryside it is impossible not to notice that there are an awful lot of trees here. What is not so obvious is that most of these trees are second or third growth. Even in the Shawnee Forest it is just about impossible to find a stand of trees whose ancestors have not been cleared for timber or farming. These are not the same forests used for cover by Revolutionary War hero George Rogers Clark; neither are they the same forests in which the Shawnee Indians or other tribes lived.

Tree silhouette at Beall Woods

Beall Woods is different. In it you'll see how the whole eastern United States looked before the Europeans came. This forest makes other stands seem puny by comparison. The 270-acre aboriginal timber stand is contained within a 635-acre conservation area. The woodland was preserved by the Beall family, but when a new owner decided to clear the land for farming, the state stepped in and saved the forest in 1965. It was later named a National Landmark and put under the supervision of the State of Illinois as a nature preserve.

The woods lie next to the Wabash River and a large creek meanders through the forest. The confluence of Coffee Creek with the Wabash River can be witnessed at the end of White Oak Trail, and Sweet Gum Trail takes the hiker by a rock-faced ravine with the creek running through it (see Hiking Section). Among the 64 identified tree species live foxes, pileated woodpeckers, deer and raccoon.

At the main trail head sits the **Red Barn**, an interpretive nature center with displays of seeds, native Illinois woods and others. Neither hunting nor camping is permitted at Beall Woods. Outside the nature preserve area is a small lake and on the west side of the lake is a boat ramp, piers, picnic tables (one sheltered) and toilets.

Beall Woods is seven miles southwest of Mt. Carmel off Illinois 1. Follow the signs off Illinois 1 around Keensburg to the forest.

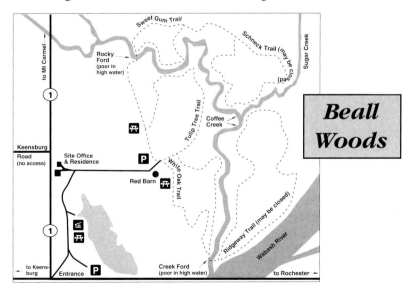

27   *Hamilton County Conservation Area*

Connecting bridge at Hamilton County Conservation Area

Several scenic trails and campgrounds surround **Dolan Lake** at this fish and wildlife area. Earthen fishing piers have been fashioned for easier bank fishing and v-bottom boats are available from the concession (use oars or bring your own motor).

The most secluded place for camping is the primitive campsite just off Shelter Trail near Rocky Point Picnic Area on the northwest side of the lake. By driving around the lake on the surrounding road you'll see several picnic areas with good views of the lake. The concession area is on the east side of the lake and has a dock and launching ramp within the complex.

Most of this 1,683-acre facility is available for hunting quail, rabbit, squirrel, dove, deer and woodcock. Fishermen will enjoy the supply of channel catfish, largemouth bass, bluegill, redear, and crappie.

The conservation area is midway between McLeansboro and Carmi off Illinois 14. A sign eight miles east of McLeansboro directs you south to the park.

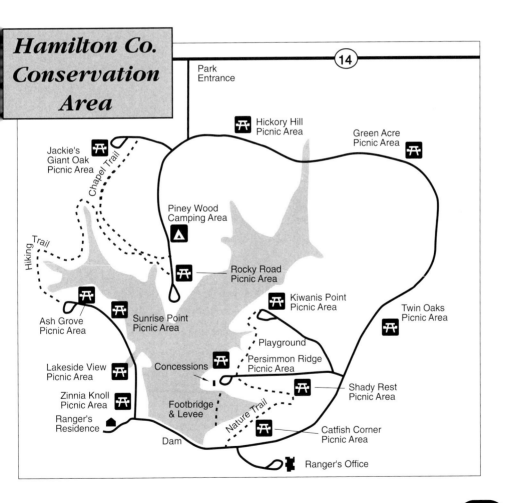

Saline County Conservation Area

As the name implies, Saline County has salt in it. Indians harvested salt from their "Great Salt Springs" before ceding the land around Equality to the United States in 1803. Since salt mining takes a lot of labor, this part of Southern Illinois was exempted from the Northwest Ordinance's general rule forbidding slaves.

Today, instead of enslaved miners, free hunters, campers, picnickers and hikers make use of this beautiful conservation area. The area is a combination of Saline River bottom land and hills indicative of the Shawnee Forest which it borders. Springs, rocky creeks and 105-acre **Glen O. Jones Lake** feature in the scenic beauty of the area.

You'll find the area's facilities on the north side of the lake. These include several camping areas for vehicles and tents, though no electricity is available, a wildlife viewing area with a picnic table and playground, two boat docks and ramps, and a concession area. The park has hiking trails and horse trails which connect with Shawnee National Forest trails, and a special equestrian campground.

Firearm hunting is allowed on the outskirts of the 1,248-acre area for deer, squirrel, turkey, rabbit, quail, doves and woodcock. Fishermen can catch largemouth bass, bluegill, redear, crappie and channel catfish.

The park features three trails. Lake Trail takes you around Glen O. Jones Lake; Wildlife Nature Trail is a loop trail between roads; Wildlife Nature Trail leads onto a ridge in the Shawnee National

Forest and ends at popular caving spot called Cave Hill.

The conservation area is at the end of a tangle of country roads at the edge of the Shawnee National Forest southeast of Harrisburg. Signs are important for finding the area. From Harrisburg take Illinois 13 east to Equality and Illinois 142. Go south (right) into Equality and stay to your right on the same road, avoiding a road heading straight where the road branches. Once outside Equality the road (which is no longer called Illinois 142) will lead you to the conservation area after traveling about six miles.

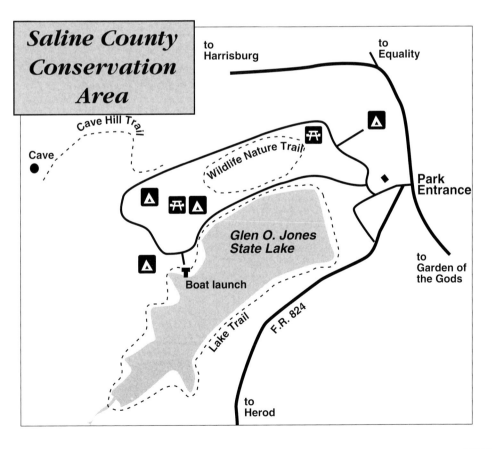

Rim Rock/Pounds Hollow

It is difficult to find a more beautiful setting to go for a swim or bathe in the sun than the 25-acre lake in Pounds Hollow. The lake was built by the Civilian Conservation Corps in 1940, but has all the appearances of a naturally formed lake in a wooded valley. The Shawnee Hills rise steeply away from the water and the heavy forestation creates the effect of a hidden waterhole.

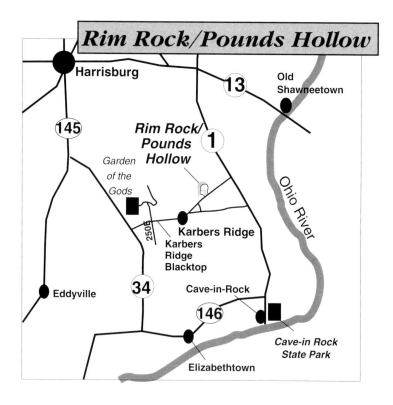

It may be hidden, but it is not primitive. Showers and a concession stand renting paddle boats and boats, equipped with trolling motors, are provided for your convenience. Picnic areas are also provided. Near the beach to the south is a campground for tent or vehicular camping.

The Rim Rock recreational trail is just west of the beach/camping area. Another picnic area bounds an interesting hiking trail which travels in a loop along bluffs and rock escarpments.

Rim Rock/Pounds Hollow is southeast of Harrisburg in Gallatin County. From Harrisburg take Illinois 145/34 south to Illinois 34. Ten miles after Illinois 34 separates from Illinois 145 turn east (left) and follow this road to Karbers Ridge then veer northeast (left) to Rim Rock/Pounds Hollow.

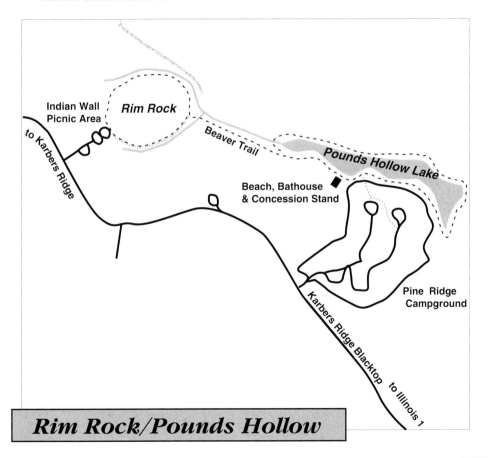

Indian Wall Picnic Area

Rim Rock

to Karbers Ridge

Beaver Trail

Pounds Hollow Lake

Beach, Bathouse & Concession Stand

Pine Ridge Campground

Karbers Ridge Blacktop   to Illinois 1

Rim Rock/Pounds Hollow

30   # Garden of the Gods

A few million years ago glaciers covered most of the Midwest and were heading for the southernmost reaches of Illinois. But a funny thing happened on the way to Cairo. The ice stopped, retreated, then melted. The result is that extreme Southern Illinois has been left with a craggy, worn and mountainous landscape of which the best example is Garden of the Gods. The area is all the more striking since the work of flattening glaciers is so obvious only a few miles to the north around Harrisburg.

Garden of the Gods is Southern Illinois' premiere attraction. Pictures of the site are always featured on brochures dipicting tourism in the area.

The recreation area boasts an impressive network of trails (some accessible to the handicapped) which give hikers breathtaking views and, at times, heavy lungs as they make their way around the rugged terrain. A campground and picnic ground are provided near the parking area. Garden of the Gods is one of the most popular nature sites in Southern Illinois so visitors should expect to be in the company of plenty of others on fair weekend days.

Garden of the Gods is southeast of Harrisburg in Saline County but at the intersection of Gallatin, Hardin and Saline Counties. It is in the vicinity of Rim Rock/Pounds Hollow. From Harrisburg follow Illinois 145/34 to Illinois 34 and turn east (left) at the sign to Garden of the Gods. Two miles on is another sign pointing north (left) leading to the Garden of the Gods.

Camel Rock at Garden of the Gods

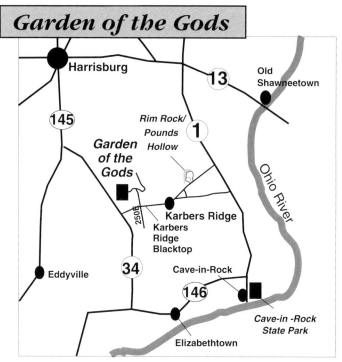

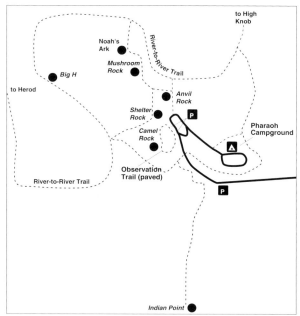

31

Bell Smith Springs

Mill Branch Creek at Bell Smith Springs and bluff

The natural bridge at Bell Smith Springs

Unquestionably one of the most beautiful places in Southern Illinois, Bell Smith Springs provides the Hunting Branch Picnic Area for an ideal setting among the rocky formations and creeks of the Shawnee National Forest. A scenic creek flows in front of the 12 shelterless picnic tables. Toilets are provided. At the parking lot next to the picnic area, another creek invites the visitor into the trails leading off into the heart of the forest. The natural bridge is a must to see.

Below this area is **Teal Pond**. Bank fishing is allowed on the pond and a small campground is provided at the secluded spot.

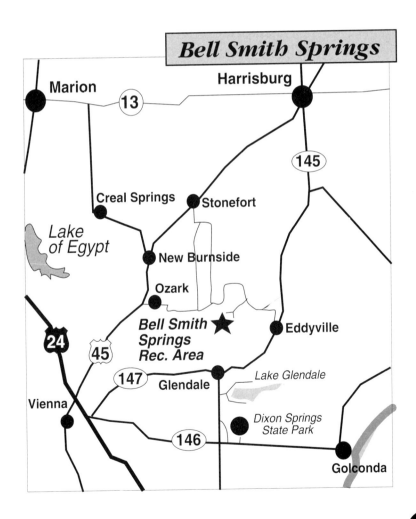

32 *Dixon Springs State Park*

A popular destination for 19th century travelers and, before that, bivouacking Indians, people have always been drawn to what the Indians called the "Great Medicine Waters" of Dixon Springs. This epithet appears appropriate since bathing in these brown sulphur-smelling waters is akin to imbibing castor oil for what ails you. More commonplace, though less odiferous, a 45-foot by 96-foot swimming pool and 45-foot water slide with on-duty lifeguard is available to visitors. The pool provides handicapped access.

Another feature which has made the 786-acre park a popular stopping place through the years is the shade provided by forest and cliff

One of several churches at the trailhead for Pine Tree Trail

overhangs. These natural air conditioners furnish shelter from the intense Southern Illinois sun. The forest is composed of oak, cypress, birch and pine trees as well as violets and lady slipper flowers. Foxes, rabbits, squirrels, deer and groundhogs thrive among the vegetation. As in many parks in extreme Southern Illinois, rock formations during and just after rain create spectacles of rivulets and waterfalls as the water drains over the cliffs and through the crags.

A self-guided 1.7 mile nature trail invites visitors into the scenic beauty of the park. And a class B trailer camping area with electricity and dumping station as well as primitive tent camping invite passers-by to stay. Cabins with numerous bunk beds are also available for groups.

Dixon Springs is about a mile east of the intersection of Illinois 145 and Illinois 146 in Pope County. It is also midway between Metropolis and Harrisburg. From Harrisburg take Illinois 145 south to just past the intersection of Illinois 147 to Illinois 146 and turn east onto Illinois 146 and then into the park. From I-24 take Exit #16 at Illinois 146 and head east on Illinois 146 until you reach the park.

33 *Lake Glendale*

This popular swimming hole for the residents of southeastern Illinois is part of the Shawnee National Forest system. A large shower and concessions building serves visitors. The concession provides paddle boats and snacks. Trolling motors are allowed on the lake where fishermen often cast for bass. Boat ramps serve the fishermen's needs and a trail circles the lake for walkers. Near the lake, though not within eyeshot, campsites and picnic areas are provided.

Lake Glendale is off Illinois 145 in Pope County, 12 miles east of Vienna. From I-24 take exit #16 at Illinois 146 and go east 11 miles to the intersection of Illinois 146 and Illinois 145. Turn north (left) and Lake Glendale is about two miles up the road.

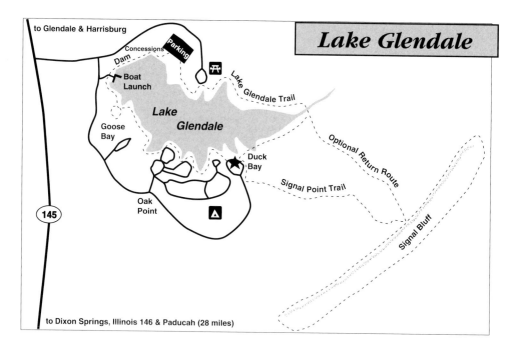

34 *Camp Ondessonk*

On the surface, Camp Ondessonk, a 1,000-acre youth camp operated by the Belleville Diocese of the Catholic Church, appears to be
just another summer camp. Each summer hundreds of kids converge
on the camp for one- or two-week sessions of hiking, horseback riding
and swimming. But, Camp Ondessonk offers much more than a brief
summer diversion for youngsters. When summer camp is not in session, the facilities of Camp Ondessonk, located just off U.S. 45 about
11 miles northeast of Vienna, are open to the public.

Located in the heart of the Shawnee National Forest, Camp
Ondessonk features some of the most beautiful scenery in the area.
The camp is crisscrossed with trails suitable for hiking and horseback

Rock overhang at Camp Ondessonk

riding. The camp maintains its own herd of 55 horses. Horseback rides can be arranged through the camp office. The horseback and hiking trails take visitors past **Cedar Falls**, an 89-foot waterfall, split-rock passages like **Fat Man's Misery**, the abandoned **Camp Pakentuck** and a prehistoric Indian stone fort.

For a nominal fee, visitors can rent the cabins used to house students during the summer sessions. The cabins are spartan, three-sided structures with bare bunks, but many are located atop limestone bluffs overlooking lakes. The splendid views make up for the lack of amenities.

Campers also have access to the boats and canoes owned by the camp.

Canoers at Camp Ondessonk

For the more faint of heart, Ondessonk provides heated dormitory accommodations, heated shower houses and complete meal packages. The camp will also provide outdoor educational programs and conservation instruction upon request. For those who wish to rough it in the lap of luxury, **St. Noel's Retreat** offers plush accommodations for business meetings as well as weekend murder mystery packages.

For more information, write Camp Ondessonk, Route 1, Ozark, IL 62972, or call (618) 695-2489.

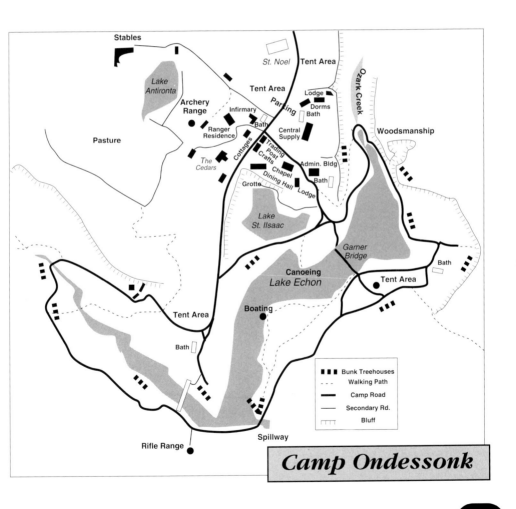

Camp Ondessonk

35   *Cave-In-Rock State Park*

Cave-In-Rock is a sleepy Ohio River town known today for its state park and one of the best views of the Ohio River in Southern Illinois.

But its past is a morbid one, filled with the unsavory characters who once laid in wait for unsuspecting sailors in the cave in the rock (for which the town is named) facing the Ohio River.

Samuel Mason, an officer in the Revolutionary War, came across the site and set up a trap for passersby in the early part of the last century. Captains and crews were lured into the cave by a sign which read, "Liquor vault and house of entertainment." Alcohol and prostitutes occupied the crew until Mason's band murdered them and stole their ship's cargo. Mason was soon joined by the sadistic Big and Little Harpe, brothers from North Carolina who had grown up with a renegade Indian tribe.

Big and Little Harpe chased a woman and her horse off one of the bluffs surrounding Cave-In-Rock. Too wild even for Mason, they were forced to leave.

The place where Mason and his gang hid out is now a state park with camping, a restaurant and cabins with superb views of the river.

The **restaurant** serves a variety of sandwiches and the ever-present catfish (see Restaurant Section). It also features an outside sitting area where patrons can view the river as they enjoy lunch or dinner.

Tent camping is available at the rear of the small park and a short path takes visitors to the bluffs overlooking the river and down into the infamous cave.

The shallow cave is filled with modern graffiti so it is hard to pick out the remnants from older times, but imagining the devilish deeds that went on inside gives the visitor a taste of the past.

Picnic areas are scattered throughout the park and playground areas are available for children.

Visitors can stay for a night or a week at the cabins which rent for $52 a day. Each cabin has a balcony which takes advantage of the fabulous view of the river. Cabins should be reserved in advance, months in advance if wanted for the peak times of June through August. Call (618) 289-4545 for reservations.

A few miles downstream or on Illinois 146 is the **Golconda Marina**. It is a full service marina with scores of covered slips, fuel, food, showers, boat rental and repair services. The marina is the gateway to the **Smithland Pool** portion of the Ohio River. The pool is a deep water 72-mile stretch created by locks and dams below Golconda extending to the Uniontown Lock to its north (see Fishing Section).

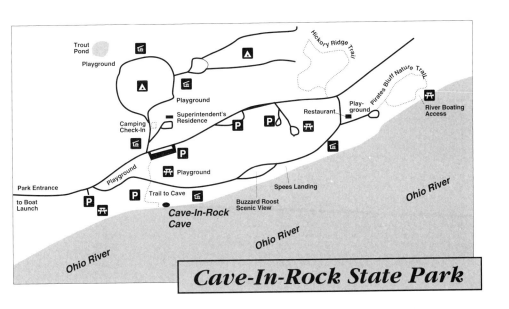

Cave-In-Rock State Park

36

Mermet Lake Conservation Area

Mermet Lake is a favorite of fishermen. Of the 231,000 visitors in 1992, some 221,000 came to fish, according to site superintendent Chris McGinness. Bluegill, carp, buffalo, channel catfish and sunfish are among the available species.

Reflecting its use, the rather bare 452-acre lake provides several docks and boat ramps. The best of these is a 30-foot permanent dock on the east side near the sheltered picnic area.

View of Mermet Lake

Duck and Canada goose hunting is another popular activity at Mermet Lake. Several blinds are provided. Squirrel, rabbit, quail, dove and archery deer hunting are also allowed.

There is a good chance at Mermet Lake to find interesting birds of prey and endangered bird species. Five **bald eagles** nest there from December through February and hawks and osprey are also common. Endangered moorhen, least bittern, and purple gallinule live on the conservation area as well.

Mermet Lake is off U.S. 45 in Massac County, 14 miles northwest of Paducah, Ky. From the north, take exit #16 off I-24 onto Illinois 146. Illinois 146 quickly intersects with U.S. 45. Go south (left) on U.S. 45 for nine miles to Mermet Lake. From the south, take I-24 to the Metropolis exit at U.S. 45. Take U.S. 45 north for 11 miles to the lake.

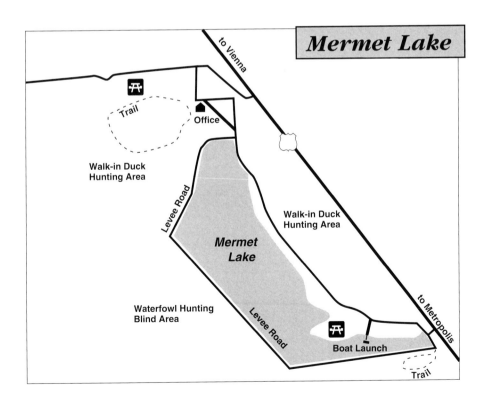

I haven't made up my mind yet.

I'm trying to decide if it is just a difference in personalities, or a basic difference in the sexes.

Every now and then I'll come home from work and suggest the family hop in the car and drive out to nearby Glen O. Jones Lake for a picnic and an evening of fishing.

To me the suggestion means quickly throwing a few things in the car and getting there. Once there, it's just a matter of grilling a few dogs and filling your face, with hands that smell like minnows or night crawlers.

Preparing for such a trip is no problem.

Les Winkeler
Sports writer

The Southern Illinoisan, June 10,1990

Don't worry about packing the rods and reels or the tackle box, chances are they're already in the back of the car.

Picnic supplies? No problem. Let's go down the list:

Hot dogs? Check.

Buns? Check.

Mustard? Check.

Onions? Check.

Potato chips? Check.

Charcoal? Check.

Lighter fluid? Check.

Cooler? Check.

There folks, is a complete picnic.

Even if the mustard is buried in the back of the refrigerator behind a decaying cantaloupe, packing that picnic should take no more than 15 minutes, 20 minutes tops.

Given a worst case scenario and it takes 20 minutes to pack lunch, that means the elapsed time from suggesting the picnic to actually fishing should be no more than 45 minutes.

This is where that sex or personality thing comes in.

My wife, who has been helping the kids find their shoes, will ask me if I've got everything packed.

With a great deal of pride, I announce that we're all set. Then it happens.

She peeks at what I've packed.

"There aren't any paper plates in here," she says. "Where's the cups? Didn't you pack any silverware? Is there a tablecloth in there?"

"Well, I just thought we could stand around the picnic table and dig the chips out with our hands," I mumble.

By this time, I know I'm in trouble. I've been married long enough to recognize that look on her face. She is going down her own checklist.

Relish? Nope.

Kraut? Nope.

Lemonade? Nope.

Watermelon? Nope.

Potato salad? Nope.

Baked beans? Nope.

I have to admit that the relish and kraut dress up a dog nicely.

And, I have been known to demolish a watermelon almost single-handedly. But, for the life of me, I don't understand the need to take baked beans on a picnic. I mean, I like baked beans, but does anybody ever say to themselves, "Man, I'd give five bucks for a plate of baked beans?"

I've never heard it.

Naturally, there won't be a baked bean in the house. That necessitates a stop at the grocery store. In the meantime, the sun and precious fishing time are slowly sinking in the west.

Shawnee National Forest

One of the first things you notice when looking at a road map of Illinois is the swath of green that covers the lower third of the state. The green patch is the Shawnee National Forest. The forest occupies a great deal of the map, over 270,000 acres, but is one of the smallest of the 156 national forests. In the western United States, national forests of 2 million acres are common. "It takes less time to travel the Shawnee from one end to the other than it takes to get from one ranger district to another in a western forest," said Tom Hagerty, a public information officer for the U.S. Forest Service. While small by some standards, the Shawnee is among the most diverse of the national forests, encompassing 55 ecological areas. **Bell Smith Springs** is among the most interesting.

Visitors to that area can see a flowering prickly pear cactus, or if their timing is perfect the flower of an hour. The flower of an hour has pink petals and blooms for just 60 minutes each year. The flower blooms on spring afternoons, usually around 1 p.m.

Many of the forest's areas receive heavy visitation, including Bell Smith Springs, but many visitors fail to notice some of its most outstanding attractions. Many visitors leave Bell Smith Springs without ever seeing the Bell Smith Springs Arch, a natural arch that is part of the bluff line that rims the canyon. A hiking trail takes visitors over a natural sandstone bridge. The arch is only about 10 minutes from the parking lot.

Mill Creek is another feature of the Bell Smith Springs area that often goes unnoticed. Located near the Hunting Branch picnic area, Mill Creek features formations where streams have cut down through bedrock. It is about a fourth mile west of Hunting Branch. **Lusk Creek Canyon**, located just west and north of Eddyville, is another such area. Visitors in early spring can see sheets of ice clinging to the sides of the sandstone bluffs towering above pristine Lusk Creek.

Burden Falls is another location that is frequently overlooked. More correctly, it is a location that is frequently driven over. Located on Forest Road 402, about five miles west of Illinois 145, the falls are not readily visible from the road. When the gravel road becomes a short concrete slab, you are there. Pull off onto the shoulder immediately. Just taking a few steps north of the roadway reveals a 30-40 foot

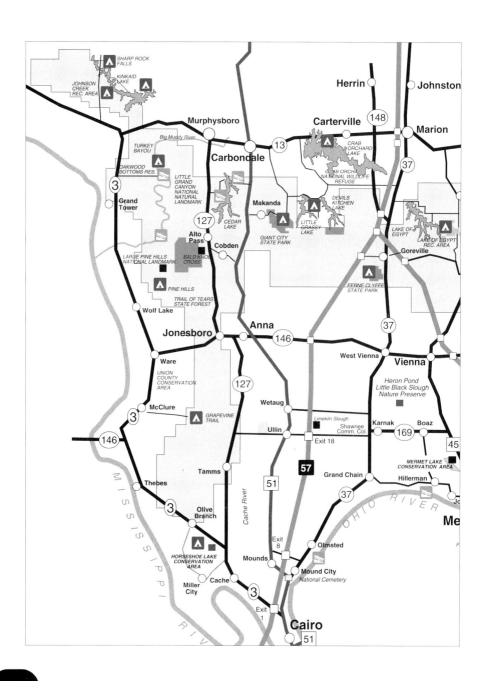

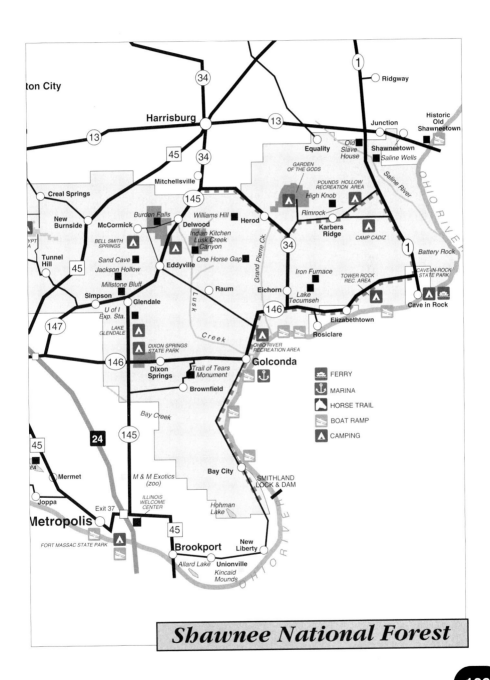

Shawnee National Forest

waterfall. The falls are likely to be dry during the summer months, but a visit in early spring can be truly inspiring.

Crow's Knob, located north of Glendale, is an excellent location to view the splendor of the forest's fall foliage. To reach Crow's Knob, take Forest Road 423 north from Glendale for about two miles. Turn east for a short distance, then take the left fork in the road until you see a small pulloff with horse hitching racks and a wooden fence. The bedrock outcrop at Crow's Knob offers an outstanding view of the forest.

The Shawnee National Forest was born in 1933. What is now considered the Shawnee National Forest was originally two separate units. The "original" Shawnee, which included land in Gallatin, Saline, Pope and Hardin counties, was merged with the Illini, which included property in Jackson, Union and Alexander counties.

Much of the forest land, particularly in the eastern portion of the forest, had been cleared in futile attempts at grain and orchard farming, meaning much of the land had to be replanted. The replanting got under way in 1934 when Civilian Conservation Corps crews planted 57 acres in jack pine. Spruce, ponderosa pine, Norway spruce, Douglas fir and red pine were planted later. Replanting reached its peak in 1941 when some 800 workers planted nearly 8,000 acres.

Historic Sites

Cairo Public Library

T he interesting history of a place is comprised of the very old and the momentous. Southern Illinois meets both of these criterion. From the launching pad for a war between the states at Cairo and the dividing line between north and south which pitted neighbor and families against each other; from the towns and locales where Lincoln walked and politicked to the prehistoric Indian remains of a lost civilization at Cahokia to the remnants of French colonial life on the Mississippi; Southern Illinois' history and artifacts are as interesting and diverse as any in the Midwest.

Many of the historic sites listed below are free of charge, but visitors are often asked to donate between $2 and $4 to keep them running.

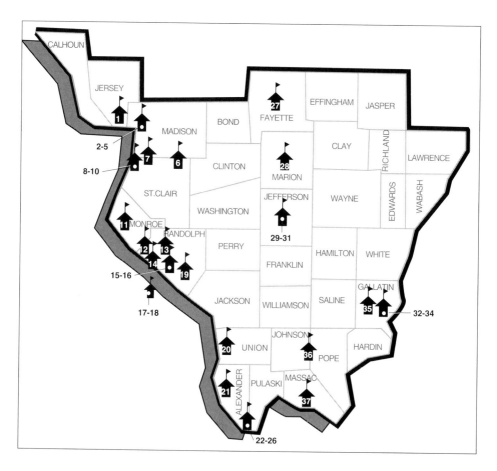

Elsah

Location: Northwest of Alton off Illinois 100 in Jersey County
Tours: (618) 374-2821 (Mary-Ann Pitchford)
Founded: 1853

The entire town of Elsah is listed in the National Register of Historic Places. This town is one of the most remarkable slices of preserved history anywhere in America. Sometimes known as New England in the Midwest, Elsah is a two-street village with idyllic limestone and brick houses. The town has been so meticulously preserved that almost nothing has been restored.

The town is a tourist haven as many of the stone houses have been converted to accommodate guests (See Bed and Breakfasts section). Elsah was founded by James Semple who, starting in 1883, provided building lots free of charge to anyone who would build a house on them. The local limestone quarry was a popular source of materials as the houses were built primarily in the styles of Greek Revival, Franco-American and Gothic Revival.

The styles tended to mimic those popular on the New England coast, but lagged several years behind the New England fashions, according to a guidebook of the town. **Elsah: A Historic Guidebook** by Charles B. Hosmer Jr., and Paul O. Williams, lays out a walking tour of the town and details the history of all the significant buildings. The book is available at the town's museum gift shop (open 1 - 4 p.m., Thursdays through Sundays).

Elsah is also home of one of the greatest concentrations of **bald eagles** in the Mississippi flyway. The eagles are in Elsah from January through the middle of March. For a tour of eagle nesting areas or other natural wonders near Elsah, contact the Riverlands Association at Elsah, IL 62028, or call (618) 374-2520.

Alton

The best way to enjoy Alton's historic and scenic offerings is by a guided motor tour; the steep streets and old houses and buildings are as varied as the Alton history. Call the Alton Tourism Office at (800) 258-6645 to arrange a tour.

As with many towns along the Mississippi Rivers , the recorded history of Alton begins with a note from Father Jacques Marquette on his journey with explorer Louis Joliet in 1673. Marquette observed the strange and terrible "Piasa Bird" (pronounced PIE-a-saw) on the bluffs facing the river. In Illini legend, this bird, with the face of horned lionesque creature, the talons and wings of a bird and the body of a reptile, was said to have a taste for Indian braves. The original image was a victim of quarrying in the 19th century and a reproduction on a billboard has been erected at the spot on the bluffs between Alton and the Pere Marquette Lodge on Illinois 100 (The Great River Road).

After statehood was granted to Illinois, and riverboat traffic became more and more important in the life of the nation, Alton bene-fited from its location at the confluence of the Mississippi and Illinois Rivers. The story of its trade, however, is eclipsed by the uncanny political importance the city played at the crossroads of American History–the Civil War.

Elijah P. Lovejoy, a committed abolitionist, agitated against slav-ery and protected printing presses at the cost of his life at the hands of an angry mob in Alton. This devotion has earned him a place in the pantheon of both civil rights and free press advocates. The monument to his life stands in the Alton City Cemetery.

Abraham Lincoln practiced law in Alton and one of its local barons retained him as a private attorney. Thus, he was on home terri-tory when the last of the seven Lincoln-Douglas Debates were held in Alton next to what is now a parking lot near the Greater Alton Convention Visitors Bureau.

A little-known, but highly influential senator, which Altonians like to refer to as "Illinois' other emancipator" worked out of Alton for years and his house still remains in pristine restored condition. **Lyman Trumbull** wrote the 13th amendment to the Constitution which freed the slaves and was one of the founders of the Republican party. His house is in the Midtown Historic District surrounded by many other beautiful 19th century homes.

With the passage of time, Alton's impact on the life of the nation became more modest. This was symbolized, perhaps, by Alton's most famous resident of the 20th century, a man known for his height rather than his accomplishments, the tallest man in recorded history, **Robert Wadlow**, Alton's "Gentle Giant."

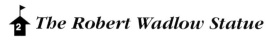

⚑ *The Robert Wadlow Statue*

Location: Corner of Clawson and College, in upper Alton

Anyone who has browsed through the Guinness Book of World Records has come across information about this Alton native, one of the book's most amazing entries. To see what it is like to stand next to a man who grew to eight feet, eleven inches, the tallest person ever recorded, travel to the north side of Alton. There stands a life-sized replica of Robert Pershing Wadlow, "Alton's Gentle Giant."

Wadlow grew at an incredible rate after he was six months old. At 18 months he weighed 62 pounds, and at 11 years old he was over seven feet, four inches. When Wadlow ran a booth in the Illinois State Fair in Springfield at age 17 he weighed 390 pounds and was eight feet, four inches tall. At his death, Wadlow weighed just over 490 pounds.

Wadlow's life story is as sad as it is interesting. At the age of 22, he died of an infection in his foot. Feet were a preoccupation with him for most of his life. They were so big that he was forced to walk up most stairs sideways and shoes, at size 37, cost his family enormous sums. At 18, Wadlow gave up on college because it was too difficult for him to get around on campus, and he and his father took up offers for the giant to act as a promoter and attraction in shows and for companies.

One of the companies he promoted was a shoe company, which provided his shoes for the rest of his life. With his father as manager, Wadlow joined the Ringling Brothers Barnum and Bailey Circus for a short stint. He and his father visited festivals across the country and it was at one of these in Michigan where death claimed him. A brace propping up a weak ankle broke the skin and Wadlow paid too little attention to the dull throb which must have seemed so far away. The infection killed him a few days later.

 *The Lyman Trumbull House*

Location: 1105 Henry Street at the corner of Union Street
Built: 1820 - 1830
Architecture: Greek Revival
Current use: Private residence

Lyman Trumbull was one of the great politicians of the Civil War-era yet his name remains obscure to the world at large. One of his works is not obscure, however, and that is the 13th amendment to the constitution which outlawed slavery.

The attractive house which bears Trumbull's name is in the neighborhood of the Middletown Historic District which is packed with other well-preserved 19th century houses. The Trumbull House is a Greek Revival House built by local architect Benjamin Ives Gilman sometime between 1820 to 1830. This national historic landmark has a federal architectural influence as well, most obviously illustrated by the double chimneys. A federal eagle (which is a replica of the original) was an early sign that the house had insurance so fire fighters would know their work would not go uncompensated.

Trumbull moved to Alton and bought the house in 1849. Trumbull was a justice of the Illinois Supreme Court while he lived in Alton. In 1855 he was elected to the U. S. Senate from Illinois as a member of the Republican Party, a party he had helped give birth to only two years before.

While a justice, Trumbull ruled that contracts of slavery were invalid in Illinois, a free state. It was this ruling which helped set the framework for the Dred Scott Decision by the U.S. Supreme Court, which overruled Trumbull and did much to set the stage for the Civil War. As a senator during the Civil War Trumbull proposed the 13th amendment after Lincoln's Emancipation Proclamation.

Trumbull was a progressive if nothing else. Before the Civil War he left the Democratic Party to help set up the Republican Party when he could not abide the northern party's toleration of slavery. After the Civil War he was effectively thrown out of the Republican Party when he refused to cooperate with a Grant administration that had become obviously corrupt. At the end of his life he argued in front of the Supreme Court for the release of socialist leader Eugene V. Debs and wrote the Populist Party platform of 1896.

Next door to the Trumbull House is a small, immaculately-preserved little structure called the **Haskell Doll House.** The Queen Anne style playhouse was built in 1885 for the five-year-old granddaughter of John E. Hayner. Lucy J. Haskell enjoyed the house only until the age of nine, however, when she died of diphtheria. The house is listed in the National Register of Historic Places.

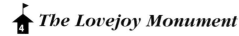

The Lovejoy Monument

Location: Corner of Fifth and Monument Street, Alton City Cemetery

In the city cemetery is another Alton landmark, to one of Illinois' martyrs to the abolitionist movement. The Lovejoy Monument commemorates a man who died defending his printing press from which he issued tracts lampooning slavery and all its works.

Elijah P. Lovejoy was at least as stubborn as he was brave. He was a school teacher from Vermont who moved to St. Louis and took up work as a newspaper editor. Incensed by his railings against slavery, townspeople forced Lovejoy to move his printing press across the river for his own safety in 1836. In Alton he refused to be driven away or diverted from his purpose. Angry mobs destroyed a succession of presses until he tried to put out the flames from a fire set to the building which housed his fourth printing press. There he was killed, a martyr to abolitionism and to the press. A tall monument stands above his grave on the top of which an angelic figure holds a trumpet to its lips.

The monument is in the Alton City Cemetery at the corner of Monument Street and Fifth. Follow Illinois 3 through lower downtown Alton, turn north onto Monument Street which leads up a hill to the cemetery.

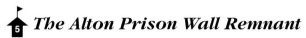

The Alton Prison Wall Remnant

Location: Broadway and Williams Streets, on the riverfront
Built: 1839
Charge: None

The Alton prison began as a civil prison, but quickly earned the wrath of prison reformer Dorothea Dix. She agitated for its closure after convincing the legislature that the prison's dirt floors and unsanitary conditions were inhumane. Shut down in 1860, it would soon reopen for the start of the Civil War. With Confederate prisoners came smallpox and an environment ripe for plague. A small, but thought provoking wall remnant remains at the site the prison once occupied by forlorn prisoners.

A sand bar in the Mississippi (now gone) was taken over as a "hospital" and quarantine for prisoners who had contracted smallpox. The death toll rose by the hundreds as some were buried at the hospital site, newly dubbed Smallpox Island, and others in a special cemetery which is today known as the **Confederate Cemetery**, located at Rozier Street in north Alton. Estimates are that between 1,000 and 5,000 died at the prison and a substantial accounting of these can be found in the list and memorial at the Confederate Cemetery.

Lebanon

Location: Junction of U.S. 50 and Illinois 4, south of Edwardsville
Phone: (618) 537-4498 (Lebanon Advertiser newspaper)
Founded: 1804
Special Events: Free tours available

The best word for Lebanon is idyllic. The high wooden store fronts and lazy, spacious pubs line a brick paved street, giving the impression of a well groomed 19th century town. McKendree College with its 19th century chapel on the northwest end of town reinforces the impression of a solid Methodist community. Many of the private homes date to the 19th century and even Charles Dickens stopped here on his excursion to Illinois.

A good way to enjoy the town is to wander through it. Park on St. Louis Street and shop in the antique shops and have a drink in the pubs. The **Mermaid House**, on the east end of the street is the former inn where Dickens stayed. It was built in 1830 and played host to the great English novelists as recorded in *American Notes*. Lebanon was one of the few destinations in America that Dickens cared for.

McKendree College, the oldest college in Illinois, is also the oldest Methodist college. The best view of the historic campus is at "front campus" facing College Road from which you get a good view of Old

St. Louis Street in Lebanon

Main, built in 1851 and the Bothwell Chapel, dating from 1858. A museum with artifacts from the college's century and-a-half history is open by appointment. Call Dr. Pat Folk at (618) 537-4481.

Indian Prehistory

At the end of the last Ice Age 12,000 years ago, a group which archaeologists refer to as Paleo Indians moved into the region for the first time. They hunted big game and made arrowheads with fluted projectile points. But Paleo Indians would soon disappear as the ice receded, giving way to bands of hunters and gatherers in the long archaic period lasting between 8,000 and 3,000 years ago. The best example of an Archaic Period site in Southern Illinois is the **Modoc Rock Shelter** near Prairie du Rocher in Randolph County. The Modoc Rock site was inhabited by a succession of Indian bands over thousands of years and archaeologists have uncovered animal remains, tools and weapons. The shelter is marked only by a state historical marker, but is listed on the National Register of Historic Places because of its importance in helping archaeologists understand Indian life before Europeans arrived.

The next phase of Indian prehistory stretching between 1,000 B.C. to 900 A.D., called the Woodland Period, is marked by the beginnings of villages and trade among Indians. This period is known for the development of burial ceremonies and burial mound building. Although these developments in other parts of the Midwest had little influence on Southern Illinois, archaeologists do find items such as sharks teeth from the Gulf of Mexico and volcanic glass from the western United States, which were transported along trading routes to the area. Southern Illinois Indians probably exchanged Cobden chert, a stone used to make arrowheads. The most recognizable remains of the Woodland Period, coming at the end of the period, are the handful of **"stoneforts"** found across the countryside. These walls may have been used as defensive positions, for herding animals, or for some other purpose which has not occurred to archaeologists.

Most of these long, low stone walls have been taken down by farmers for use as building materials, but an easily accessible one remains in Giant City State Park, near Makanda (See Parks section). Another Woodland and Mississippian site is at **Millstone Bluff** which has an interpretive trail and petrogylphs carved by ancient peoples. Millstone Bluff is in the Shawnee Forest in Pope County near the tiny town of Robbs.

The last, and most advanced, phase of Indian prehistory is the Mississippian. Mississippians sustained their settlements by cultivating corn and other crops so their settlements tended to grow up near rich alluvial (river) bottom farmland. The richest in Southern Illinois is in the American Bottom, what is now called the Metro East area. And it was here that the great city of Cahokia became the center of commerce, social and political power for Mississippian culture in the Midwest. Known for their elaborate burial and tribal rituals, these culminate in the giant mounds at **Cahokia Mounds Interpretive Center** in Collinsville.

Mississippian civilization disappeared about 1500, just before the first Europeans arrived in Illinois. These were the last of the truly "native Southern Illinoisans" since the historic tribes of the region like the Illini and Shawnee came from farther north. These tribes tended to be on better terms with French settlers than with the English, or later Americans, who eventually drove them onto reservations farther west. In the present-day town of Cahokia, for example, the Indians lived, and sometimes inter-married with the French settlers. The museum in the Cahokia Courthouse (see below) describes relations between French settlers and Indians at the time.

Cahokia Mounds

Location: Collinsville (Illinois 111 and Collinsville Road)
Phone: (618) 346-5160
Age: 700 A.D. - 1500 A.D.
People: Mississippian
Charge: None
Handicapped access: See below

Current use: Interpretive site

Hours: Interpretive Center: daily, 9 a.m. - 5 p.m.; March - Nov., closed Mon. and Tues.

Tours: June - Aug.: Wed. - Sat. 10 a.m. and 2 p.m.; Sunday, 12 noon and 2 p.m.; April - October: Sat. and Sun., 2 p.m.

There is simply nothing like them north of Mexico. The Cahokia Mounds are what remains of the most advanced Indian civilization outside of Latin America: huge earthen monuments to a society that disappeared just before Europeans arrived on the scene. It is not clear why the center of Mississippian culture was deserted around 1500. Warfare, disease, social unrest and decimation of crops through climactic change are all candidates.

Whatever the reason for its collapse, modern day archaeologists have dug up Cahokia's remains and recreated the city in an elaborate interpretive center on the site. Inside the interpretive center archaeological finds await visitors. Accompanying the art, pottery, tools and weapons is a wealth of explanatory displays describing the culture of the Mississippian civilization with a special emphasis on Cahokia itself, center of a thriving metropolis. The life-size diorama invites visitors to wander through a "neighborhood" in the recreated city of Cahokia, looking in on child care in the huts and craft work in the streets. Before wandering through the displays, it is a good idea to view the orientation show, a dramatic overview of Cahokia Mounds and its parent, the Mississippian civilization. By watching the orientation, visitors will better appreciate the individual displays in the center. A gift shop offers books and tokens relating to the subjects on display.

Outside the interpretive center is the **Nature/Culture Hike** (a guidebook is available in the gift shop) which takes visitors around the mounds themselves. In a public works project reminiscent of the Egyptian pyramids, Indians labored to haul tons of earth dug with tools of wood, stone or shell. The earth was transported to the mounds on human backs as three types were created: platform mounds with flat tops used for ceremonies and the dwellings of powerful tribesmen, conical mounds and ridgetop mounds, both used for the burial of dignitaries.

At the northwest corner of the trail is a reproduction of the

Cahokians' calendar, **Woodhenge**. Its name is derived from England's Stonehenge because it is thought to serve the same function as that ancient stone calendar. As the name implies, Woodhenge was composed of wooden rods. At certain times during the year these lined up with the sun, giving the Mississippians an exact sense of changing seasons and reliable festival dates. Woodhenge has been recreated by scientists at the spot where it once stood.

Due east from Woodhenge is the highlight of the trail, **Monk's Mound**. It is the most massive earthen structure in the pre-Columbian New World and represents the figurative as well as literal apex of the Cahokian metropolis. The mound earned its name after 18th century French monks built a chapel on the first terrace.

Climbing the stairs, which have been built where the Indians once laid them, you'll find yourself 100 feet above the ground on a flat topped mound covering 15 acres at its base. From this vantage point the ruler of Cahokia lived and surveyed his fief. The mound was built in stages between 900 A.D. and 1200 A.D. with a succession of buildings on top of it accompanying its growth.

⚑ *Modoc Rock Shelter*

Location: Randolph County, near Prairie du Rocher
Age: 8000 B.C. - 1000 B.C.
People: Archaic Indian

Modoc Rock Shelter is a small site with only a roadside sign describing its significance. But this significance is great indeed for the understanding of the life of Southern Illinois' first inhabitants. The shelter was inhabited over thousands of years by a succession of Indian bands. The remains of campfires, tools, weapons and animals give archaeologists a sense for the living patterns of Archaic Indians. It turns out that these Indians depended on much the same flora and fauna as is found in Southern Illinois today: deer, turtles, waterfowl, rabbits and fish lie buried in the layers of earth, while nuts were also gathered from the earliest times.

Modoc Rock Shelter is west off Illinois 3 between the tiny town of

Modoc and Prairie du Rocher. From the south on Illinois 3, turn at the Roots Junction and follow the road past Modoc to the site. From the north, take Illinois 3 to Illinois 155 into Prairie du Rocher and follow the road leading southeast towards the town of Modoc. The interpretive sign is before Modoc.

 *Millstone Bluff*

Location: Near Robbs in Pope County & the Shawnee National Forest
Phone: (618) 253-7144
Age: 8000 B.C. to about 1500 A.D.
People: Woodland and Mississippian
Charge: None
Current Use: Interpretive nature trail
Handicapped access: No

Millstone Bluff is a short interpretive trail in the Shawnee National Forest near the major attraction of the Garden of the Gods. Although it is located in an out-of-the-way place, rock carvings (petroglyphs) at the end of the trail are probably the most accessible in Southern Illinois outside of a museum. At the end of the trail are a few admittedly faded carvings of a thunderbird, a runner and a cross inside a circle, probably made by the Woodland Indians. Along the trail is a clearing where an interpretive sign tells you that this was once the site of a Mississippian Indian dwelling. The Mississippian Indian culture came after Woodland Indians and disappeared just before white men arrived in the area.

To get to Millstone Bluff from I-24, take the Vienna exit #16 east (away from Vienna) on Illinois 146 to Illinois 147 and go eight miles on Illinois 147 to a left turn at the sign pointing towards the site.

Cahokia

The town of Cahokia was an old French trading center and later the original St. Clair County seat. As such, it has retained prime examples of French Colonial architecture in the Mississippi valley as well as an aristocratic turn of the 18th century mansion.

Many of the towns along the Mississippi River were settled when an Indian tribe was joined by Catholic missionaries who intended to convert them to Catholicism. This story is true of Cahokia. Named for a tribe of the Illini federation, Cahokia's first European building, a log church, was erected by priests in 1698. The descendant of this church was built in 1799 and is still in use today.

Thanks to amicable relations between the French and Indians the French transferred their goods as well as their religion to the Indians, and Cahokia was considered the most important trading center between the French and Indians during the French occupation.

When the Illinois country fell into British and later American hands, trade with the Indians continued. But Nicholas Jarrot, a French Canadian immigrant realized that it would be more lucrative to trade with the settlers passing through on their way to the western frontier. In 1810 the **Jarrot Mansion**, which still still stands today, was erected. It was financed by the fruits of his trade, which were not always acquired in an honest fashion.

St. Clair is a county east of St. Louis, but when the county was created in 1790 there was no state of Illinois, only the Illinois country which included much of the present-day Midwest. St. Clair County stretched to the Canadian border.

Instead of building a new courthouse as the Northwest Ordinance suggested, it was decided to use the nicest house in town. The former Saucier home, which dated to the middle of the 18th century, would become the **Cahokia Courthouse**. The courthouse was the county seat to thousands of miles of uncharted wilderness. As a river town, Cahokia was prone to floods that proved troublesome. When the county was shrunk to a more manageable size in 1814, the county seat was moved to Belleville, a town farther from the Mississippi and less apt to flood.

Cahokia celebrates its heyday each year featuring its historic buildings in the **Fete du Bon Vieux Temps**. The Festival of the Good Old Days is held in February and includes, during the day, music at the Cahokia Courthouse, story telling and dancing at the Jarrot Mansion and tours of the Holy Family log church. At night there is usually a traditional dance with fiddle music (see Festivals Section).

 *Cahokia Courthouse*

Location: Elm Street, Cahokia
Phone: (618) 332-1782
Built: 1740
Charge: None
Architecture: French Colonial, post-on-foundation
Handicapped access: Yes
Current use: Museum
Hours: Thurs. - Sat., 1 - 5 p.m.
Special Events: Fete du Bon Vieux Temps

The courthouse at Cahokia is a four-room log and mortar building which dates back to the time before English was spoken in Illinois. Built in 1740, it is one of the few remaining upright log "post-on-foundation" structures in the United States.

The building was converted from a private home when the Northwest Ordinance established St. Clair County in 1790. Cahokia was named the county seat and the courthouse was equipped with a courtroom and other necessities from 1793 - 1814.

Though it has had other functions before and since, the interpretive display in the courthouse-museum takes advantage of the judicial and governmental status. One of the rooms is a recreated courtroom from the period. Elaborate interpretive displays in other rooms use a few artifacts, original documents and many replicas to give a feel for the law and society of French Colonial and early American times in the St. Clair County area.

The building itself had been taken apart and put back together before becoming one of the few structures under the direction of the Illinois Historic Preservation Agency. It has been dismantled and re-erected three times since 1900, making appearances in the 1904 St. Louis World's Fair and at Chicago's Jackson Park. Each of these rebuildings left the courthouse smaller than before. It was returned to

Cahokia in the 1930s. Intensive research led to the present structure, which historians believe is an accurate depiction of the original.

 *Holy Family Parish Log Church*

Location: E. 1st and Church Street
Phone: (618) 332-1782
Built: 1740
Charge: None
Architecture: French Colonial, post-on-foundation
Handicapped access: No (only one step, however)
Current use: Church
Hours: By appointment
Special Events: Fete du Bon Vieux Temps

The Holy Family Church is the only church in the country with upright timber post architecture. It has been well maintained through its lifetime and is still used for church services.

There are no regular hours, but an attendant will let visitors in or one can call ahead for an appointment. There is no arranged historical display, but the building is itself history. Though built after the territory of Illinois had already become a part of the United States, the church's architecture is a throwback to the French Colonial days. But this fact is unsurprising since the parishioners at the time would have spoken French and their government records were likewise kept in that language. Like a little Quebec, the settlements in the Mississippi Valley hung tenaciously to their French culture and language.

🏠 *Jarrot Mansion*

Location: 124 E. First Street, Cahokia
Phone: (618) 332-1782
Built: 1810
Charge: None
Architecture: Frontier Federal
Handicapped access: No
Current use: Empty
Hours: Thurs. - Sat., 1 - 5 p.m.
Special Events: Fete du Bon Vieux Temps

Unlike most inhabitants of the area, Nicholas Jarrot was not from the French settlements along the Mississippi or from Quebec. He was from France itself. He left during the dark days of the French Revolution and came to America in 1794 to make his fortune. Jarrot took up capitalism with a vengeance, and, although he came to a French speaking region, he was determined to fit into the society's elite. This, he believed, meant imitating the eastern establishment. The Jarrot Mansion, built in 1810, was the result: federal architecture reminiscent of Baltimore high society which Jarrot believed demonstrated that he had entered their class.

The mansion is the oldest masonry building in Illinois. It is an historical testament to its builders, who received little else from their hard work as Jarrot refused to pay many of them for their services. He was known for driving a hard bargain and taking advantage of people passing through on their way west.

It must of been all the more galling for the carpenters whose wages Jarrot withheld to find that they were being bamboozled by a judge of the territorial court. As a literate bilingual English-French speaker, Jarrot was an indispensible asset in running the courts. Added to these activities was Jarrot's penchant for land speculation, his most lucrative business.

The mansion is under renovation and open only for special events like the Fete du Bon Vieux Temps. Plans are for interpretive displays to accompany tours of the house.

Maeystown

Location: Southwest of Prairie du Rocher, off Illinois 3 in Monroe County.
Tours: (618) 458-6660 (Dave Braswell)
Founded: 1852

The history of this village, buried deep in Monroe County, lives in the descendants of its original 19th century founders and the buildings dating from the same era. The village's continuity is astounding and probably why (lock, stock and barrel) it has been listed on the National Register of Historic Places.

The town is populated mainly by direct descendants of its first inhabitants, mostly of immigrants from Germany who came to Maeystown after the failed European revolutions for liberty at mid-century. Establishments like the **Hoefft's Village Inn**, a tavern and restaurant, are still owned by people named Hoefft. One of the town's two most prominent historians, Gloria Bundy, is a direct descendant of Maeystown founder, Jacob Maeys.

As in many German burgs, street gutters are lined with flagstones. An especially elegant German custom, especially around Switzerland, is to build houses into the mountain side. There are no mountainsides in Maeystown, but houses are built directly into the hillsides. In addition to the limestone and brick buildings, two bits of 19th century town walls of are still standing. One of these is at the **Corner George Inn** which is owned by David Braswell, the town's other helpful historian and a "Yankee," as they used to call the non-German stock who came here. But this Yankee has contributed greatly to Maeystown's revival through his restoration of the inn, a stonewall foundation building, three bricks thick.

The tiny town can be readily toured by walking. It is one of the few slices of little Germany left in Illinois.

To get to Maeystown turn off Illinois 3 at Waterloo onto Maeystown Road and follow it southwest for about five miles to the tiny town.

St. John's Church in Maeystown

Fort de Chartres

Location: Four miles west of Prairie du Rocher
Phone: (618) 284-7230
Charge: None

Architecture: Reproduction of 18th century French fortification
Handicapped access: Yes
Current use: Museum, state historic site
Hours: Daily, 9 a.m. - 5 p.m.
Special Events: Kid's Day

"Never a volley from France's folly," said one sharp-witted Frenchman upon hearing that the grand Fort de Chartres on the banks of the Mississippi had fallen to the British without so much as a shot fired in her defense. The westernmost outpost of France's empire was erected in 1720. The fort was rebuilt a number of times over three decades, but the army could not seem to keep its forts in repair against the periodic onslaught of a flooding Mississippi. The French finally opted for a stone fort and limestone was floated down river from the quarries north of Prairie du Rocher.

When completed around 1760, it was a model of modern efficiency and power. A dry moat surrounded the fort to slow attackers. Fifteen feet high and three and-a-half foot thick walls equipped with sentry boxes and cannon towers protected the garrison from siege. The walls enclosed four acres and included barracks, a powder magazine, guards' and priest's rooms and other buildings.

Barely three years after the fort's completion it was turned over to the British in the Treaty of Paris. Ceding virtually all of their holdings east of the Mississippi, the French turned over Fort de Chartres with their defeat in the French and Indian War. France's state-of-the-art fort did them no good against the British. Their less technologically advanced ally was more effective. Continued fighting by the Indian chief Pontiac kept the British out of the fort until 1765 when they took it over from the French garrison. The British abandoned the place in 1771 when the flooding Mississippi River wrecked the fort once again.

The State of Illinois has reconstructed much of the grandeur of the stone fort for which the French once held such high hopes. Inside the massive walls stands the oldest building in Illinois. **The powder magazine** was one of the original structures in the stone fort. Along with the walls, the guards' house and the king's storehouse have been rebuilt. The buildings consisting of only a skeleton of wooden planks are meant to be interpretive devices. Historians are not sure what the barracks and government house looked like so they have "ghosted" them to give a feel for the space within the fort's walls.

The **Piethman Museum** has been installed inside the king's store house. Visitors will find artifacts, including a tomahawk, trade silver, and a cannon, from the French reign, and informative displays describing life in and around the fort. Other buildings in the fort also have historical artifacts and displays. A gift shop called the Trading Post offers memorabilia.

Kid's Day, held on the first weekend in May is a fair with 18th century games, crafts and songs. Another special event is the Rendezvous held the first weekend in June featuring musket firing competitions with the competitors dressed in buckskins or colonial military gear. The Rendezvous also includes dancing, music, food, traders and craftsmen.

Creole House

Location: Market Street, Prairie du Rocher
Phone: (618) 282-2245
Built: Circa 1800
Charge: $2 adults, $1 children
Architecture: Mississippi Valley transitional
Handicapped access: No
Current use: Museum
Hours: Fri., 10 a.m.-2 p.m.; Sun. 12 noon.-5 p.m., and by appointment

The Creole House is in one of the original French settlements along the Mississippi and is built in the French style with the roof overhanging the porch. Though the town dates from 1722, the house was built around 1800 and has seen several additions since. Today it houses documents and artifacts, many dating from the 19th century and earlier.

Pierre Menard Home

Location: Illinois 150 north of Chester (off Illinois 3)
Phone: (618) 859-3031
Built: Circa 1800
Charge: None
Architecture: Southern French Colonial
Handicapped access: No
Current use: Museum
Hours: Daily, 9 a.m. - 5 p.m.
Special Events: Christmas open house in Dec.; Candlelight tour in
    June

"Pierre Menard and the Menard Home occupy a position for Illinois much like that of Washington and Mount Vernon for the nation," wrote Southern Illinois historian John Allen. In fact, the house is sometimes referred to as "the Mount Vernon of the West." A solid citizen of the Illinois territory, Menard became Illinois' first lieutenant governor in 1818. No sooner had the state constitution been written than it was amended to allow Menard, who had not been a United States citizen for 20 years as the constitution required, to serve as lieutenant governor.

Menard came from Montreal to the Illinois country in the 1780s and became one of the premiere merchant traders in the area. By the end of the 18th century his trade reached north to Canada, east to the coast and south to Louisiana. The traditionally amicable relationship of French settlers with the Indians allowed him to trade with them as well as settlers heading west. The Menard Home reflects the wealth of its occupants.

Built about 1800, its porch and sloping roof is typical of the French Colonial style. Presumably, the Menards filled their home with fine things. Unfortunately, little is left from their residence, but house period pieces and mid-19th century pieces are on display. Some of Menard's belongings which do remain are the family Bible (in French) and a crib, chest of drawers and wardrobe.

A slide show describing Menard's life and times is available on the lower floor of the house and adjoining is a room with artifacts from the Menard era. On display are descriptions of the politics of early Illinois, the trade of Menard along with the ledger book he used to record it.

Fort Kaskaskia State Historic Site is just down the road from the Pierre Menard Home. It rests on the site where the French built a fort in the mid-18th century to protect the Kaskaskia settlement from feared British attack. The British never attacked, but at the end of the French and Indian War they took control of the territory. Finding the fort in disrepair, the British opted for a stone building in Kaskaskia itself. The old French fort's ruins later burned.

Today the fort is gone and the town washed away by the Mississippi River. A great view of the Mississippi remains, however, and the old headstones and some of the graves have been moved from Kaskaskia to the historic site. **Garrison Hill Cemetery** contains hundreds of headstones dating throughout the 19th century. Many of the names are French, reflecting the original settlers of the area.

Fort Kaskaskia looks like a park and provides the amenities of one. Picnic shelters supply great views of the Mississippi and camping is available for tents or vehicles with electricity available. Two playgrounds at either end of the site will keep the kids happy and the camp sites provide handicap access, as do the toilets at the entrance/exit point to the site.

The **Fort Kaskaskia Traditional Music Festival** brings bluegrass, folk, and country musicians to the site on the last weekend in September. Food, wagon rides and crafts displays are also offered at this popular annual event.

Kaskaskia Island

Arriving at Kaskaskia, a visitor finds little more than a score of houses and three prominent red brick buildings lined up side by side. Though the smallest of towns, few communities could rival its history and artifacts. A rare combination of American and French colonial history are combined on the island called Kaskaskia.

"French Kaskaskia" dates back to 1703 when a group of Kaskaskia Indians, with French Jesuit priests in tow, moved their village on the banks of the Kaskaskia River, four miles north of its confluence with the Mississippi. The Indians left a few years later, but the French remained and the town grew in size and importance.

Kaskaskia apparently was known in France for its glamorous social life. It had caught the attention of the king himself and in 1741, Louis XV presented the "Versailles of the West," with a church bell. Cast in La Rochelle, France, the bell bears the inscription, "For the Church of Illinois, with the compliments of the King from beyond the sea" (in French, of course).

The North American colonies of France and Great Britain soon became entangled in a world-wide conflict between the great powers. During the French and Indian War, the inhabitants of Kaskaskia became frightened that the British would attack their town. In response to their pleas, the French built Fort Kaskaskia overlooking the town across the Mississippi River.

The British won the war without fighting in the Kaskaskia area, and took over all of North America east of the Mississippi. The French colonial settlements were left mostly undisturbed, but the Revolutionary War brought George Rogers Clark to Kaskaskia on his mission to liberate the West from the British. The townspeople welcomed him. To celebrate their "liberation" from the British they rang the church bell they had received from their former king. From then on the bell was known as the **Liberty Bell of the West**. Kaskaskia was submerged during the flood of 1993 and the Liberty Bell of the West was once again used, this time to toll for the desertion of the island in the face of a broken levee and rising waters.

When Illinois was admitted to the union in 1818, Kaskaskia was named its capital. But only a year later, legislators, noting the propensity for flooding, decided to move the capital to drier ground in Vandalia. More than a century and-a-half later, the town finds itself an island on the wrong side of the Mississippi. A change of the river's course in 1881 put the town on the Missouri side of the river. But it is still a part of Illinois, the only part west of the Mississippi.

After the flood, some Kaskaskians picked up and moved to the center of the island that had been created by the river's change of course. They also moved their church and rebuilt it brick by brick. The mission's history reaches back to the first Europeans in the Illinois country and it retains relics from the 17th century to prove it.

 *Immaculate Conception Church*

Location: Kaskaskia
Phone: (618) 366-2622 (Old Kaskaskia Trading Post)
Built: 1894
Charge: None
Architecture: Roman Gothic
Current use: Church services
Hours: By appointment and summer day times
Special Events: Christmas displays

The Church of the Immaculate Conception was built in 1843 in "old" Kaskaskia and it was moved to its present location in the center of the island in 1894. But the history of the mission dates back to the original French explorers and missionaries in Illinois in the 17th century. The church and parish retain priceless relics from this era which visitors can view.

The latest incarnation of the Church of the Immaculate Conception is in the Roman Gothic style. Its prominent spire is an addition to the simpler design of the Gothic church which preceded it. The interior of the church, however, is much the same. The altar dates to 1736 and is a fine example of French colonial art, as are its 17th century statues of saints. Damaged by a flood in 1973, the statues are, nonetheless, rare and valuable artifacts from the 17th century. The altar stone is another relic from the 17th century. Town tradition has it, and at least one historian agrees, that the stone was the property of Father Marquette himself, the priest who accompanied Joliet on the first exploration of the Illinois country in the 17th century.

The most prized relic of the parish was another of Father Marquette's possessions, a silver chalice made in Mexico in the 1500s.

137

The chalice depicts the centuries-old symbol of Mexico—an eagle perched on a cactus enclosed by a circle.

Some of the parish's relics may be viewed by appointment only or on special occasions like the Christmas displays. To get an impromptu tour or just to get the door of the church unlocked ask at the **Old Kaskaskia Trading Post** at the far end of the street. The shop (open every day) offers food as well as pamphlets and booklets describing the history of the town.

Kaskaskia Bell State Memorial
(The Liberty Bell of the West)

Location: Kaskaskia
Phone: (618) 366-2622 (Old Kaskaskia Trading Post)
Cast: 1741
Charge: None
Design: 18th century French
Handicapped access: Yes
Hours: Open upon request
Special Events: None

Cast as a gift to the citizens of Kaskaskia by Louis XV, the bell came from La Rochelle, France in the 1740s, years before anyone had heard of the United States. When George Rogers Clark came to Illinois to take the area from the Redcoats, he stopped in Kaskaskia to liberate its French inhabitants. Acknowledging him, Kaskaskians rang the bell they had received from the French king. Thus was born the "Liberty Bell of the West."

It's a few years older than the one in Philadelphia and also sports a crack (though smaller) on its side. The bell is housed in a bell shrine of red brick, next to two other buildings of similar design and coloration, the priest's house and the Church of the Immaculate Conception.

The "Liberty Bell of the West" is visible from the barred door, but to get the door unlocked and have a closer look, ask at the **Old Kaskaskia Trading Post** at the far end of the street.

Mary's River Covered Bridge

Location: Near Bremen, east of Illinois 150 in Randolph County
Built: 1854

Mary's River Covered Bridge looks as quaint as it sounds. It has been featured on so many Christmas cards that you might experience *deja vu* when you arrive. The bridge is one of only a handful of covered bridges left in Illinois and the country. This one has weathered its time well thanks to restoration by the state.

When Chester was an important port of call on the Mississippi

Mary's River Covered Bridge (Carbondale Convention & Tourism Bureau photo)

River, wheat, timber, corn and other products were transported by wagon and ox carts from the interior to the river. To make this trade run more smoothly, a private toll road was built between Bremen and Chester which included this covered bridge. Now it is used as a tourist attraction with a few picnic tables and bathrooms nearby. Built in 1854, the bridge was put out of commission in 1930 when Illinois 150 was built.

To find the bridge, take Illinois 150 east out of Chester for about five miles to an intersection with a county road near Bremen.

Bald Knob Cross

Location: Northwest of Cobden, off Illinois 127 in Union County
Phone: (618) 893-2344
Built: 1963
Size: 112 feet high, 63 feet across
Visitor center hours: Daily, Nov. - April, 11a.m. - 4p.m.
Special events: Easter Sunrise Service

The **Cross of Peace** was the dream of a Southern Illinois man named Wayman Presley who, in 1937, wondered aloud about a non-denominational site to worship God. As Bald Knob Cross manager Barbara Casey said, "To have a place where people could gather and leave their denominational differences at the bottom of the hill."

After help from pig farmers and a lucky break on a national television show, Presley managed to raise the money for building the largest Christian monument in North America.

The pigs came into the picture when one of Myrta Clutts' sows had a triple litter of piglets in the mid 1950s. That gave her the idea to use the piglets to help Presley raise money for his cross. Pigs were given to farmers across Southern Illinois who sold them and returned the money as donations for the cross. $30,000 was raised in this manner.

Presley's continuing crusade for the cross brought him to the attention of television producers for "This is Your Life." After being fea-

Cross of Peace at Bald Knob (Carbondale Convention & Tourism Bureau photo)

tured on the show, he got hundreds of thousands of individual donations from people all over the country.

While the huge cross is impressive in itself, its backdrop is magnificent. Located outside the tiny town of Alto Pass and up a long, winding road, the landscape opens up at the top of the hill and gives visitors
a breathtaking view of the Southern Illinois countryside.

A visitor center and souvenir shop at the cross is open November
through April, depending on good weather.

Thebes Courthouse

Location: Thebes, Illinois 3, north of Cairo
Phone: (618) 764-2600
Built: 1844 - 1845
Charge: None
Architecture: Greek Revival
Handicapped access: Ground floor only
Current use: Museum
Hours: April 1 - Oct. 31, Mon. - Sat., 10 a.m. - 4 p.m.; Sunday, 12 noon - 5 p.m.
Special events: None

Overlooking the Mississippi River and the Missouri countryside is an attractively renovated example of one of Illinois' early courthouses. The old courthouse at Thebes, however, is more than an old law building. Three central figures prominent in events leading to the Civil War likely used the Thebes courthouse. Lawyer Abraham Lincoln may have argued law there, General John A. Logan practiced politics there; the runaway slave Dred Scott may have been imprisoned in the Thebes Courthouse jail.

The Greek Revival structure sits on a bluff facing the river. There is great view of the Mississippi from the rear of the building and standing on the upper terrace. In the front is a southern colonial style porch with columns.

The jail cells were in the basement and this is where Dred Scott might have been kept for the night. Scott was an escaped slave whose master sued for his return. The case eventually went to the Supreme Court of the United States which ruled that escaped slaves could still be treated as property on free soil and returned to their masters. The decision rocked the abolitionist movement and did much to mobilize feelings against slavery.

It is uncertain whether Scott was actually kept for the night. The evidence is local legend. A mysterious entry in the log book for the jail at about the right time lists an unnamed black prisoner with no crime specified. Was it Dred Scott? People around Thebes think so.

Abraham Lincoln's connection with the courthouse is also some-what tenuous. He probably visited the Lightner family in Thebes and local legend holds that he argued cases in the courthouse. There is no record of this occurring, but then some of the court records are lost.

There are no doubts about the association of John A. Logan, Civil War general, U.S. congressman, senator and vice presidential nominee, with the court at Thebes. Logan was state's attorney for the circuit and argued cases at the courthouse. When he left his post, Logan became a powerful force in Illinois politics. In 1861 he returned to Thebes to make a speech in the courthouse, rallying the divided citizens to the Union cause.

Cairo

In 1840 Charles Dickens made a voyage to America and during his travels, Cairo was one of the many places which suffered from his acerbic wit. Despite Dickens' opinion and a financial collapse in the early part of the 19th century, trade boomed for this little city at the confluence of the Mississippi and Ohio Rivers. During the Civil War, 20,000 soldiers were garrisoned within it, and the town became a bustling center of commerce and steamboat manufacturing.

In addition to serving as a trading port, Cairo played a pivotal strategic role in the war, first as a shield against Confederate incursion, then as a spearhead for General U.S. Grant's campaign in the West. After his presidency, the Civil War hero returned to his first major headquarters and saw the fruits of commerce that had made the town prosper.

A **Customs Building**, designed by architect A.B. Mullet, was erected to cope with the steamboat traffic paddling up the Mississippi. The building, which was also a post office and federal courthouse, served in Cairo as the admission center for an international port of entry. Stately southern mansions with names like Riverlore populated "Millionaire's Row" on Washington Avenue. Another of the houses on Millionaire's Row, The **Galigher Home** (Magnolia Manor), where

Grant stayed during his visit, was paid for with milled flour and hard-tack Charles Galigher sold to the Union army during the war.

Cairo continued to prosper during the 19th century, but its heyday passed when trade began to bypass the small town in favor of a direct route to the population centers of St. Louis and Chicago. The building of the Erie Canal in the Great Lakes region and the connection of St. Louis to other trade centers by railroad earlier in the century meant that Cairo would eventually be excluded from the trade on which it depended.

Even so, the old wealth of the town seemed to hang on and in 1884 Anna Eliza Safford built a beautiful Queen Anne library as a memorial to her husband. Presenting the library to her town she declared that it should "do the greatest good for the greatest number." Her precedent has been keenly observed in Cairo, and particularly in the **Cairo Public Library** which she established, as rare antiques and works of art from Europe, America and the Far East have found their way into Cairo's public historical buildings.

🚩 *The Customs House and Museum*

Location: Corner of 14th St. and Washington Avenue
Phone: (618) 734 -1019
Built: 1867 - 1872
Architecture: Victorian Italianate
Current use: Museum
Charge: None
Schedule: Monday through Friday, 10 a.m. - 12 p.m., 1 - 3 p.m.
Handicapped access: Yes (call ahead)

One of the outstanding historical and architectural buildings on Cairo's main street, Washington Avenue, is the Customs House. Designed by the famed architect Alfred B. Mullet (also responsible for the United States Treasury Building in Washington, D.C. and the San Francisco Mint), the Customs House was completed in 1872 and served as the administrative center to Cairo in its capacity as a port of entry on the Mississippi River. As such, ships from all over the globe docked at Cairo's harbor to register their goods and crews. The first floor of the building served as the post office and the third floor as a federal courthouse. The second was reserved for use by customs agents.

The architect's creative hand can be seen in the cantilevered ceilings which are made to be self-supporting and are one of Mullet's trademarks. The building's Italianate design and graceful arched windows remind visitors that these bureaucratic headquarters were once part of one of 19th century America's most important trading centers.

It is now the elegant location for a museum to the Cairo area's illustrious past. Included within the museum is a display featuring the desk of General U. S. Grant and other memorabilia from his Civil War time in Cairo. At the rear of the first floor is an 1865 man-pulled fire engine pumper and at the front is a reproduction of the turn of the century post office. Next to the post office reproduction is the safe used during that time with the decorative watercolor still adorning its door.

These are just a few of the displays on the first floor. Rooms on the second floor are devoted to the local history of medical and pharmaceutical, agricultural, railroad and lumber and grain. The third floor is a restored turn of the century court room.

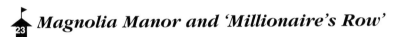 *Magnolia Manor and 'Millionaire's Row'*

Location: 2700 Washington Avenue
Phone: (618) 734-0201
Built: 1872
Architecture: Victorian Italianate
Current use: Museum and private home
Special events: Magnolia festival in May; Holiday House in Dec.
Charge: $3.50, children 4 to 12, $2, Under 4, free
schedule: April - Dec.: Mon.-Sat., 9 a.m. - 5 p.m.; Sun., 1 - 5 p.m.,
          Jan. - March: Mon. and Tues. closed
Handicapped access: No

A Victorian mansion with more than its share of history and architectural splendor sits on the inner drive of Washington Avenue.

Originally grouped with four other post-Civil War mansions earning the neighborhood its designation, "Millionaire's Row," Magnolia Manor stands as the house that hosted the North's victorious general and the 18th president of the United States, Ulysses S. Grant. It was completed by Cairo flour merchant Charles Galigher in 1869.

Before completion of the house Galigher and his family had befriended Grant during his assignment in Cairo. Following the war, and upon Grant's completion of his second term in the White House, Grant and his family enjoyed a world tour, visiting with dignitaries and heads of states as they traveled. On the way back to their home town of Galena, Grant stopped at Cairo to see old friends from the war days and the house they had built. As might be expected, he was met with great excitement by Cairo and the surrounding area as thousands came to get a glimpse of the war hero-president.

Galigher accommodated Grant and his wife on the third floor of the four story mansion, in the master bedroom. Grant's wife stayed in the adjoining room (connected by an interior corridor). The bedroom where Grant slept and the rest of the house can be seen much as it was during that 1880 visit. Most of the furniture and paintings in the house were owned by the Galigher family and all the pieces date from the Victorian era or earlier.

A tour of the house reveals an extraordinary collection of antique furniture and paraphernalia. The first floor is the enormous kitchen and pantry. A large stove dominates the room and was a novelty since most grand houses of the day installed their stoves in a separate building from the main house. A great deal of brick surrounds the stove for safety.

Guests were met and entertained on the second floor. The anteroom leads into a library, drawing room and dining room as well as the magnificent spiral staircase leading to the upper floors. Deserving special attention in the library are a handsome bookcase, carved by Galigher's wife, Kate, and a grandfather clock dating from 1736. The drawing room was the elegant setting for musical, dramatic and ballroom entertainment. Though not an original, the square grand piano in this room was a popular addition in houses of the well-to-do at this time.

Up the spiral staircase and onto the third floor, visitors find the bedrooms. The master bedroom, where Grant stayed, features several 19th century presidential photographs and lithographs. On the wall is a painting the Galighers acquired on one of their European excursions. Authorship is unknown but it is a 1551 portrait of Ambrois Pare, surgeon to Henry II and other French kings. The governess' bedroom features a rosewood sleigh bed and several Victorian vanity items. The ornate silver handled curling iron with a similarly decorated stand is especially luxurious.

In the hallway is a secretary (desk and book case combined) that is distinctive for its lack of ornamentation. The secretary pre-dates the Victorian period and was owned by the first governor of Illinois, Shadrach Bond.

The curator of the house, Myra Polson, and her husband live in the manor. Unlike many historic buildings, all of the house is accessible and visitors are encouraged to stroll around the rooms at their leisure or even try out the old furniture. "The thing that gives this house its uniqueness is that it feels like a home," said Mrs. Polson. Special events add to the fun as Holiday House, beginning on Thanksgiving, shows visitors a festively decorated mansion and guides dressed in Victorian attire.

There were originally five mansions on this corner of Washington Avenue and 28th Street. The other two that remain were built by the Halliday family. Next door to Magnolia Manor is a bed and breakfast called **Windham Bed and Breakfast**, 2606 Washington Avenue (see Bed & Breakfast section). Though somewhat less grand than the manor, Windham House is still an impressive 19th century Italianate mansion. It was built in 1876 by Thomas Halliday, Cairo businessman, mayor and congressman. As are all three of the mansions, it is listed on the National Register of Historic Places for architecture and history.

Helen Bishoff, the owner, is a local historian and has gone to great pains to fill the house with only high caliber period furniture (rosewood, mahogany and walnut) as well as her own collection of paintings ranging from the year 1660 to 1880. The decor is a rich combination of Empire and Revival pieces. The sofa in the main room, for example, is a Regency dating from 1840. Bishoff conducts prearranged group house tours for $2.75 per person, phone (618) 734 - 3247.

The most spectacular of the three mansions stands diagonally across the street on Washington Avenue. **Riverlore** is a virtual castle whose high white fence (it does not obstruct the view) displays its name prominently. The house was built in 1865 by the eldest and richest of the Halliday brothers, William Parker. It remains a private home and is not open for public tours. But from the street it is still possible to admire the second empire elegance and opulent grandeur of the white French style mansion with a slate roof.

Customs House in Cairo

⛳ *Cairo Public Library*

Location: 1609 Washington Avenue
Phone: (618) 734-1840
Built: 1884
Architecture: Queen Anne
Current use: Public library
Special events: Christmas decorations
Charge: None
Schedule: Mon. - Fri., 10 a.m. - 5 p.m; Saturday, 9 a.m. - 12 noon
      and by appointment
Handicapped access: No

There can be few more elegantly furnished or designed public libraries in America. The library was built in 1884 as a memorial to one of the prominent citizens of late 19th century Cairo, A.B. Safford, by his wife, Anna Eliza Safford. The wealthy have continued to support the library with rare and fabulous antiques and works of art.

The attractive symmetry of the building catches the eye as you drive by on Washington Street. Standing in front of the pleasing Queen Anne structure is an original sculpted bronze fountain. It is called *Fighting Boys* and was made by Janet Scudder, one of America's outstanding sculptors.

Just inside the doorway is a brightly-colored, oddly-shaped drinking fountain, courtesy of the Depression-era Works Project Administration. Highlights of the antiques on display include, on the first floor in the adult reference room, a replica of the steamboat *City of Cairo* with a collection of Cybis Porcelain. In the adjoining room, the adult reading room, the unusual periodical shelves are of mid-19th century origin. Several of the pieces in this room were original furniture in the Cairo Customs House including two federal style cabinets and the mantle over the fireplace which is marble in the Italianate style.

On the first landing you'll find a Tiffany grandfather clock, one of only four in the world. On the second landing is an exquisite 14th century Italian credenza and up the stairs is an elaborately carved 17th century Florentine rosewood table and chair set. On the second floor, often used for recitals and community meetings, is a sparkling chandelier taken from the Cairo Opera House. In the auditorium with the chandelier is a desk that once belonged to President Andrew Jackson, which he kept at the Bank of the United States in Philadelphia.

 *Fort Defiance State Park*

Location: U. S. 51, south of Cairo
Date: 1861
Current Use: State park
Charge: None

Today Fort Defiance is a barren state park with little more than an observation point from which visitors can view the meeting point of two of America's most romantic rivers, the Ohio and Mississippi. But during the Civil War, it was a vital staging ground for the Union's war in the West (at this time Illinois was in the west of the nation) and the first posting from which a drunken Union soldier called U.S. Grant would show his mettle on the battle field and rise to become overall commander of Union forces and eventually president.

With the outbreak of fighting at Fort Sumter in 1861, it was evident to the North and the South that Cairo was a key to the western theater of war. Standing at the confluence of the Mississippi and the Ohio, the North would hold a firm position for sallies into Tennessee, as well as secure its flank for attacks to the West across Missouri. The south could similarly deprive northern forces of this advantage by capturing Cairo as well as securing a base of military operations in a region whose sympathies were divided.

The spot, a dividing line between slave and free states, became the object of a race between Confederate and Union forces when the local militia declared that it would take a stance of "armed neutrality" towards the combatants. In practice, this meant that whether Union or Confederate, the first forces on the ground would secure the position.

On April 19, 1861 Governor Yates of Illinois sent a Chicago militia to garrison Cairo. The troops were assembled and put on the

Illinois Central Railway. In the meantime, Confederate troops had been making their way up muddy roads toward Cairo for days. Three days after Yates issued the order, the militia arrived at Fort Defiance and took the site. The Confederates were some 12 miles to the south.

"Those first Union troops to reach Cairo were a motley group," wrote historian John W. Allen. Their uniforms did not match, they were ill-trained and their weapons were not standard. Yet through a superior transportation system, they had secured a vital post for the Union, fortification from which Grant would launch his campaign in the West representing the first Union successes of the war. The winning of Cairo would be an auger of things to come. It represented the overwhelming industrial might of the North, against which the South could not, in the end, hold out.

▲ *Mound City National Cemetery*
26

Location: Junction of U.S. 51 and Illinois 37
Date: 1862
Charge: None
Current use: Veteran's cemetery
Handicapped accessible: Yes

Authorized by an act of Congress July 18, 1862, at the height of the Civil War, Mound City National Cemetery is a burial ground for thousands of veterans starting with the Civil War dead who were at that time buried in plots in the surrounding area. These bodies were gathered up and deposited at Mound City near the major Union base, Fort Defiance. Most of the Civil War dead were Union soldiers but at least a few, indicated by pointed headstones, were Confederate.

At this lonely stretch of highway on the way to Cairo, the biggest cemetery in Illinois is an impressive site. In the center of the grounds is a 72-foot high granite memorial with the names of hundreds of war dead. Along the cemetery path are plaques with stanzas of *The Bivouac of the Dead* by Theodore O'Hara. Written to honor Kentucky soldiers killed in the Mexican-American War, the poem has come to commemorate all American dead in war.

The Old State Capitol at Vandalia

Built: 1836
Charge: None
Phone: (618) 283-1161
Handicapped access: North side of building, first floor only
Architecture: Federal
Current use: Museum
Hours: Feb.–Dec. daily, 9 a.m. - 5 p.m.; Closed Mon. and Tues.
Special events: Candlelight tours in December and Father's Day weekend

The capitol building in Vandalia is not an architectural marvel, but it is one of the premiere historical sites in the state. Full-time tour guides take patrons back to everyday political life in what was the state's capital between 1836 and 1839.

The state legislature decided to move the capital from Kaskaskia to Vandalia in 1819 and the Old State Capitol building in Vandalia was the third in a succession of capitols. The last was built quickly when Vandalians felt there was a danger that the seat of government would be moved out of town. But to no avail, it was a young Springfield representative named Abraham Lincoln who was instrumental in getting the capital site moved in 1839.

Vandalians appear to have forgiven Lincoln for depriving them of the capital. They have been gracious enough to place a life mask of the Great Emancipator at the entrance of the building. The mask, which greets the visitors to the old state capitol, was made just before he took over the presidency. Lincoln began his legislative career in Vandalia and served as a state representative for the Whig Party in the House of Representatives chamber on the second floor. Lincoln's political rival, Douglas also served in the House, but on the opposite side of the chamber, as a Democrat. The room opposite from the House of Representatives is the Senate chamber. Both are filled mainly with reproduction furniture from the period.

On the first floor are the offices of the constitutional office holders, such as the secretary of state, plus a room where the Supreme Court was held. The Supreme Court room is especially interesting with its comb backed Windsor chairs and old fashioned writing quills. The guide will give you a chance to test your penmanship with these Victorian instruments.

Furniture on the first floor are all period pieces and a few, like the secretary cabinet in the secretary of state's office is an original. It belonged to the fourth governor of Illinois.

In the front lawn of the Old State Capitol is one of twelve statues in the United States commemorating the old Cumberland Road. Also called the National Road, this wagon trail was America's first inter-state highway, starting in Cumberland, Maryland, and ending in Vandalia after squabbling Illinois and Missouri politicians could not agree on a crossing point to Missouri. **The Madonna of the Trail** is a powerful sandstone representation of a pioneer woman with a baby at her bosom and another child clinging to her waist.

William Jennings Bryan Birthplace

Built: 1852
Charge: None
Phone: (618) 548-7791
Handicapped access: No
Architecture: Open frame structure
Current use: Museum
Hours: Daily, 1 - 5 p.m., closed Thurs.
Special events: A tea on Bryan's birthday, March 19

The great orator, three-time presidential candidate and secretary of state William Jennings Bryan, was born and raised in Salem, Illinois. The Salem Historical and Patriotical Commission has preserved the Bryan home and turned it into a museum with a collection of numerous photographs and items of interest from Bryan's life and political career.

The house was built in 1852 by Silas Bryan. His son, William, was born in 1860. Mariah Elizabeth Jennings Bryan taught her oldest surviving son at home until the age of 10 when he started public school. By the time the family moved out of the house to the outskirts of Salem in 1886, the young man had already formed a taste for politics and oratory with his participation in the Salem High School debating club called "the Senate."

The museum is filled with the paraphernalia from Bryan's career. A glass cabinet displays campaign ribbons from his congressional tenure from Nebraska and Democratic nominations for president. An 1896 photograph of Bryan, his running mate and their wives relates the drama of a turn of the century campaign rally. A hundred-year-old tape recording of the Cross of Gold speech delivered at the 1896 Chicago Democratic convention is a rare recording of the "silver tongued orator's" most famous speech. Also included in the museum are photographs of the "Scopes Monkey Trial," in which Bryan prosecuted John T. Scopes, also a Salem native, for teaching evolution in Tennessee where it was forbidden by law.

Mt. Vernon

Appellate Courthouse in Mt. Vernon

Location: 14th and Main streets
Phone: (618) 242-2130
Built: 1857
Charge: None
Architecture: Greek Revival
Handicapped access: Yes
Current use: Appellate court proceedings
Hours: Business hours, tours upon request
Special events: None

Mt. Vernon's luxurious appellate courthouse was originally a division of the Illinois Supreme Court and stands today as a testimony to the grand architecture of the mid-19th century. A tour guide will show visitors around the second floor of the courthouse upon request (the first floor judge's quarters and are not available to tour).

The guide pulls out an old legal tome which records Abraham Lincoln's argument before the court. When court is not in session you will be escorted through the courtroom. Court is in session approximately one week a month. The public may attend the proceedings.

Appellate Courthouse in Mt. Vernon

Southern Illinois Genealogy Collection

Location: C.E. Brehm Memorial Library, 101 S. Seventh Street
Phone: (618) 242-6322
Handicapped Access: Yes
Hours: Mon. - Thurs., 9 a.m. - 8 p.m.; Fri., 9 a.m. - 5 p.m.; Sat., noon-
   6 p.m.; Sun., 1 - 5 p.m.

The roots of Southern Illinois are in Mt. Vernon. To be specific, a collection of 17,000 items relating to the history and genealogy of Southern Illinoisans are housed in the C.E. Brehm Memorial Library. This is one of the biggest circulating collections of its kind, according to administrative librarian, Kendi Kelly. The library focuses on migratory information for Americans moving from southern states like Virginia, North and South Carolina, Kentucky and Tennessee. It also contains a small selection on European immigration, with titles like "The Famine Immigrants."

The collection is housed on the south wing of the first floor and facilities for microfilm copying are provided. The items in the collection are stored on computer and can be accessed from branch Shawnee Library systems. A Shawnee Library System card (available with membership in a local library) entitles anyone to check out books from the collection.

Mitchell Museum

Location: Richview Road, Mt. Vernon
Phone: (618) 242-1236
Opened: 1973
Architecture: Neoclassical
Charge: None
Handicapped Access: Yes
Special Events: See below
Hours: Tues. - Sat., 10 a.m. - 5 p.m.; Sun. 1 - 5 p.m.; closed Mon.

In the 1960s, a successful Mt. Vernon entrepreneur and his art teacher wife, decided to turn their enthusiasm for art into a legacy for the community in which they had grown up. The result is that the center of Southern Illinois is endowed with an elegant museum of 19th and 20th century art and an active program for traveling exhibits and the performing arts.

The Mitchell Museum, named for John R. and Eleanor R. Mitchell, and the Cedarhurst grounds are the headquarters for paintings, sculptures, chamber music and children's art. The Mitchells had the museum built on the grounds of Cedarhurst and left their entire estate, including financial assets as a foundation for the art complex.

Much of the museum's permanent collection was donated by the Mitchells. The collection includes paintings by American Impressionists like Mary Cassatt and Maurice Prendergast. George Bellows is also represented. In the administration building is a gallery featuring traveling exhibits as well as a permanent collection of artistic furniture. This art is functional as well as beautiful and includes a piece by the American architect Mies van der Rohe.

There are three galeries in the Mitchell Museum. One is for the permanent collection, one is for traveling art exhibits and the other is for traveling children's art exhibits. "My interest," said curator Bonnie Speed, "is showing the best art possible from all over the country and even all over the world." To this end, the staff and volunteers work hard to put together high quality international and national exhibits. "The International Critics Choice," organized by the Mitchell Museum and shown in 1993, was a collection of contemporary art from Europe and the Americas. The children's gallery features exhibits like "Art of the Comic Book."

The performing arts are included in Cedarhurst's mission as several chamber music performances are brought to Southern Illinois each year. These include the Burgundian Consort who play medieval Spanish tunes and various classical chamber musicians.

Special events are an integral part of the museum's programs. In addition to the traveling exhibits, art lectures are given for the public, children's stories are told and dinner theater is presented (see Performing Arts Section). The **Cedarhurst Craft Fair**, held the first weekend after Labor Day, draws crafts artists from all over the country and food and craft demonstrations are plentiful. For a list of current programs write or call the museum.

Old Shawneetown

Before motor vehicles and railroads, America's inland waterways were the best method for getting great quantities of goods and people from one place to another. The new territory of Illinois was best accessed from the east on the Ohio River, and in an early attempt at central planning, the U.S. Congress itself surveyed. Shawneetown is the only town in the nation besides Washington D.C. to have that distinction. In 1810 Shawneetown was founded on the banks of the Ohio.

By 1816, two years before the territory would become a state, the first bank in Illinois had been set up in the house of John Marshall, a prominent citizen. It printed its own money and had a stormy career as periodic runs on the bank forced it to shut down several times before its final closure in the mid 19th century. Before its demise, the first bank was joined by the First State Bank in Illinois. Built in 1839, the Greek Revival structure was a grand addition to what had promised to be a grand city.

An illustration of the town's stature was the stop by French Revolutionary War hero, General Marquis de Lafayette on his visit to America in 1825. He was treated to a banquet and dance at the **Rawlings Hotel**, built only a few years before his arrival. Prominent Illinois citizens lived and were buried in the Shawneetown **Westwood Cemetery**. One of these was Major General James Harrison, the Civil War general who apprehended the fleeing president of the Confederacy, Jefferson Davis, at the end of the Civil War. General Harrison sent Davis to prison, but sent his horse to graze in Shawneetown.

However, by the time the First State Bank had been established things were changing for Shawneetown. The river trade on which it depended began to dry up as railroads and the new Erie Canal in the Great Lakes area combined to divert trade to the north. The river, which had spurred the idea for a town at the site in the first place, proved a great hazard to life and property. Periodic and extreme flooding caused a levee to be built. The great flood of 1937, when many structures were wholly submerged in the Ohio, convinced most residents to leave. With the help of the federal government, inhabitants packed up and moved to higher ground, dragging houses and a water tower with them.

Today, little remains of Old Shawneetown. A few 19th century buildings with water marks remind visitors of the floods and a score of residential houses remain as a reproach to ill-considered central planning. Bill Rister (618) 269-3542, head of the Shawneetown Historical Society, will show individuals or groups around the old town free of charge.

⚑ The First Territorial Bank of Illinois
32

Location: Main Street, Old Shawneetown
Phone: (618) 269-3542 (Bill Rister, president, Shawneetown
        Historical Society)
Built: 1812
Charge: $1.25; $1 each for groups of ten or more
Architecture: Georgian
Current use: Museum
Handicapped access: No
Hours: By appointment
Special events: None

The first bank in Illinois was an improvised affair. John Marshall had the only brick house in town so he got the 1816 charter for Illinois' first bank and ran the business out of his front room, dropping deposits into a hole in the floor which led to his basement. To protect the money the cashier slept with it every night.

The bank suffered a roller coaster history, closing for short and long periods of time before it was shut for good in 1834. In a time before insurance against loss, the confidence of a bank's depositors was fragile and a loss of confidence meant a run. The bank presumably did little to help itself when, in 1830, it refused a loan to men trying to start a new town called Chicago in northern Illinois. "It's too far away from Shawneetown to ever amount to anything," was the alleged response.

The bank issued its own currency, as was common at the time, and some of it is on display at the entryway along with early land grants for Gallatin County. The bank acquired a vault before its final closure and the original is on display. In addition, fine portraits of John Marshall and his wife, Amy Leech Marshall are on display. The furniture is not original to the house, but is generally 19th century pieces from the federal period.

In front of the old bank is an 1820 log cabin built by John Seats and moved from near Equality. There are no displays inside.

 *Shawneetown Bank*

Location: Main Street, Old Shawneetown
Phone: (618) 269-3303
Built: 1840
Charge: None
Architecture: Greek Revival
Current use: State historic site
Handicapped access: No
Hours: Wed. - Sun., 8 a.m. - 4 p.m.
Special events: None

The Shawneetown Bank is worn by age and floods, but the four story columned building still presents one of the grandest facades in Southern Illinois. "The oldest structure in Illinois built specifically as a bank," says the Illinois Historic Preservation Society, the bank is a symptom of the optimism in 1830s Shawneetown. Gearing up for expansion, the bank which started in John Marshall's house was looking for new branches throughout the state.

The biggest and best of these was to be in Shawneetown, housed in a structure of reassuring solidity and strength. The stone columns were floated down the Ohio from Pennsylvania especially for the bank, and

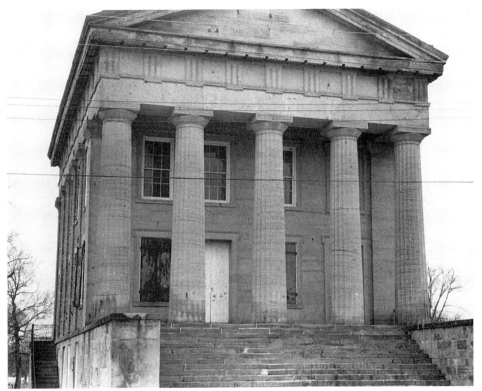

Shawneetown Bank

a metal gabled roof was inserted above. The five columns, however, are unusual for a building of this style. Most Greek Revival structures have an even number of columns. It is speculated that an extra column was installed by the unknown architect in order to hide the awkward front double entrance arrangement.

Restoration of the building has been going on since the 1970s and continues slowly. There are no displays inside the building, although the original vault is there. A state employee will escort visitors inside.

North of the bank facing the levee, is the old **Rawlings Hotel** built in 1822. Lafayette stayed there during his 1825 visit to Shawneetown. A plaque in front of the the old hotel recounts its history, but the structure is in an extreme state of disrepair and cannot be entered.

Westwood Cemetery

Location: Galt Road, between Shawneetown and Old Shawneetown
Begun: 1815
Handicapped access: No
Current use: Local cemetery

In one of the oldest cemeteries in Illinois rest the prominent citizens of Shawneetown. At the back of the small cemetery are most of the early 19th century graves. A monument to General Thomas Posey, 1750 - 1816, describes the life of this officer in the Revolutionary War who went on to become a United States senator and a governor of the Indiana territory.

Another of Shawneetown's illustrious residents interred at the site is Major General James Harrison, who apprehended Jefferson Davis, the president of the Confederacy, at the close of the Civil War. Many other grave stones dating from the 19th century are to be found in this cemetery.

The Crenshaw House
(The Old Slave House)

Location: Illinois 1, six miles west of Shawneetown
Phone: (618) 276-4410
Built: 1834 - 1838
Charge: $4
Architecture: Greek Revival
Handicapped access: No
Current use: Museum and private home
Hours: April 15 - Nov. 15; daily 9 a.m. - 5 p.m.
Special events: None
Restrictions: No tour buses

The Crenshaw House, formerly the Old Slave House, is probably the best known historic site in Southern Illinois. Its diabolical history is intertwined with its first owner, John Crenshaw, who made his money with the government concession on salt mines at the nearby Saline River.

Mining salt required lots of labor and early Illinois was in short supply of the sort of landless workers who would do the job. For this reason, the Illinois constitution had exempted the concessionaire of the salt mines from the general prohibition against slaves in Illinois. Crenshaw was allowed to "lease" slaves from Kentucky and use them to work the mines.

Apparently, Crenshaw was not satisfied with this arrangement and there is much evidence to suggest that he participated in the illegal trade of slaves and possibly their "breeding" as well. Crenshaw was accused by a Gallatin County grand jury of selling free indentured blacks into slavery. He was said to be running an underground slave railroad in reverse. Crenshaw was acquitted of the crime, but his great power and influence could have strongly swayed a jury taken from a population reluctant to convict any white man for crimes against blacks.

The house itself suggests participation in this illicit trade. An attractive Greek Revival home, Crenshaw's house has verandas on the first and second floors with the third story forming a pediment with a single large window at its peak. These outwardly stately features conceal the interior architecture which was specially designed to accommodate slaving activities. Though altered today, the house was built to allow carriages to enter at double doors and discharge its passengers inside. A narrow stairwell leads directly to the third floor where there are many small rooms with imprints on their frames left from the locks and doors removed early this century. Also on this floor are two structures which appear to be whipping posts. The third floor is completely sound proofed from the rest of the house thanks to double ceilings and floors.

In addition to the upstairs slave quarters, visitors will find the 7,500 square feet of this stately house crammed with period antiques, many of them original to the house since the present owner's family bought the house from the Crenshaw family in 1906. The spot was chosen because it is near the salt springs, but also for its panoramic view of the Saline River Valley. Authentic slave cabins from Tennessee are also available for inspection on the grounds.

The owner takes groups of no more than 12, meaning most bus tours are not welcome.

Fort Massac State Park

Location: Exit #37 off I-24, Metropolis
Charge: None

Fort Massac combines the allure of an historic fort and museum with the scenic beauty of the Ohio River. Perched on the river border between Illinois and Kentucky, the site has seen at least two fortifications come and go The structures were destroyed by Indians and demolished by earthquakes. The current fort was built just east of the original in 1973 and is architecturally based on the late 18th century American fortification.

Today the fort houses a museum of artifacts uncovered at the site. Artifacts date from the 1750s to the early 1800s and include charred timber from a fort burned at the spot, French and British military clothes, weapons and everyday settler dress. The fort also hosts an annual re-enactment of a battle waged between British, French and Indian troops during the French and Indian War. On this October weekend there are scores of booths in the park filled with vendors dressed in the 18th century garb of soldiers and frontiersmen.

Facilities available throughout the year around tent and trailer sites with a sanitary dump station, water, electricity showers. Several picnic tables are available within sight of the fort's ramparts and two self-guided walking trails, one of which skirts the Ohio River. A boat ramp is provided on the river and recreational boating, and of course, fishing, is permitted. Also permitted is hunting for squirrel, woodcock, dove and rabbit as well as bow hunting for deer.

Bill Bullock, dressed in period costume, greets visitors to Fort Massac
(*Photo courtesy of Fort Massac State Park*)

Festivals, Fairs, Exhibits & Gatherings

The Sweetcorn & Melon Festival at Mt. Vernon (Southern Illinoisan Photo)

T he richness of life is exemplified by the way people gather to celebrate their cultural uniqueness. Fairs and festivals, exhibits and gatherings of various types abound in Southern Illinois. There is something for everyone to enjoy!

Activities range in size from the Du Quoin State Fair which draws hundreds of thousands of visitors yearly to small town parades and festivals with only a few hundred participants. We can only begin to

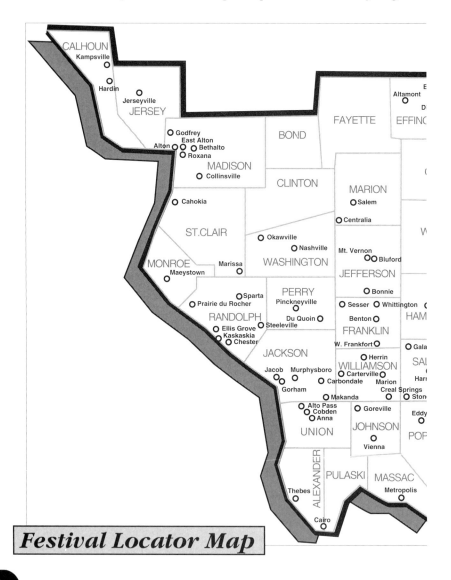

Festival Locator Map

list the activities in Southern Illinois. Many events are held one time only and others are held annually with fairly predictable times. We suggest you call and verify the specifics for any particular event. If we have inadvertently omitted your favorite event, write us and give us the details for future editions. Meanwhile, take a look through the listing that follows and enrich your life by participating.

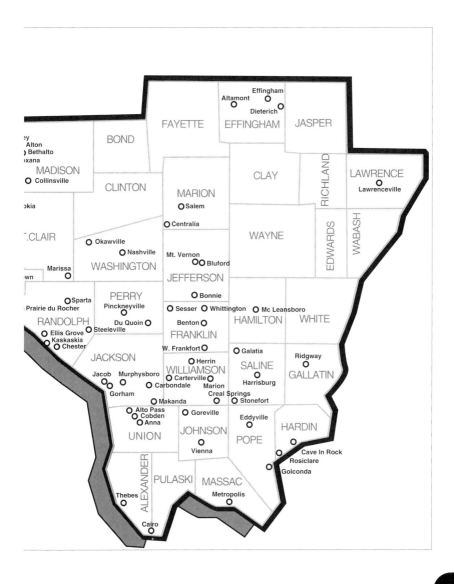

Listing of Events by Month

These events may be held in different months from year to year. Please check with organizers for specific times of events.

JANUARY

Ellis Grove
TWELFTH DAY OF CHRISTMAS CELEBRATION

Okawville
BIG BUCK CLASSIC

Prairie du Rocher
TWELFTH NIGHT DINNER AND BALL

FEBRUARY

Cahokia
FETE DU BON VIEUX TEMPS

Carbondale
ORCHIDS, TRAINS, PLANES & STAMP SHOW
SPRING SPORTS AND RECREATION SHOW

Creal Springs
SWEETHEART SPAGHETTI AND MEATBALL FEST

Maeystown
ST JOHN'S CHURCH FESTIVAL

Mt. Vernon
MIDWESTERN HERB SHOW

Murphysboro
GENERAL LOGAN BIRTHDAY BREAKFAST

Prairie du Rocher
FRENCH AND INDIAN WAR WOODS WALK

MARCH

Carterville
ILLINOIS BIG BUCK & TURKEY EXPO

Murphysboro
ST. PATRICK'S DAY FESTIVAL & IRISH STEW COOK-OFF

APRIL

Across the southern tip of Illinois
RIVER-TO-RIVER RELAY

Carbondale
SPRINGFEST

Carterville
SOUTHERN ILLINOIS EARTH SCIENCE CLUB GEM SHOW

Maeystown
FRÜEHLINGFEST

Salem
CHAMBER OF COMMERCE HOME SHOW/COMMUNITY
EXPOSITION

MAY

Altamont
SPRING HERB FESTIVAL

Benton
REND LAKE WATER FESTIVAL

Carbondale
AIRSHOW
GREAT CARDBOARD BOAT REGATTA
MAKE IT YOUR HOME FESTIVAL

Collinsville
INTERNATIONAL HORSERADISH FESTIVAL

Effingham
CRUISE NITE
BLUEGRASS MUSIC FEST

Galatia
GALATIA OLD SETTLERS DAYS

Herrin
HERRINFEST ITALIANA

Mt. Vernon
MT. VERNON OPEN TENNIS TOURNAMENT

Murphysboro
GENERAL JOHN A. LOGAN DAYS

Prairie du Rocher
KIDS DAYS

Sesser
MEMORIAL DAY FLEA MARKET

Thebes
THEBES ARTS AND CRAFTS FESTIVAL AND MEMORIAL
DAY BARBECUE

Whittington
SOUTHERN ILLINOIS FESTIVAL OF ARTS AND CRAFTS

JUNE

Alton
ALTON LANDING RIVER FESTIVAL

Bonnie
STRAW AND HAY DAYS

Cairo
MAGNOLIA FESTIVAL

Du Quoin
STREET MACHINE NATIONALS

Ellis Grove
PIERRE MENARD HOME CANDLELIGHT TOUR & OPEN
HOUSE

Godfrey
SPORTSFEST

Maeystown
MAEYSTOWN HOMECOMING

Makanda
    MAKANDA FEST
McLeansboro
    HAMILTON COUNTY FAIR

Metropolis
    SUPERMAN CELEBRATION

Nashville
    WASHINGTON COUNTY FAIR

Okawville
    HERITAGE DAYS

Pinckneyville
    PERRY COUNTY FAIR

Prairie du Rocher
    FORT DE CHARTRES RENDEZVOUS

Roxana
    ROXANA AUTO SHOW AND TROPHY MEET

Salem
    SUMMERFEST

Sesser
    SESSER REND LAKE DAYS HOMECOMING

Wayne Fitzgerrell State Park (Whittington)
    REND LAKE SKI SHOW

JULY

Altamont
    EFFINGHAM COUNTY FAIR

Alton
    ALTON DRUM AND BRASS REVIEW
    FIREWORKS ON THE MISSISSIPPI

Anna
    JULY 4 CELEBRATION

Bluford
    ILLINOIS ENGINE SHOW

Cave-In-Rock to Golconda
DAVY CROCKETT OHIO RIVER RELAY RACE

Collinsville
GREAT AMERICAN TRAIN SHOW

Du Quoin
FREEDOM FEST, JULY 4 CELEBRATION

Eddyville
JULY 4 CELEBRATION

Goreville
JULY 4 CELEBRATION

Harrisburg
SALINE COUNTY FAIR

Herrin
JULY 4 CELEBRATION

Jacob
JACOB DAY

Jerseyville
JERSEY COUNTY FAIR

Kaskaskia Island
JULY 4 CELEBRATION

Metropolis
MASSAC COUNTY YOUTH FAIR

Mt. Vernon
ALL-AMERICAN SALUTE TO FREEDOM

Murphysboro
JULY 4 CELEBRATION

Okawville
JULY 4 CELEBRATION

Rend Lake
JULY 4 CELEBRATION

Sparta
RANDOLPH COUNTY FAIR
SPARTAFEST

Steeleville
JULY 4 CELEBRATION

Altamont
FANTASTIC FLOWER FAIR

Alton
MASS OF CELEBRATION

Centralia
BALLOONFEST

Cobden
COBDEN PEACH FESTIVAL

Du Quoin
DU QUOIN STATE FAIR

East Alton
EAST ALTON CENTENNIAL CARNIVAL & CRAFT SHOW

Ellis Grove
ELLIS GROVE ANNUAL PICNIC

Jerseyville
JERSEYVILLE AMERICAN LEGION STRASSENFEST

Kampsville
ARCHAEOLOGY DAY

Madison
SOUTHWESTERN ILLINOIS GRAND PRIX

Marissa
MARISSA COAL FESTIVAL

Maeystown
SOMMERFEST

Mt. Vernon
SWEETCORN AND WATERMELON FESTIVAL

Murphysboro
ST. ANDREW'S PARISH FESTIVAL

Stonefort
STONEFORT REUNION

Pinckneyville
AMERICAN THRESHERMAN'S ANNUAL SHOW

Pulaski
PULASKI COUNTY FAIR

Sparta
CORN FEST

Whittington
WHITTINGTON GUN CREEK DAYS

SEPTEMBER

Altamont
SCHUETZENFEST

Alton
ALTON EXPOSITION

Bethalto
LABOR DAY BETHALTO HOMECOMING

Carbondale
CASCADE OF COLORS BALLOON FESTIVAL

Carterville
CARTERVILLE FREE FAIR
NATIONAL HUNTING & FISHING DAYS

Chester
CHESTER'S POPEYE PICNIC

Collinsville
ITALIAN FEST

Creal Springs
CREAL SPRINGS WONDER WATER REUNION

Effingham
OLD SETTLER'S REUNION

Ellis Grove
FORT KASKASKIA TRADITIONAL MUSIC FESTIVAL

Fidelity
FIDELITY FALL FESTIVAL

Goreville
RURITAN GOLF SCRAMBLE

Harrisburg
PAST TO PRESENT FESTIVAL

Metropolis
LABOR DAY CELEBRATION

Mt. Vernon
CEDARHURST CRAFT FAIR

Murphysboro
MURPHYSBORO APPLE FESTIVAL
MURPHYSBORO & ILLINOIS STATE BBQ CHAMPIONSHIP

Okawville
OKAWVILLE FAIR AND WHEAT FESTIVAL

Prairie du Rocher
COUNTRY FAIR AND APPLE FETE

Ridgway
GALLATIN COUNTY FAIR AND POPCORN DAYS

Sesser
LABOR DAY FLEA MARKET

West Frankfort
OLD KING COAL FESTIVAL

OCTOBER

Alto Pass
FALL FESTIVAL

Alton
    ECHOES OFF THE RIVER MARCHING BAND
        COMPETITION
    HERITAGE DAYS
    LANDMARK HISTORIC HOUSE TOUR

Cairo
    RIVERBOAT DAYS FESTIVAL

Cahokia Mounds, Collinsville
    HERITAGE AMERICA

Carbondale
    ARTS IN CELEBRATION

Centralia
    CENTRALIA HALLOWEEN PARADE

Dieterich
    SORGHUM FEST

Fort Defiance, Cairo
    CIVIL WAR ENCAMPMENT AT FORT DEFIANCE

Golconda
    FALL FESTIVAL

Jacob
    JACOB WURST MART

Kampsville
    KAMPSVILLE OLD SETTLERS DAYS

Marion
    MARION COUNTRY FEST

Maeystown
    OKTOBERFEST

Metropolis
    ANNUAL FORT MASSAC ENCAMPMENT

Pope, Johnson, Union and Alexander Counties
    TRAIL OF TEARS WAGON TRAIN

Prairie du Rocher
  FRENCH AND INDIAN WAR ASSEMBLAGE

Pinckneyville
  AMERICAN THRESHERMAN FALL FESTIVAL
  MARDI GRAS FESTIVAL
  OCTOBER FALL FESTIVAL

Rosiclare
  FLUORSPAR FESTIVAL

Sesser
  OKTOBERFEST CRAFT FAIR

Steeleville
  STEELEVILLE OKTOBERFEST

Union County
  FALL COLORFEST

Vienna
  JOHNSON COUNTY HERITAGE FESTIVAL

Whittington
  CHILDREN'S ART FESTIVAL

NOVEMBER

Alton
  GREAT RIVER ROAD RUN
  CELEBRATION OF CHRISTMAS

Anna
  VETERAN'S DAY PARADE

Belleville
  BELLEVILLE GINGERBREAD WALK
  WAY OF LIGHTS

Cairo
  MAGNOLIA MANOR HOLIDAY HOUSE

Carbondale
  GREAT SALUKI TAILGATE

Carterville
AUTUMNFEST PRE-HOLIDAY CRAFT FAIR

Effingham
KALEIDOSCOPE OF CRAFTS SHOW

Golconda
POPE COUNTY DEER FESTIVAL

Harrisburg
SOUTHEASTERN ILLINOIS HERITAGE FESTIVAL

Okawville
CHRISTMAS BAZAAR

Prairie du Rocher
FORT DE CHARTRES WINTER RENDEZVOUS

The Great Cardboard Regatta –Carbondale (Carbondale Convention & Tourism Bureau photo)

DECEMBER

Alton
OLDE ALTON ARTS AND CRAFTS FAIR
CHRISTMAS HISTORIC HOUSE TOUR

Carbondale
LIGHTS FANTASTIC

Dieterich
CHRISTMAS LIGHT DISPLAY

Du Quoin
DU QUOIN CHRISTMAS STROLL

Ellis Grove
PIERRE MENARD HOUSE CHRISTMAS OPEN HOUSE

Godfrey
CHRISTMAS CAROUSEL

Metropolis
OLDE-TYME CHRISTMAS

Murphysboro
MURPHYSBORO TOUR OF HOMES

Okawville
CHRISTMAS STROLL & FESTIVAL OF TREES
CHRISTMAS HOUSE TOUR & LIVE NATIVITY PAGEANT

Prairie du Rocher
LA GUIANNEE

Sesser
COUNTRY CHRISTMAS STROLL AND LIGHTED PARADE

Alphabetical Description of Festivals

AIRSHOW
This annual event shows off aircraft from the civil, military and experimental areas. Air show performances, also.
When: May
Where: Southern Illinois Airport, Carbondale
Phone: (618) 529-1721
Admission: Call for admission price

ALL-AMERICAN SALUTE TO FREEDOM
This fireworks display, the largest in the southern half of Illinois, rivals any across the U.S. Fireworks start at dusk, but the fun runs all day with model boat races, craft fair on the grounds.
When: July
Where: Mt. Vernon Airport, Illinois 15 east
Phone: (618) 242-3151
Admission: Free

ALTON DRUM AND BRASS REVIEW
"Seventy-six trombones..." Strike up the band and head for Alton for this drum and bugle corp competition, a Drum Corp International Event, sponsored by Alton Band and Orchestra Builders.
When: July
Where: Alton Public School Stadium, State Street
Phone: (618) 465-8281
Admission: Reserved seats $10, general admission $7

ALTON EXPOSITION
Riverfront celebration with carnival rides, top name entertainment, food booths, and exhibitions.
When: September
Where: Alton Riverfront Park
Phone: (618) 463-3526
Admission: Inquire

ALTON LANDING RIVER FESTIVAL
Annual festival held in the heart of the Alton Antique District with over 50 antique and specialty shops. Also features arts and crafts, collectibles, food and entertainment.

When: June
Where: Broadway Street in downtown Alton
Phone: (618) 462-1337
Admission: Free

AMERICAN THRESHERMAN SHOW

This annual event features threshing demonstrations with steam tractors and horse power. Other features include antique machinery demonstrations and antique car shows, swap meet, flea market and lots of food and drink .
When: Third weekend in August, all day and evenings
Where: Perry County Fairgrounds, Pinckneyville
Phone: (618) 336-5268
Admission: $3 per person

AMERICAN THRESHERMAN FALL FESTIVAL

This festival highlights fall activities including apple butter, hominy and molasses making, corn shredding and husking, rail splitting and other crafts, with some threshing and animal teams on the grounds. Consignment auction sale of antiques is held on Sunday.
When: October
Where: Perry County Fairgrounds, Pinckneyville
Phone: (618) 336-5268
Admission: $3 per person

ARCHAEOLOGY DAY

This is the annual open house for the Center for American Archaeology, and features site tours, displays and demonstrations, replicated Indian village and much more. Fun and educational!
When: August
Where: Center for American Archaeology, Kampsville
Phone: (618) 653-4316
Admission: Adults $10; 55+ $7.50; students $5; children under 12 free

ARTS IN CELEBRATION

The biennial Arts in Celebration festival is the premiere arts and cultural event of Southern Illinois. The festival showcases performance, visual, literary and musical talent from throughout the Midwest. The festival acts as a catalyst for future arts and musical events in the area and provides strong motivation for area cultural growth. Call for events and ticket information.

When: A biennial event to be held in 1994
Where: Evergreen Park, Carbondale
Phone: (618) 529-4147
Admission: Call for admission price

AUTUMNFEST PRE-HOLIDAY CRAFT FAIR
See over 120 arts and crafts exhibitors with items for sale at this 19th annual festival. Craft demonstrations and music. Free admission. A time to start your Christmas shopping!
   When: Second full weekend in November
   Where: John A. Logan College, Carterville
   Phone: (618) 985-3741, ext. 416 or 365
   Admission: Free

BALLOONFEST
Balloonfest boasts over 50,000 participants, 45 or more hot air balloons, craft fair, balloon races, crafts and good eats. Saturday night features symphonic music and tethered, lighted balloons of all shapes. A true favorite for young and old alike.
   When: Third weekend in August
   Where: Centralia
   Phone: (618) 532-6789; sponsored by the Chamber of Commerce
   Admission: $1

BELLEVILLE GINGERBREAD WALK
Window-shop for Christmas presents while you savor delectable gingerbread creations in shops on historic Main Street.
   When: December-January
   Where: East Main Street, Belleville
   Phone: 1-800-782-9587
   Admission: Free

ILLINOIS BIG BUCK & TURKEY EXPO
Hunters bring your deer mounts and compare! Seminars, shows, and taxidermy skills are all here for the avid hunter.
   When: March
   Where: Carterville
   Phone: 1-800-433-7399
   Admission:$6 adult; $5 with deer mount; $3 child

BIG BUCK CLASSIC
Celebrating the white-tailed deer, this festival features displays and

vendor booths, plus various seminars. In some years over 200 mounts have been displayed–this year should be better yet!

When: January
Where: Okawville
Phone: (618) 243-5694
Admission: Inquire

BLUEGRASS MUSIC FEST

Pickin' and grinnin' at a lively, foot-stomping music festival in the beautiful surroundings of the Lake Sara Campgrounds! Bring your own instrument because jammers are welcome.

When: May
Where: Lake Sara Campgrounds near Effingham
Phone: (217) 682-3340
Admission: Call for admission price

CARTERVILLE FREEFAIR

This annual town celebration provides a place for old friends and neighbors to make new ones at the flea market, carnival, midway, music, parade, food and contests. Queen crowned Thursday, rodeo on Sunday 2 p.m. at Cannon Park.

When: September evenings and all day Saturday
Where: Division Street, Carterville
Phone: (618) 985-4956
Admission: Free except for rodeo

CASCADE OF COLORS BALLOON FESTIVAL

A new entry in the festival arena, this is a balloon festival complete with food, music and carnival rides.

When: September
Where: Southern Illinois Airport, Carbondale
Phone: 1-800-526-1500
Admission: Free

CEDARHURST CRAFT FAIR

This national juried invitational show featuring the handcrafted work of more than 150 artists, with activities for children, entertainment, demonstrations and unusual foods, draws more than 20,000 visitors each year. Provides an opportunity to meet with the artists. Shuttle bus from 34th Street and Doctor's Park, $1 each way.

When: September
Where: Mitchell Museum, Richview Road, Mt. Vernon

Phone: (618) 242-1236
Admission: Preview Party $10 advance; $12 at the door; Craft Fair $2; children under 12 free

CELEBRATION OF CHRISTMAS
Lighted Christmas display in the park, running Monday through Friday until December 26.
When: November
Where: Rock Spring Park, Alton
Phone: (618) 466-8858
Admission: Inquire

CENTRALIA HALLOWEEN PARADE
Come dressed as your favorite...whatever! Parade boasts over 25,000 participants, floats by local businesses, costumes, etc.
When: Last Saturday in October
Where: Centralia
Phone: (618) 532-6789; sponsored by the Chamber of Commerce
Admission: Free

CHAMBER OF COMMERCE HOME SHOW/COMMUNITY EXPOSITION
With emphasis on home building and improvement, the local businesses display their products.
When: Usually the first week in March
Where: Activity Center, E. Oglesby & Rotan Ave, Salem
Phone: (618) 548-3010
Admission: Inquire

CHESTER'S POPEYE PICNIC
You'll find spinach and hamburgers...and much more at this festival! A commemoration of Chester native Elzie Segar, the creator of Popeye, this event features a parade, carnival, sporting events, dances, contests, food, races, pageants and fireworks display. Call for times.
When: September
Where: Church street, Chester
Phone: (618) 826-5114 or 826-2326
Admission: Free

CHILDREN'S ART FESTIVAL
Bring out the kids and let their creative juices flow. Activities include a children's store, food, demonstrating artists, entertainment.

When: October
Where: Southern Illinois Arts & Crafts Marketplace, Whittington, Exit 77 off I-57
Phone: (618) 629-2220
Admission: Free

CHRISTMAS BAZAAR

This is an opportunity to start your Christmas shopping early!
When: November 20, 9 a.m. to 3 p.m.
Where: St. Peter's Catholic Church, Okawville
Phone: (618) 243-5417
Admission: Free

CHRISTMAS CAROUSEL

Craft fair featuring handmade items from members of the Godfrey Women's Club. Luncheon served.
When: November
Where: Alton-Wood River Sportsman's Club, Godfrey
Phone: (618) 466-4679
Admission: Free

CHRISTMAS HISTORIC HOUSE TOUR

Tour of historic homes, filled with antiques and decorated for Christmas (some with as many as 12 Christmas trees!), in three historic districts.
When: December
Where: Alton
Phone: 1-800-ALTONIL
Admission: Inquire

CHRISTMAS HOUSE TOUR & LIVE NATIVITY PAGEANT

House tour and live nativity pageant, free admission. Shuttle service (free) available for house tour. Call for times.
When: December
Where: Okawville
Phone: (618) 243-5694
Admission: house tour $5; nativity pageant free

CHRISTMAS LIGHT DISPLAY

Set in rural Effingham County, this lights display features 130,000 lights! Take the kids and get in the holiday spirit.
When: December, all month, dusk to 10 p.m.

Where: South of Dieterich to Ingraham Road, then left to Mullin's
Christmas Farm; watch for lights
Phone: (618) 752-2460
Admission: Free

CHRISTMAS STROLL & FESTIVAL OF TREES
Come and take a stroll through the participating businesses all deco-
rated for the holiday. Have your card stamped and you'll be eligible
for an attendance prize. Visit the Festival of Trees, located at the
Okawville High School and enjoy a variety of decorations you can
only imagine.
When: December
Where: Okawville
Phone: (618) 243-5694
Admission: Festival of Trees $1, stroll free

CIVIL WAR ENCAMPMENT AT FORT DEFIANCE
Held in conjunction with the "Battle of Belmont," approximately 250
Union troops will be camped at Fort Defiance and transported to the
battle by barge. A battalion hospital tent will be erected at the Fort,
and wounded from the battle will be returned to Fort Defiance for
care. Come see how it was back then.
When: October
Where: Fort Defiance, Cairo
Phone: (618) 734-0371
Admission: Free, but donations are accepted

CIVIL WAR RE-ENACTMENT AT MAKANDA
When: Inquire, every other year beginning in 1995
Where: Makanda
Phone: (618) 457-4779
Admission: Free

COBDEN PEACH FESTIVAL
A summertime festival in honor of that popular sweet Southern Illinois
fruit, the peach. Queen contest, carnival, exhibits, games, parade, bar-
beque, peach cobbler, sliced peaches and ice cream.
When: August
Where: Cobden High School ball park
Phone: (618) 893-2776
Admission: Free

CORN FEST
Go here to fill up on summertime fare! Serving all the corn-on-the-cob and sliced tomatoes you can eat, fried chicken, homemade bread, Indian pudding and ice cream. Also features a country store and musical entertainment.
When: August
Where: Charter Oak School, Schuline Road, off Illinois 4 south of Sparta
Phone: (618) 965-9525 or 282-2245
Admission: Free

COUNTRY CHRISTMAS STROLL AND LIGHTED PARADE
All the surrounding communities and organizations are invited to bring a float (must be lighted). No entry fee. Prizes are given for best entries! Sesser merchants have special sales for this event, and the historic Opera House usually has a special show right after the parade.
When: Usually during first week in December
Where: Main Street, Sesser and the Sesser Opera House
Phone: (618) 625-56366
Admission: Free

COUNTRY FAIR AND APPLE FETE
Features numerous artists and craftspeople, country store, guided house tours, musical entertainment, horsedrawn carriage rides, log sawing contest, children's petting zoo, famous homemade apple fritters, apple pie, apple butter, apple cider, Mulligan Stew, kettle corn, pork rinds and much more, all in the setting of this historic French settlement!
When: September
Where: Creole House, Prairie du Rocher
Phone: (618) 282-2245
Admission: Free

CREAL SPRINGS WONDER WATER REUNION
Contests, carnival, flea market, crafts and food all centered around the mineral water which flows from the towns namesake source. Parade Saturday, 11 a.m., rodeo Saturday 2:30 p.m,. Gospel sing Sunday afternoon.
When: September
Where: Creal Springs
Phone: (618) 996-3064 or 996-3073
Admission: Free except for rodeo

189

CRUISE NITE

Turn back the clock and drop the top on the T-bird for this open car show and display. Judging in several classes will be held.

When: May
Where: Village Square Mall, U.S. 45, Effingham
Phone: (217) 347-0623
Admission: Free

DAVY CROCKETT OHIO RIVER RELAY RACE

A 25-mile race with flatboats, canoes, kayaks, sailboats. Celebrate Pope County's anniversary with special entertainment and events. Turtle races, state champion frog jumping contest, games and dances.

When: July
Where: Cave-in-Rock to Golconda
Phone: (618) 285-3457
Admission: Free for spectators; $10 entry fee for boats

DU QUOIN CHRISTMAS STROLL

Dress warmly and come out to enjoy the holiday sights. Horse-drawn carriages are available for touring. See a gigantic Christmas tree, Santa and his sleigh, gingerbread houses and a brilliant display of decorated trees in Du Quoin's municipal building. Costumed teddy bears and wreaths for sale.

When: December
Where: Downtown Du Quoin
Phone: (618) 1-800-455-9570
Admission: Free

DU QUOIN STATE FAIR

This downstate 10-day event features Grand Circuit harness racing, ARCA and USAC races, commercial exhibits, foods, Agriland field demonstrations, home show, livestock, concerts. You'll also find a midway and LOTS of tempting goodies!

When: Aug.-Sept
Where: Du Quoin State Fairgrounds, U.S. 51, Du Quoin
Phone: (618) 542-9373 or 542-3000
Admission: Inquire

EAST ALTON CENTENNIAL CARNIVAL & CRAFT SHOW

Event kicks off with a parade which leads to a carnival, craft booths, entertainment and more.

When: August

Where: East Alton
Phone: (618) 259-0106
Admission: Free

ECHOES OFF THE RIVER MARCHING BAND COMPETI-TION

Over 20 marching bands from high schools in Missouri and Illinois compete in this competition sponsored by the Alton Band and Orchestra Builders.
When: October
Where: Alton Public School Stadium, State St., Alton
Admission: Adults $4; students $2

EFFINGHAM COUNTY FAIR

Traditional county fair with all the trimmings–entertainment, queen contest, tractor pull, demolition derby, agricultural displays and much more.
When: July-Aug
Where: Effingham County Fairgrounds, Altamont
Phone: (217) 342-4147
Admission: Free

ELLIS GROVE ANNUAL PICNIC

Spend the day in Ellis Grove for the village's picnic. Parade at 1 p.m. Food and drink stands.
When: August
Where: Village Hall Park, Ellis Grove
Phone: (618) 859-2101 or 859-2541
Admission: Free

FALL COLORFEST

Activities throughout Union County in honor of the beautiful fall foliage. Arts and crafts shows, quilt show, farm tours, historic home tours, antique car show. Call for brochure with map.
When: October
Where: Union County, Anna
Phone: (618) 833-6311 or 1-800-248-4373
Admission: Free

FALL FESTIVAL

Enjoy breathtaking fall vistas from high atop Bald Knob Mountain. Highlights include a slide show of the area, live music, a barbecue and

craft demonstrations.
   When: October
   Where: Bald Knob Mountain Recreation Area, Alto Pass
   Phone: (618) 893-2344
   Admission: Call for admission price

FALL FESTIVAL

The courthouse lawn will be full of antiques, art and collectibles for your browsing and purchasing. Lots of handmade items, exhibits, and games for the kids.
   When: October
   Where: Main Street, courthouse lawn, Golconda
   Phone: (618) 672-4317
   Admission: Free

FANTASTIC FLOWER FAIR

A full day of tours, talks and demonstrations at beautiful Alwerdt's Gardens at the height of the summer flower season.
   When: August
   Where: Alwerdt's Gardens, one mile south of I-70 exit at Altamont
   Phone: (618) 483-5798
   Admission: Call for admission price

FETE DU BON VIEUX TEMPS

Translated this French phrase means "Festival of the Good Old Days." There is an 18th century reception with period music, dancing, and a Colonial fashion show
   When: Usually, the last week of February
   Where: 107 Elm St., Cahokia
   Phone: (618) 332-1782
   Admission: Free

FIDELITY FALL FESTIVAL

Fall festival and fish fry with games and raffles. Features many crafts booths.
   When: September
   Where: Fidelity Park, Fidelity
   Phone: (618) 729-3720
   Admission: Free

FIREWORKS ON THE MISSISSIPPI

Celebrate the birthday of our nation with fireworks and boat races. Top name entertainment, food, and arts and crafts round out the festival.

When: July 3 and 4
Where: Alton Riverfront
Phone: (618) 465-4936 or 1-800-258-6645
Admission: Free

FLUORSPAR FESTIVAL
Carnival rides, flea market, and a parade are all part of this festival, celebrating a locally abundant mineral.

When: October
Where: Rosiclare
Phone: (618) 287-2491 or 285-6825
Admission: Free

FORT DE CHARTRES RENDEZVOUS
Recreating the period from 1750 - 1820, this festival is a favorite with historians who set up camp in the partially reconstructed 18th-century French fort for this two day event. Traditional craft demonstrations and flag ceremonies twice daily highlight the event.

When: June
Where: Fort de Chartres, Prairie du Rocher
Phone: (618) 284-7230
Admission: Call for admission price

FORT DE CHARTRES WINTER RENDEZVOUS
What was it like in a military camp during the winter in the 18th century? Come see for yourself. Winter camp life between 1750-1820 is depicted at this festival, a favorite of history recreationists.

When: November
Where: Fort de Chartres, Prairie du Rocher
Phone: (618) 284-7230
Admission: Free

FORT KASKASKIA TRADITIONAL MUSIC FESTIVAL
Annual traditional music festival featuring regional talent performing bluegrass, cajun, country, folk and mountain music. Food and drink stands on site. Bring your lawn chairs and blankets. Craft demonstrations and sale held both days, too.

When: September
Where: Fort Kaskaskia State Historic Site, Ellis Grove
Phone: (618) 859-3741 or 859-3031
Admission: Free

FORT MASSAC ENCAMPMENT

A military encampment recreating life from 1720 to the 1830s. Both days begin with the posting of colors. Highlights of the event include mock battles and tactical demonstrations, traders and craftspeople in authentic costumes. Also featured are traditional children's games, music and food preparation.

When: October
Where: Fort Massac State Park, Metropolis
Phone: (618) 524-9321
Admission: Call for admission price

FRENCH AND INDIAN WAR ASSEMBLAGE

Life at Fort de Chartres life during the period of 1750 to 1760 is depicted. A flintlock shoot is held which the public may see from a distance.

When: October
Where: Fort de Chartres State Historic Site, Prairie du Rocher
Phone: (618) 284-7230
Admission: Free

FRÜEHLINGFEST

German for spring fest, this festival features craft demonstrations, carriage rides, tours of the bed and breakfast inn, music and food. Visit historic Maeystown.

When: April
Where: Main and Mill Streets, Maeystown
Phone: (618) 458-6660
Admission: Free

GALATIA OLD SETTLERS DAYS

Arts and crafts to enjoy and purchase, lots of good food, flea market, carnival rides, music and a parade. Bingo games round out the fun. Call for times.

When: May-June
Where: Galatia High School grounds
Phone: (618) 268-4296
Admission: Free

GALLATIN COUNTY FAIR AND POPCORN DAYS

Traditional county fair with arts and crafts, beauty contest, talent contest, tractor pull, horse and livestock shows, all set in the popcorn capital of the world!

When: September
Where: Gallatin County Fairgrounds and downtown Ridgway
Phone: (618) 272-8971
Admission: Free

GENERAL JOHN A. LOGAN DAYS

Annual event showcasing the Logan Museum, dedicated to General John A. Logan. City walking tour, historic expositions, memorial services, historic tour of the cemetery, picnic in the park. Crafts demonstrated, carnival, western shoot-out.

When: May
Where: 1619 Edith St., Murphysboro and downtown
Phone: (618) 684-6421
Admission: Call for admission prices to some events

GENERAL LOGAN BIRTHDAY BREAKFAST

A traditional breakfast celebrating Gen. John A. Logan's birthday. This morning festival includes casserole and fruit. Several hundred individuals usually attend.

When: Usually the first Saturday in February
Where: 2125 Spruce, Murphysboro
Phone: (618) 684-6421 or 684-2688
Admission: $5 donation

GREAT AMERICAN TRAIN SHOW

"All aboard!" This two-day model train show, with over 10,000 trains, gathers collectors and railroad buffs alike.

When: July
Where: Gateway Center, One Gateway Drive, Collinsville
Phone: (708) 834-0562
Admission: Call for admission price

GREAT CARDBOARD BOAT REGATTA

This is perhaps the most interesting and unique event in Southern Illinois. Conceived by Dr. Richard Archer 20 years ago as a final exam for his freshman design class, the regatta has grown to become a copyrighted event held throughout the United States. Students build their own boats out of cardboard as a creative problem solving exercise. They race against time as well as compete for judges awards of the Many sink or capsize in the process making this a wonderful spectator sport.

When: One week prior to final exams for SIU students; in May or April
Where: Southern Illinois University, Campus Lake, Carbondale
Phone: (618) 453-5761
Admission: No charge for entrants or spectators

GREAT RIVER ROAD RUN

Annual river road run (flat course), now in it's 34th year. Includes 10K run and 2 mile fun run. Age group awards, T-shirts to all entrants.

When: November, 10 a.m.
Where: Downtown Alton
Phone: 1-800-ALTONIL
Admission: $10 prior to Nov. 22, $15 after

GREAT SALUKI TAILGATE

Show your Saluki pride and try to win great prizes for the best tailgate celebration! Themed competition with prizes in various categories and groups.

When: November
Where: McAndrew Stadium, Southern Illinois University at Carbondale
Phone: (618) 453-5311
Admission: Call for entry fee

HAMILTON COUNTY FAIR

Traditional county fair with livestock judging, rides, and lots of food and drink. Also, floral hall exhibit, demolition derby, and horse pulls

When: August
Where: McLeansboro
Phone: (618) 643-3531
Admission: Free

HERITAGE AMERICA
The American Indian Heritage is celebrated with events such as tribal dancing and exhibits and good food.
> **When:** Last week in September
> **Where:** Cahokia Mounds State Historic & World Heritage Site, Collinsville
> **Phone:** (618) 344-9221 or 346-6160
> **Admission**: Inquire

HERITAGE DAYS
Fine recreation of history from 1700-1840. Admission is free to those arriving in costume from that period.
> **When:** October
> **Where:** Alton
> **Phone:** (618) 465-4020
> **Admission**: Adults $2; students $1; children's area 75¢

HERITAGE DAYS
Tour Heritage House Museum, enjoy various old-time crafts being demonstrated, children's prairie games, storytellers. Food and beverages located on grounds.
> **When:** June
> **Where:** West Walnut, Okawville
> **Phone:** (618) 243-5694
> **Admission:** Free

HERRINFEST ITALIANA
Do you have a "bigga nose?" Bring it to this ethnic festival and you could win a prize! Four day festival featuring a golf tournament, carnival, crafts, car show, ethnic food, games, parade, nightly entertainment and more. Call for times.
> **When:** May
> **Where:** Downtown Herrin
> **Phone:** (618) 942-5163
> **Admission**: Free

ILLINOIS ENGINE SHOW
Revisit the past at this engine show, with gasoline and steam engines, threshing machines and an antique tractor pull. A flea market rounds out the show.
When: July
Where: Bluford, northeast of town
Phone: (618) 755-4458
Admission: Call for admission price

INTERNATIONAL HORSERADISH FESTIVAL
When you are a top producer of horseradish then that's cause for celebration. In the acclaimed "Horseradish Capital of the World." A host of horseradish-related events including a horseradish eating contest.
When: First week in May
Where: Woodsland Park, Collinsville
Phone: (618) 344-2884
Admission: Free

ITALIAN FEST
Cultural & social events feature Italian food, bocce tournament, parades and free entertainment. There is even a grape stomp.
When: Usually the third week of September
Where: Downtown Collinsville
Phone: (618) 344-2884
Admission: Free

JACOB DAY
Come enjoy this local celebration in the tiny town of Jacob, in the fertile Mississippi valley. Event features softball games, food, crafts.
When: July
Where: Jacob Community Park
Phone: (618) 763-4748
Admission: Free

JACOB WURST MART
Fans flock to this celebration to purchase the homemade sausage sold in bulk. Pork and liver sausage for sale. You have to get there early, though, because it sells out fast! Plate lunches of delicious pork sausage, sauerkraut and mashed potatoes from 11 a.m. to 2 p.m. Crafts, children's games, music, dancing in evening.
When: October
Where: Jacob Community Park

Phone: (618) 763-4748
Admission: Free

JERSEY COUNTY FAIR

Traditional week-long county fair featuring queen contest, tractor and truck pulls, livestock judging, and demo derby. Highlights also include a sanctioned rodeo, harness racing and parade.

When: July
Where: Jerseyville American Legion Park, Jerseyville
Phone: (618) 498-5848
Admission: Adults $1; children under 13 free

JERSEYVILLE AMERICAN LEGION STRASSENFEST

Polka, polka, polka! German food and German music abound at this festival which also features crafts, games and a flea market.

When: Aug. 6-8
Where: American Legion Grounds, Jerseyville

JOHNSON COUNTY HERITAGE FESTIVAL

Family event featuring arts and crafts booths, music, food and games for everyone. Sock hop Friday night. Country music Saturday night. Parade on Saturday. Car show on Sunday.

When: October
Where: Vienna Community Park, Vienna
Phone: (618) 658-2511 or 658-9255
Admission: Free

JULY 4 CELEBRATION

Rend Lake: Enjoy music, entertainment, food, a pageant, carnival and fireworks at dusk on the 4th; $2 parking fee per car.

When: July
Where: Rend Lake Visitors Center
Phone: (618) 724-2493
Admission: Inquire

JULY 4 CELEBRATION

Steeleville: This delightful festival has been an annual celebration since 1866. It includes a huge parade, picnic, crafts, a car show and fireworks. Baseball games. Nightly entertainment and dancing.

When: July 3-5
Where: City park and Legion Park, Steeleville
Phone: (618) 965-3134

Admission: Free

JULY 4 CELEBRATION
Murphysboro: Ball games, carnival, fireworks, crafts, music, stage show and more. Call for details.
   When: July 2-4
   Where: Riverside Park
   Phone: (618) 684-6421
   Admission: Free

JULY 4 CELEBRATION
Anna: Celebration includes fireworks display, barbecue, food stands, ball games and other sports activities.
   When: July 4
   Where: City Park
   Phone: (618) 833-6311
   Admission: Free

JULY 4 CELEBRATION
Herrin: Features a carnival, live music, flea market, and a fireworks display at dusk on the 4th. Food booths.
   When: July 2-4
   Where: City Park
   Phone: (618) 942-3326
   Admission: Free

JULY 4 CELEBRATION
Goreville: Goreville's 15th annual Independence Day gala. Parade at 1 p.m. July 3. Fireworks at dusk July 4 next to Goreville Baptist Church. Gospel music, food.
   When: July 3, 4
   Where: Downtown, Illinois 37
   Phone: (618) 995-2511
   Admission: Free

JULY 4 CELEBRATION
Eddyville: Barbecue, entertainment, gospel sign and fireworks July 4.
   When: July 3, 4
   Where: Community Center Grounds, Eddyville
   Phone: (618) 672-4222
   Admission: Free

JULY 4 CELEBRATION
Kaskaskia Island: Annual patriotic program on the island, first capitol of Illinois, climaxed by the ringing of the Liberty Bell of the West. The bell was received from Louis XV of France in 1743.
When: July 4, noon - 3 p.m.
Where: Immaculate Conception Church grounds, Kaskaskia Island
Phone: (618) 366-2622
Admission: Free

JULY 4 CELEBRATION
Beach Blast: Day-long event of sporting activities.
When: Prior to July 4, all day
Where: Youth Association Park, Okawville
Phone: (618) 243-5694
Admission: under $5

JULY 4 CELEBRATION
Freedom Fest: Du Quoin's first celebration. Craft and flea market, square dancing, ski show, volleyball tournament, fireworks at dusk both days.
When: July 3, 4 all day
Where: Du Quoin State Fairgrounds
Phone: (618) 542-8338
Admission: Call for admission price

KALEIDOSCOPE OF CRAFTS SHOW
Do your Christmas shopping in the holiday atmosphere of this annual craft fair. Handmade items abound, food and drink available.
When: November
Where: Knights of Columbus building, Effingham
Phone: (217) 342-4147
Admission: $1

KAMPSVILLE OLD SETTLERS DAYS
The arrival of Pere Marquette and Louis Joliet is reenacted on the riverfront during this celebration of life in Calhoun County in pioneer days. Mountain men encampment with traditional craft demonstrations and live entertainment.
When: October
Where: Kampsville Riverfront Park
Phone: (618) 232-1108
Admission: Free

KIDS DAYS
Eighteenth century games, contests, crafts, and activities for children of all ages.
> **When:** May
> **Where:** Fort de Chartres State Historic Site, Prairie du Rocher
> **Phone:** (618) 284-7230
> **Admission:** Free

LA GUIANNEE
A New Year's Eve celebration held continuously since 1699 in Illinois. Members of La Guiannee Societe dressed in period costume sing old French songs as they stroll from house to house. Singers continue performance at the Creole House, local homes and eating establishments. The singers receive gratuities of food and drink from their hosts.
> **When:** Dec. 31, 7 p.m.
> **Where:** Fort de Chartres and Creole House, Prairie du Rocher
> **Phone:** (618) 284-7230
> **Admission**: Free

LABOR DAY BETHALTO HOMECOMING
Annual event featuring carnival rides and games, free entertainment, arts and crafts, lots of food and BINGO!
> **When:** September
> **Where:** Bethalto City Park
> **Phone:** (618) 377-8695
> **Admission:** Free

LABOR DAY CELEBRATION
Highlights of this annual celebration, sponsored by the Lions Club, include live musical entertainment and fireworks on the Ohio River.
> **When:** Labor Day, 10 a.m. - 9:30 p.m.
> **Where:** The courthouse and Fort Massac State Park, Metropolis
> **Phone:** (618) 993-6101
> **Admission**: Free

LABOR DAY FLEA MARKET
Bluegrass music and over 100 booths to browse through. A great place to find bargains!
> **When:** Labor Day weekend, 8 a.m. - 6 p.m.
> **Where:** Main Street in Sesser
> **Phone:** (618) 625-6366

Admission: $15 for booth set up; no fee to general public

LANDMARK HISTORIC HOUSE TOUR
Once a year chance to see all historic homes decorated with antiques.
When: October
Where: Historic districts, Alton
Phone: (618) 465-6676
Admission: Tickets available at Landmarks and Convention and Visitors Bureau

LIGHTS FANTASTIC
Annual lighted parade including floats, bands, cars. Refreshments, special lighted displays and storefront artwork displays. Holiday sing and Santa Claus.
When: December
Where: Downtown Carbondale
Phone: (618) 529-4147
Admission: Free

MAEYSTOWN HOMECOMING
Enjoy barbershoppers crooning your favorite tune, cut a rug, eat good food, play some games and watch the parade on Sunday all at this traditional hometown homecoming.
When: June
Where: Mill Street, Maeystown
Phone: (618) 458-6660
Admission: Free

MAGNOLIA FESTIVAL
Amid the beautiful blooming magnolia trees which this festival celebrates, you will find a wealth of activities, including tours of Magnolia Manor, barbecue dinners, arts and crafts, Christmas decorations and more.
When: June
Where: Magnolia Manor, 2700 Washington Ave., Cairo
Phone: (618) 734-0201
Admission: Call for admission price

MAGNOLIA MANOR HOLIDAY HOUSE
Ring in the holiday in a traditional manner. Annual holiday celebration features a 14-room Victorian mansion with period furnishings, decorated with handmade Christmas decorations. The decorations may be

purchased. Refreshments.
   When: November
   Where: 2700 Washington Ave., Cairo
   Phone: (618) 734-0201
   Admission: Call for admission price

MAKANDA FEST
Arts, crafts and music festival featuring a juried arts and crafts show, demonstrations by local artisans, live music, food and drink, all on the boardwalk in Makanda.
   When: June
   Where: Downtown Makanda
   Phone: (618) 457-8508 or 529-1783

MAKE-IT-YOUR-HOME FESTIVAL
Annual get-acquainted day with informational booths, food, music, games for kids. Free admission.
   When: May
   Where: Town Square, Carbondale
   Phone: (618) 549-6013
   Admission: Inquire

MARDI GRAS FESTIVAL
Festival features flea market, food stands and a variety of special events. The highlight is a large parade featuring costumed participants and area marching bands. Parade begins at 7:30 pm.
   When: October
   Where: Downtown Pinckneyville
   Phone: (618) 357-2211
   Admission: Free

MARION COUNTRY FEST
Bluegrass and gospel music ring through the air. An annual celebration, the event also features carnival rides, arts and crafts, car show, children's parade on Saturday, auction and bratwurst dinner.
   When: October
   Where: Marion, various locations
   Phone: (618) 997-6311
   Admission: Free

MARISSA COAL FESTIVAL
Three-day festival features antique tractor pull, kiddie pedal pull, vol-

leyball tournaments, crafts, queen contest, nightly entertainment, nightly bingo, carnival, coal museum, parade on Sunday, various foods and more.

When: August
Where: City Park, South Main Street, Marissa
Phone: (618) 295-2562
Admission: Free

MASS OF CELEBRATION

African-American celebration in honor of St. Augustine, Father Augustins Toltin, the first black priest in America who was assigned to Alton in 1886, and Dr. Martin Luther King, Jr. Celebration begins at St. Mary's Church, Henry St, in Alton, followed by a motorcade to Old Cathedral, State St., Alton.

When: August 28, 10 a.m.
Where: Alton

MASSAC COUNTY YOUTH FAIR

Youth from 13 Southern Illinois counties exhibit hundreds of livestock and projects. See the greased pig contest and tractor pull.

When: July
Where: Massac County High School, Metropolis
Phone: (618) 524-2714
Admission: Free

MEMORIAL DAY FLEA MARKET

Bluegrass music and over 100 booths to browse through. A great place to find bargains!

When: Memorial Day weekend, 8 a.m. - 6 p.m.
Where: Main Street in Sesser
Phone: (618) 625-6366
Admission: $15 for booth set up, no fee to general public

MIDWESTERN HERB SHOW

Herb products exhibition with demonstrations.

When: February
Where: Times Square Mall (42nd & Broadway), Mt. Vernon
Phone: (618) 242-3151
Admission: Free

MT. VERNON OPEN TENNIS TOURNAMENT

Thrill to the excitement of a tennis tournament, sanctioned by the

United States Tennis Association, featuring the best players in Southern Illinois and surrounding states. Call for times and entry fee.
When: May
Where: Mt. Vernon City Park
Phone: (618) 242-6890
Admission: Call for admission price

MUPRHYSBORO TOUR OF HOMES

Come visit area homes festively decorated for the holidays. The event is sponsored by the Junior Women's Club.
When: December
Where: Murphysboro
Phone: (618) 684-6421
Admission: Call for admission price

MURPHYSBORO AND ILLINOIS STATE BARBECUE CHAMPIONSHIP

Use your favorite barbecue recipe to win cash prizes and trophies in categories such as ribs, shoulders and whole hog. This competition is sanctioned by "Memphis in May." The competition is fierce, with team skits included. Music and dancing as well.
When: September
Where: GM&O Railroad site at 17th and Pine, Murphysboro
Phone: (618) 684-2775 or 684-6421
Admission: Free to public, call for entry fee information

MURPHYSBORO APPLE FESTIVAL

The crisp fall air is the perfect backdrop for this annual celebration that features a carnival, apple pie contests, entertainment, food, parade, and "Apple-L-Ympics," marching band competition and a queen contest. Golf tournament rounds out the event.
When: September
Where: 17th and 18th Streets, Murphysboro
Phone: (618) 684-3200 or 684-6421
Admission: Free

NATIONAL HUNTING AND FISHING DAYS

Always a favorite with the sportsman, but this event will appeal to all. Archery, field dog trials, boat and RV dealers, sportsmen's clubs, turkey and duck calling contests, and the World Open Goose Calling Championships are all featured.
When: Fourth Saturday and Sunday in September

Where: John A. Logan College Campus, Illinois 13, Carterville
Phone:1-800-851-4720 (ext. 416)
Admission: Free

OKAWVILLE FAIR AND WHEAT FESTIVAL
Agricultural fair includes free entertainment, lots of home-cooked food, an antique tractor pull, horse judging and a float parade Sunday.
When: September
Where: Community Club Park, Okawville
Phone: (618) 243-5694
Admission: Free

OCTOBER FALL FESTIVAL
This agricultural fair includes free entertainment, home-cooked food, and old-time cooking and craft demonstrations. There is a fiddler's contest and consignment sale.
When: October
Where: Community Club Park, Okawville
Phone: (618) 243-5694
Admission: Inquire

OKTOBERFEST
Celebrate fall this quaint Southern Illinois town with good German food. See the arts and crafts display.
When: October
Where: Maeystown
Phone: (618) 458-6660
Admission: Free

OKTOBERFEST CRAFT FAIR
Many different types of crafts displayed by vendors from Southern Illinois. Variety show on Saturday night at the historic opera house.
When: Second weekend in October
Where: Sesser City Park
Phone: (618) 625-6366
Admission: Free

OLD KING COAL FESTIVAL
Old King Coal was a merry old soul, and you will be too if you attend this celebration featuring a Princess Flame, Little King Coal and Old King Coal pageants. Carnival, food, crafts. Parade, Saturday at 11 a.m. Antique car show Sunday.

When: September
Where: East Main Street, West Frankfort
Phone: (618) 932-2181
Admission: Free

OLD SETTLER'S REUNION
Day-long event celebrating the founding of Effingham County. Events include a craft show, flea market, antiques, demonstrations, contest, speakers and music.
When: September
Where: Effingham County Courthouse lawn, Effingham
Phone: (217) 342-4147
Admission: Free

OLDE ALTON ARTS AND CRAFT FAIR
Crafts festival featuring over 250 artisans from a 500 mile radius. Food, including specialty desserts, breakfast and lunch.
When: December
Where: Alton High School Annex Bldg., College Ave, Alton
Phone: (618) 465-6123
Admission: inquire

OLDE-TYME CHRISTMAS
The museum and visitor's center are festively decorated by the garden club with 1750's style decorations. Take in the sights and enjoy music and refreshments.
When: December
Where: Fort Massac State Park, Metropolis
Phone: (618) 524-9321
Admission: Free

ORCHIDS, TRAINS, PLANES & STAMP SHOW
Exhibits featuring orchids, model trains, planes & stamps from the pre-eminent collectors in the area. This festival features something for all ages.
When: February
Where: 1900 W. Sycamore, Carbondale
Phone: (618) 549-5346
Admission: Free

PAST TO PRESENT FESTIVAL
Turn back the hands of time to days gone by, when making lye soap,

caning chairs and making cider was a way of life. Crafts, antique sale, heritage demonstrations, food stands.

When: September
Where: Saline County Fairgrounds, Harrisburg
Phone: (618) 252-8391
Admission: $1 per car

PERRY COUNTY FAIR

Traditional county fair with western horse show, livestock show, horse racing, rodeo, demolition derby, tractor pull, queen pageant, donkey softball game. Call for times.

When: June
Where: Perry County Fairgrounds, Pinckneyville
Phone: (618) 357-9222 or 357-5002
Admission: Call for admission price

PIERRE MENARD HOME CANDLELIGHT TOUR AND OPEN HOUSE

Begins at dusk on Saturday. Grounds and home will be lit by candle-light. Entertainment featured on rear porchway. Sunday will feature an open house and quilt show.

When: June
Where: Pierre Menard Home, Ellis Grove
Phone: (618) 859-3031
Admission: Free

PIERRE MENARD HOUSE CHRISTMAS OPEN HOUSE

The home of Illinois' first lieutenant governor will be decorated for the holidays with native greenery, herbs and fruit displays on tables and fireplace mantles. Tour guides and participants in period dress. Music from French Colonial and early Illinois times. French pastries and hot cider are served.

When: December
Where: Pierre Menard House, Ellis Grove
Phone: (618) 859-3031
Admission: Free

POPE COUNTY DEER FESTIVAL

Three-day extravaganza for wild game hunters. Parade on Saturday, queen contest, arts, crafts, music and food, fireworks and barbecue.

When: November
Where: Courthouse Square, Golconda

Phone: (618) 672-4222
Admission: Free

PULASKI COUNTY FAIR

Traditional county fair features a horse show, mule pull, 4-H exhibits, tractor pulls, arts and crafts, demolition derbies, carnival, concession stands, food and crafts judging.
  When: August
  Where: Pulaski County Fairgrounds, Pulaski
  Phone: (618) 342-6212
  Admission: $2 per car

RANDOLPH COUNTY FAIR

Fun-packed traditional county fair with a variety of activities, including horse shows, demolition derby, carnival rides, food concession stands. Demolition derby with a twist (they use combines!), mud bog, livestock judging, rabbit show on Saturday, horse pull and tractor pull. Call for times.
  When: July
  Where: Randolph County Fairgrounds, Sparta
  Phone: (618) 443-2007
  Admission: Call for admission price

REND LAKE WATER FESTIVAL

Week-long event. Air show, carnival, pageants, car show, 5K race, parade on Saturday and more. Call for times and location of events.
  When: May, to be announced
  Where: Benton
  Phone: (618) 438-2121
  Admission: Inquire

REND LAKE SKI SHOW

Earth, air and sky are all featured at this festival. Ski shows, skydiving, food, live music, carnival, craft fair. Displays of fishing and sporting boats, campers, motor homes.
  When: June
  Where: Wayne Fitzgerrell State Park, Whittington
  Phone: (618) 629-2211
  Admission: Free

RIVER-TO-RIVER RELAY

A true test of endurance...and a lot of fun! That's how participants describe this race. An 80-mile race for teams of eight runners, each person running three legs of 3.3 miles. The route follows beautiful roads and trails through the Shawnee National Forest. Call for time and entry fee.

When: April
Where: Across the southern tip of Illinois
Phone: (618) 997-3690 or 1-800-433-7399
Admission: Inquire

RIVERBOAT DAYS FESTIVAL

A celebration of Cairo's river history, this festival includes a children's art show, variety show, carnival, and a formal ball on Saturday evening. Craft fair, tours of historic buildings and landmarks, musical entertainment and a Civil War encampment at Fort Defiance add to the fun. Call for times.

When: October
Where: Cairo–on the riverfront
Phone: (618) 734-2737 or 734-0456
Admission: Call for admission price

ROXANA AUTO SHOW AND TROPHY MEET

Jalopies or jaguars, you'll see them all at this auto show!Antique, classics and custom cars and trucks displayed for judging in the park. Many food stands, so bring the kids and picnic. A swimming pool is also available if the weather gets too hot.

When: June
Where: Roxana Park, Roxana
Phone: (618) 462-1337
Admission: Free

RURITAN GOLF SCRAMBLE

Join this fun-loving civic group in golfing and fun as they support small-town community development.

When: September
Where: Lake of Egypt Country Club, North of Goreville
Phone: (618) 995-2511
Admission: $60 donation

SALINE COUNTY FAIR

Traditional county fair with western horse show, demolition derby, tractor pull, mud bog. Big bands, midget car races, bull mania, wild cow milking and riding. What more could you ask for? Call for times.

When: Last week in July
Where: Saline County Fairgrounds, Harrisburg
Phone: (618) 252-3575
Admission: Call for admission price

SESSER REND LAKE DAYS HOMECOMING

Local bands nightly. Friday and Saturday nights feature "Grand Ole Opry" stars from Nashville. Roasted corn and barbecue sandwiches. Carnival, flea market and parade at 4 p.m Saturday.
When: Third weekend in June, Wed. - Sat.
Where: Sesser Main Street and City Park
Phone: (618) 625-6366
Admission: Free

SCHUETZENFEST

One day German festival featuring fine German food, dance, games and contests. Come out and find out what Schuetzenfest really means!
When: September
Where: Effingham County Fairgrounds, Altamont
Phone: (217) 342-4147
Admission: Call for admission price

SOMMERFEST

Come see the antique vehicle show, crafts, music and enjoy the German food.
When: August
Where: Maeystown
Phone: (618) 458-6660
Admission: Free

SORGHUM FEST

Come and satisfy your sweet tooth while you help make sorghum in the crisp autumn air. Held amid the beautiful historic surroundings of the Kremer's Starvation Farm this celebration is a sure crowd-pleaser.
When: October
Where: Kremer's Starvation Farm, rural Dieterich
Phone: (217) 739-2338
Admission: Call for admission price

SOUTHEASTERN ILLINOIS HERITAGE FESTIVAL

Over 160 booths of crafts and art lets you get a head start on your Christmas shopping while you enjoy entertainment, food.

When: November
Where: Southeastern Illinois College, seven miles east of Harrisburg
Phone: (618) 252-6376, exit. 420
Admission: Free

SOUTHERN ILLINOIS EARTH SCIENCE CLUB GEM SHOW
Gem and mineral show, Indian artifacts, fossil demonstrators, art, artisans, wire wrapping of gems, lapidary work.
When: April
Where: Carterville Junior High School Gymnasium
Phone: (618) 242-2931 or 549-2402
Admission: Free

SOUTHERN ILLINOIS FESTIVAL OF ARTS AND CRAFTS
Watch craftsmen from Illinois and the Midwest ply their craft skills. Special demonstrations of 18th century crafts. Food booths. Entertainment.
When: May
Where: Southern Illinois Arts & Crafts Marketplace, Whittington, Exit 77 off I-57.
Phone: (618) 629-2220
Admission: Inquire

SOUTHWESTERN ILLINOIS GRAND PRIX
"Gentlemen, start your engines!" This event gathers exotic race cars to compete in high speed races.
When: August
Where: Madison, Illinois 203 and I-55/70
Phone: (618) 782-9587
Admission: Call for admission price

SPARTAFEST
This festival has fun all over town, from the airport for the airshow to the Randolph County Fairgrounds for the rodeo. Also enjoy the Little Miss pageant, arts, crafts and flea market, basketball, volleyball and horseshoe contests, hot air balloon show, and fireworks Sunday.
When: July - August
Where: Sparta. VFW, airport, fairgrounds, downtown
Phone: (618) 443-2145
Admission: Free except for rodeo

Springs Sports & Recreation Show at SIU-C Arena

SPORTSFEST

Live entertainment, craft show, beer garden, and food tents, set in a carnival atmosphere.

    When: June

    Where: Alton-Wood River Sportsman's Club, 3109 Godfrey Road, Godfrey

    Phone: (618) 466-3042

    Admission: None

SPRING HERB FESTIVAL

Join us at beautiful Alwerdt's Gardens to learn about cooking with herbs. A full day of tours, talks and demonstrations. Call for more information.

    When: Third week of May, 9 a.m. until 5 p.m.

    Where: Alwerdt's Gardens, one mile south of I-70 exit at Altamont

    Phone: (217) 483-5798

    Admission: Free

SPRING SPORTS AND RECREATION SHOW

The SIU Arena offers over 65,000 square feet of exhibit space for visitors to shop for the latest in grown-up "toys." The 10th anniversary of the Spring Sports and Recreation Show provides a variety of displays from retailers, distributors, and manufacturers of sports, recreation, and related products and services.

    When: Usually held the first or second week in February

    Where: Southern Illinois University at Carbondale, the Arena

    Phone: (618) 453-2321

    Admission: $3 adults; children 12 and under free with adult

SPRINGFEST

This event on the campus of Southern Illinois University at Carbondale features the Doc Spackman Memorial Triathlon, carnival rides and outdoor concerts. Call for times and entry fees.

    When: April

    Where: Southern Illinois University at Carbondale

    Phone: (618) 536-3393

    Admission: Free

ST. JOHN'S CHURCH FESTIVAL

Celebrate the German Heritage of this quaint Southern Illinois town with German pancakes and sausage dinner in an historic church.

    When: February

Where: St. John's Catholic Church, Maeystown
Phone: (618) 458-6660
Admission: Inquire

ST. ANDREW'S PARISH FESTIVAL
A two-day celebration of summer at the local Catholic church, just like you remember from your childhood. Music, food, more.
When: August
Where: St. Andrew's Church, 724 Mulberry St., Murphysboro
Phone: (618) 684-2013 or 684-6421
Admission: Free

ST. PATRICK'S DAY FESTIVAL AND IRISH STEW COOK-OFF
Enjoy St. Patty's Day with a parade featuring a bagpipe band, 5K run and walk, plus an Irish stew cook-off. Call for times.
When: March
Where: Walnut Street, Murphysboro
Phone: (618) 684-6421
Admission: Free

STEELEVILLE OKTOBERFEST
Start the day at the craft fair on Sparta Street (you'll also find plenty to eat!), then continue on up to the car show with 14 classes of awards. Finish up the day cuttin' the rug at the street dance and cheer the crowning of the king and queen.
When: October
Where: Steeleville, various locations
Phone:(618) 965-3134
Admission: Free

STONEFORT REUNION
Hometown celebration in the small community of Stonefort featuring square dancing, beauty contest, music every night.
When: August
Where: Stonefort
Phone: (618) 777-2807
Admission: Free

STRAW AND HAY DAYS
Gospel music, queen contest, craft fair and more at this festival! Food booths open every evening and all day Saturday. Round out the event

with the parade on Saturday.
   When: June
   Where: Bonnie Park, Third St. in Bonnie (eight miles south of Mt. Vernon on Illinois 37)
   Phone: (618) 242-5646
   Admission: Free

STREET MACHINE NATIONALS
This celebration draws huge crowds from all over the United States and Canada to view the more than 3,500 street machines (1949-present day models) and sport trucks. Vintage vehicles from 37 states and Canada. Competition and seminars.
   When: June
   Where: Du Quoin State Fairgrounds, U.S. 51 south, Du Quoin
   Phone: (317) 236-6515
   Admission: Adults $8 advance, $10 gate

SUMMERFEST
Annual two-day festival for the whole family, sponsored by St. Theresa Catholic Church. The event features a carnival and games for the kids.
   When: June
   Where: St. Theresa Catholic Church, West Main Street, Salem
   Phone: (618) 548-0899
   Admission: Free

SUPERMAN CELEBRATION
Come on down to the hometown of the Man of Steel. Join participants for a day of fun, including super trek bike ride, food booths, road race, entertainment, games, all under the watchful eye of the new Superman statue. On Saturday, events also include classic car show, parade, fireworks, tennis tournament, tours of gardens and the historic Curtis House. Admission to tours, others free.
   When: Second weekend in June
   Where: On the riverfront, Metropolis
   Phone: (618) 524-2714
   Admission: Free

SWEETCORN AND WATERMELON FESTIVAL
A weeklong festival held at various sites in Mt. Vernon. Nightly activities include bed, tricycle and go-cart races. The week culminates in a parade on Saturday and free sweetcorn and watermelon downtown.

When: August
Where: Downtown Square, Mt. Vernon
Phone: (618) 242-5725
Admission: Free

SWEETHEART SPAGHETTI AND MEATBALL FEST

Take your honey out for Valentine's Day and enjoy entertainment, door prizes, dance and spaghetti meatball dinner.
When: February
Where: Fire House, Creal Springs
Phone: (618) 996-3064
Admission: Call for admission price

THEBES ARTS AND CRAFTS FESTIVAL AND MEMORIAL DAY BARBECUE

Country music and rides, lots of arts and crafts to browse among, drawing and prizes throughout the day, barbecue.
When: Memorial Day weekend

Murphysboro Apple Festival (Carbondale Convention & Tourism Bureau photo)

Where: Thebes Courthouse and River Park
Phone: (618) 764-2240
Admission: Free

TRAIL OF TEARS WAGON TRAIN

This festival is part of Native American Awareness Month and Day in Illinois, and highlights the trail used for the forced removal of the Cherokee nation from 1838 to 1893.
When: October
Where: Pope, Johnson, Union and Alexander Counties
Phone: (618) 833-8697
Admission: Free

TWELFTH DAY OF CHRISTMAS CELEBRATION

Old French songs, dancing, traditional French pastries and hot mulled cider, tours of the Pierre Menard Home. This celebration marks the end of the Christmas season. There is an opportunity to tour the Pierre Menard Mansion
When: January- usually the first week
Where: Pierre Menard Home, Ellis Grove
Phone: (618) 859-3031
Admission: Free

TWELFTH NIGHT DINNER AND BALL

This annual event consists of a five-course dinner and dance in the atmosphere of the French Colonial Era. There coronation of the Twelfth Night king and queen is held. There are carriage rides to Twelfth Night Ball at American Legion Hall. The Twelfth Night celebration continues on the next day at the Pierre Menard Home.
When: January, usually the first week
Where: Prairie du Rocher
Phone: (618) 284-3463
Admission: Admission to the dance is $5. Inquire about other fees.

VETERAN'S DAY PARADE

Be patriotic and honor those who made America a great place to live at this parade through downtown Anna.
When: November
Where: Anna, downtown
Phone: (618) 833-5182
Admission: Free

WAY OF LIGHTS

The crib of the Christ child awaits you at the end of this illuminated path. Christmas scenes are outlined in over 150,000 white lights. Come indoors to warm up and enjoy a Christmas tree display and children's choir.

When: November
Where: National Shrine of Our Lady of the Snows, Illinois 15, Belleville
Phone: 1-800-782-9587
Admission: Call for admission price

WASHINGTON COUNTY FAIR

Traditional, fun-packed county fair with activities, including horse shows, demolition derby, carnival rides, food concession stands. Demolition derby, mud bog, livestock judging, horse pull and tractor pull. Call for times.

When: July
Where: Washington County Fairgrounds, Nashville
Phone: (618) 327-3298
Admission: Call for admission price

WHITTINGTON GUN CREEK DAYS

Five nights of fun! Tractor pulls (big ones and pedal pull for the kids!), hog calling, fine country music and dancing on the largest round dance floor in Southern Illinois. Gun demonstrations and competitions, too.

When: August
Where: Ball park, Whittington
Phone: (618) 629-2190
Admission: Free

WILLIAMSON COUNTY RODEO

Yippee aye oh! Bring the buckeroos down for a fun time at this rodeo! Calf roping, barrel racing and more are on tap. Call for times.
When: June
Where: Williamson County Fairgrounds, Marion
Phone: (618) 997-3690
Admission: $4 per performance for adults, children 6-12 $2.50, under 12 free; passes also available, $10 adult pass, all performances, $5.50 children

Exercise, Fitness & Health Centers

T wenty years ago there were virtually no established fitness or
health centers in Southern Illinois. Now over 50 are known
to be in operation. These serve a variety of needs from aero-

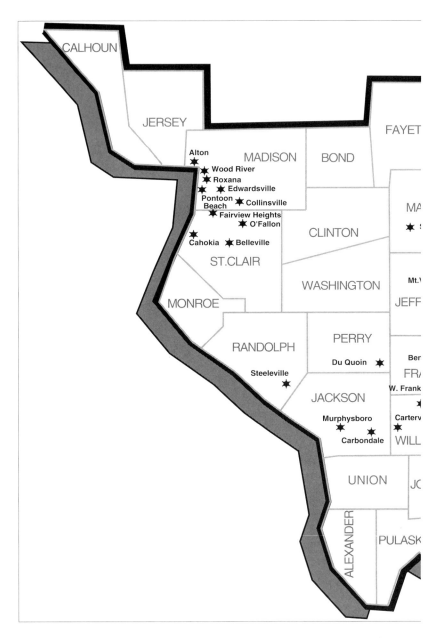

bic exercises like basketball, swimming, racquetball to body building or weight management. Some even have baby sitting or day care centers and amenities like spas or whirlpools, saunas and tanning equipment.

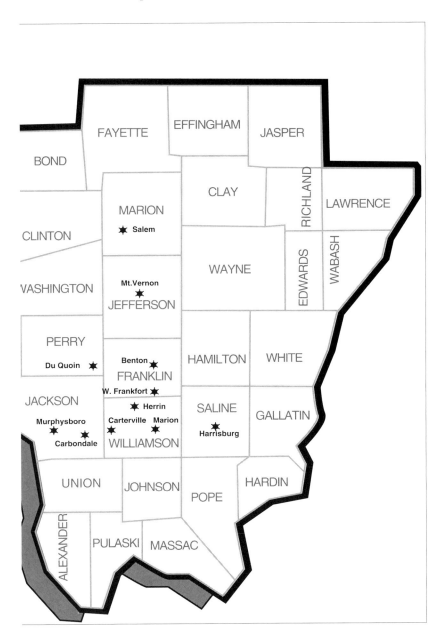

Adventure US Inc

Membership: Open
Facilities: 25-acre adventure park with 50-foot climbing and rappelling tower, high adventure course, low challenge course and high adventure elements. Call for open climbing schedule. Associated with Metro Sports Complex. Park and Club rental available.
Fees: Inquire
Location: 2300 N. Henry, Alton
Phone: (618) 462-3110

Nautilus Fitness-Racquet Centre

Membership: Open
Facilities: Racquetball, handball, basketball, volleyball, indoor pool, free weights, Nautilus, LifeCircuit strength training, Parmount Equipment, Lifecycles, recumbent life rollers, Stairmasters, treadmills, Nordic Track, gravitrons, kids programming, aerobics, stretch, step and aqua classes, Yoga, playland and martial arts.
Fees: Prices vary; individual memberships $24-$44/month; per family $30-$59/month
Location: 4425 Industrial Dr. Alton
Phone: (618) 466-9115

Piasa Martial Arts Academy

Membership: Open
Facilities: Martial arts classes (Tae Kwon Do)
Fees: Inquire
Location: 2300 Main, Alton (two studio locations)
Phone: (618) 465-8914

Metro Sports Inc.

Membership: Open
Facilities: Gymnastics, martial arts, batting cage, aerobics, tan-

ning, nursery, olympic size swimming pool, senior programs, Nautilus, volleyball, basketball, weights, BBQ patio

Fees: Inquire
Location: 2300 N. Henry, Alton
Phone: (618) 462-1066

Belleville

Belleville Fitness Center

Membership: Open, oldest operating club in Midwest or state
Facilities: Weights, lifecycle, indoor pool, tanning, gym, Nautilus, Universal, free weights, largest and deepest pool in county, lap and open swimming, aerobics
Fees: Individual $180 or $225/ year for family (indoor pool and Nautilus)
Location: 1234 Centreville Ave, Belleville
Phone: (618) 235-2833

Belleville Health & Sports Center

Membership: Open
Facilities: Cardiovascular center, racquetball, aerobics, Nautilus, whirlpool, sauna, steam room, Stairmasters, lifecycles, indoor track, personal fitness assessment and programs
Fees: Inquire; discounts offered to seniors 55 and older
Location: 1001 S. 74th St, Belleville
Phone: (618) 398-2778

Belleville Weightlifting Club

Membership: Open
Facilities: Weightlifting
Fees: Inquire
Location: 1401 Lebanon Ave, Belleville
Phone: (618) 235-4608

Body Perfect

Membership: Open
Facilities: Toning tables, treadmill and stationary bike, tanning beds
Fees: $4/visit, other payment plans
Location: 19 S. High, Belleville
Phone: (618) 277-7377

Encore Dance Academy

Membership: Open
Facilities: Dance floor and floor gymnastics
Fees: 1 hour/ week, $22/month
Location: 1403 W. Main, Belleville
Phone: (618) 277-0428

Liverite Fitness Center

Membership: Open
Facilities: Olympic indoor pool, Nautilus, treadmills, lifecycles, Stairmaster, step aerobics, racquetball courts, basketball, weights, saunas, whirlpools, tanning, fitness instruction, nursery, arthritis program
Fees: Inquire
Location: 1024 Carlyle Ave, Belleville
Phone: (618) 236-2882

World Class Gymnastic Centre

Membership: Open
Facilities: Gymnastic facilities, gymnastic classes
Fees: Inquire
Location: 5700 Old Collinsville Rd., Belleville
Phone: (618) 632-4555

Benton

Super Circuit Fitness Center

Membership: Open
Facilities: Stationary bikes, fitness machines, free weights, tread-

mill, rowing, stair steppers
Fees: $35/month for everything or $25/month for weights
Location: Illinois 37 N., Benton
Phone: (618) 439-2600

Leisure World Health Club

Membership: Open
Facilities: Olympic size pool, Nautilus, aerobic dance classes, racquetball, basketball, saunas, tanning, cardiovascular center, free weights, whirlpool, free child care.
Fees: $33/month; discounts offered to corporations.
Location: 139 E. Bethalto Dr., Bethalto
Phone: (618) 377-2104

Cahokia Fitness Center

Membership: Open
Facilities: Aerobics, weight lifting, cardiovascular training, power lifting team, youth basketball, eight week summer programs
Fees: $14/month
Location: 200 W. 3rd, Cahokia
Phone: (618) 337-9520

Great Shapes Fitness Center

Membership: Women only
Facilities: Aerobics, weight control, tanning, jacuzzi, sauna, massage therapy, kid's dance, cardiovascular equipment
Fees: Inquire
Location: U.S. 51 S., Carbondale
Phone: (618) 549-4404

Sports Center

Membership: Open

Facilities: Tennis, racquetball, aerobics, Nautilus, Paramount, free weights, exercise equipment, treadmills, bicycles rowing machines, indoor basketball, sauna

Fees: Inquire, numerous packages available

Location: 1215 E. Walnut, Carbondale

Phone: (618) 549-3272

Student Recreation Center- SIU-C

Membership: Must be affiliated with Southern Illinois University

Facilities: Facilities are comprehensive and undoubtedly the best in Southern Illinois. Facilities include Olympic swimming pool, several gyms, racquetball, squash, weights, frisbee, walking and running tracks, aerobics, wrestling, wall climbing, numerous outdoor activities planned throughout Southern Illinois. Intramural sports are organized by the SIU Recreation Center.

Fees: Students get membership with student fees. Faculty and alumni inquire for yearly or semester rates.

Location: SRC Grand Ave, SIU, Carbondale

Phone: (618) 453-1225

Carterville

Delta Health Club

Membership: Open

Facilities: Indoor pool, sauna, whirlpool, Nautilus, treadmills, stationary bikes, hydra steps, Jacuzzi, step and Aqua aerobics, teddy bear aerobics aqua-arthritis class, martial arts, self defense instruction.

Fees: Three months, $138, 12 months, $386; inquire about other rates; discounts to seniors on classes only

Location: One Tip Dr., Illinois 13, Carterville

Phone: (618) 997-3377

Aerobiflex Fitness

Membership: Open
Facilities: Nautilus, weights, aerobics, toning tables, tanning, instruction
Fees: Inquire
Location: 1081 W. Broadway, Centralia
Phone: (618) 532-6514

H & B Health & Fitness Inc

Membership: Open
Facilities: Aerobics, circuit training, weights, cardiovascular training, free weights, power lifting, sauna
Fees: Monthly, or yearly; inquire; discounts for students
Location: 225 S. Locust, Centralia
Phone: (618) 533-2991

Leisure World Health Club

Membership: Open
Facilities: Treadmills, stair steppers, bicycles, rowing machines, Nautilus, Pro Star Freeway, whirlpool, sauna, Olympic size swimming pool, racquetball, volleyball, basketball, tanning beds, child care, aerobics classes
Fees: Inquire, monthly rate
Location: 9 Collinsport Dr., Collinsville
Phone: (618) 344-3095

New Creation Health Spa

Membership: Open
Facilities: Step aerobics, tanning beds
Fees: $4 /visit
Location: 22 N. Mulberry, Du Quoin
Phone: (618) 542-3633

Body Designer

Membership: Open
Facilities: Passive exercise session, tanning
Fees: $6/session
Location: 1210 N. Main, Edwardsville
Phone: (618) 656-7202

Student Fitness Center at SIU-E

Membership: Students, alumni, faculty and staff of SIU-E
Facilities: Weight room, racquetball courts, pool, gym, child care, aerobics, indoor track
Fees: Free to students, $125/year for others
Location: Campus of SIU-E
Phone: (618) 692-2233(BFIT)

Ballys Vic Tanny Health Club

Membership: Open
Facilities: Indoor jogging, aerobics, weights, indoor pool
Fees: Inquire
Location: 5925 N. Illinois Ave., Fairview Heights
Phone: (800) 695-8111

Flip-Flops & Fitness

Membership: Open for children
Facilities: Gymnastics floor and equipment
Fees: $20-$35/month
Location: 26 E. Locust, Harrisburg
Phone: (618) 252-8537

A J Tumbling Center

Membership:	Open for children
Facilities:	Gymnastics classes for children
Fees:	$5 per lesson
Location:	300 E. Cherry, Herrin
Phone:	(618) 988-1772

Vigiano's Fitness Center

Membership:	Open
Facilities:	Free weights, cardiovascular equipment,various weight equipment, trainer available evenings, 24-hour key facility
Fees:	$30/month
Location:	300 E. Cherry, Herrin
Phone:	(618) 988-8878

Cleopatra Health Spa

Membership:	Open to women only
Facilities:	Step aerobics, group exercises, individual exercise and diet programs, whirlpool, sauna, tanning beds, eucalyptus room, nursery
Fees:	Inquire
Location:	802 N. Russell, Marion
Phone:	(618) 997-6359

Omni Athletic & Health Club

Membership:	Open
Facilities:	Pool, racquetball, volleyball, basketball, sauna, hot tub, stair climber, bicycles, free weights, circuit machines, aerobics
Fees:	Inquire
Location:	303 W. Commercial, Marion
Phone:	(618) 997-2033

Tumble Town

Membership: For all children
Facilities: 4,000 sq. feet fully equipped gymnasium
Fees: $20/year registration fee; inquire; discounts for two or more family members
Location: 114 E. Main, Marion
Phone: (618) 997-2571

Mt. Vernon

Mount Vernon Health & Fitness Center

Membership: Restricted to drug-free individuals
Facilities: Weights, aerobics, tanning, weights, Universal machines, cardiovascular cycles and steppers, martial arts
Fees: Student discounts
Location: 2601 Veterans Memorial Dr., Mt. Vernon
Phone: (618) 244-6227 or 244-4220

Murphysboro

Cathy's Tone N Tan

Membership: Open
Facilities: Motorized exercise tables, tanning
Fees: Inquire
Location: 1107 Locust, Murphysboro
Phone: (618) 687-1644

Motel Murphysboro & Apple Dome

Membership: Restricted, inquire
Facilities: Swimming pool, Jacuzzi, locker rooms, showers, weight room, free weights, Universal equipment, tanning bed
Fees: $120 to join, $35-45/month
Location: 100 N. 2nd, Murphysboro
Phone: (618) 687-2345

Tumble Town

Membership: Open for children
Facilities: Fully equipped gymnasiums, 10,000 square feet
Fees: $20/year registration fee; inquire; discounts offered to two or more family members
Location: RR 3, Murphysboro; on Illinois 127
Phone: (618) 687-2133 or 687-2571

O'Fallon

Adams School of Dance Inc.

Membership: Open to children 4 - 18 years of age
Facilities: Dance and acrobatic classes
Fees: $24/month (includes one hour per week)
Location: 119 E. First, O'Fallon
Phone: (618) 632-2216

Dance Station

Membership: Open
Facilities: Dancing for exercise
Fees: Inquire
Location: 220 W. State, O'Fallon
Phone: (618) 632-1217

Pontoon Beach

Hard Body Gym

Membership: Open
Facilities: Operated by Dan McGuire, former Mr. Missouri and Mr. St. Louis, one racquetball court, one aerobics room, free weights, personalized training, aerobics, Nautilus, Universal, cable machines
Fees: High school and college students $180/year; others $210/year and family rates
Location: 3710 Illinois 111, Pontoon Beach
Phone: (618) 931-8714

Roxana Recreation Dept.

Membership: Open
Facilities: Weight room, basketball, outdoor pool (summer), ball diamonds
Fees: $3 adults, $2 students, season tickets available
Location: Gymnasium at 3rd & Center, Roxana
Phone: (618) 254-6919

Health & Fitness Inc

Membership: Open
Facilities: Nautilus, free weights, tanning, aerobics, personal trainer, child care
Fees: Commercial discount for faculty employees; student discount, individual, $50 initial and $26 per month
Location: 306 S. Broadway, Salem
Phone: (618) 548-3255

Pro Fitness Centre

Membership: Open
Facilities: Aerobics, free weights, Nautilus, cardiovascular conditioning, karate, gymnastics, tanning
Fees: Inquire
Location: 1507 E. Main, Salem
Phone: (618) 548-6685

Southwestern Illinois Gymnastic Academy

Membership: Open to children ages 3-18

Facilities: Gymnastic classes, team competes in levels 4-6 gymnastics, recreational classes

Fees: $20 per month which includes four 1-hour sessions; yearly insurance fee of $18

Location: 3 Industrial Park, Steeleville

Phone: (618) 965-9711

Sloan's Gymnastic School

Membership: Open to children ages 2-18

Facilities: Gymnastics and tumbling classes, cheerleading, gymnastics team competing at levels 1-6

Fees: $24 for four 1-hour sessions, $23 for preschool classes lasting 45 minutes each; discount for early payment

Location: 502 E. Oak, West Frankfort

Phone: (618) 937-3136

The Body Shop

Membership: Open

Facilities: Nautilus, Universal, gym, free weights, tanning

Fees: $20/month, tanning (free)

Location: 48 East Ferguson, Wood River

Phone: (618) 251-5809

❧ *Fishing: Lakes & Rivers* ❧

Jay Zapp with a nice bass at Cedar Lake (Southern Illinoisan photo)

A local angler once said the biggest decision faced by a Southern Illinois fisherman is trying to decide where to fish. He was right. The fishing possibilities here are almost endless.

The area is surrounded by the Mississippi and Ohio rivers and criss-crossed by their tributary rivers and creeks. In addition, lakes, man-made and natural, dot the landscape. Largemouth bass, crappie, catfish and bluegill are the prevalent game species, but some lakes and rivers offer more exotic fare such as trout, muskie, pike, walleye and sauger. Generally, the avid angler can find nearly anything that strikes his or her fancy.

Probably the quickest way to profile the area's diverse fishery is to look at **Devils Kitchen Lake**, about 10 miles southeast of Carbondale, and **Horseshoe Lake**, just north of Cairo. Devils Kitchen is the area's deepest lake with depths up to 90 feet. This man-made lake is in the Crab Orchard National Wildlife Refuge. Heavily forested bluffs jut out into the crystal clear water. Ironically, this deep lake is probably best known for its huge bluegill, a shallow water fish. During the spring spawning season the chirping of crickets is a common sound on the lake as fishermen head out in search of bluegill beds.

Although huge spawning beds can be found throughout the 900-acre lake, Carbondale fisherman Lloyd Nelson prefers the extreme south end of the lake. This area of the lake is isolated, filled with fields of lily pads and nearly impossible to reach. The angler has to be determined and patient to negotiate the submerged timber to reach the southernmost bluegill beds. It is not unusual to see a fisherman rocking a boat from side to side, trying to dislodge it from a stump, actually the top of a tree protruding from 30 to 40 feet of water.

"I come down here because I can be by myself," Nelson said. "Not many guys make it this far. I've caught just as big bluegill up by the marina. I've caught more down here. I don't know, It's the fishing pressure I guess. I like the lily pads for some reason. It's a little more classic."

This type of bluegill fishing is relatively simple. The fisherman moves up and down the banks looking for the darkened beds. A cricket placed on a small hook set about 18 inches below a float will usually result in a fish in the boat. Bluegill can be caught in this fashion at least through July. Later in the year, the bluegill search out the cooler water. In late summer and fall, the unusual sport of deep-water bluegill fishing begins. Fishermen probe 25 feet down into the submerged timber in quest of the tasty sunfish.

"A lot of people don't like to fish them on the banks," said Dian Powell, a former employee of the lake's lone marina. "They wait until they go back to the treetops. We've even converted some of the bass fishermen." There are certain advantages to the treetop approach. Most of the fish caught are keeper size and this type of fishing requires fewer casts. "A lot of people don't like to cast into the bank time after time," Powell said. "You can't sit there and relax. It's hard work catching them on the banks. It's easier to catch them deep." Ironically, it is the relative infertility of the lake that has created the excellent bluegill fishery. Chuck Surprenant, a fisheries assistance

The word is that they are good eating (Southern Illinoisan photo)

An albino catfish (Southern Illinoisan photo)

officer at the Crab Orchard National Wildlife Refuge, said the quality of bluegill and redear fishing is the product of a relatively low population of those species.

"When numbers are down, the food availability for individual bluegill is high," he said. "The individual bluegill that survive can grow." Surprenant said the midsummer migration of bluegill to the treetops is unique and quite a challenge for the fisherman. "For a person who wants a challenge, they'll have a 1,000-acre lake to themselves," he said.

Devils Kitchen is one of the few trout fisheries in Southern Illinois. Rainbow trout are stocked as part of a federal program. Trout fishing on Devils Kitchen in no ways resembles the classic fly fishing approach. Most trout are caught at night in front of the dam at 20- to 25-foot depths. Preferred baits are pinches of nightcrawler or wax worms.

On the other end of the spectrum, and at the southern tip of the state, is Horseshoe Lake in Alexander County. Horseshoe Lake is a natural 1,890-acre oxbow. The maximum depth of the lake is six feet. The lake may be the most unique spot in Southern Illinois, more closely resembling a Louisiana bayou than a typical Southern Illinois lake. Cypress and tupelo trees dominate the landscape. Only the absence of Spanish moss and alligators will convince visitors that they are not in Louisiana.

Horseshoe Lake is primarily a bluegill and crappie lake, although large bass and catfish are not uncommon. It is the quiet beauty of the lake and the possibility of catching a cooler full of bluegill, redear or crappie that keeps Delmar Hunziker of Murphysboro coming back to the lake week after week. Hunziker fishes with one hand on the sculling paddle and the other on his fly rod. Using spinning gear in the heavily forested areas of the lake would be nearly impossible. It's just not as practical as a fly rod or a telescoping crappie pole.

Delmar Hunziker

"You don't need fancy equipment down here," Hunziker said. Like Devils Kitchen, Horseshoe Lake is known to produce large bluegill. "When you can't get your hands around them, that's when I call them a bluegill," Hunziker said.

Although fishing is excellent, a trip to Horseshoe Lake is worthwhile just to view the stately elegance of the cypress and tupelo groves. The duckweed floating on the motionless water amid ancient cypress trees gives the lake a mystical, almost surreal quality. "I think that's part of the enjoyment," Hunziker said. "I'm around machinery all week. I can come down here and enter another world. It's just part of God's creation and I enjoy it."

Major Lakes of Southern Illinois

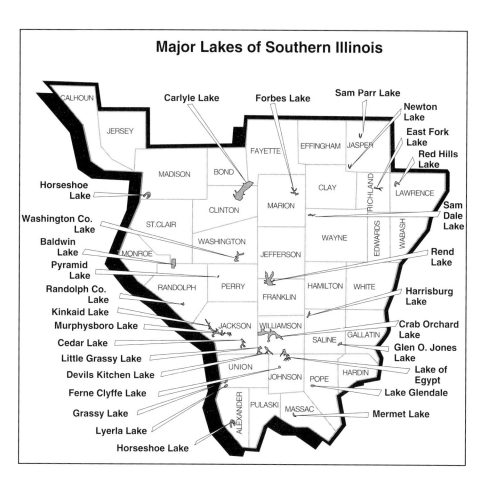

Lakes

Baldwin Lake

This 2,018-acre lake in Randolph County is one of the most popular spots among anglers during the winter. The lake serves as a cooling basin for the Illinois Power Company's Baldwin power plant. Baldwin Lake is leased to the Illinois Department of Conservation to provide recreational benefits for fishermen and hunters. The lake provides excellent fishing for largemouth bass, hybrid stripers, bluegill and channel catfish.

Location: North of Illinois 154 in Randolph County
Acres: 2,018
Maximum depth: 35 feet
Shoreline: 15 miles
Motor limit: 50 horsepower
Boat rental: No
Launch facilities: Yes
Frequently caught species: Largemouth bass, bluegill, crappie, channel catfish, hybrid stripers

Carlyle Lake

Carlyle Lake is known as one of the Midwest's top sailing lakes. Illinois' largest inland lake is located on the prairie of Clinton County. The vast open areas of the 26,000-acre impoundment draw sailors from throughout the United States. The lake is 15 miles long and up to 3.5 miles wide.

Carlyle Lake is growing in popularity as a bass fishery and is a highly productive white bass lake. If fishing variety is what you seek, the Carlyle Lake tailwater is a must. Anglers have caught 52 species of fish, ranging from the smallest sunfish to 60-pound flathead catfish.

Location: On Illinois 127 and U.S. 50 at about the midway point between I-64 and I-57
Acres: 26,000
Maximum depth: 40 feet
Motor limit: None
Boat rental: Yes
Launch facilities: Yes
Frequently caught species: Largemouth bass, bluegill, crappie, channel catfish, flathead catfish, walleye

Cedar Lake

Although most anglers utilize the lake for its bass, bluegill, crappie and catfish action, Cedar Lake is one of the few lakes in Southern Illinois that contains walleye. Anglers have been known to catch walleye on the rocky shelves and points of Cedar Lake's rugged shoreline, at this, another of the area's deep, clear lakes.

Location: Four miles south of Carbondale between U.S. 51 and Illinois 127
Acres: 1,750
Maximum depth: 80 feet
Shoreline: 92 miles
Motor limit: 10 horsepower
Boat rental: No
Launch facilities: Yes
Frequently caught species: Largemouth bass, bluegill, crappie, channel catfish, walleye, striped bass

Crab Orchard Lake

Perhaps the best known lake in Southern Illinois is Crab Orchard. The 6,965-acre lake is generally regarded as one of the most productive bass lakes in the Midwest. The Southern Illinois Bass Busters, the oldest bass club in Illinois and one of the first clubs in the nation, is based at Crab Orchard Lake. In addition to bass, anglers find excellent crappie, bluegill and catfish action on Crab Orchard. Crab Orchard is the largest of the three lakes on the Crab Orchard National

Wildlife Refuge and is also popular for its water skiing, sailboating, camping and picnicking.
Location: East of I-57 on Illinois 13

Acres: 6,965
Shoreline: 125 miles
Motor limit: None
Boat rental: Yes
Launch facilities: Yes
Frequently caught species: Largemouth bass, crappie, bluegill, channel catfish, flathead catfish, white bass

Devils Kitchen

Devils Kitchen, located on the Crab Orchard National Wildlife Refuge, is deep and clear. The lake, 90 feet deep in some locations, is one of the few places in Southern Illinois where anglers can catch rainbow and brown trout. The trout are not a native species, but are stocked through a federal program. The lake is also popular with bass and bluegill fishermen. No swimming is allowed in the 810-acre lake.

Location: Southeast of Carbondale on Giant City Blacktop
Acres: 810
Shoreline: 24 miles
Motor limit: 10 horsepower
Boat rental: Yes
Launch facilities: Yes
Frequently caught species: Largemouth bass, bluegill, crappie, channel catfish, trout, yellow perch

Dolan Lake

Dolan Lake is managed by the Illinois Department of Conservation. Dolan is one of the few lakes in the area with a walleye population. The lake is also noted for its big redear.

Location: Five miles southwest of the intersection of U.S. 45 and Illinois 14

Acres: 71
Maximum depth: 18 feet
Shoreline: Three miles
Motor limit: 10 horsepower
Boat rental: Yes
Launch facilities: Yes
Frequently caught species: Largemouth bass, bluegill, crappie, redear, walleye

East Fork Lake

Bass and bluegill are the dominant species in this Richland County lake. Bass average nearly two pounds in the 935-acre lake.

Location: One mile north of Olney
Acres: 935
Maximum depth: 40 feet
Shoreline: 25 miles
Motor limit: None
Boat rental: Yes
Launch facilities: Yes
Frequently caught species: Largemouth bass, crappie, bluegill, channel catfish and walleye

Ferne Clyffe Lake

This 16-acre lake was built in Ferne Clyffe State Park in 1960. A mile-long trail circles the lake, which features bankfishing exclusively. A trout stocking program was a popular feature at Ferne Clyffe, but was discontinued due to Department of Conservation cutbacks in 1991. This program is scheduled for reinstatement in 1994.

Location: One mile south of Goreville on Illinois 37
Acres: 15.8
Maximum depth: 21 feet
Shoreline: 0.9 miles

Motor limit: Boats not allowed
Boat rental: No
Launch facilities: No
Frequently caught species: Largemouth bass, bluegill, channel catfish, redear

Forbes Lake

Located in the Stephen A. Forbes State Fish and Wildlife Area, this 585-acre lake was completed in 1963. The lake was stocked with largemouth bass, bluegill, redear, crappie, channel catfish and hybrid striped bass. Fishing is also permitted at several smaller ponds surrounding the lake. Unlike most fish and wildlife area lakes, there is no motor restriction on Forbes Lake. There is a fisheries research center on the grounds that is open for tours Monday through Friday.

Location: Fourteen miles northeast of Salem
Acres: 585
Maximum depth: 28 feet
Shoreline: 18.4 miles
Motor limit: None
Boat rental: Yes
Launch facilities: Yes
Frequently caught species: Largemouth bass, bluegill, redear, crappie, channel catfish

Glen O. Jones Lake

Located in the Saline County Conservation Area, Glen O. Jones Lake is a picturesque lake nestled in the hills of Southern Illinois. Glen O. Jones is off the beaten path, and is a good location for anglers seeking solitude. The lake offers excellent bankfishing opportunities.

Location: Five miles south of Illinois 142 at Equality
Acres: 105
Maximum depth: 33 feet
Shoreline: 2.7 miles

Motor limit: 10 horsepower
Boat rental: Yes
Launch facilities: Yes
Frequently caught species: Largemouth bass, bluegill, redear, channel catfish, crappie

Grassy Lake

Not to be confused with its larger counterpart (Little Grassy), Grassy Lake is located in Union County. This small, 310-acre lake is shallow, but a haven for bluegill and redear enthusiasts.

Location: About three miles southeast of Ware
Acres: 310
Maximum depth: Five feet
Shoreline: Three miles
Motor limit: 10 horsepower
Boat rental: No
Launch facilities: Yes
Frequently caught species: Largemouth bass, bluegill, redear, crappie and channel catfish

Harrisburg Lake

Harrisburg Lake provides good bass fishing and drinking water to the nearby city of Harrisburg. There is a six-horsepower limit.
Location: Six miles north of Harrisburg on Illinois 34

Location: Six miles north of Harrisburg on Illinois 34
Name: Harrisburg Lake
Acres: 209
Maximum depth: 30 feet
Shoreline: 6.5 miles
Motor limit: 6 horsepower
Boat rental: No
Launch facilities: Yes
Frequently caught species: Largemouth bass, bluegill, channel cat

Horseshoe Lake (*Alexander County*)

Perhaps the most unique lake in Southern Illinois, this natural oxbow is dotted with cypress and tupelo groves. In addition to excellent fishing, Horseshoe Lake is one of the goose hunting hotspots of the Midwest. Anglers are drawn to the lake by the prospects of catching stringers of big bluegill, redear and crappie. Dedicated bass fishermen have been known to pull huge largemouth bass from around the cypress trees.

Location: Just south of Illinois 3 at Olive Branch
Acres: 1,890
Maximum depth: Six feet
Shoreline: 20 miles
Motor limit: 10 horsepower, except during goose season when no
   motors are allowed
Boat rental: Yes
Launch facilities: Yes
Frequently caught species: Largemouth bass, crappie, bluegill,
   redear, channel catfish

Horseshoe Lake (*Madison County*)

This Horseshoe Lake is also an ancient oxbow, but is located near Granite City. The two lakes have more in common than just their names. Both were formed from the Mississippi River, both are shallow and both have outstanding fishing potential.
Location: Take I-70 to Illinois 111
Acres: 2,107
Maximum depth: 5 feet
Motor limit: 25 horsepower
Boat rental: Yes
Launch facilities: Yes
Frequently caught species: Largemouth bass, bluegill, crappie,
   channel catfish

Kinkaid Lake

Along with the crystal clear waters, sheer limestone bluffs and the beauty of the Shawnee National Forest, Kinkaid Lake offers the only muskie fishing in Southern Illinois. Muskies as big as 25 pounds have been pulled out of Kinkaid's deep, clear waters. The irregular shoreline offers literally hundreds of coves that the muskies call home. The lake also provides excellent white bass and crappie action. A few walleye are caught on occasion.

Location: Just west of Murphysboro on Illinois 149
Acres: 2,750
Maximum depth: 80 feet
Shoreline: 92 miles
Motor limit: None
Boat rental: Yes
Launch facilities: Yes
Frequently caught species: Largemouth bass, bluegill, crappie, channel catfish, walleye, white bass, muskie

Lake of Egypt

A power plant lake, Lake of Egypt is popular with fishermen all year around, but particularly in the winter and early spring. Bass anglers catch fish in the moss beds at the northern end of the lake with small grubs even in the dead of winter. Lake of Egypt offers excellent crappie fishing, and has a limited population of hybrid striped bass. Anglers must purchase an annual or daily pass to fish the lake.

Location: Eight miles south of Marion accessed by Illinois 37
Acres: 2,300
Maximum depth: 52 feet
Shoreline: 92 miles
Motor limit: None
Boat rental: Yes

Launch facilities: Yes
Frequently caught species: Largemouth bass, crappie, bluegill, channel catfish, hybrid stripers

Lake Murphysboro

Lake Murphysboro is the principal attraction at Lake Murphysboro State Park. The 145-acre lake was built in 1950 by the state's Division of Fisheries. The state manages the lake by controlling submerged vegetation and draws down the water level at times to control the small panfish population. The lake is well suited to bank fishermen.

Location: Just north of Illinois 149, a mile west of Murphysboro
Acres: 145
Maximum depth: 40 feet
Shoreline: 7.5 miles
Motor limit: 10 horsepower
Boat rental: Yes
Launch facilities: Yes
Frequently caught species: Largemouth bass, bluegill, redear, crappie, channel catfish

Lake Glendale

Located in the heart of the Shawnee National Forest, Lake Glendale offers an excellent bass and bluegill fishery. Although the lake covers just 79 acres it has been known to yield bass over nine pounds.

Location: Just west of Illinois 145 about 20 miles south of Harrisburg
Acres: 79
Maximum depth: 14 feet
Shoreline: 2 miles
Motor limit: No motors allowed
Boat rental: Yes
Launching facilities: Yes
Frequently caught species: Largemouth bass, bluegill

Little Grassy

Little Grassy is Devils Kitchen's sister lake on the Crab Orchard National Wildlife Refuge. Like Devils Kitchen, Little Grassy is deep and clear. Bass, bluegill, crappie and channel catfish anglers all flock to Little Grassy. The lake is particularly popular in late April when spring sunshine brings the crappie and bluegill to the wooded shorelines to spawn. To use any of the lakes on the Crab Orchard National Wildlife Refuge, patrons must purchase a federal duck stamp at the ranger station on Illinois 148.

Location: Southeast of Carbondale on Giant City Blacktop
Acres: 1,000
Maximum depth: 77 feet
Shoreline: 28.3 miles
Motor limit: 10 horsepower
Boat rental: Yes
Launch facilities: Yes
Frequently caught species: Largemouth bass, bluegill, crappie, channel catfish

Lyerla Lake

Located in Union County, Lyerla Lake is a sister to Grassy Lake. Like Grassy Lake, Lyerla provides excellent bluegill and redear action. This bottomland lake has also been known to yield big crappie.

Location: About three miles southeast of Ware on Illinois 3/146
Acres: 260
Maximum depth: Nine feet
Shoreline: 3.8 miles
Motor limit: 10 horsepower
Boat rental: No
Launch facilities: No wet weather launch
Frequently caught species: Largemouth bass, bluegill, crappie, redear, channel catfish

Mermet Lake

Like the southernmost Horseshoe Lake, Mermet Lake provides anglers with a chance to work cypress roots and lily pads for large-mouth bass and sunfish. Topwater enthusiasts are particularly fond of Mermet. The lake also yields large crappie and channel catfish.

Location: On U.S. 45 near I-24
Acres: 452
Maximum depth: 12 feet
Shoreline: 4.6 miles
Motor limit: 10 horsepower
Boat rental: No
Launch facilities: Yes
Frequently caught species: Largemouth bass, crappie, bluegill, redear, channel catfish

Newton Lake

The lake is leased from the Central Illinois Public Service Company by the Illinois Department of Conservation.

Like most power plant lakes, Newton Lake provides excellent fishing opportunities year around. Largemouth are particularly good around the points and weed beds.

Location: Eight miles southwest of Newton
Acres: 1,750 acres
Maximum depth: 40 feet
Shoreline: 52 miles
Motor limit: 10 horsepower
Boat rental: No
Launch facilities: Yes
Frequently caught species: Largemouth bass, bluegill, crappie, channel catfish

Pyramid Lakes

Located in Pyramid State Park, the lakes are actually a series of 24 abandoned strip pits. The water is as clear as any a fisherman will ever encounter. Boats are allowed on all the lakes, but not all have launching facilities. The area is particularly renowned for large bluegill.

Location: Just east of Illinois 127 about five miles south of Pinckneyville
Acres: Ranges from 0.5 to 39.8 acres
Maximum depth: Range from 13 to 44 feet
Shoreline: Range from 0.1 to 5.7 miles
Motor limit: 10 horsepower
Boat rental: No
Launch facilities: Some lakes
Frequently caught species: Largemouth bass, bluegill, channel catfish

Randolph County Lake

Randolph County Lake offers fishermen one of the few opportunities in the area to catch smallmouth bass. There is also a limited walleye fishery in this Illinois Department of Conservation lake.

The lake was completed in 1961.

Location: Five miles north of Chester on County DD
Acres: 65
Maximum depth: 35 feet
Shoreline: 4 miles
Motor limit: 10 horsepower
Boat rental: Yes
Launch facilities: Yes
Frequently caught species: Largemouth bass, smallmouth bass, bluegill, redear, crappie, channel catfish, walleye

Red Hills Lake

The lake was formed in 1953 by impounding Muddy Creek, a tributary of the Embarass River. Gas motors are not permitted on the 40-acre lake which provides good bass, bluegill and catfish action.

Location: U.S. 50 just west of Lawrenceville divides the park in half
Acres: 40
Shoreline: 2.5 miles
Motor limit: Electric only
Boat rental: Yes
Launch facilities: Yes
Frequently caught species: Largemouth bass, bluegill, channel cat-
fish

Rend Lake

Rend Lake is a huge, 18,900-acre, U.S. Army Corps of Engineers impoundment of the Big Muddy River that offers outstanding fishing for largemouth bass, crappie, white bass, hybrid stripers and catfish.

Although the lake is one of the largest in Illinois, it is user friendly. There are 23 boat ramps located around the lake, making nearly all areas available even to anglers in small jon boats. In addition, the Corps of Engineers have constructed fish shelters and placed them under water. The fish attractors are clearly marked with buoys. Many of the fish shelters are accessible to bank fishermen.

A truly unique experience is fishing in the tailwater in springtime. Persistent anglers are known to carry away stringers of several hundred pounds of rough fish. Archers like to fish for carp in this manner.

Location: On I-57 north of Benton and south of Mt. Vernon
Acres: 18,900
Maximum depth: 30 feet
Shoreline: 162 miles
Motor limit: None
Boat rental: Yes
Launch facilities: Yes

Frequently caught species: Largemouth bass, crappie, bluegill, channel catfish, flathead catfish, white bass, hybrid stripers

Sam Dale Lake

This 194-acre lake, located in Wayne County, is one of the few lakes in Southern Illinois with a yellow perch population. The lake is located between the communities of Zenith and Orchardville.

Location: Ten miles south of U.S. 50 near Zenith
Acres: 194
Maximum depth: 18 feet
Shoreline: 8.4 miles
Motor limit: 10 horsepower
Boat rental: Yes
Launch facilities: Yes
Frequently caught species: Largemouth bass, bluegill, crappie, channel catfish, yellow perch

Sam Parr Lake

Located in Jasper County, Sam Parr Lake offers largemouth, bluegill and channel catfish action. The lake is surrounded by rolling, timbered hills.

Location: On Illinois 33 east of Newton
Acres: 180
Maximum depth: 28 feet
Shoreline: 9.5 miles
Motor limit: 10 horsepower
Boat rental: No
Launch facilities: Yes
Frequently caught species: Largemouth bass, bluegill, crappie, channel catfish

Washington County Lake

Washington County Lake is another area maintained by the Illinois Department of Conservation. Bass, bluegill, crappie and channel catfish are the dominant species. The lake has a loading ramp designed for handicapped access.

Location: Just east of Illinois 127 about five miles south of Nashville
Acres: 248
Maximum depth: 25 feet
Shoreline: 12 miles
Motor limit: 10 horsepower
Boat rental: Yes
Launching facilities: Yes
Frequently caught species: Largemouth bass, bluegill, redear, crappie, channel catfish

Sailing on Crab Orchard Lake (Carbondale Convention & Tourism Bureau photo)

Site-Specific Fishing Regulations

Unless otherwise noted, state regulations apply in all state waters. State regulations establish a daily catch limit of six for black bass, which includes largemouth bass, smallmouth and spotted bass. A daily creel limit of six also applies to walleye, sauger and walleye/sauger hybrids.

Baldwin Lake:
   Crappie–25 fish daily creel limit, nine-inch minimum length limit.
   Bass–18-inch minimum length limit.
   Striped, white or hybrid bass–17-inch minimum length limit, three fish daily creel limit.

Bay Creek Lake:
   Channel catfish–Six fish daily creel limit.

Cedar Lake:
   Large or smallmouth bass–15-inch minimum length limit.
   Striped, white, hybrid bass–17-inch minimum length limit, three-fish daily creel limit.
   Walleye or sauger–14-inch minimum length limit.

Crab Orchard Lake:
   Striped, white, hybrid bass–ten fish daily creel limit, only three of which can be over 17 inches.

Crab Orchard Lake and Refuge Ponds:
   Large or smallmouth bass–15-inch minimum length limit, except Visitor Pond.

Dutchman Lake:
   Channel catfish–six-fish daily creel limit.

Ferne Clyffe Lake:
   Channel catfish–six-fish daily creel limit.

Harrisburg New City Reservoir:
Channel catfish–six-fish daily creel limit.

Horseshoe Lake:
Large or smallmouth bass–14-inch length limit.
Channel catfish–six-fish daily creel limit.

Glen O. Jones Lake:
Large or smallmouth bass–14-inch length limit.
Channel catfish–six-fish daily creel limit.

Kaskaskia River and tributaries:
Walleye and sauger–14-inch minimum length limit.

Kinkaid Lake:
Large or smallmouth bass–18-inch minimum length limit.
Muskellunge–36-inch minimum length limit.
Walleye or sauger–14-inch minimum length limit.

Lake Glendale:
Channel catfish–6-fish daily creel limit.

Lake Murphysboro:
Bluegill or redear–25-fish daily creel limit.
Channel catfish–six fish daily creel limit.
Large or smallmouth bass–15-inch minimum length limit.

Lake of Egypt:
Large or smallmouth bass–16-inch minimum length limit.
Crappie–30 fish daily creel limit.

Little Grassy Lake:
Channel catfish–six fish daily creel limit.
Large or smallmouth bass–12-15-inch slot limit.

Lyerla Lake:
　　Channel catfish–six fish daily creel limit.

Mermet State Lake:
　　Channel catfish–six fish daily creel limit.
　　Large or smallmouth bass–14-inch minimum length limit.

Mississippi River (between Illinois and Missouri):
　　Northern pike–one fish daily creel limit.
　　Walleye and sauger–eight fish daily creel limit.

Nashville City Lake:
　　Channel catfish–6 fish daily creel limit.
　　Large or smallmouth bass–18-inch minimum length limit.

One Horse Gap Lake:
　　Channel catfish–six fish daily creel limit.

Pounds Hollow Lake:
　　Channel catfish–six fish daily creel limit.

Pyramid State Park Ponds:
　　Channel catfish–six fish daily creel limit.

Randolph County Lake:
　　Channel catfish–six fish daily creel limit.
　　Large or smallmouth bass–14-inch minimum length limit, three
　　　　fish daily creel limit.
　　Walleye or sauger–14-inch minimum length limit.

Rend Lake:
　　Largemouth or smallmouth bass–14-inch minimum length limit.

Sparta City Lakes:
　　Channel catfish–six fish daily creel limit.
　　Large or smallmouth bass–15-inch minimum length limit.

Visitor Pond Crab Orchard:

Large or smallmouth bass–21-inch minimum length limit.

Washington County Lake:

Channel catfish –six fish daily creel limit.
Large or smallmouth bass–14-inch minimum length limit.
Striped, white or hybrid bass–17-inch minimum length limit, three fish daily creel limit.

West Frankfort City Lakes:

Channel catfish –six fish daily creel limit.

Whoopie Cat Lake:

Channel catfish –six fish daily creel limit.

Rivers

Although Southern Illinois is crisscrossed by rivers, lakes are the area's major fishing resource. For anglers who prefer fishing river systems, Illinois has plenty to offer in the Smithland Pool, the Kaskaskia River Fish and Wildlife Area and the Big Muddy River.

The **Smithland Pool** was formed when the Smithland Dam was built across the Ohio River. The dam caused water levels in tributary creeks to rise nearly 12 feet, in effect creating a 27,000-acre fishing paradise.

Fishing is excellent in the **Ohio River** and tributary creeks on both the Illinois and Kentucky sides. Largemouth bass, crappie and catfish are caught in the river and the creeks. Hybrid stripers and sauger are caught in the river while the creeks provide outstanding bluegill fishing. A state of-the-art marina is located in Golconda.

The **Kaskaskia River Fish and Wildlife Area** was created when the lower 22 miles of the Kaskaskia River were channelized for navigation purposes. Although there is some bass and catfish fishing done in the main channel, most anglers flock to the oxbows which were the original river channel. Largemouth bass, crappie and catfish are the dominant species. A modern, full-service marina is located at New Athens.

In the extreme northern portions of the region, fishing has improved greatly on the **Alton Pool of the Mississippi River**. Bass and crappie fishing are both excellent in that area. Generally speaking, fishing on the Mississippi is best from Alton north. In fact, The Bass Anglers Sportsman's Society (BASS) held one of its major tournaments on the Alton Pool in 1992. Another area growing in popularity among Southern Illinois fishermen is the lower Kaskaskia River. The river was channelized for navigation in the 1970s, but most of the good fishing remains in the oxbows of the old river channel. The lower Kaskaskia is home to many local and regional bass tournaments.

The upper Kaskaskia also contains excellent fishing. In fact, the area just below the Carlyle Dam is one of the few places in Southern Illinois where anglers can regularly catch walleye. However, the upper Kaskaskia, like most of the other rivers in Southern Illinois, is narrow and access is limited.

The Big Muddy River provides excellent crappie and white bass action, but again, access is limited. Anglers wishing to fish the smaller rivers would be well advised to contact local guides.

The Smithland Pool on the Ohio River is the most popular destination for river fishermen.

Name: Smithland Pool
Acres: 23,000
Length in Southern Illinois: 70 miles
Motor limit: None
Boat rental: Yes
Launch facilities: Yes
Frequently caught species: Largemouth bass, catfish, crappie, white bass, hybrid stripers, bluegill, sauger.
Camping: Yes

The Smithland Pool is Illinois' last frontier. It came into existence in 1980 when the Smithland Dam was built across the Ohio River. The

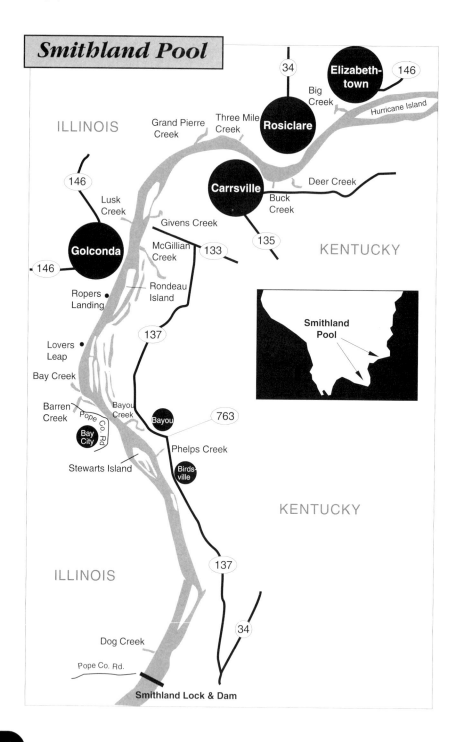

Smithland Pool

ILLINOIS

Grand Pierre Creek

Three Mile Creek

34

Big Creek

Elizabeth-town

146

Rosiclare

Hurricane Island

146

Lusk Creek

Carrsville

Deer Creek

Buck Creek

Givens Creek

Golconda

McGillian Creek

133

135

146

Ropers Landing

Rondeau Island

KENTUCKY

Lovers Leap

137

Bay Creek

Barren Creek

Bayou Creek

Bayou

763

Smithland Pool

Pope Co. Rd.

Bay City

Phelps Creek

Stewarts Island

Birds-ville

KENTUCKY

ILLINOIS

137

34

Dog Creek

Pope Co. Rd.

Smithland Lock & Dam

dam raised water levels about 12 feet in the river and its tributary creeks, creating a fishing paradise.

Gary Hise, a Golconda native, is a tournament fisherman and guide on the Smithland Pool. "There really wasn't any fishing (before the Smithland Dam) other than in isolated pools in some of the creeks that you could get to maybe with a four-wheel drive vehicle," he said.

The Smithland Dam resulted in a pool of 23,000 acres that is home to largemouth bass, crappie, bluegill, catfish, white bass, hybrid stripers and even some walleye and sauger.

The main tributaries on the Illinois side of the Ohio are (starting from the south): Dog, Barren, Bay, Lusk, Grand Pierre, Three Mile and Big creeks. Persons holding an Illinois fishing license can fish the Ohio River and Illinois tributaries. Fishing the Kentucky tributaries requires a Kentucky license.

Although fishing opportunities abound, access is limited. The southernmost access ramp is located about 7.5 miles upstream from the Smithland Dam, near Barren Creek. The two-lane concrete ramp is located about 10.5 miles south of Golconda. Some of the creeks can be reached only by boat traveling on the Ohio. The best access point is Golconda. Not only is Golconda centrally located, but it has a modern marina. There is immediate access to the Ohio River from the **Golconda Marina**.

"They have covered slips as long as 50 feet, and as small as whatever you want to put in there," Hise said. "From what I've been around, and I've fished the Red Man circuit in Kentucky and Iowa, we have a Cadillac of a facility."

In addition to the marina, there is another access ramp in Golconda. The ramp is at the end of Main Street. This ramp provides direct access into the river. There is also a Lusk Creek access ramp in Golconda. This ramp, which includes parking for about 20 rigs, is located just off Illinois 146 on the west edge of Golconda. The only other public access ramps on the pool are located in Rosiclare and Elizabethtown. The Elizabethtown ramp is located just north of Big Creek.

Although the pool is a popular site for tournaments, anglers can fish in virtual seclusion during the week. The small towns located on the river remain virtually as unspoiled as the scenery on the creeks.

"You can get out and have a pretty darned good day out here, and it's had pretty heavy pressure the last few years," Hise said. "Midweek is by far the best. It will look like it's deserted almost. If you've got a boat you can really run around in, you can hit three or four creeks and maybe see only two or three other boats all day."

The scenery is also breathtaking. The small feeder creeks flow through the hilly terrain of the Shawnee National Forest. Seeing wild turkey strut along the creek bank or whitetail deer sneak a drink of water is not unusual.

Jim Ocker of Fishing Hot Spots spent several weeks on the Smithland Pool in 1991 mapping the river and feeder creeks. He was quite impressed by the area. "It's unique to the Midwest, not just Southern Illinois," he said. "There is good vegetation. I had no intention of finding anything like that when I came here."

The really adventurous anglers can fish the river channel where hybrid stripers, walleye, sauger and huge catfish roam. "There's always a chance when fishing in the river you'll get a strike, all your line will be gone, there's a snap, and you don't know what it was," Hise said.

The river presents other perils, especially in periods of high water. "If there is high water and trash coming down, you have to be really careful," Hise said. "There can be something floating out there larger than you under the water. There can be good fishing in the spring whenever that's occurring. That could be bad if you're going to launch at Golconda and go to Bay Creek on that fast muddy water."

Jimmy Waddell (SIU-C) studies the bass population (Southern Illinoisan photo)

Compare Your Catch to the Illinois State Record

Species	Illinois Record Holder	Weight	Where Caught	Date Caught
Bass, Largemouth	Edward Wibel	13lb./1oz.	Stone Quarry Lake	2/15/76
Bass, Smallmouth	Mark Samp	6lb./7oz.	Strip Mine (Fulton Co.)	3/26/85
Bass, Spotted	Richard Leonard	7lb./3.125oz.	Strip Mine (Fulton Co.)	3/15/92
Bass, Striped	Jerry Podmarsky	31lb./0oz.	Heidecke Lake	6/20/93
Bass, Hybrid	Dave Guelsvich	20lb./3oz.	Lake of Egypt	6/22/89
Bass, White	Bruce Wilson	4lb./14oz.	Kaskaskia River	10/7/61
Bass, Yellow	Bob Stewart	1lb./13oz.	Strip Mine (Fulton Co.)	6/5/80
Bluegill	Darren May	3lb./8oz.	Farm Pond (Jasper Co.)	5/10/87
Bowfin	Charles Keller	16lb./6oz.	Rend Lake	9/23/64
"	Dan Nugent	16lb./6oz.	Bay Creek	8/14/92
Buffalo	C. B. Merritt	48lb./0oz.	Mississippi River	1936
Bullhead, Black	Justin White	5lb./6oz.	Strip Mine (Fulton Co.)	4/24/88
Bullhead, Brown	Andrea Horzog	2lb./9oz.	Weldon Springs	4/14/85
Bullhead, Yellow	Bill Snow	5lb./4oz.	Fox River	1955
Carp	Clarence Heinze	42lb./0oz.	Kankakee River	5/30/26
Catfish, Blue	Ernest Webb	65lb./0oz.	Alton Lake	1956
" "	Andrew Coats Jr.	65lb./0oz.	Alton Lake	1956
Catfish, Channel	Todd Baumeyer	45lb./4oz.	Baldwin Lake	2/7/87

Species	Illinois Record Holder	Weight	Where Caught	Date Caught
Catfish, Flathead	Paul Campbell	64lb./0 oz.	Carlyle Lake	4/13/91
Crappie, Black	John Hampton	4lb./8oz.	Rend Lake	5/15/76
Crappie, White	Kevin Donnie	4lb./7oz.	Farm Pond (Morgan)	4/8/73
Drum	Joe Rinella	35lb./0oz.	DuQuoin City Lake	1960
Goldeye	Jacob Chinderle	1lb./12oz.	Kankakee River	4/23/64
Muskellunge	Dan Becker	32lb./0oz.	Otter Lake	9/2/92
Muskie, Tiger	David Pan	26lb./2.88oz.	Summorset Lake	8/4/89
Northern Pike	Walter Klanzak	26lb./15oz.	Strip Mine (Kankakee)	11/9/89
Perch, Yellow	Joeseph Grogs	2lb./8.75oz.	Arrowhead Club	1/5/74
Sauger	Bill Rolando	5lb./12.6oz.	Mississippi River	7/30/67
Sauger-Walleye	John Regina	5lb./6.24oz.	Illinois River	10/25/87
Sturgeon	Allen Trout, Jr	5lb./2.66oz.	Rock River	5/30/58
Sunfish, Green	John Stain	2lb./1oz.	Farm Pond (DeWittt)	6/28/81
Sunfish, Hybrid	Georgia Holland	2lb./4.48oz.	Farm Pond (Jersey)	6/16/90
Sunfish, Redear	Mike DeMattei	2lb./12.3oz.	Marion City Lake	9/7/85
Trout, Brown	Walter Henkels	28lb./8oz.	Lake Michigan	5/2/75
Trout, Rainbow	Margo Anne Kobs	24lb./13oz.	Lake Michigan	5/26/85
Walleye	Fred Gosalin	14lb/0oz.	Kankakee River	1961
Warmouth	Wesley Mills	1lb/13oz.	Farm Pond (Cumberland)	5/22/71

Last summer the American Fishing Tackle Manufacturing Association commissioned its second study of fishing habits in the United States.

Can you imagine that?

A survey of fishermen? Come on, give me a break.

What do you think the margin of error on this thing is, 80 to 90 percent?

Fishermen do not tell the truth.

They never have. They never will.

Les Winkeler
Sports writer

Reprinted from the Southern Illinoisan

There's even a biblical precedent for fishing lies.

Remember the kid who had the loaves and fishes?

He said he had just two fish. But, according to the story, several thousand people were fed with these two fish, and then they had to pick up the leftovers.

To me, that sounds like a crappie fisherman covering his tracks.

Several levels of liars have evolved among fishing types since that time.

At the top of the list is the secretive angler.

If this angler caught a minnow, he wouldn't give you a straight answer about how he did it. Although it may take a compass, a map, the north star and the light of the moon to find his favorite fishing hole, he won't even tell you which lake the fish was caught in.

The secretive fisherman believes that every fish in the lake is a private possession. He believes that if word gets out that he is catching fish, every jon boat, Ranger and Basstracker in the hemisphere will descend upon this hallowed fishing hole.

The second level of liar is less dangerous, but no less annoying.

If he is catching bass on crank baits, he or she will tell you spinner baits. If crappie are hitting jigs, this person will tell you minnows. If bluegill are destroying crickets, he will tell you to buy red wigglers.

Finally, there are guys like me.

If I do happen to catch a fish, a three-pounder becomes a five-pounder, 12-pound test line becomes six-pound test and 10 crappie spontaneously multiply to 25 or 30.

It's not a malicious thing, it's just that five-pounders make for better stories.

Anyway, these are the types of people AFTMA dealt with for their research.

The information collected by AFTMA reveals that the average angler fishes 1 to 19 times per year, but would like to fish more. Most anglers, 46 percent, said work interferes with their fishing time.

Now that is un-American.

I say oppressed workers of this country UNITE. Most people have sick days and personal days. I don't think it would be asking too much of employers to give each worker 1-19 fishing days.

Continuing with this profile, the average fisherman lives in a rural area and listens to country music or oldies rock. That makes sense to me. Somehow, I just can't visualize a fisherman working a jig through a fallen tree while dancing to the Hammer.

According to AFTMA's research, the average angler is between 35 and 44 years old, has had some college education and makes between $35,000-$50,000 per year.

I don't know anyone, fisherman or not, that makes $35,000. This "average" guy doesn't live in my neighborhood.

The survey also indicates that anglers are 68 percent more likely than non-fishermen to appear at a hospital emergency room with a hook in their finger.

(I made that one up. I've got to get in practice. Fishing season is just around the corner.)

Finally, the average fisherman has no children, but would rather fish with family or friends than fish alone.

Maybe if this person wouldn't spend so much time in a boat, he might have some friends to take fishing, or even some children.

It's a scary thought.

A Suggested Recipe for Bluegill

Bluegill are often described as the best "eatin" fish around. Bluegill is versatile as chicken in the manner and variety of ways in which it may be prepared. We include this highly recommended recipe brought to our attention by Margie Parr of Carbondale from "Measure of Love," a recipe donated by Kathy Tomilin.

Stuffed Bluegill Fillets

For fish:

> 2 pounds bluegill fillets (Crappie work fine as well)
> 1 tsp salt
> dash pepper
> 2 tbsp. melted butter
> paprika

For stuffing:

> 1 cup chopped onion
> 1/4 cup melted butter or margarine
> 2 cups dry bread cubes
> 1 cup grated cheddar cheese
> 2 tbsp. chopped parsley
> 2 tsp. powdered mustard
> 1 tsp. dried dill

Sprinkle fish with salt and pepper. Place half the fillets in a well-greased baking dish, about 12 x 8 x 2. Mix all stuffing ingredients in a large bowl. Place stuffing on each and cover with remaining fillets. Brush with melted butter and sprinkle with paprika. Bake at 350 degrees for 30-35 minutes Serves six. Enjoy!

Hiking

Hiking is one of the most under rated activities and certainly the most under-utilized recreational activity in Southern Illinois. Some Southern Illinois trails do well to see one hiker per day, a tragedy given the abundance of wonderful trails in this region.

Plan a hiking trip, a wonderful activity to replace an afternoon of television, shopping or simply loafing. It's beneficial to your health and a joy to be out experiencing nature. Hike not only in spring, summer and fall but especially in the winter. A brisk winter walk, as long as the weather is not prohibitive, will generate body heat that will keep you warm and invigorated. The best panoramic views are when the foliage is off. There are no insects to bother you and the ice and snow can enhance the best scenery. Do it! Chances are you won't regret it!

When hiking, observe the posted rules. Leave time to complete your hike before darkness sets in. Make sure others are aware of your plans. Wear appropriate clothing for the weather and if there is any doubt about the trail, check with the site superintendent before beginning your walk. Trails are under constant revision by park officials so obtain the most recent map from the site officials. On some hikes it would be a service to take a plastic trash bag and pick up litter left by inconsiderate hikers.

Hiking trails have been catalogued in deep Southern Illinois, for the most part, in a separate publication, *Fifty Nature Walks in Southern Illinois* by Alan McPherson. The book may be obtained from Cache River Press, Route 3 Box 239c, Vienna, IL 62995. Due to the extensive coverage of this book, we have limited our coverage of hiking herein to those trails primarily north and west of Illinois 13. All trails are accessible to the public and most are maintained by the State of Illinois. Virtually all have been hiked by one or more of the authors. The authors' feelings about the various trails may be evident in the descriptions that follow.

The hikes described below vary from the very short, appropriate for the family with small children, to the vigorous all day hike of ten or more miles that will challenge the avid hiker. While it is generally believed that virtually all hiking is located in deep Southern Illinois we have found that hiking sites are scattered throughout the region above Illinois 13. The map below shows the overall location of hikes. Site maps are provided with each hike. The numbers on the map refer to the hikes in the order in which they are covered.

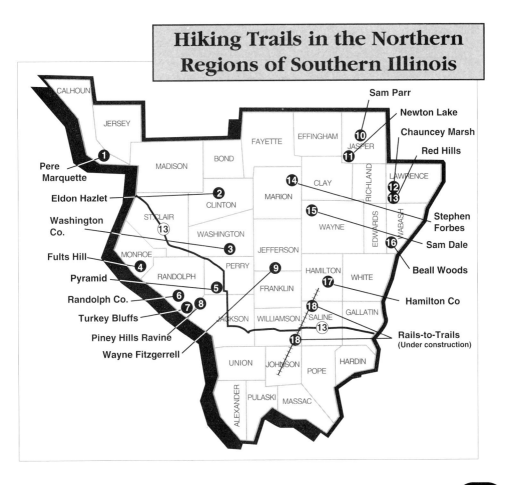

Hiking Trails in the Northern Regions of Southern Illinois

1 *Pere Marquette State Park*

The Visitor's Center– the trailhead for several trails at Pere Marquette

Visitors come to Pere Marquette State Park for many reasons, but perhaps the best reason is to hike the trails. There are a total of 15 miles of high quality hiking trails available to the public. The best vistas of the Illinois and Mississippi rivers can be obtained from the hiking trails. All trails are well blazed and identified by number and color codes. Their difficulty ranges from easy to difficult. Be sure to take this book or a map with you to see how the various trails merge. You won't forget your hiking experiences at Pere Marquette State Park.

Goat Cliff Trail (trail #1; yellow blazed) is two miles one way and begins close to the parking lot near the park road, between it and the Visitor's Center. It stretches for some distance between the park road and the along the bottoms of the bluffs. Shortly after you start walking, there is an "upheaval of rocks" that marks the Cap Au Gres fault where the land once rose out of the sea. Evidence of ancient sea creatures may be found in the limestone bluffs along the trail. The trail eventually winds up the bluffs to provide breathtaking (your breath may already be short from the climb) vistas of the area. A short side trail leads you to Goat Cliff where the vista is superb. Just a little further along the trail, it joins trails #3, #4 and #5. We suggest you continue your hike to make an extended loop rather than retracing your steps.

Dogwood Trail (trail #2; dark blue blazed) begins very close to the Visitor's Center and is marked by the large trail sign and map. It is the most frequently traveled trail because the trailhead is obvious near the Visitor's Center. It is a loop trail only three-fourths mile in length with one excellent vista of the Illinois River valley. The trail climbs steeply from the beginning and about midway allows the hiker the option of skipping over to trail #3 or returning on the Dogwood Trail. A nature brochure is usually available at the beginning of this hike to aid the hiker.

Ridge Trail (trail #3; light blue blazed) is a short one-half mile trail, but steep and because of its steepness is classified as difficult. It allows a short-cut access to trail #5 which provides access to McAdams' Peak.

Ravine Trail (trail #4; green blazed) is a one mile, one-way trail along an intermittent stream. A branch in the trail allows you to join trail #5 or to continue up to McAdams' Peak. The path steepens near the top where a bench has been placed for you to recuperate from the climb.

Hickory Trail (Main) (trail #5; red blazed), although only three-quarters of a mile long, is considered the main trail of the park since it connects with most of the other trails. This trail takes the hiker along the ridge line from one beautiful vista, McAdams' Peak, to another, Twin Shelters. Twin Shelters can be accessed by car when the paved park road is open and thus can serve as a trailhead for those "comfort" hikers that want the best views without making the effort to hike up the steep trails. Hikers will see breathtaking vistas from Hickory Trail and will see the McAdams' Peak Hill Prairie Natural Area. However you reach Hickory Trail, it is a hiking must.

Oak Trail (trail #6; pink blazed) is a three-quarter mile trail connecting trails #5 and #8. It is suggested as a short cut from the Lodge to McAdams' Peak. The slope is not excessively steep and the path is wide.

Hickory North Trail (trail #7; red with white bar blazed) is a mile long and extends from trail #5 to the park road and also connects with trail #8. This trail winds over hills and down into deep valleys. Trees are large and there is a special "deep, dark woods" feeling that makes this trail especially suited for reflection about life's joys and tribulations.

Hickory South Trail (trail #8; red with white circle blazed) is one and a half miles long and leads from an area north of the lodge to trails #9 and #7 and the park road. The trail is popular since it is easily accessible to lodgers. The trail may also be accessed from a spur trail near the water plant. From the park road the hiker may travel north to Twin Shelters vista and gain access to trail #5.

Fern Hollow Trail (trail #9; orange blazed) is the longest trail and one of the most out-of-the-way trails. Because of its length and relative inaccessibility it is the most private of the trails and the hiker is most likely to see wildlife here. The trail may be accessed from trails #7 or #8 or the park road.

Rattlesnake Trail (trail #10; orange with white bar blazed) is

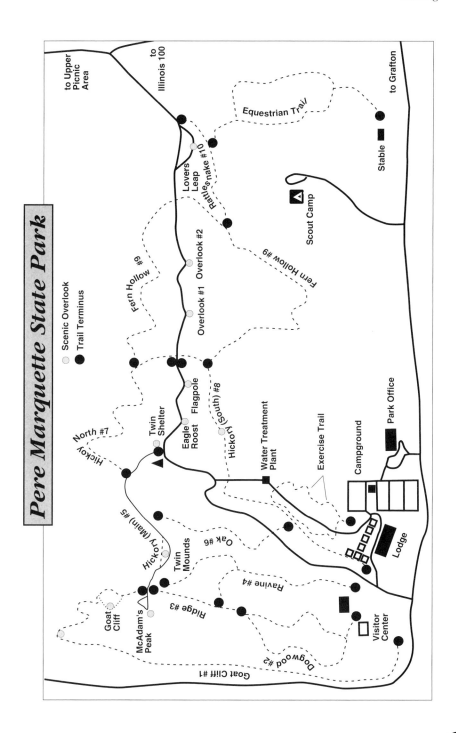

Pere Marquette State Park

Scenic Overlook
Trail Terminus

to Upper Picnic Area
to Illinois 100
to Grafton

Equestrian Trail

Lovers Leap
Rattlesnake #10

Stable

Scout Camp

Fern Hollow #9

Fern Hollow #9

Overlook #2
Overlook #1

North #7
Hickory

Twin Shelter
Eagle Roost
Flagpole
Hickory (South) #8

Water Treatment Plant

Exercise Trail

Campground
Park Office

Hickory (Main) #5

Oak #6

Lodge

Twin Mounds

Ravine #4

Goat Cliff
McAdam's Peak
Ridge #3

Dogwood #2
Goat Cliff #1

Visitor Center

Vista from hiking trail at Pere Marquette State Park

three-fourths of a mile long. Although this is the trail in which the visitor is most likely to see timber rattlesnakes along the rocky bluffs and outcrops, they are rarely seen. The trail may be accessed from trail #9 or along the park road at the south. The trail intersects with the equestrian trail, which is off-limits to hikers.

For a full day hike, the authors recommend taking trail #1 (Goat Cliff) to trail #5 (Hickory Main). Hike to Twin Shelters and then backtrack and take trail #7 (Hickory North) to trail #9 (Fern Hollow) around to where it joins trail #8 (Hickory South). Take Hickory South to its trailhead behind the area near the lodge. If you go the distance you have been seven miles and seen most of the park. Pack a lunch and make a day of it, resting where you feel like it and enjoying the vistas. Chances are you will sleep well that night.

2 *Eldon Hazlet State Park*

Eldon Hazlet State Park is an isolated but major recreation area in central Southern Illinois at Carlyle Lake. The park has abundant wildlife, especially birds. Bald eagles, osprey and herons are some of the 155 species of birds that may be seen by the hiker. Hikers may also enjoy the wildflowers that abound in the spring.

The park has five interconnecting trails, the longest of which is about one and a half miles. The first four (numbered on the map) have been collectively termed the Cherokee Hiking Trails. These pass through a hardwood forest toward the lake and return to the point of origin or to another loop trail. The Cherokee Trail #1 (our numbering) is the northernmost trail skirting the lake and takes the hiker down to the shoreline in certain spots. The middle trail (#2) and the lower trail (#3) provide higher elevation views of the lake. In addition, Cherokee trail #2 takes you along the Burnside Cemetery. Fourteen gravestones, primarily of the Burnside family, date from 1830 to 1861. The Cherokee trail has bridges that traverse creeks emptying into Carlyle Lake.

Two new trails have been recently added to the south of the Cherokee Trails. These trails pass through successional fields and have no lake views.

Near the Carlyle Lake dam off Lake Road, which can be accessed from Illinois 127, are small nature trails developed by the **Corps of Engineers**. Chipmunk Trail, the Little Prairie Nature Trail, and Willow Pond Nature Trail provides handicapped access and is located next to the visitor's center.

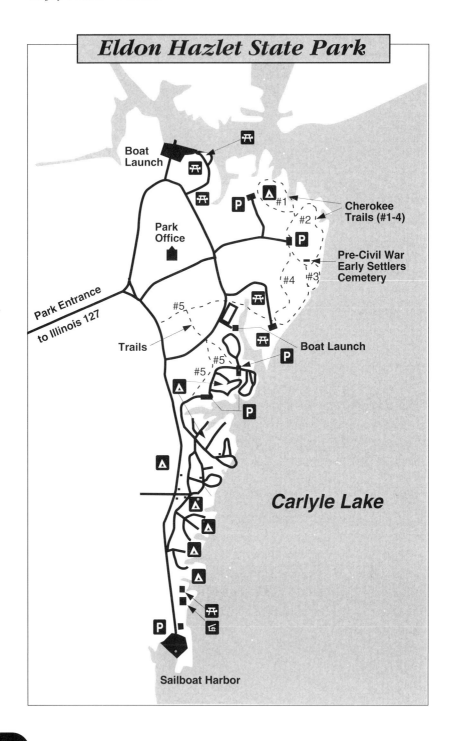

Eldon Hazlet State Park

Boat Launch

Park Office

Park Entrance to Illinois 127

#1
#2
Cherokee Trails (#1-4)

Pre-Civil War Early Settlers Cemetery

#4
#3

#5

Trails

#5

#5

Boat Launch

Carlyle Lake

Sailboat Harbor

❸ *Washington County Conservation Area*

A thorny locust at Washington County Conservation Area

Washington County Conservation Area (WCCA) has one major trail of seven miles in length. The trail, known as the **WCCA Trail** follows the roads of the park. Over the north end of the lake where there is no park road, the trail becomes a conventional hiking trail through the woods. If you wish to hike only the wooded portion of the trail you must either have transportation back to the trailhead or retrace your steps.

The wooded portion of the trail begins as the park road changes to private road at the north end of the park. A sign on the west side of the road indicates the trailhead. The trail extends for about 2.5 miles through bottomland and across creeks. Be careful in crossing creeks since at the time of this writing some bridges were in a poor state of repair. Some interpretive signs posted by a Boy Scout troop in Nashville help with tree identification. About midway the trail ascends to the ridge above the stream feeding the lake and follows the contour of the lake. Excellent views are found in this region. When we hiked this trail we were fortunate to see an owl. At one point the trail branches and goes on a spur to the lake. If you take this short trail, backtrack to the main trail.

The wooded portion of the trail moves away from the lake to terminate at a parking lot and camping area along the northwestern edge of the lake. We suggest that if you have come to Washington County Conservation Area to hike that you only hike the wooded trail. For overnight campers with plenty of time or those with two cars, we suggest that the entire trail be hiked. The seven-mile walk around the lake is pleasant, but will take about 4 to 5 hours.

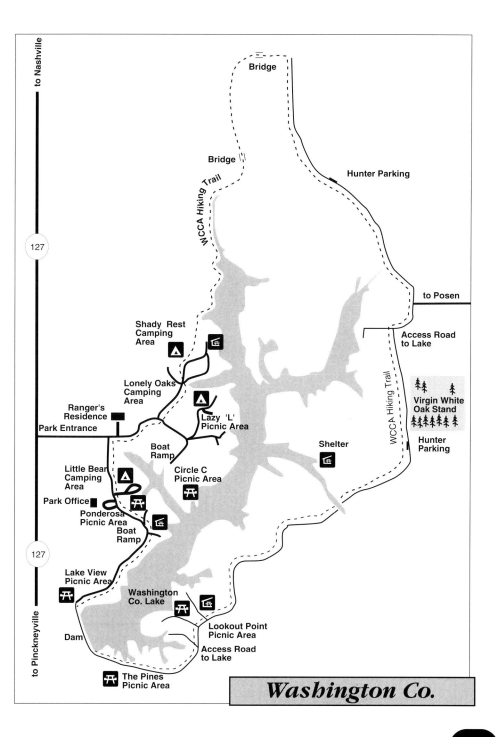

to Nashville

to Pinckneyville

127

127

Bridge

Bridge

Hunter Parking

to Posen

Access Road to Lake

WCCA Hiking Trail

Shady Rest Camping Area

Lonely Oaks Camping Area

Ranger's Residence

Park Entrance

Lazy 'L' Picnic Area

Boat Ramp

Circle C Picnic Area

Shelter

Virgin White Oak Stand

Hunter Parking

WCCA Hiking Trail

Little Bear Camping Area

Park Office

Ponderosa Picnic Area

Boat Ramp

Lake View Picnic Area

Washington Co. Lake

Dam

Lookout Point Picnic Area

Access Road to Lake

The Pines Picnic Area

Washington Co.

283

4 *Fults Hill Prairie Nature Preserve*

There is a high bluff where the Mississippi River has, over millions of years, dug its channel. Visitors of Fults Hill Prairie Nature Preserve may view the panorama of the Mississippi River lowlands from the blufftops that adjoin Bluff Road. There are two trailheads at the parking space that steeply ascend the bluffs. We recommend you take the one to the left (north) and complete the hike by coming down the one at the right (south). When you reach the summit a small user-made spur leads you to a panoramic overlook of the lowland. You will find this a climb where you may need to rest several times to catch your breath, but once on top, the vista to the west into Missouri from the summit is spectacular. Bald eagles may be seen in winter and hawks and turkey vultures year around.

Fults Hill Prairie Nature Preserve can be reached from Illinois 3. (To reach Illinois 3 see directions from Randolph County Conservation Area.) Take Illinois 155 from Ruma 20 miles north of Chester or five miles south of Red Bud and proceed west to Prairie du Rocher. Take the Bluff Road north from Prairie du Rocher. Just before reaching the little village of Fults, there will be a roadside parking area where the two trailheads are located for the loop trail.

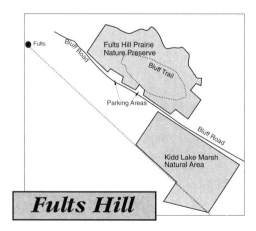

5 *Pyramid State Park*

The abundance of near-to-the-surface coal in Southern Illinois has encouraged strip mining. One only need fly over certain parts of Southern Illinois to see the dramatic impact of past strip mining on the contour of the land. Pyramid State Park was mined between 1932 and 1950 and takes advantage of the rugged contour formed by rows upon rows of coal mining excavations, forming a state park with unique topographical features for the hiker. The many lakes formed by the pitted land encompass a total of 135 acres of water. The lakes are especially clear and the water is said to be exceptionally pure.

The hikes are described as moderately difficult because of all the ups and downs formed by past excavation. Most hiking trails are dual use trails for both hikers and horseback riders, although horseback riders have not extensively muddied them. The land is wooded, primarily with softwood species of the kind that thrive in old strip mines. Pine trees have also been planted in certain areas. The heavily wooded and hilly terrain gives the hiker a sense of privacy. Generally, the hiker or hiking group can find and enjoy one of the smaller lakes with plenty of privacy.

Pyramid State Park boasts hike-in camping on the **Pyramid Trail** which circles the interior of the park and has spurs that lead to lakes and connect with the **Ten-Mile Trail**. The Ten-Mile Trail, a challenging one day hike, is primarily a dual use trail that circles most of the park and passes the largest of the lakes, Boulder Lake. **Ridge Run Trail** and **Split Lake Trail** connect the main park road with the Pyramid Trail. **Red Squirrel Run** and **Blackjack Fork** take the hiker from the main road to small lakes.

One especially nice option open to the hiker is to hike along the scenic Ten-Mile Trail from the boat launch at the south end of Boulder Lake and along Wesseln Lake. Just past Wesseln Lake is the north entrance to the park where you may arrange to meet someone for transportation back to your car at the south entrance.

To reach the main entrance of Pyramid State Park exit I-57 at Marion and proceed west through Carbondale to the outskirts of Murphysboro. Go north on Illinois 13/127 to where a sign will direct you westerly on Illinois 152. The entrance of the park is on the right approximately 2.4 miles west of Pyatts. The park ranger's office is usually manned if you need information or assistance.

Alternatively, to reach Pyramid State Park take exit #50 onto Illinois 13/127. Go south through Pinckneyville for approximately six miles to the intersection and proceed as described above.

There is a northern, lesser-used, signed entrance to the park about 2.5 miles south of Pinckneyville. Go west from Illinois 13/127 at the sign for about two miles watching carefully for the park entrance road on the left side of the road.

Do not plan to hike during deer hunting season. Trails are closed to hikers for obvious safety reasons.

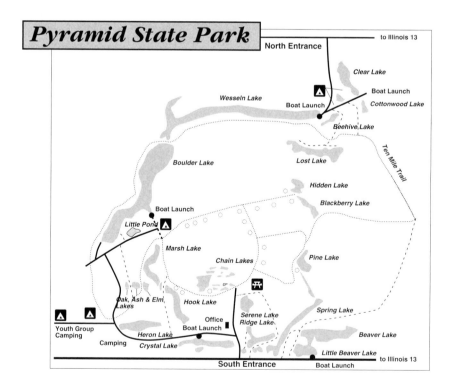

6 *Randolph County Conservation Area*

The trails at Randolph County Conservation Area are primarily dual use trails for both horseback riders and hikers. They are well maintained and not muddy from overuse. Horseback riding is seasonally restricted. The terrain is generally wooded and rather level. A few trails marked in the brochure for hikers are really designed as access trails to Randolph County Lake.

The Boy Scouts of Troop 305 in nearby Chester have taken the initiative to create an interpretive nature walkway through the park called the **Oak Ridge Trail**. The half-mile trail extends from Shelter 4 to Shelter 1 and has two loops. An interpretive book designed by the Boy Scouts may be obtained at the park office. The book has 25 items of interest listed for hikers to see as they walk along Oak Ridge Trail. The items are marked along the trails in easy view. Most are native trees. Hikers are asked to return the books to a box at the end of the trail.

There is a nice, wet weather waterfall on the foot trail extending west from Randolph County Lake. The waterfall is just north of where the trail intersects with a dual use trail (see map).

This region is especially suited for family hiking. There are many play and picnic areas, the land is relatively flat and the hikes, except for horse trails, are relatively short.

To reach Randolph County Conservation Area, take Illinois 150 north from Chester. Chester is a small community that lies on Illinois 3 along the Mississippi River about equidistant from St. Louis and the southern tip of Illinois.

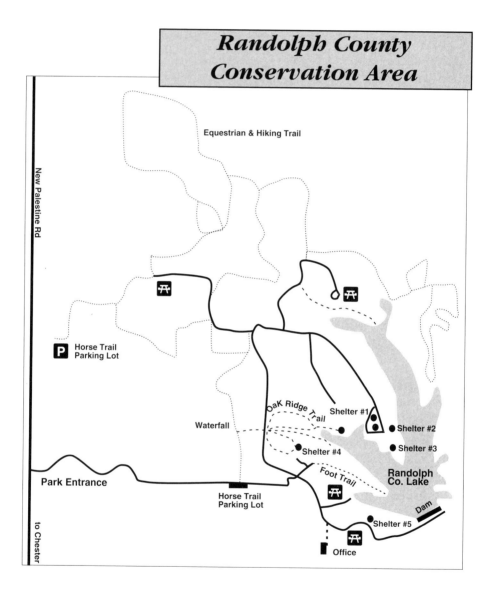

Randolph County Conservation Area

Equestrian & Hiking Trail

New Palestine Rd

Horse Trail
Parking Lot

Oak Ridge Trail

Waterfall

Shelter #1

Shelter #2

Shelter #3

Shelter #4

Foot Trail

Randolph
Co. Lake

Park Entrance

Horse Trail
Parking Lot

to Chester

Dam

Shelter #5

Office

7 *Turkey Bluffs*

View of the Mississippi from Turkey Bluffs

Hunting and fishing are the main attractions at Turkey Bluffs Fish and Wildlife Area but there is one main hiking trail.

The trailhead begins at the end of the road that almost encircles this area. The signs encourage hikers to begin their hike on the right side of this loop trail. If you follow the right (east) trail, it will take you down into the lowlands alongside the ridge overlooking the Mississippi River. Here you will find typical Southern Illinois oak-hickory forest. After about a mile, the hike turns sharply upward in a breath taking walk to the summit of the ridge overlooking the Mississippi River. In the winter there are good panoramic views of the river, although the views could be improved by selective clearing of trees at one or two sites along the ridge-top trail. The ridge-top trail is relatively level and takes you back to the trailhead. We recommend that unless you plan to take the entire loop, begin your hike on the left (west) side and where the trail veers off the ridge eastward you should retrace your steps to the beginning of the trail.

To reach Illinois 3 from I-57, take exit #54 at Marion and proceed west on Illinois 13 through Carbondale and take Illinois 149 north at the outskirts of Murphysboro for about eight miles until the road intersects Illinois 3. Also, to reach Turkey Bluffs Fish and Wildlife Area proceed south on Illinois 3 from East St. Louis or north on Illinois 3 from Cairo. From Missouri, Illinois 3 can be accessed from I-55 at the Perryville exit via Missouri 51 going east to the bridge at Chester where the two highways meet. Turkey Bluffs State Fish and Wildlife Area is located on Illinois 3 about 3.5 miles south of Chester. The large sign is positioned on the west side of the road. Access is on the east side of the road.

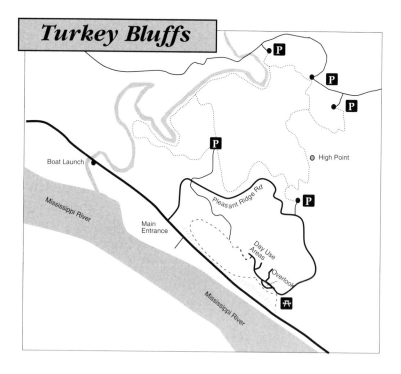

⑧ *Piney Hills Ravine at Piney Creek Nature Preserve*

Bluff overhang at Piney Hills Ravine

Foot for foot, this little known site is perhaps the best hiking trail in Southern Illinois. Its scenic wonder has been underemphasized due to its isolation from easy access roads. We strongly recommend that you visit this site and discover for yourself the serene beauty of the ravine, Piney Creek and tributaries that flow therein. The Natural Heritage Division of the Department of Conservation has set aside this 500-plus acre tract as a nature preserve.

From the parking lot, the hiker must walk about half a mile and traverse fields to gain access to the trailhead. Administrating officials might consider extending the road to the trailhead.

The trailhead is well marked with a sign showing the loop trail. The trail is moderately difficult and begins by descending the ravine. It is not long before the hiker views a large waterfall formed at the beginning of one of the tributaries of Piney Creek. The trail continues to descend along the ravine where views of the creek and the steep rock formations become more spectacular. At the bottom, the blazed

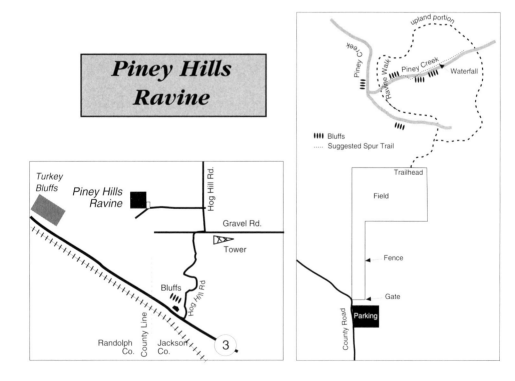

trail crosses Piney Creek. We suggest you leave the marked trail and walk up the creek on your right to see the large pools, waterfalls and ravine walls. Retrace your steps to the trail and continue along Piney Creek. Rock walls are tall and are undercut by the creek. A short distance along the creek the trail turns abruptly to the right (north) and steeply ascends the ravine. The trail winds toward a field and then eventually along a high rock wall which contains Indian petroglyphs and graffiti dating back to the early 1800s. Please respect the area and do not add to the damage. You will cross the creek again before joining the trail again near the trailhead. For more information about the site, check with the ranger at Randolph County Conservation Area.

To reach Piney Hills Ravine at Piney Creek Nature Preserve requires attention to directions as there are no directional signs showing the way to this isolated spot. The directions to Randolph County Conservation Area provide directions to Chester. Proceed south from Chester on Illinois 3 for about 11 miles carefully noting the passing of the sign that indicates you have entered Jackson County. Take the first paved road on the left (north) side of the road (Hog Hill Road). Go four miles north and the road will make a "T." Take a right (east) for only about 50 yards and make an immediate left (north) on a gravel road for 1.2 miles. Turn left and proceed for about 1.6 miles. The small parking lot will be located to your right. A gate indicates the beginning of the path to the trailhead.

The administrating officials for Piney Creek Nature Preserve are based at Randolph County Conservation Area.

⑨ *Rend Lake, Wayne Fitzgerrell State Park & Other Sites*

Tree "art" at Rend Lake

Two hiking trails are found at Rend Lake. One in Wayne Fitzgerrell State Park is an unnamed 1.4 mile loop trek through the woods. The well marked trailhead begins along a park road and soon crosses another of the park's roads. The path is wide and easily traversed. The major portion of the hike winds through relatively flat terrain but does not allow a good view of the lake. Good examples of black oak trees, with their low hanging dead branches may be found along the trail. On the return portion of the loop the hiker again passes the park road before ending the walk near the trailhead. The walk passes through a relatively young hardwood forest. The second hiking trail, **Blackberry Trail**, is on the west side of the lake at South Sandusky Recreation Area in a section maintained by the Corps of Engineers. A canopied information building serves as the trailhead for this three-quarter mile, relatively easy hike. Allow 30 minutes for a leisurely hike. A brochure describing the trail and native tree species along the trail is available. Hikers may match the numbers placed on trees to numbers on a brochure that contains information about the species. The trail passes through forested hardwoods and contains

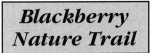

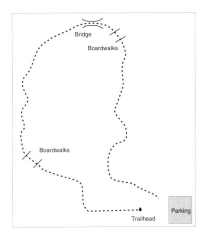

295

three boardwalks and a "halfway" bridge.

To reach Rend Lake Wayne Fitzgerrell Park take exit #77 off I-57 and proceed west on Illinois 154 past the Arts and Crafts Center to cross a major finger of the lake on the causeway. Take the park entrance on your right (north). To reach Blackberry Trail continue on Illinois 154 west and take either county road, 800E or 850E, to your left (west). These roads intersect at the North Sandusky Area. Turn right and skirt the park by making a left (south) on county road 750 E. Bear left (east) on county road 1300N. The trail entrance is just a few tenths of a mile on this road on your left. Look for the small shelter building.

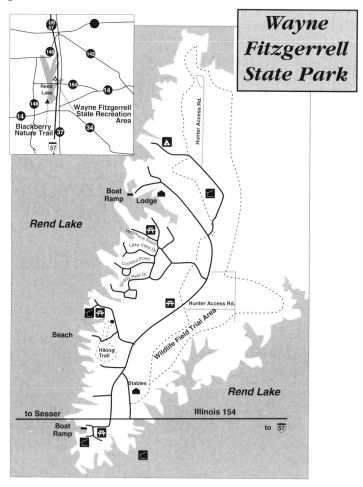

⑩ *Sam Parr State Park*

Trail head at Lake Side Trail

Sam Parr State Park has both hiking and equestrian trails, although the latter are designated for both hikers and horses.

The only trail, exclusively for hiking, **Lake Side Trail**, is on the south and southeast sides of the lake. This two-plus mile hike (one way) does not bring you back to the trailhead so arrange to retrace your steps or have some one meet you at the trail's end. Begin the hike at the picnic area where you immediately cross the dam. Past the dam the trail winds extensively to follow the contour of the lake. Good lake views make this hike extremely enjoyable. The hike is easy to moderate and the trail is blazed with red flags. It will take a brisk walker about 35-40 minutes to accomplish the one-way hike.

The equestrian/hiker trail is 13 miles long. Use for horses has been restricted from April 1 to August 25 to preserve the trail. The trailhead begins at the parking area on the east side of the lake. The trail winds close to the lake in several areas. Three loops are present, one on the west side of the lake and two on its east side.

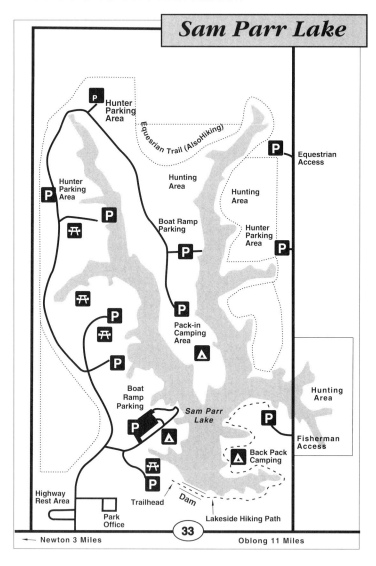

Sam Parr Lake

Hunter Parking Area

Equestrian Trail (Also Hiking)

Equestrian Access

Hunter Parking Area

Hunting Area

Hunting Area

Boat Ramp Parking

Hunter Parking Area

Pack-in Camping Area

Boat Ramp Parking

Sam Parr Lake

Hunting Area

Fisherman Access

Back Pack Camping

Highway Rest Area

Trailhead

Dam

Park Office

33

Lakeside Hiking Path

Newton 3 Miles

Oblong 11 Miles

⑪ *Newton Lake*

Newton Lake offers some of the longest hikes in Southern Illinois. The lake has very few access points and except for the power plant, remains relatively unspoiled. One large trail extends down the west side of the lake. The trail is multi-use for horseback riders, cross-country skiers, and hikers. From October 15 to April 15 it is shut down to horse travel to minimize muddying of the trail. Hikers can select the length of their hike by choosing return loops. Since return loops are relatively straight in comparison to the main trail that follows the "ins and outs" of the lake, the trip back to the trail head is shortened by taking a return loop. The entire trail is 22.5 miles if one retraces their steps, but is only 15.1 miles using the return loops. A park brochure describes the length of each segment and the return loops.

Lake view from trail at Newton Lake

The trailhead is at the north end of the lake close to the park office. The trail winds up and down the hills and ravines that adjoin the lake. Lake views are numerous along the trail. Prairie chickens, rare in Illinois, may be seen. In 1992, a pair of bald eagles nested along the shoreline of the lake and raised a single eaglet. During this time the park superintendent closed off a portion of the trail and also placed buoys to keep lake traffic away. It is not known if the eagles will return. Please consult with the park superintendent for the status of the trail prior to beginning your hike. Also note that there is a south access to the lake but the trail does not reach that far south. Thus, all hikers must return to the north access.

To reach the north access of Newton Lake from I-57 take any of the exits to Effingham and proceed southeast on Illinois 33 for about eight miles to the town of Dieterich. Turn right (south) on the county road and proceed for about 10 miles until you see a bait shop. Turn east (left) and go about five miles to the park entrance. Many maps do not show the west-east road leading to the park entrance.

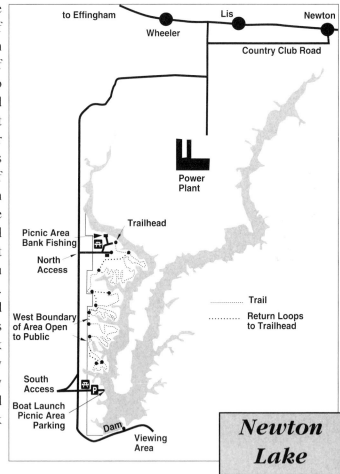

⑫ *Chauncey Marsh Nature Preserve*

Chauncey Marsh Nature Preserve is a satellite area administered by Red Hills State Park. It offers one main hiking area when conditions permit. Note that this area is lowland and will become impassable in prolonged wet weather.

The trail distance has never been measured with certainty but appears to be less than two miles. The trailhead first heads south from a field adjoining a township road. It loops back and travels east in a rectangular pattern that eventually leads to the opposite end of the

Crawfish tower

same field. The trail is almost all wooded with species of hickory best suited to the bottom land. The preserve contains both wet and dry marshes.

To reach Chauncey Marsh Nature Preserve proceed north through Red Hills State Park for about 5.5 miles to the Chauncey Road (1800 N) and go east for about one mile. Turn north on township road 600 E. You will see the entrance at the field about two thirds of a mile north.

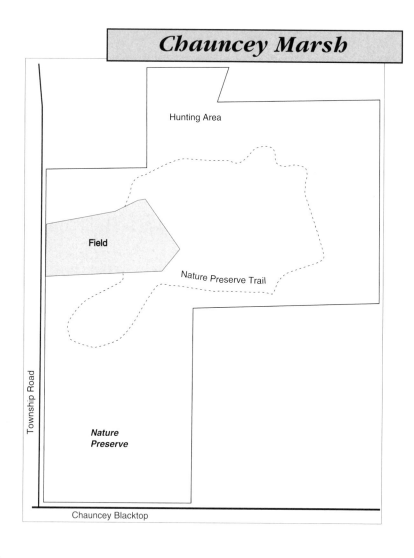

Chauncey Marsh

Hunting Area

Field

Nature Preserve Trail

Township Road

Nature Preserve

Chauncey Blacktop

⓭ *Red Hills State Park*

Like many state parks in Southern Illinois, Red Hills has dual use trails that are long and skirt a major portion of the park. It also has trails exclusively for hikers. U.S. 50 divides the park into a northern section and a southern section.

The northern part of the park has three trails that form loops with segments of the loops in common. These loops are named **Indian Treaty, Robin** and **Tulip Trails**. The Indian Treaty trailhead is the suggested beginning point. It is marked by a large sign at the northern

Historical sign at Red Hills

entrance of the park on the right (east). The trails meander along the side of Red Hill, the highest point in the area. Oak, hickory, ash and tulip poplar predominate on these moderately difficult trails. Each loop is described as about one mile long although there is some variability.

The northern and southern portions of Red Hills State Park are divided by U.S. 50. The dual use hiker/equestrian trail encircles the southern portion of the park. It provides the longest hike, five miles, and traverses fields and forest. Most of the walk is some distance from the park lake. Check with the site superintendent about the condition of the trail since horses in wet periods can cause deterioration of the trail.

To reach Red Hills State Park exit I-57 at exit #116 and proceed east 60 miles. The park entrance is on the north and south side of the road about 15 miles east of Olney.

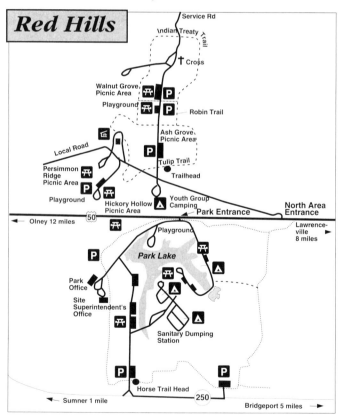

⑭ *Stephen A. Forbes State Park*

Old gravestone on Henneman Cemetery Trail

Stephen A Forbes State Park has one long hiking trail, three short trails, and a major equestrian trail that also serves hikers.

The longest is the **Oak Ridge Trail**. The well-marked trailhead is located near the shower house on the north side of the lake. This moderately difficult trail winds up and down the hilly lakeside. A brisk walker can traverse the trail in less than 50 minutes. We suggest that runners would also enjoy the challenge of the up and down terrain. This wooded walk, about 100 feet above the lake, provides a very nice view of the lake. Views of the lake panorama, floating dock across the lake and the concession stand. There are occasional benches and picnic tables for those who wish to rest or bring their food. While hiking this trail the authors saw four turkey hens and a large doe. As one turns west of the lake and hikes along a small finger of the lake there is an unusually shaped oak tree on the right. The atypical shape was caused by bending or breaking of the tree toward the ground. One of the major branches of the tree grew upward seeking light and became dominant. The trail crosses several small creeks. Views are best in the winter.

The foot trail to **Marlow Pond** is one-third of a mile in length (0.7 miles round trip) and leads down a hill, following a stream. It eventually crosses a bridge and climbs above the stream to the large Marlow Pond. The trail is shared with horses and can be muddy. Follow the trail sign to avoid getting lost. After enjoying the scenery at Marlow Pond, retrace your steps to the trailhead.

Henneman Cemetery Trail is about one-fourth mile round trip. The trail crosses a bridge and terminates at a deep ravine containing a stream. Graves in Henneman Cemetery date back into the early 1800s. About 15 headstones, many in poor condition, dot the cemetery.

Phillips Creek Trail is very short and provides access to the east side of the lake from the road.

For the veteran hiker, the 15-mile horse trail proves a challenge. The trail is virtually all wooded and encircles the park with loops on the northwest and southeast portions of the trail.

To reach Stephen A. Forbes State Park from I-57, take exit #127 and proceed east through Kinmundy for about five miles. Turn south at the directional sign and proceed for three miles to the park entrance.

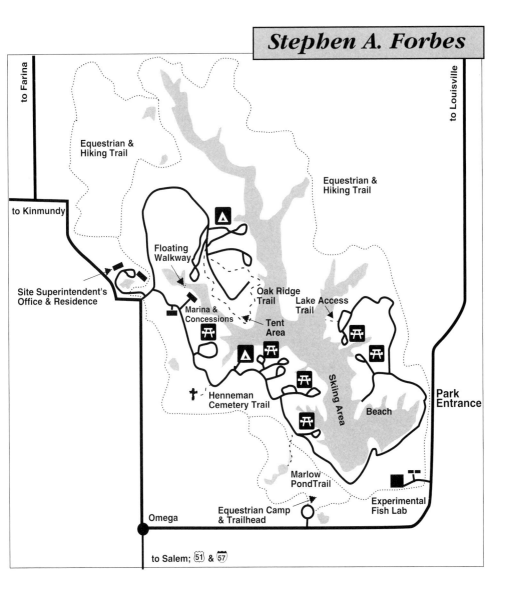

Stephen A. Forbes

to Farina

to Louisville

Equestrian &
Hiking Trail

Equestrian &
Hiking Trail

to Kinmundy

Floating
Walkway

Oak Ridge
Trail

Lake Access
Trail

Site Superintendent's
Office & Residence

Marina &
Concessions

Tent
Area

Henneman
Cemetery Trail

Skiing Area

Park
Entrance

Beach

Marlow
PondTrail

Experimental
Fish Lab

Omega

Equestrian Camp
& Trailhead

to Salem; 51 & 57

307

⑮ *Sam Dale Lake Conservation Area*

Sam Dale Lake provides a beautiful setting for a hike. It offers three main hiking trails encompassing a total of about 4.5 miles.

On the north side of the lake at the end of the park road is a 2.75-mile unnamed trail composed of three loops. Loops allow the hiker to choose the hike length. The first loop is three-fourths of a mile and begins near the playground and toilet, and ends at a field along the park. The loop provides views of the lake and traverses hardwood forest with some planted pine. The trails are broad and well marked. The second loop is about 2.5 miles in length and skirts the lake on the south side. The third loop takes origin from the second and is a greater

Sam Dale Lake as viewed by the hiker

distance from the lake. All loops are of easy to moderate difficulty. Turkey may occasionally be seen along the trail.

Two trails extend nearly the whole length of the southern face of the lake. **Pine View Trail** extends about three-fourths of a mile from the parking area at the west end of the road and generally follows the lake contour. It ends at the parking lot on the main spur road to the dining area and playground. The second trail, **Fox Run Trail**, extends one mile from the boat launch and crosses two roads leading from the park road to the lake and ends near the youth group camp. The trail gets its name from the fox that inhabit this region. These trails are excellent for children since there is little chance of getting seriously lost. They traverse oak-hickory forest and planted pine.

To reach Sam Dale Lake Conservation Area take Exit #109 and proceed west from I-57 on Illinois 161 about nine miles. Follow the signs north to the park entrance.

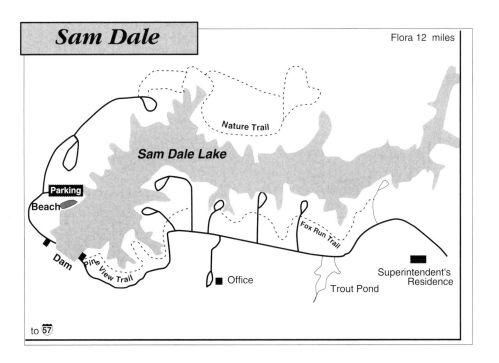

16   *Beall Woods*

Evidence of a lightning strike at Beall Woods

One of Illinois' natural gems is located on the Wabash River south of Carmi. Beall Woods is a small park located near a small lake, but is mainly a hiking mecca. There are four open loop trails and one "connector trail" that total ten miles. Three of these are in current use. Unfortunately, Beall Woods has suffered the effects of state budget cuts although recently some monies have been restored to state budgets.

In spite of the lack of maintenance of some trails, the Beall Woods area offers some of the most beautiful scenery in Southern Illinois. These areas are best hiked in the fall, winter and spring since insects may be a problem in the summer. Make sure to take insect repellent in the summer.

White Oak Trail is about 1.75 miles long and is a loop trail. All trails begin at the same trailhead near the red barn that serves as a nature center. White Oak Trail is signed and begins to the right of the entry way. It is frequently signed with an oak leaf symbol. The trail heads from an upland region down into the bottomland along Coffee Creek. A short distance down the trail one is impressed with the large size and variety of the trees. Beall Woods is the largest tract of virgin timber east of the Mississippi River. Over the years many trees have been struck by lightning and are interesting to study.

There is clearly an unusual, almost eerie atmosphere, in the bottomland as one walks near the creek. Along White Oak Trail the author was fortunate to see a pileated woodpecker and eight white-tailed deer, among which was a stately buck. At the turn-around point on the loop trail you can hike out to the confluence of Coffee Creek and the Wabash River. Walk out to the confluence and see the moaning oil derrick across the creek. The return is up a stairway along high ground. An interpretive sign describes a tree that was 16-feet in diameter that once stood along the creek.

Ridgeway Trail was not accessible on our visit since there was no easy ford to Coffee Creek. The site superintendent notes that the trail has been closed since 1978, but funds have been allocated to build a bridge in the near future. At one time it was signed by a cardinal, a tribute to the ornithologist, Robert Ridgeway. To gain entrance to the Ridgeway Trail, Coffee Creek must be forded or one must walk across a fallen tree over the creek. This is not recommended unless the creek is exceptionally low and easily passable. Check with the site superintendent for the status of the trails. Once across Coffee Creek, the loop trail eventually borders the Wabash River and turns away to run along a pecan orchard and along planted Kentucky coffee trees. The variety of trees along the trail is enormous. The loop trail returns to Coffee Creek and the creek must be forded again. Please note that you must return by White Oak Trail to the trailhead.

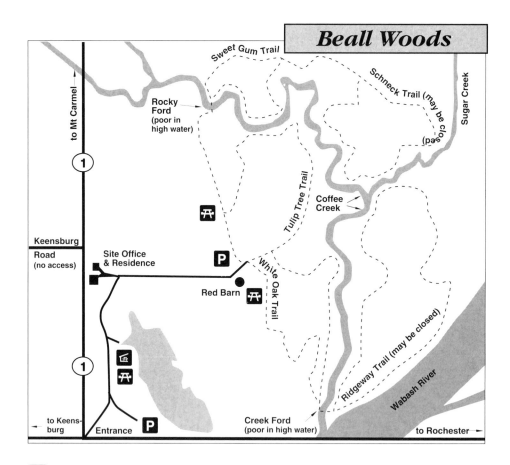

Tulip Tree Trail is primarily an upland forest trail that lies in the center of the trails region of the nature preserve. The trail is easy, wide and not blazed. Several interpretive signs describe plant and tree species. The trail is a 1.5-mile long loop trail and follows Coffee Creek along a small cliff.

The trail leading to the rocky ford was once part of a stage coach trail and can only be reached from the west part of Tulip Tree Trail loop. This branch connects Tulip Tree Trail to **Sweet Gum Trail**. The creek must be forded when low or the hiker must find a fallen tree to cross the creek. We recommend that caution be exercised when doing either. No good ford exists in high water. If you manage to access Sweet Gum trail there is a rewarding hike along the bottomland trail ahead. The right portion of the loop trail extends along the creek and you will see a ravine. The trail ascends a hill before circling back to Rocky Ford Trail to cross Coffee Creek.

To reach Beall Woods Conservation Area and Nature Preserve take exit #132 from I-57 and proceed north on Illinois 1 for about 12 miles. You will see the signed entrance to Beall Woods on the right (east) about three miles south of Mt. Carmel.

17

Hamilton County Conservation Area

The giant oak at Hamilton County Conservation Area

Hamilton County Lake has three easy trails which primarily serve picnicking and camping visitors. Trails are through hardwood forest and occasionally cross creeks or drainage areas. The trails skirt the lake although lake views do not abound. Since the trails are one-way, you must retrace your steps or have a car waiting for you.

On the east side of the lake a three-fourths mile-long trail begins near the dam and proceeds north along the contour of the lake. About one-half mile along the trail it crosses a park road and proceeds another one-third mile to the Kiwanis Point Picnic Area.

Two trails are found on the northwest portion of the lake. Well

The trailhead for Shelter Trail

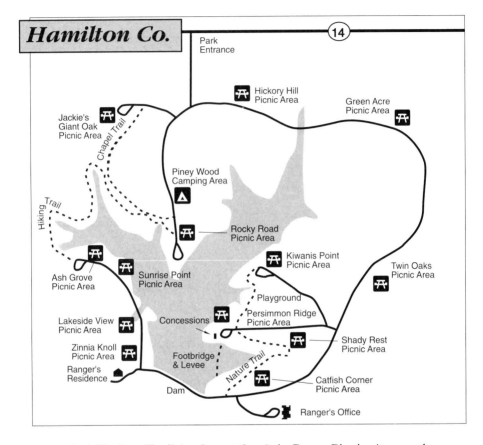

marked **Shelter Trail** begins at the Ash Grove Picnic Area and proceeds generally north along the lake. It winds around the lake eastward through a segment of planted pine and ends at the Rocky Point Picnic Area. Just north of the trail terminus a second trail, **Chapel Trail**, begins. Note that this trail is well marked since there is one other possible cleared path that may be confused with the trailhead. Also the trail widens at a clearing. Do not follow the clearing but bear left at the clearing to stay on the trail. The half-mile trail is wooded and ends at a spectacular swamp oak tree, over five feet in diameter.

To reach Hamilton County Conservation Area take exit #71 from I-57 at Benton. Follow U.S. 14 east for 24 miles through McLeansboro. Continue east along Illinois 14 about six miles; the signed entrance road to the park is on your right.

18 *Rails to Trails*
(under development)

The Illinois Department of Conservation has announced plans for a unique hiking and biking development that will, undoubtedly, be popular among hikers and cyclists. The development, commonly referred to as *Rails to Trails* is a conversion of an abandoned Norfolk Southern Corporation railway line into a hiking and biking trail.

The proposed 43-mile trail begins at Harrisburg and stretches to Karnak, a small town southwest of Vienna. The headquarters will be located in Vienna near the city park. Contracts have been awarded for the first phase of development. Completion is scheduled for 1994. Plans call for the initial development of a 17-mile section between Tunnel Hill and Vienna.

The beginnings of Rails to Trails

The trail will have no more than a one-percent grade, meaning it will present no terrain difficulties for bikers and hikers. The trail is virtually (99%) all wooded. There are numerous rest stops planned along the way at nearby towns, allowing hikers and bikers to take advantage of as little or as much of the trail as they desire. A tunnel and bridges will be highlights for hikers.

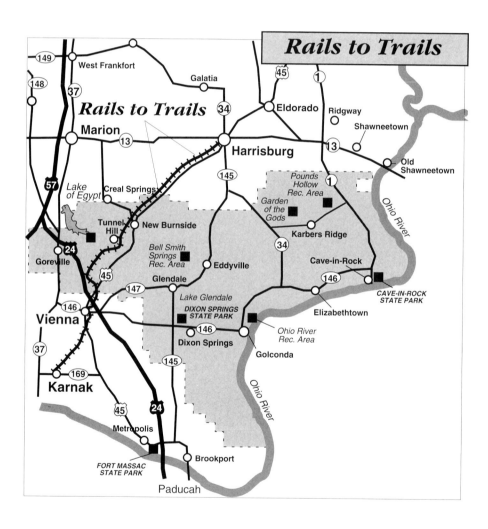

A fter four hours of wandering around the woods, I had no idea where I was. To make matters worse, I had no idea how to find out where in the world I was.

The entire mess began innocently enough.

I awoke early Sunday morning to the sound of birds singing. Our cabin at Camp Ondessonk sat on a bluff overlooking a lake. It was an idyllic experience about to turn idiotic.

Let's dwell on the idyllic for a few more moments.

Since I was the first to arise, I

Les Winkeler
Sports writer

The Southern Illinoisan, Oct. 8, 1992

started a campfire. Within a few moments people began stumbling down from the cabins for a hearty pre-hike breakfast.

Our destination–Pakentuck.

Pakentuck was the site of a Boy Scout camp at one time, if memory serves me correctly. It is a beautiful place, imposing limestone bluffs, a small waterfall and a clear mountain pool. It is a favorite spot with hikers and horseback riders.

Pakentuck is easy to find.

"Take any path east out of the camp, you can't miss it," we were told.

Actually, that's fairly accurate. We traveled east, and we did find Pakentuck with a minimum of difficulty.

What I object to is people telling me, "you can't miss it." I learned to despise that phrase as the day wore on.

We enjoyed the beauty of Pakentuck for about an hour, then decided it was time to get back to the old campsite. For various reasons, we decided to take a different route back to camp. That was our first mistake.

We stopped to ask directions from an approaching horseback rider.

We were very specific.

"If uh, we follow this, um, trail, will it take us like back to a bigger trail which leads to a road?" is basically what we asked her.

Amazingly, she responded.

Not surprisingly, her answer was nearly as convoluted as our question. However, she seemed to say the trail did indeed lead to Ondessonk.

I don't know who this young lady was. She is probably a wonderful person. I'm not blaming her for getting us lost. She was just a piece of the puzzle.

We followed the path that she suggested. During that portion of the trek at least four other horseback riders verified the trail would take us back to Camp Ondessonk.

"You can't miss it," they all said.

After about 90 minutes–the walk to Pakentuck was supposed to take only about 30 minutes–I had this sneaking suspicion we were lost.

Somehow, I felt my daughters also sensed this fact.

The youngest was lying on the ground in the fetal position. My oldest daughter had this look of sheer terror in her eyes, the look that is usually reserved for the times she thinks we will make her do the dishes when Beverly Hills 90210 is on the tube.

Finally, we heard horses approaching.

We were told we were going in completely the wrong direction.

I could buy that, but then the directions the guy gave us supposedly took us through a swamp. At this point, I should have asked him how much it was going to cost me to buy the bridge through the swamp, but we had nothing else to go on.

We followed his directions until another couple approached on horseback.

"Excuse me, but just out of curiosity, will this path take us back to Camp Ondessonk?" I asked.

"I don't know," the man replied.

Finally, someone willing to tell me the truth!

However, they did tell us how to get back to Pakentuck.

To make a long story, nearly five hours, short, the swamp directions were all wet. We eventually backtracked and found our way back to Pakentuck again. It was kind of like, although we really didn't know where we were, we kind of knew where we were even if we didn't know exactly where we were at.

Know what I mean?

Finally, we made our way back to the original path and limped back to Camp Ondessonk.

Camp was there all the while, I don't know how we could have missed it.

Hunting

Photo courtesy of the Southern Illinoisan

I f the quality of deer hunting in Southern Illinois was measured on a scale of 1 to 35, Mark Guetersloh of Murphysboro would probably rate it at least a 32. In 1990, within the span of 10 days, Guetersloh killed two 16-point bucks. The larger of the two still ranks among the top 20 scores internationally.

Like all good hunters, Guetersloh did his homework, scouting the deer for nearly a year. On the morning of Oct. 2, just the second day of hunting season, he was sitting in his deer stand and he saw "his" deer about 35 yards away, just out of range. The deer was standing with another buck of almost equal size, and Guetersloh virtually resigned himself to the fact that taking the deer would have to wait until another day.

Then, fate intervened. Another deer, "only" an eight-point buck came crashing through the underbrush directly under Guetersloh's stand. That drew the two bigger bucks in for a closer look. In this case, curiosity, and Guetersloh, killed the deer. The 16-point brute field dressed at 219 pounds. The rack had a gross score of 204 and five-eighths on the Pope and Young system. After deductions, the official score was 185 and one-eighth. "Antler growth here is excellent," said Mickey Stewart, an owner of the Wildlife Refuge in Carbondale, which serves as a deer check-in station. "We don't have to take a backseat to anybody here."

A veteran hunter, Guetersloh was prepared to spend many long days in the woods passing up shots at lesser deer to have the opportunity to take "his" deer. He and his hunting partner Mike Porter, also of Murphysboro, scouted the deer for nearly a year. "We scouted him out pretty heavily," Guetersloh said. "Probably in May or June, we saw him in velvet. We built stands accordingly. You see an animal like that, and you say, 'That's the animal I want to hunt.' I said 'that's the animal I want to hunt all season.' I didn't expect to see him that close, that soon."

Guetersloh's deer was a trophy of a lifetime, or so he thought. What transpired Oct. 11, surprised even Guetersloh. He was sitting in his stand, hoping to fill his second permit with a 10-point buck with two drop tines that he had been scouting, when a 16-point non-typical buck walked into range. "This was a new deer," he said. "I sat and watched him for 15 minutes to decide if I should shoot him because I didn't want my season to be over." It didn't take him long to decide.

The second buck had a gross score of 152 and a net of 133 and one-eighth. Although both deer are remarkable specimens, Guetersloh said there are plenty more in the woods of Southern Illinois just like them. "Definitely, I hunt private property, but I'll tell you that there are a lot of places on public property that produce that kind of deer. The opportunities there (on public land) are as good as anything, especially for the bowhunter," Stewart said. "It's a little tougher for the shotgun hunter because he's got to apply for a permit for a specific county."

The only prohibitions against hunting in the Shawnee National Forest is that firearms cannot be discharged within 150 yards of an established campground. The only other areas in the forest that are

Canada geese (Photo courtesy of the Southern Illiniosan)

off-limits to hunters are those places designated natural areas. Illinois' deer herd is burgeoning, particularly in Southern Illinois. Despite the ever-increasing population, Illinois has maintained a quality herd, both in terms of size and rack production. "The further north you go (in the United States), the larger the body," Guetersloh said. "We've

Carp hunting (Photo courtesy of the Southern Illinoisan)

got a pretty good balance here. A 300-pound deer in Texas would rewrite the record books."

With the growing herd, Illinois hunting laws are becoming more liberal. In the early 1990s, Illinois added extra days to the shotgun season, added a handgun season and a muzzleloading season. "Illinois deer hunting laws are in turmoil because we have a lot of people that want to get the population down," Guetersloh said. "That will affect the quality of trophy hunting, but they're going to have a ton of deer down here from here on out."

Turkey Hunting

As late as the 1960s, wild turkeys were just a fond memory in Southern Illinois.

Turkey hunting returned to the area in the early 1970s. Southern Illinois now has shotgun seasons in the spring and fall and an archery season in the fall. "They are two different sports," says Mickey Stewart, owner of Wildlife Refuge in Carbondale. "In the spring, you're making hen sounds to attract the gobblers. The fall can be easier with a shotgun because there are a lot more young birds out there. The spring, in my mind, is a lot more fun."

More and more counties are opening to turkey hunting each year. The hunter-success ratio is about 20 percent.

"We have so much public hunting," Stewart said. "If a hunter spends the time and does the right things, he will definitely locate and have a chance to kill a few birds. In that respect, it's as good a place to hunt as anywhere else." Stewart said any of the counties within the Shawnee National Forest are excellent for turkey hunters. There are spectacular fringe benefits for the turkey hunter. "If a guy looks, he will hunt in some of the most spectacular landscape he has ever been in," Stewart said. "It ranks high anywhere. It's a pleasure being in the woods in the morning, when you're working birds, it's just a bonus. I get a whole lot of intrinsic value other than hunting the birds, it's good for the head."

Dove Hunting

Dove hunting opportunities abound on public and private land.

Many state parks and conservation areas grow sunflowers and other grain crops, specifically to attract doves. Stewart said dove hunting in the area ranges from spotty to excellent. He said the quality of hunting depends on how much time the hunter is willing to invest in scouting potential hunting areas. "Many landowners will let you hunt them," Stewart said. "At least in the past they have let them hunt." Stewart qualified his statement by adding that landowners approached in an orderly and polite fashion have been cooperative with dove hunters.

The dove is the most avidly hunted game bird in the area. Illinois hunters may benefit from the fact that the dove is classified as a songbird and cannot be hunted in some neighboring states.

Waterfowl

Southern Illinois likes to bill itself as the goose hunting capital of the world. The area is located on the **Mississippi Flyway**, resulting in an annual winter flock of at least one million birds.

Goose hunting is big business in Southern Illinois.The Williamson County Tourism Bureau estimates that goose hunting brings $7.5-$10 million into the economy of Williamson, Jackson, Alexander and Union counties each year. There are ample public hunting opportunities, and the countryside is littered with private hunting clubs. The average cost of a day's hunting at a private club is about $75, which includes guide and decoys.

"The best public hunting is by boat on Crab Orchard or Rend Lake," Mickey Stewart said. "You need a big boat, and you need to know what you're doing because it can get pretty ugly out there." Although harvest numbers are down in recent years, the area still remains one of the premiere goose hunting areas in the country.

The decline in hunter success has generally been attributed to two factors, an aging goose flock and mild winters. The mature-to-immature ratio of the flock has increased in recent years. The mature birds are less likely to be fooled by decoy spreads, and are generally more difficult to harvest. "The birds have been hunted harder up and down the flyway," Stewart said. "The birds are adapting well. They're living on golf courses, they live on little ponds in suburbs." In addition, warm weather has resulted in plentiful food and open water on the area refuges. The warmer winters have also meant that many of the birds never fly as far south as Southern Illinois, wintering in the central part of the state.

Although the numbers in the duck flock have been dwindling nationwide, some areas in Southern Illinois provide excellent hunting. "Rend Lake is premiere duck hunting," Stewart said. "It has everything from open water to flooded timber to flooded grains. It's premiere shooting." Public hunting areas that provide good duck hunting include Mermet Lake in Massac County and Oakwood Bottoms in Jackson County. Stewart said Southern Illinois also has a large resident wood duck population.

There are about 60 goose hunting clubs in the Southern Illinois area. Most clubs offer hunting on a daily basis while some are moving toward annual memberships. Hunting at a public club ranges from $40 to $90 per day. That price includes the use of the pit and decoys.

Hunters should have reservations in advance. Many of the clubs do not book hunters on a stand-by basis.

Hunters unable to book reservations at a club can try the public hunting areas at Rend Lake, the Crab Orchard National Wildlife Refuge, Horseshoe Lake and the Union County Refuge.

Public Hunting Areas

Finding land to hunt is more difficult than finding game for most hunters. Not so in Southern Illinois where hunters have nearly 140,000 acres of public hunting land at their disposal. Some of the land is controlled by the federal government; other areas are under the state's jurisdiction. Hunters should check site specific regulations before hunting. Note: written permission must be obtained to hunt on private land. The following areas are open to public hunting:

Bluff Lakes

Location: Union County, near Jonesboro
Phone: (618) 833-8576
Site classification: Federal land
Huntable acres: 275
Youth or controlled hunt: No
Species: Waterfowl, deer, turkey, rabbit, dove, squirrel, wood-cock, raccoon, opossum, fox, coyote
Regulations: Site specific regulations for waterfowl. Statewide regulations apply for all other species.

Calhoun Point

Location: Calhoun County, near Grafton
Phone: (618) 376-3303
Site classification: Federal land
Huntable acres: 2,300
Youth or controlled hunt: No
Species: Waterfowl, deer, turkey, squirrel, rabbit, dove, quail, woodcock, raccoon, opossum, fox, coyote
Regulations: Site specific regulations with check station or sign-in/out policy for waterfowl. Statewide regulations apply to all other species.

Campbell Pond

Location: Perry and Jackson counties
Phone: (618) 833-5175
Huntable acres: 160
Youth or controlled hunt: No
Species: Waterfowl, squirrel, deer, rabbit, dove, quail, pheasant, woodcock, raccoon, opossum, fox, coyote
Regulations: Statewide regulations for waterfowl. Statewide regulations with check station or sign-in/out policy.

Carlyle Lake

Location: RR 2, Vandalia, 62471
Phone: (618) 425-3533

Site classification: Wildlife management area

Huntable acres: 16,881

Youth or controlled hunt: No

Species: Waterfowl, turkey, deer, rabbit, dove, quail, pheasant, woodcock, raccoon, opossum, fox, coyote

Regulations: Statewide regulations for firearm deer season. Site specific waterfowl regulations with check station or sign-in/out policy. All other species subject to site specific regulations.

Crab Orchard National Wildlife Refuge

Location: Williamson County, near Carterville

Phone: (618) 997-3344

Site classification: Federal land

Huntable acres: 4,400

Youth or controlled hunt: No

Species: Waterfowl, squirrel, turkey, rabbit, dove, quail, woodcock.

Regulations: Site specific regulations with check station or sign-in/out policy for waterfowl. Site specific firearm deer season regulations. Statewide regulations apply for all other species.

Diamond/Hurricane Island

Location: Calhoun County, near Hardin

Phone: (618) 376-3303

Site classification: Wildlife management area

Huntable acres: 2,607

Youth or controlled hunt: No

Species: Waterfowl, squirrel, deer, turkey, rabbit, dove, quail, woodcock, raccoon, opossum, fox, coyote.

Regulations: Site specific regulations with check station or sign-in/out policy for waterfowl. Statewide regulations apply to all other species.

Dog Island

Location: Dixon Springs State Park, RR 2, Golconda, 62938

Phone: (618) 949-3394

Site classification: Wildlife management area

Huntable acres: 220

Youth or controlled hunt: No

Species: Waterfowl, squirrel, deer, turkey, rabbit, dove, quail, raccoon, opossum, fox, coyote

Regulations: Statewide regulations apply to all species. Check station or sign-in/out policy in effect.

Eldon Hazlet State Park

Location: Keyesport Road, Carlyle, 62231

Phone: (618) 594-3015

Huntable acres: 2,300

Youth or controlled hunt: Pheasant

Species: Waterfowl, deer, squirrel, rabbit, dove, quail, pheasant, woodcock, raccoon, opossum, fox, coyote

Regulations: Site specific pheasant permit required. Site specific regulations apply for all other species.

Ferne Clyffe State Park

Location: Box 120, Goreville, 62939

Phone: (618) 995-2411

Huntable acres: 450

Youth or controlled hunt: No

Species: Squirrel, deer, turkey, rabbit, dove, quail, pheasant, woodcock

Regulations: Site specific regulations with a check station or sign-in/out policy for squirrel. Site specific regulations for firearm deer season. Site specific permit required with check station or sign-in/out policy for spring turkey season. Statewide regulations with check station or sign-in/out policy for all other species.

Fort DeChartres
　　Location: Prairie du Rocher, 62277
　　Phone: (618) 284-7230
　　Site classification: Historic site
　　Huntable acres: 800
　　Youth or controlled hunt: No
　　Species: Waterfowl, squirrel, deer, turkey, rabbit, dove, quail, woodcock, raccoon, opossum
　　Regulations: Muzzle loaders only. Site-specific regulations for waterfowl. Statewide regulations with check-in station or sign-in/out policy.

Fort Massac
　　Location: Box 708, Metropolis, 62960
　　Phone: (618) 524-9321
　　Site classification: State park
　　Huntable acres: 984
　　Youth or controlled hunt: No
　　Species: Squirrel, deer, rabbit, dove, quail, pheasant
　　Regulations: Site specific regulations with check-in station or sign-in/out policy for squirrel and dove. Statewide regulations with check-in station or sign-in/out policy for other species.

Fuller Lake
　　Location: Calhoun County, near Hardin
　　Phone: (618) 376-3303
　　Huntable acres: 1088
　　Youth or controlled hunt: No
　　Species: Waterfowl, squirrel, deer, turkey, rabbit, quail, dove, pheasant, woodcock, raccoon, opossum, fox
　　Regulations: Site specific regulations for waterfowl. Statewide regulations apply for all other species.

Giant City State Park
　　Location: RR 1, Makanda, 62958

Phone: (618) 457-4836
Huntable acres: 1,900
Youth or controlled hunt: No
Species: Squirrel, deer, turkey, rabbit, dove, quail, woodcock.
Regulations: Check-in station or sign-in/out policy for all species. Site specific regulations apply for squirrel, rabbit, dove and quail. Statewide regulations for all other species.

Hamilton County Conservation Area
   Location: RR 4, McLeansboro, 62850
   Phone: (618) 773-4340
   Site classification: Conservation area
   Huntable acres: 1,400
   Youth or controlled hunt: No
   Species: Squirrel, deer, rabbit, dove, quail, pheasant, woodcock.
   Regulations: Check-in station or sign-in/out policy for all species. Statewide regulations apply for deer. All other species subject to site specific regulations.

Horseshoe Lake (Alexander County)
   Location: Box 77, Miller City, 62962
   Phone: (618) 776-5689
   Site classification: Conservation area
   Huntable acres: 3200
   Youth or controlled hunt: Geese
   Species: Waterfowl, squirrel, deer, rabbit, dove, quail, woodcock
   Regulations: Check-in station or sign-in/out policy for all species. Site specific waterfowl permit required. Site specific regulations apply to all other species.

Horseshoe Lake (Madison County)
   Location: P.O. Box 1307 Granite City, 62040
   Phone: (618) 931-0270
   Site classification: Conservation area
   Huntable acres: 2,000

Youth or controlled hunt: Quail and pheasant (controlled), pheasant and dove (youth)

Species: Waterfowl, rabbit, dove, quail

Regulations: Site specific regulations for all species. Check-in station or sign-in/out policy for waterfowl.

I-24

Location: Johnson County, near Vienna

Phone: (618) 995-2411

Site classification: Wildlife management area

Huntable acres: 70

Youth or controlled hunt: No

Species: Squirrel, deer, turkey, rabbit, dove, quail, woodcock, raccoon, fox, opossum

Regulations: Check station or sign-in/out policy for all species. Site specific regulations for dove. Statewide regulations apply for all other species.

Kaskaskia River

Location: RR 1, Baldwin, 62217

Phone: (618) 785-2555

Site classification: Fish and wildlife area

Huntable acres: 14,000

Youth or controlled hunt: No

Species: Waterfowl, squirrel, deer, rabbit, dove, quail, woodcock, raccoon, opossum, fox, coyote

Regulations: Site specific regulations with check station or sign-in/out policy for all species.

Kidd Lake

Location: Randolph County Conservation Area

Phone: (618) 826-2706

Site classification: State natural area

Huntable acres: 400

Youth or controlled hunt: No

Species: Waterfowl, woodcock.

Regulations: Statewide regulations with check station or sign-in/out policy.

Kinkaid Lake

Location: RR 4, Box 144, Murphysboro, 62966
Phone: (618) 684-2867
Site classification: Fish and wildlife area
Huntable acres: 4,500
Youth or controlled hunt: No
Species: Waterfowl, squirrel, deer, turkey, rabbit, dove, quail, woodcock, raccoon, opossum, fox, coyote
Regulations: Statewide regulations for waterfowl. Statewide regulations with check station or sign-in/out policy for all other species.

LaRue Swamp

Location: Union County, near Alto Pass
Phone: (618) 833-8576
Site classification: Federal land
Huntable acres: 1,000
Youth or controlled hunt: No
Species: Waterfowl, squirrel, deer, turkey, rabbit, quail, dove, woodcock, raccoon, opossum, fox, coyote.
Regulations: Site specific regulations for waterfowl and deer (firearms). Statewide regulations apply for all other species.

Little Black Slough

Location: Johnson County, near Cypress
Phone: (618) 995-2411
Site classification: State natural area
Huntable acres: 3,300
Youth or controlled hunt: No
Species: Waterfowl, squirrel, deer, rabbit, dove, quail, woodcock, raccoon, opossum, fox, coyote
Regulations: Check station or sign-in/out policy for all species.

Site specific regulations for waterfowl and coyote. Statewide regulations apply for all other species.

Lower Cache River

Location: Ferne Clyffe State Park
Phone: (618) 995-2411
Site classification: State natural area
Huntable acres: 1,200
Youth or controlled hunt: No
Species: Waterfowl, squirrel, deer, rabbit, dove, quail, pheasant, woodcock, raccoon, opossum, fox, coyote
Regulations: Check station or sign-in/out policy for all species. Waterfowl, coyote and squirrel subject to site specific regulations. Statewide regulations apply for all other species.

Mermet Lake

Location: RR 1, Belknap, 62908
Phone: (618) 524-5577
Site classification: Conservation area
Huntable acres: 1,700
Youth or controlled hunt: No
Species: Waterfowl, squirrel, deer, rabbit, dove, quail
Regulations: Check station or sign-in/out policy for all species. Statewide regulations for archery deer season and rabbit and quail. Site specific regulations apply for all other species.

Mississippi River (Pool 25)

Location: RR 1, Grafton, 62037
Phone: (618) 376-3303
Site classification: Fish and wildlife area
Huntable acres: 386
Youth or controlled hunt: No
Species: Waterfowl, squirrel, deer, turkey, raccoon, opossum, fox, coyote
Regulations: Site specific regulations for waterfowl. Statewide

regulations apply for all other species.

Mount Vernon Game Propagation Center
Location: RR 4, Game Farm Road, Mt. Vernon, 62864
Phone: (618) 242-0830
Huntable acres: 450
Youth or controlled hunt: Doves (youth)
Species: Deer (archery), doves
Regulations: Site specific regulations with check station or sign-in/out policy.

Oakwood Bottoms
Location: Jackson County near Murphysboro
Phone: (618) 687-1731
Huntable acres: 3,000
Youth or controlled hunt: No
Species: Waterfowl, squirrel, deer, turkey, rabbit, quail, woodcock, raccoon, opossum, fox, coyote
Regulations: Statewide regulations for deer and turkey. Site specific regulations apply for all other species.

Pere Marquette State Park
Location: Box 158, Grafton, 62037
Phone: (618) 786-3323
Huntable acres: 6,500
Youth or controlled hunt: No
Species: Squirrel, deer, turkey (spring)
Regulations: Statewide regulations apply for squirrel and firearms deer season. Site specific regulations for archery deer season. Site specific permit required and check station or sign-in/out policy in effect for spring turkey hunting.

Pyramid State Park
Location: RR 1, Box 115-A, Pinckneyville, 62274
Phone: (618) 357-2574

Huntable acres: 2,350
Youth or controlled hunt: No
Species: Squirrel, deer, rabbit, dove, quail, woodcock.
Regulations: Check station or sign-in/out policy for all species. Statewide regulations for deer and woodcock. Site specific regulations apply for all other species

Randolph County
    Location: RR 1, Box 345, Chester, 62233
    Phone: (618) 826-2706
    Site classification: Conservation area
    Huntable acres: 700
    Youth or controlled hunt: No
    Species: Squirrel, deer (archery), rabbit, dove, quail, woodcock, raccoon, opossum, fox, coyote.
    Regulations: Check station or sign-in/out policy applies for all species. State regulations for deer, rabbit, dove and woodcock. Site specific regulations apply for all other species

Red Hills
    Location: RR 2, Sumner, 62466
    Phone: (618) 936-2469
    Site classification: State park
    Huntable acres: 725
    Youth or controlled hunt: No
    Species: Squirrel, deer (archery), rabbit, dove, quail, pheasant, woodcock
    Regulations: Check station or sign-in/out policy for all species. Statewide regulations apply to squirrel and deer. Site specific regulations in effect for all other species

Red's Landing
    Location: Calhoun County, near Hardin
    Phone: (618) 376-3303
    Site classification: Wildlife management area
    Huntable acres: 785
    Youth or controlled hunt: No

Species: Waterfowl, squirrel, deer, turkey, rabbit, dove, quail, woodcock, raccoon, opossum, fox, coyote

Regulations: Statewide regulations apply for all species.

Rend Lake

Location: RR 4, Box 68, Benton, 62812

Phone: (618) 439-3832

Site classification: Fish and wildlife area

Huntable acres: 6,734

Youth or controlled hunt: No

Species: Waterfowl, squirrel, deer, rabbit, dove, quail, pheasant, woodcock, raccoon, opossum, fox, coyote

Regulations: Site specific regulations with check station or sign-in/out policy for waterfowl. Statewide regulations apply to all other species.

Richland County

Location: Richland County, near Olney

Phone: (618) 393-6732

Site classification: Conservation area

Huntable acres: 3,867

Youth or controlled hunt: Pheasant (youth and controlled)

Species: Pheasant

Regulations: Site specific regulations with check station or sign-in/out policy.

Riprap Landing

Location: Calhoun County, near Mozier

Phone: (618) 376-3303

Site classification: Wildlife management area

Huntable acres: 1,232

Youth or controlled hunt: No

Species: Waterfowl, deer, squirrel, turkey, rabbit, dove, quail, pheasant, woodcock, raccoon, opossum, fox, coyote.

Regulations: Site specific regulations in effect for waterfowl. Statewide regulations apply for all other species.

Saline County Conservation Area
    Location: RR 1, Box 30, Equality, 62934
    Phone: (618) 276-4405
    Site classification: Fish and wildlife area
    Huntable acres: 900
    Youth or controlled hunt: No
    Species: Waterfowl, squirrel, deer, turkey, rabbit, dove, quail, pheasant, raccoon, opossum, fox, coyote
    Regulations: Check station or sign-in/out policy for all species. Statewide regulations for deer and turkey. Site specific regulations apply to all other species.

Sam Dale Lake
    Location: RR 1, Johnsonville, 62850
    Phone: (618) 825-2292
    Site classification: Conservation area
    Huntable acres: 930
    Youth or controlled hunt: No
    Species: Squirrel, deer (archery), rabbit, dove, quail, pheasant, woodcock
    Regulations: Check station or sign-in/out policy for all species. Statewide regulations in effect for deer. Site specific regulations apply for all other species.

Sam Parr State Park
    Location: RR 5, Box 220, Newton, 62448
    Phone: (618) 783-2661
    Site classification: State park
    Huntable acres: 704
    Youth or controlled hunt: Dove (youth)
    Species: Squirrel, deer (archery), rabbit, dove, quail, pheasant, woodcock
    Regulations: Check station or sign-in/out policy for all species. Statewide regulations for deer. Site specific regulations apply to all other species.

Shawnee National Forest
>   **Location**: Jackson, Union, Alexander, Johnson, Williamson, Massac, Pope, Hardin, Gallatin and Saline counties
>   **Phone**: (618) 253-7114
>   **Site classification**: Federal land
>   **Huntable acres**: 26,200
>   **Youth or controlled hunt**: No
>   **Species**: Waterfowl, squirrel, deer, turkey, rabbit, dove, quail, woodcock, raccoon, opossum, fox, coyote
>   **Regulations**: Site specific regulations for waterfowl. Statewide regulations apply for all other species.

Stephen A. Forbes State Park
>   **Location**: RR 1, Kinmundy, 62854
>   **Phone**: (618) 547-3381
>   **Site classification**: State park
>   **Huntable acres**: 2,300
>   **Youth or controlled hunt**: Dove (youth)
>   **Species**: Waterfowl, squirrel, deer (archery), rabbit, dove, quail, pheasant, woodcock, raccoon, opossum, fox, coyote
>   **Regulations**: Check station or sign-in/out policy for all species. Site specific permits required for raccoon, opossum, fox and coyote. Statewide regulations for deer and woodcock. Site specific regulations apply for all other species.

Ten Mile Creek
>   **Location**: RR 1, Box 179, McLeansboro, 62859
>   **Phone**: (618) 643-2862
>   **Site classification**: Fish and wildlife area
>   **Huntable acres**: 5,800
>   **Youth or controlled hunt**: No
>   **Species**: Waterfowl, squirrel, deer, rabbit, dove, quail, pheasant, woodcock, raccoon, opossum, fox, coyote.
>   **Regulations**: Site specific permit required for all species.

Trail of Tears State Forest
    Location: RR 1, Box 182, Jonesboro, 62952
    Phone: (618) 833-6125
    Site classification: State forest
    Huntable acres: 4,665
    Youth or controlled hunt: No
    Species: Squirrel, deer, turkey, rabbit, dove, quail, woodcock, raccoon, opossum, fox, coyote
    Regulations: Check station or sign-in/out policy for all species other than raccoon, opossum, fox and coyote. Site specific permits required for raccoon, opossum, fox and coyote. Statewide regulations apply for all other species.

Turkey Bluffs
    Location: RR 1, Box 345, Chester, 62233
    Phone: (618) 826-2706
    Site classification: Fish and wildlife area
    Huntable acres: 2,250
    Youth or controlled hunt: No
    Species: Waterfowl, deer, squirrel, turkey, rabbit, dove, quail, woodcock, pheasant, raccoon, opossum, fox, coyote.
    Regulations: Check station or sign-in/out policy for all species. Statewide regulations for waterfowl, turkey, deer, squirrel, rabbit, quail, and woodcock. Site specific regulations apply for all other species.

Union County Conservation Area
    Location: RR 2, Box 181-A, Jonesboro, 62952
    Phone: (618) 833-5175
    Site classification: Conservation area
    Huntable acres: 2,400
    Youth or controlled hunt: Geese (youth and controlled)
    Species: Waterfowl, squirrel, deer, turkey, dove
    Regulations: Statewide regulations for turkey. Check-station or sign-in/out policy for all other species. Site specific permit required for waterfowl. Site specific regulations apply to all other species.

Washington County Conservation Area
> **Location**: RR 3, Nashville, 62263
> **Phone**: (618) 327-3137
> **Site classification**: Conservation area
> **Huntable acres**: 750
> **Youth or controlled hunt**: Quail, pheasant, rabbit (controlled)
> **Species**: Squirrel, deer (archery), rabbit, dove, quail, pheasant, woodcock, raccoon, opossum, fox, coyote
> **Regulations**: Site specific regulations and check station or sign-in/out policy for all species. Site specific permits required for pheasant and quail.

Wayne Fitzgerrell State Park
> **Location**: RR 4, Box 68, Benton, 62812
> **Phone**: (618) 279-3110
> **Site classification**: State park
> **Huntable acres**: 1,200
> **Youth or controlled hunt**: Pheasant (controlled)
> **Species**: Deer, dove, pheasant
> **Regulations**: Check station or sign-in/out policy for all species. Site specific permit required for pheasant. Site specific regulations for dove and deer.

Wildcat Hollow
> **Location**: Stephen A. Forbes State Park
> **Phone**: (618) 547-3381
> **Site classification**: Wildlife management area
> **Huntable acres**: 320
> **Youth or controlled hunt**: No
> **Species**: Squirrel, deer (archery), rabbit, dove, quail, pheasant, woodcock, raccoon, opossum, fox, coyote
> **Regulations**: Statewide regulations for all species.

Goose Hunting Clubs

Club Name	Contact person	Phone
		(618 area code unless specified)

Alexander County

B&M, Dan Maronie 776-5561
Benchmark Farms Inc., Fred McRoy Jr. 734-0648
Bend-View Farms, Charles Bonifield 776-5505
Billings Hunting Club, Darold D. Billings 776-5649
Blakemore Hunting Clubs, Frank Blakemore 776-5233
C&S, Ed Caul 776-5438
Nate Burnett Club, Nate Burnett ....(314) 683-2666
Doug's Hunting Club, Douglas Miller, ...(314) 264-2442
Gene Pecord Hunting Clubs, Orval E. Pecord 776-5626
Grace Hunting Club, Ken Masterson 776-5798
Guns & Feathers, Brent Bauer 254-4938
Horseshoe Farms Hunting Club, Greg Patton 776-5531
John Blakemore Hunting Club, John Blakemore 776-5458
Lakeside Hunting Club, Gene Fore 776-5401
Low & Slow Hunting Club, Robert Mueth 566-7571
M&H, Bob Hall 776-5438
Marlin Hunting Club, Gerald and Jerry Clutts 776-5870
McGaughey Construction, Rick McGaughey 776-5438
Miller Brothers, Jack Collins..776-5816
Muddy Bottoms, Kenneth Farris 776-5486
Mueth Hunting Club #1, Robert Mueth 566-7571
Mueth Hunting Club #2, Troy Sauerhage 566-4253
Oakwood Hunting Club, Karl K. Fraley ....776-5566 or 684-4217
Patton Hunt Club, Greg Patto 776-5570
Pecord & Volner Hunting Club, Milton A. Pecord 776-5125
River Road Hunting Club, Darold Billings 776-5649
Royal Dicks Hunting Club, James Tiemann.................................... 259-7138
Southside Hunting Club, William Crowell ....(314) 471-2867
Sunset Club, Peggy Shipley 776-5813
TCT, John Gernidus 776-5438
Whistling Wings Hunting Club, James Farley 524-7002
Whitaker Hunting Club, Darold Billings ....776-5649 or 776-5573
Williams Hunting Club, Charles Williams 776-5905
Willis Hunting Club, Chesley K. Willis 776-5551
Willis and Oehler, David C. Willis 776-5535
Worthington Hunting Club, C.J. Worthington 776-5333
Grandpa's Outfitters, Anthony DeLaRosa ....(314) 471-3887

Union County
B & C Hunting Club, Steve Tuma 833-2013
Brown's Hunting Club, Carlos L. Brown 833-2096
Clear Creek Club, James Pickel 833-5989
DBJ, Bart Carr ....(314) 334-9131
Davis Farms Hunting Club, Bill Davis 833-2506
Double C Hunting Club, Leven Cox ....(314) 471-9366
Grassy Lake, Collin Cain 833-7890
K&V Hunting Club, James Keistler 833-3264
Lloyd's North Gate Flyway, Lloyd Arras 281-4373
Lyerla Lake Farm, Irwin E. Fuchs 833-5900
Run-N-Lake, Luella Morgan 833-2679
Shawnee Farms Duck Club, Lee Roy Rendleman 833-4613
Skydusters, Roger Von Bokel 233-4088
Stains, Vick Eck 833-4269
Flyway Clubs & Wolf Lake Hunting Club, Kerry Glasco 833-3377
Wild Wings Hunting Club, Terry Taylor ....(314) 335-0838

Williamson and Jackson Counties
Carl Benson ....(314) 231-1575 Ext. 3232
Leon Berg 942-5687
Big Muddy Refuge, Bruce Jones 596-2931
Bob's Hunt Club, Robert Williams 684-2219
Burns Goose Club, Tom Burns 964-1806
Bush Hunting Club, Paul Bush 964-1142
Canadian Flyway Goose Club, Robby Wessel 243-5205
Country Kitchen Hunting Club, Alfred Fluck 997-2697
Crab Orchard Lake Campground, Richard Pearson 985-4983
Creekpaum's Goose Club, Neal Creekpaum 996-2076
D-J Goose Club, Richard Dempsey ....(708) 789-0071
D & M, Mark Schaede 993-8914
DRC Hunt Club, David Campbell ....(314) 889-0106
Dan's Hunting Club, Daniel Quirey ....(812) 423-5228
Don Hagan Goose Club, Donald Hagan 475-3653
Equality Hunting Club, Bobby Simpson 253-8585
Everdave's, David McBride 457-6808
Ferrell's Hunting Club, Laverne L. Ferrell 985-4561
Fox Ridge Goose Club, Dave Neuner 233-4424
Gander's Landing Hunting Club, Randy Stierley ....(812) 783-1078
Dennis Glisson 669-2643
Grafton Hunting Club, Duey Skinner 964-1335
Grassy Knob Hunting Club, Franklin Petersohn ....(812) 425-4518
Gray Feather Hunting Club, Cabell Williams Jr. ....(812) 425-7152
Green Acres Goose Club, Lewis Fosse 997-6139
Gunner Goose Club, Frank Baird 667-0193
Happy Hollow, Fred D. Nolen 457-7611

Rick Herren 964-1881
Honker Farms, Gary Lukuc 244-4770
Honker Hill, Don R. Lucas 932-3322
Honkers' Corner Goose Club, Larry Bonifield 985-6542
Honker's Haven, Charles Heyde 997-4457
Honker's Knob, Morris Dabb 498-5378
J&N Hunting, Jon Hilty ....(309) 928-9295
Jake and Norb's Gun Club, Pete Harry ....(812) 838-5732
Just Good Friends Hunting Club, John Hooker ......(217) 785-9080
Ken's Goose Club, Kenneth J. Samuel 985-2484
L & D Goose Hunting Club, Glenn R. Lancaster 997-6119
Leland's Wolf Creek Hunt, Paul M. Leland 964-1680
M&B, Mark Bayer 244-2438
Mackey Bend, Steven Hahn ....(812) 422-8122
Mac's Club, Edward Hamlin 259-4900
McVicker Goose Club, James McVicker 942-4242
North Winds Goose Club, James Henrekin ....(815) 438-3798
Old Orchard Club, Ltd., Caroline Keene 985-2261
Osman Hunt Club, Ronald Osman 827-3547
Pat's Hunting Club, David E. Comp 985-4676
Pike's Hunting Club, Terry Pike 997-1124
David Pittman 457-6714
Pop's Hunting Club, Tony Zedolck 877-2458
Roach Goose Club II, Ron Reeder 687-4051
Robinson's Goose Club, James Robinson 964-1893
Edward B. Sasse 457-7249
Snider's, George Stout 658-8842
South Market Hunting Club, Dennis Vahle 234-5001
Southern Valley Hunting Club #1, Ronald W. Tinges 964-1133
Southern Valley Hunting Club # 2, Donald Portell 654-4426
Southern Valley Hunting Club #3, Jerry Brosam 964-1133
Steve's Hunting Club, Steven Morris 985-6946
Supergan's Hunting Club, Frank V. Supergan 964-1136
Timberline Hunting Club, Steve Hahn ....(812) 422-8122
Tim's 40, John Sytsma 457-7827
W-H Goose Club, Delbert L. Webb 259-0668
Young's Hunting Club, Brett Young 985-2274

Private Hunting Preserves

For hunters who do not wish to hunt public land or have no access to private land, there is a third possibility–hunting preserves. Hunting preserves are licensed areas that offer hunting from Sept. 1 to April 15, some are open year-around, for pheasants, quail, chukar, partridge, mallards or even wild turkeys. Preserves are open to the public on a daily fee or annual membership basis. Most of the hunting preserves offer experienced guides and trained dogs.

Calhoun Hunting Club

Owner: Jerry Corbett
Location: French St, Hardin
Phone: (618) 576-2221
Game: Pheasant, quail, mallards

Elm Shade Farm

Owner: Adolph Hitzemann
Location: Rt. 2, Red Bud
Phone: (618) 282-2492
Game: Pheasant, quail, chukar

Feather Hill Preserve

Owner: Kenneth and Janice
  Wiseman
Location: Rt. 3, Metropolis
Phone: (618) 524-5463
Game: Pheasant, quail

Frisco Game Preserve

Owner: Norris Webb
Location: Rt. 1, Ewing
Phone: (618) 629-2527
Game: Pheasant, quail, chukar

Grizzle's Game Birds

Owner: Terry C. Grizzle
Location: Rt. 2, Brighton
Phone: (618) 372-8672
Game: Pheasant, quail,
  chukar

Heggemeier Hunting Club

Owner: Robert and David
  Heggemeier
Location: Rt. 2, Nashville
Phone: (618) 327-3709
Game: Pheasant, quail,
  turkey, mallards, chukar

Knights Prairie Hunt Club

Owner: Jerry MacKenzie
Location: Rt. 1, Box 142,
  McLeansboro
Phone: (618) 736-2390
Game: Pheasant, quail

Land O'Sports Ranch Unlimited

Owner: John Schwarz
Location: Rt. 1, Box 140, Smithboro
Phone: (618) 326-7196
Game: Pheasant, quail, chukar

Otter Creek Hunt Club

Owner: Mike Runge
Location: Rt. 3, Box 124 AB, Jerseyville
Phone: (618) 376-7601 or 498-6791
Game: Pheasant, quail, chukar, turkey

Shady Rest, The

Owner: Curtis O'Dell
Location: Box 101, Cave-In-Rock
Phone: (618) 289-4323
Game: Pheasant, quail, chukar, turkey

Streamline Hunt Club

Owner: Ronald K. Doering
Location: Rt. 1, Box 204, Percy
Phone: (618) 497-2526
Game: Pheasant, quail, chukar, turkey

Southern Illinois Sporting Clays

Owner: Bill and Sharon Mandrell
Location: Rt. 1, Box 175 AA, Thompsonville
Phone: (618) 982-2906
Game: Pheasant, quail, chukar

Trail of Tears Sportsman's Club

Owner: Debra Charles
Location: Rt. 1, Old Cape Rd., Jonesboro
Phone: (618) 833-8697
Game: Pheasant, quail, chukar, turkey

Wild Acres Quail Preserve

Owner: Orba Blades
Location: Rt. 1, Box 68, Thompsonville
Phone: (618) 937-1548
Game: Quail

World Class Shooting Preserve

Owner: James R. Moore
Location: Rt. 1, Box 448, Johnston City
Phone: (618) 983-8758
Game: Pheasant, chukar, quail

Shooting Ranges

The outstanding hunting in Southern Illinois has spawned satellite recreational centers such as 3-D archery ranges, indoor archery ranges and indoor shooting ranges. The following facilities are open to sportsmen:

Crossroads Sporting Goods

Owner: Mike and Greg Simmons
Location: New Rt. 13, south frontage road, Carterville
Phone: (618) 985-2058
Facilities: Indoor pistol and .22 rifle range

Doug's Sport Shop

Owner: Doug Hollenkamp
Location: Rt. 50 west, Carlyle
Phone: (618) 594-3737
Facilities: Indoor range, dart target video system.

Dunn's Sporting Goods

Owner: Dennis Dunn
Location: 1904 W. Rendleman, Marion
Phone: (618) 997-3626
Facilities: Indoor range.

Ferrell's Sporting Clays

Owner: Laverne Ferrell
Location: About a mile and a half south and east of Carterville
Phone: (618) 985-4561
Facilities: Five-station sporting clays

Hill's Archery

Owner: Les and Bonnie Hill
Location: 2.5 miles south of Steeleville on Rock Castle Creek Road
Phone: (618) 965-3665
Facilities: 3-D range.

Lusch's Archery

Owner: Randy Lusch
Location: 3201 Bryant Ln. Salem
Phone: (618) 548-3300
Facilities: 3-D range, video range, and 12 indoor lanes

Mike's Archery

Owner: Mike Kottkamp
Location: 203 East Croan, St. Irvington
Phone: (618) 249-6641
Facilities: Indoor range.

Pine Tree Archery

Owner: Mike and Pam Collins
Location: Just north of Carterville
Phone: (618) 985-3238
Facilities: Indoor range and 3-D course.

Pawn and Gun\The Firing Line

Owner: David Dennison and Corey Partridge
Location: Rt. 45 N, Harrisburg
Phone: (618) 253-5300
Facilities: Indoor archery range, indoor pistol range, indoor rifle range, dart target video system.

Shawnee Marketing

Owner: Ken and Nina Hall
Location: On Glendale gravel road off Illinois 145
Phone: (618) 695-3333
Facilities: Pro shop and an indoor range

Southern Illinois Sporting Clays

Owner: Bill and Sharon Mandrell
Location: Rt. 1, Box 175 AA, Thompsonville

Phone: (618) 982-2906
Facilities: Walk-through sporting clays

Town Hall Archery

Owner: Jack, Dian, Monty and Scott Hoffarth
Location: 1991 South 59th, St., Belleville
Phone: (618) 235-9881
Facilities: 32 indoor lanes, 3-D shooting.

Whispering Pines

Owner: Rick Sharp and Dale Russell
Location: Off I-57, exit 36 near Lick Creek
Phone: (618) 833-6342
Facilities: 3-D range

I had never met Gus Lorenz, George Brand, Dick Helwig or Sergio Meilman before last Thursday. When I left them at about noon Friday, I felt like old friends.

I met these guys at a deer camp at Carol Mullins' farm in Pope County. I really didn't have much in common with any of them.

Gus, George and Dick are neighbors in Chicago. They have been friends for years. George and Dick have been coming to Pope County to hunt together for nearly 30 years.

Les Winkeler
Sports writer

The Southern Illinoisan, Nov. 21, 1991

These guys are from a different generation. They grew up in the city. The experiences that shaped their lives are radically different than the circumstances I have known.

Sergio fits outside this group. He met the rest of the guys through hunting at Carol's deer camp.

Although Sergio is roughly my age (probably younger, but I've never bothered to ask), he and I have radically different tastes.

That was evident by the diverse discussions we had, ranging from favorite movies to book reviews.

Imagine that–a bunch of supposed testosterone-crazed guys about to embark on a killing expedition talking about movies and books.

This has to be about (anti-hunting and anti-male contingents can cringe here) male bonding.

I realize male bonding, and indeed anything positive about males is unpopular these days, so I'm not going to get all syrupy and philosophical about what a beautiful experience the deer camp was, but I will tell you I had a good time.

Most of my friends know me as a person who rarely shuts up.

However, I can be quite reserved among strangers. I can't explain it. Maybe it's a lack of confidence.

Anyway, I didn't have long to worry about the psychological ramifications of the fear of interpersonal communications with strangers because after just a few minutes everybody was friends.

I'm not exactly sure how that happened.

Gus and George were the first two guys I met.

Obviously old friends, they could barely speak without cross-referencing stories for one another. When they weren't helping each other fill in the gaps in their stories, they were slinging barbs back and forth.

These were my kind of guys.

My wife has never understood my relationship with my closest friends. In reality, I guess I don't really understand it either, but we are happiest when we are ripping each other apart.

One of the pseudo-psychologists at the office said it's because males are taught to suppress their emotions. By using insults, men can express and mask their emotions at the same time.

I'm not smart enough to argue with that, so I'll buy it.

At any rate, these guys made me feel right at home.

They sat and argued about nearly anything that was of mutual interest–hunting, movies, politics and religion.

George was the object of derision because he has the nerve to bet against the Chicago Bears.

The others delighted in the story of George's harrowing opossum experience the night before. Mullins has a pet opossum named Hang Ten. He is still a baby, about the size of a rat.

Opossums are shy, so Hang Ten didn't show his face, and Mullins forgot to tell her guests about him. George woke up the entire house when Hang Ten crawled across his face at about 2 a.m.

Fortunately, neither was hurt.

Through it all, you get the feeling that they make the annual journey to Pope County to enjoy each other's company. The success of the hunting trip does not hinge on bringing home some venison.

Golfing

Sixteenth hole at Crab Orchard Golf Club

The golf boom that has been sweeping the nation the past few years has not ignored Southern Illinois. The landscape is dotted with established public and private courses and at least two new 18-hole public courses are scheduled to be open soon. The Governor's Run Country Club is scheduled to open in 1994. This new 18-hole championship course will be located on the shores of Carlyle Lake. Construction began in the spring of 1993. Carbondale opened an 18-hole course, Hickory Ridge, in the summer of 1993. Cedar Oaks Golf Course is an 18-hole course that is under construction near Vienna, at the intersection of I-24 and Illinois 146. Developers hope to have the first nine holes of the public course ready for play in 1994. Visitors to the area should have no problem getting a tee time at any of the area's public and semi-private courses.

The quality of the courses should be a pleasant surprise to most visitors. "They're getting better than ever," said Bob Tierney, 1993 president of the Southern Illinois Golf Association. "There are a half-dozen courses, in the last 10 years, that have improved their facilities. It's just amazing." Rend Lake Golf Club is annually recognized by major golf publications as one of the top public courses in the Midwest. Tierney also cited Jackson Country Club, Crab Orchard Golf Club, Green Hills Country Club and Greenview Golf Course as some of the premiere courses in the area. "These are all 18-hole courses. "There aren't any courses in the cities that do it any better," he said. "It seems people are putting more money into their courses. People realize that there is some competition for the golfing dollar." In addition, there are plenty of nine-hole facilities. Tierney said starter courses such as Green Acres and Midland Hills are good for beginners. Most courses in the area require tee times for weekend play. Call to check each course's policy. Cart prices are for two people sharing one cart, unless otherwise noted.

A locator map showing Southern Illinois golf courses and a listing providing basic information about them follows.

Golf Course Locator Map

1 ....Rolling Hills Golf Club	39 ....Salem Country Club
2............................Alton Municipal	40 ....Colonial Golf Club
3 ....Cloverleaf Golf Course	41 ....Meadow Woods Golf Club
4......Spencer T. Olin Golf Course	42..............Greenview Golf Course
5 ....Rock Springs	43...........Green Hills Country Club
6 ....Belk Park Golf Course	44 ....Homestead Golf Course
7 ....Fox Creek Golf Course	45.............Indian Hills Golf Course
8 ....Sunset Hills Country Club	46.......North County Country Club
9 ....Lake James Golf Course	47 ....Sparta Country Club
10 ....Oak Brook Golf Club	48 ....Chester Country Club
11 .....St. Catherine's Golf Course	49 .Southwestern Lakes Golf Club
12 ....Legacy Golf Course	50 ....Jackson Country Club
13................Arlington Golf Course	51.........Midland Hills Golf Course
14. ....Fairmont Golf Course	52 .....Union County Country Club
15.........Grand Marais Golf Course	53 ....Egyptian Country Club
16. ....Tamarack Country Club	54..............Rend Lake Golf Course
17 ....Locust Hills Golf Course	55 ....Benton Country Club
18 ....St. Clair Country Club	56 ..Franklin County Country Club
19 ....Triple Lakes Golf Course	57 ....Green Acres Golf Club
20 ....Elmwood Golf Club	58 ....Crab Orchard Golf Club
21 ....Clinton Hills Golf Course	59..Stardust
22 ....Westhaven Golf Course	60.......................Fairway Golf Club
23 ....The Orchards	61 ......Lake of Egypt Country Club
24 ....Jefferson Barracks G. C.	62.......................St. Elmo Golf Club
25 ....Columbia Golf Club	63 ....Effingham Country Club
26 ....Waterloo Country Club	64.... Jasper County Country Club
27 ....Annbriar	65 ....Richland Country Club
28........Ridge Golf & Country Club	66 ....East Fork Par 3
29 ....Yorktown Par 3	67 ......Lawrence Co. Country Club
30 ......Cardinal Creek Golf Course	68.....................Flora Country Club
31 ....Greenville Country Club	69...............Fairfield Country Club
32 ....Highland Country Club	70 ...Mt. Carmel Muni. Golf Course
33 ....Twin Oaks Golf Course	71 ....McLeansboro Golf Club
34 ....Carlyle Lake Golf Club	72 ....Carmi Country Club
35......Bent Oak Muni. Golf Course	73 Saline Co. Golf & Country Club
36 ....Okawville Golf Course	74 .....Shawnee Hills Country Club
37......Nashville Muni. Golf Course	75 ....Hardin County Golf Club
38 ....Vandalia Country Club	76 ....Metropolis Country Club

❶ *Rolling Hills Golf Club*

Location: 5801 Pierce Lane, Godfrey.
Phone: (618) 466-8363
Membership: Public
Distance: 5,718 yards, par 71
Fees: Weekdays $12 for 18 holes. Weekends $14 for 18 holes. Cart rental $9 per person for 18 holes. Driving range: $2.50.
PGA pro: Todd Cress

❷ *Alton Municipal*

Location: Homer Adams Parkway, midtown Alton, next to the Ramada Inn.
Phone: (618) 465-9861.
Membership: Public
Distance: 3,003 yards, par 35
Fees: $7 weekdays, $8 weekends. Cart rental, $8.

❸ *Cloverleaf Golf Course*

Location: Near Alton, on Fosterburg Road, a mile north of Illinois 140.
Phone: (618) 462-3022
Membership: Public
Distance: 5,514 yards, par 70
Fees: Weekdays, $6.50 nine holes, $11 for 18; Weekends, $7.50 for nine holes, $12.50 for 18 holes.
PGA pro: Michael Graner

❹ *Spencer T. Olin Community Golf Course*

The Spencer T. Olin Community Golf Course was selected as the

No. 1 public golf course in 1991, 1992 and 1993 by both the St. Louis Post Dispatch and Golf Scene magazine. The course was also selected as one of the top 50 public golf courses in America by USA Today.

Location: 4701 College Ave. (Illinois 140), Alton.
Phone: (618) 465-3111
Membership: Public
Distance: 6,941 yards, par 72
Fees: Weekday $36 for 18 holes, includes cart. Weekends, $42 including cart. Driving range, $3.
PGA pro: Jon DePriest.

5   ## *Rock Springs Golf Course*

Location: Rock Springs Park, Alton.
Phone: (618) 465-9898
Membership: Public
Distance: 3,052 yards, par 35
Fees: Weekdays, city residents of Alton $5 for nine holes, non-resident $6.50. Weekends, $6 for residents and $7 for non-residents.

6   ## *Belk Park Golf Course*

Location: 880 Belk Park Road, Wood River,
Phone: (618) 251-3115
Membership: Public
Distance: 6,741 yards, par 72
Fees: Weekdays $12 for nine holes, $17 for 18 holes. Weekends $13 for nine holes, $19 for 18 holes. Cart rental $10 for nine holes and $18 for 18 holes. Driving range: $1.
PGA pro: Mark Marcuzzo

❼ ## *Fox Creek Golf Club*

Location: Near Edwardsville, about seven miles north of I-270 on Illinois 159.
Phone: (618) 692-9400
Membership: Semi-private
Distance: 6,987 yards, par 72
Fees: Weekdays $25 for 18 holes, Weekends $29 for 18 holes, includes cart. Driving range: $3.
PGA pro: Mike Walsh

❽ ## *Sunset Hills Country Club*

Location: Just off I-270 near Edwardsville.
Phone: (618) 656-8088
Membership: Private
Distance: 6,725 yards, par 72
Fees: Public must play with members. Weekdays $27, weekends $32.
PGA pro: Victor Whipp

❾ ## *Lake James Golf Course*

Location: Near Edwardsville, off Illinois 140, left on St. James Drive for 2.5 miles.
Phone: (618) 656-4653
Membership: Public
Distance: 5,937 yards, par 72
Fees: Weekdays, $5.50 nine holes, $10 for 18 holes. Weekends, $7 for nine holes, $13.50 for 18 holes. Cart: $3.50

⑩ ## *Oak Brook Golf Club*

Location: Near Edwardsville, one fourth mile east of Illinois 4 on Fruit Road.
Phone: (618) 656-5600
Membership: Public
Distance: 6,250 yards, par 71
Fees: Weekdays, $6 for nine holes, $11 for 18 holes, Weekends, $7 for nine holes. $13 for 18. Carts $8 for nine holes. Driving range: $1.50.
PGA pro: Larry Suhre

⑪ ## *St. Catherine's Golf Course*

Location: North of Edwardsville on Illinois 157.
Phone: (618) 656-4224
Membership: Public
Distance: 2,811 yards, par 35
Fees: Weekdays $5.50 for nine holes, $9 for 18 holes. Retirees and teenagers have discount. Cart rental $8 per nine holes.

⑫ ## *Legacy Golf Course*

Location: 3500 Cargil, Granite City.
Phone: (618) 931-4653
Membership: Public
Distance: 6,327 yards, par 71
Fees: Weekdays, $9 for nine holes, $17 for 18 holes. Weekends, $12 for nine holes, $20 for 18 holes. Cart rental: $4 per person for nine holes, $8 per person for 18 holes. Driving range: $2.50 and $4.

⑬ *Arlington Golf Course*

Location: Between Illinois 111 and Illinois 157, off Horseshoe
Lake Road.
Phone: (618) 931-5232
Membership: Semi-private
Distance: 7,000 yards, par 72
Fees: Mon., Wed., Fri., $14; Tues. and Thur., $12;
Weekends, $22 all day. Driving range: $3.

⑭ *Fairmont Golf Course*

Location: 4000 Collinsville Road, Fairmont City.
Phone: (618) 874-9554
Membership: Public
Distance: 2,248 yards, par 33
Fees: Weekdays, $4 for nine holes, $6 for 18 holes.
Weekends and holidays, $5 for nine holes, $8
for 18 holes. Driving range: $3, $2.

⑮ *Grand Marais Golf Course*

Location: From I-64, take Illinois 111 south until the road ends,
then turn right.
Phone: (618) 398-9999
Membership: Public
Distance: 18 holes, 6,506 yards, par 72
Fees: Weekdays, $7 for 9 holes, $12 for 18. Weekends and
holidays, $8 for nine holes, $13 for 18. Carts:
$7.50 for 9 holes during the week, $8 per nine
holes on weekends and holidays.

⑯ *Tamarack Country Club*

Location: Near O'Fallon. From I-64, exit at U.S. 50 north, then
turn right on South Lincoln Road.

Phone: (618) 632-6666
Membership: Public
Distance: 18 holes, 6,450 yards, par 71
Fees: Weekdays, $8 for nine holes, $12 for 18 holes.
                Weekends and holidays, $10 for nine holes,
                $15 for 18. Carts: $8 per nine holes, $16 for
                18 holes. Driving range: $1.50

⓱ *Locust Hills Golf Course*

Location: Half-mile west of the town square in Lebanon.
Phone: (618) 537-4590
Membership: Public
Distance: 6,500 yards, par 71
Fees: Weekdays, $7 for nine holes, $12 for 18 holes. ($6
                and $10 for college students and senior citi-
                zens.) Weekends and holidays, $9 for nine
                holes, $15 for 18 holes. Carts: $9 per nine
                holes, $16 for 18 holes.

⓲ *St. Clair Country Club*

Location: From I-64, go south on Illinois 157, then left at Foley
                Drive, Belleville.
Phone: (618) 398-3402
Membership: Private
Distance: 6,536 yards, par 71

⓳ *Triple Lakes Golf Course*

Location: Between Columbia and Millstadt. From Illinois 3,
                take Illinois 158 east, then turn left at the
                Farmers Inn.
Phone: (618) 476-9985
Membership: Public
Distance: 6,227 yards, par 72

Fees: Weekdays, $6.50 for nine holes, $9.50 for 18 holes.
                   Weekends and holidays, $13 for 18 holes.
                   Carts: $9 for nine holes, $16 for 18 holes.

20   # *Elmwood Golf Club*

Location: West of Illinois 13 at 1400 Eiler Road, Belleville.
Phone: (618) 538-5826
Membership: Public
Distance: 3,030 yards, par 36
Fees: Weekdays, $6.50 for nine holes, $10 for 18.
                   Weekends and holidays, $8 for nine holes,
                   $11.50 for 18. Carts: $7 per nine holes.
PGA pro: Joseph Idoux

21   # *Clinton Hills Golf Course*

Location: 3700 Old Collinsville Road, Belleville
Phone: (618) 277-3700
Membership: Public
Distance: 6,600 yards, par 71
Fees: Weekdays, $9 for 9 holes, $13 for 18. Weekends and
                   holidays, $12 for 9 holes, $16 for 18. Carts:
                   $9 per nine holes. Driving range: $2.

22   # *Westhaven Golf Course*

Location: One half-mile south of Belleville on Illinois 159.
Phone: (618) 233-9536
Membership: Public
Distance: 2,986 yards, par 35
Fees: Weekdays, $6.50 for 9 holes, $11 for 18 holes.
                   Weekends and holidays, $7.50 for 9 holes,
                   $12 for 18. Carts: $8 per nine holes.

㉓ # *The Orchards*

Location: Three miles east of Belleville on Illinois Route 15, then left on Greenmount Road
Phone: (618) 233-8921
Membership: Semi-private
Distance: 6,405 yards, par 71
Fees: Weekdays, $16 for nine holes, $26 for 18 holes before noon (mandatory cart is included); $8 for nine holes, $16 for 18 holes after noon with no cart. Weekends and holidays, $13 for nine holes, $25 for 18 holes before noon (mandatory cart is included); $13 for 9 holes, $25 for 18 holes after noon with no cart. Driving range: $2, $3, $5.
PGA pro: Bill Bals

㉔ # *Jefferson Barracks Golf Course*

Location: Half-mile southeast of I-255 near Columbia.
Phone: (618) 281-5400
Membership: Public
Distance: 3,090 yards, par 36
Fees: Weekdays, $8 for nine holes, $14 for all day; $6 for senior citizens, $10 all day. Weekends, $10 for nine holes and $16 for 18 holes. Carts: $4 per person per nine holes. Driving range: $2.

㉕ # *Columbia Golf Club*

Location: One mile north of Columbia on Illinois 3.
Phone: (618) 286-9653
Membership: Public
Distance: 5,980 yards, par 71. An additional nine holes are under construction.

Fees: Weekdays, $9.50 for 9 holes, $14 for 18 holes. Weekends and holidays, $12 for nine holes, $18.50 for 18 holes. Senior citizens, $10.50 for 18 holes through the week. Carts: $5 per person for nine holes, $9 per person for 18 holes.

PGA pro: Bob Furkin

26 *Waterloo Country Club*

Location: North edge of Waterloo.
Phone: (618) 939-6311
Membership: Private
Distance: Nine holes
Fees: Weekdays, $10 all day. Weekends and holidays, $12

27 *Annbriar*

Location: Near Waterloo on Illinois 3, 9.4 miles south of I-255, turn right on HH road, 2.1 miles east on HH, then turn left 400 yards.
Phone: (618) 939-4653
Membership: Public
Distance: 6,841 yards, par 72
Fees: Summer rates $34 weekdays, $38 weekends, including cart. Driving range: $3.
PGA pro: Jon Lark

28 *Ridge Golf & Country Club*

Location: Near Waterloo, 1.5 miles east of Illinois 3 on Hamacher Road.
Phone: (618) 939-4646.
Membership: Semi-private
Distance: 3,200 yards, par 36
Fees: Weekdays, $8 for nine holes, $10 for 18. Cart: $8 per

nine holes. Weekends, $15 for nine holes, $23
for 18 holes, cart included. Driving range: $2,
$3 and $4.

PGA pro: Kevin Triefenbach

㉙ *Yorktown Par 3*

Location: From I- 64, take U.S. 50 exit at O'Fallon, go south,
then left on Hartman Lane, left on Shiloh
Road and right on Anderson Road

Phone: (618) 233-2000

Membership: Public

Distance: 2,166 yards

Fees: Weekdays, $5 for nine holes, $7 for 18. Weekends and
holidays, $5.50 for nine holes, $8 for 18 holes
holes. Night rates (any day after 6 p.m.), $6
for 9 holes, $9 for 18. Carts: $6 per nine
holes, $11 for 18 holes holes. Driving range,
$2, $1.

㉚ *Cardinal Creek Golf Course*

Location: Scott Air Force Base.

Phone: (618) 744-1400

Membership: Private

Distance: 6,484 yards, par 72

Fees: Play is limited to military personnel and civilian
employees of Scott Air Force Base.

㉛ *Greenville Country Club*

This 18-hole course is private. The par-72 course plays 6,670
yards. For more information, call (618) 664-1536.

㉜ # *Highland Country Club*

Location:	Three miles northeast of Highland off Illinois 40
Phone:	(618) 654-4653
Membership:	Private
Distance:	3,200 yards, par 36
Fees:	Non-members must play with a member

㉝ # *Twin Oaks Golf Course*

This mildly hilly nine-hole course, located near Carlyle Lake, has large undulating greens with a wide-open layout.

Location:	Nine miles north of Carlyle on Illinois 127.
Phone:	(618) 749-5611.
Membership:	Semi-private
Distance:	3,190 yards, par 36
Fees:	Weekdays, $7 for nine holes, $10 for 18 holes. Weekends and holidays, $8 for nine holes, $12 for 18 holes. Carts: $8 per nine holes. Driving range: $1.

㉞ # *Carlyle Lake Golf Club*

A nine-hole course that has improved dramatically in the past few years with the addition of bunkers and watered fairways. The course is located just minutes from Carlyle Lake.

Location:	Half-mile south of Carlyle on Illinois 127.
Phone:	(618) 594-2758
Membership:	Public
Distance:	3,285 yards, par 36
Fees:	Weekdays, $7 for nine holes, $10 all day. Weekends and holidays, $8 for nine holes, $12 all day. Carts: $8.50 per nine holes. Driving range: $2.75 and $1.75.

(35) *Bent Oak Municipal Golf Course*

This new course opened in July 1993. The fully-irrigated course is being operated by the City of Breese. Driving range and cart rental fees are still to be established.

Location: 1725 S. Broadway, Breese.
Phone: (618) 526-8181
Membership: Public
Distance: 3,400 yards, par 36
Fees: Weekdays, $6 for nine holes. Weekends and holidays, $8 for nine holes.

(36) *Okawville Golf Course*

This is one of the newer courses in Southern Illinois, opening in August of 1992. The course features a bar and a restaurant with a dinner and luncheon menu.

Location: From I- 64, take Illinois 177 into Okawville. Take first road to right, Waterworks Road, north one-fourth mile.
Phone: (618) 243-6610
Membership: Public
Distance: 3,040 yards, par 36
Fees: Weekdays, $7 for nine holes, $12 for 18 holes. Weekends, $8 for nine holes, $14 for 18 holes. Carts: $8 per 9 holes.

(37) *Nashville Municipal Golf Course*

Location: Nashville Community Park, several blocks east of Illinois 127
Phone: (618) 327-3821
Membership: Public
Distance: Nine holes, 3,026 yards, par 36

Fees: Weekdays , $6 for nine holes, $9 for 18 holes. Weekends and holidays, $7 for nine holes, $12 for 18 holes. Carts: $8 per nine holes.

㊳ *Vandalia Country Club*

Location: On Eighth Street in Vandalia
Phone: (618) 283-1365
Membership: Private
Distance: 2,864 yards
Fees: Weekdays, $8 for 18 holes. Weekends and holidays, $10 for 18 holes. Carts: $10 for nine holes, $15 for 18 holes.

㊴ *Salem Country Club*

A new driving range will opened in the spring of 1994 and an additional nine holes were scheduled to open July 1.

Location: 700 Divot Drive, Salem
Phone: (618) 548-2975
Membership: Private
Distance: 5,970 yards, par 36.
Fees: Out-of-town golfers need not play with a member. Weekdays, weekends and holidays, $7 for nine holes, $13 for 18. Carts: $8 per nine holes.

㊵ *Colonial Golf Club*

Location: South edge of Sandoval on old U.S. 51.
Phone: (618) 247-3307
Membership: Public
Distance: 5,667 yards, par 70
Fees: Weekdays, $5.50 for nine holes, $7.50 for 18. Weekends and holidays, $6 for nine holes and

$8 for 18 holes. Carts: $7 for nine holes, $14 for 18 holes.

⓵ *Meadow Woods Golf Club*

Location: North of Centralia Coca-Cola plant.
Phone: (618) 532-1121
Membership: Private
Distance: 3,004 yards, par 36
Fees: Members of other clubs may play by calling for a tee time. Weekdays, weekends and holidays, $7 for 9 holes, $12 for 18.

⓶ *Greenview Golf Course*

This 18-hole course features watered fairways. The back nine is characterized by narrow fairways carved out of the woods.

Location: One mile south of Centralia on U.S. 51
Phone: (618) 532-7395
Membership: Semi-private
Distance: 6,500 yards, par 72
Fees: Weekdays, $7 for nine holes, $13 all day. Weekends and holidays, $8 for nine holes, $15 all day. Carts: $9 for nine holes, $18 for 18 holes.
PGA pro: Tom Wargo

⓷ *Green Hills Country Club*

This 18-hole course features hills, water hazards and medium-sized greens.

Location: Four miles north of Mt. Vernon and Illinois 15 on Old Fairfield Road
Phone: (618) 244-3961
Membership: Semi-private

Distance:	6,460 yards
Fees:	Weekdays, $15 for all day, $22 with cart. Weekends and holidays, $20 all day walking, $27 with cart. Carts: $5 per person for nine holes, $9 per person for 18 holes. Driving range: $3.
PGA pro:	Mike Tucker

44 *Homestead Golf Course*

Location:	1.5 miles north of Mt. Vernon on Illinois 37
Phone:	(618) 242-5015
Membership:	Public
Distance:	Nine holes, 2,613, par 35
Fees:	Weekdays, weekends and holidays, $4 per nine holes. Carts: $2,50 per person per nine holes. Driving range: $1 and $1.50

45 *Indian Hills Golf Course*

Location:	Half-mile west of the Methodist Children's Home on Indian Trail Drive in Mt. Vernon.
Phone:	(618) 244-4905
Membership:	Public
Distance:	6,000 yards, par 72
Fees:	Weekdays, $7 for nine holes, $10 for 18 holes. Weekends and holidays, $7 for nine holes, $12 for 18 holes. Carts: $5 per person for nine holes, $8 per person for 18 holes. Lighted driving range: $2.50

46 *North County Country Club*

Location:	Just off Illinois 3, three blocks west of the downtown intersection in Red Bud
Phone:	(618) 282-7963
Membership:	Public

Distance: 2,664 yards, par 35

Fees: Weekdays, $7 for nine holes, $10 for 18. Weekends and holidays, $11 for nine holes, $15 for 18 holes. Carts: $8 per nine holes. Driving range: $2, $3.

❹❼ *Sparta Country Club*

Location: Near the Randolph County Fairgrounds in Sparta .

Phone: (618) 443-4911

Membership: Private

Distance: Nine holes

❹❽ *Chester Country Club*

Location: One mile north of Chester on Illinois 3.

Phone: (618) 826-3168

Membership: Semi-private

Distance: 3,500 yards, par 36

Fees: Weekdays, $8 for 18 holes. Weekends and holidays, $14 for 18 holes. Carts: $7 per nine holes. Driving range: $2 and $1.

❹❾ *Southwestern Lakes Golf Club*

This is a tight, hilly course. There are plans to open a second nine holes. Watered fairways have been added recently.

Location: Three miles south of Percy on Illinois 4.

Phone: (618) 497-8484

Membership: Public

Distance: Dual tees, 6,640 yards, par 36

Fees: Weekdays, $7 for nine holes, $12 for 18. Weekends and holidays, $8 for nine holes, $14 for 18 holes. Carts: $8 for nine holes, $15 for 18 holes. Driving range: $2.25.

50 *Jackson Country Club*

This 18-hole course is fully watered and is renowned for its zoysia fairways and slick greens. Members of other clubs may play the course, but must make arrangements with the pro. Greens-fee players must play with members.

Location: Four miles west of Carbondale on Illinois 13, then one mile south on Country Club Road.
Phone: (618) 684-2387
Membership: Private
Distance: 5,897 yards
Fees: Weekdays, $17 for 18 holes. Weekends and holidays, $20 for 18 holes. Carts, $8 per person per 18 holes.
PGA pro: Jesse Barge

51 *Midland Hills Golf Course*

Midland Hills is the oldest golf course in Southern Illinois, and is quite possibly the hilliest.

Location: Four miles south of Carbondale on U.S. 51, then one mile south on Old U.S. 51, then one mile west on Midland Hills Road
Phone: (618) 529-3698
Membership: Public
Distance: 3,052 yards
Fees: Weekdays, $6 for nine holes, $10 all day. Weekends and holidays, $6.50 for nine holes, $10.50 for 18 holes. Carts: $8 for nine holes, $15 for 18 holes, $4 for a single rider per nine holes.
PGA pro: Wally Young

52 *Union County Country Club*

Location: End of Jefferson Ave. in Anna.
Phone: (618) 833-7912
Membership: Semi-private
Distance: Dual tees 6,625 yards, par 71
Fees: Weekdays, $7 for nine holes, $12 for 18 holes. Weekends and holidays, $8 for nine holes, $14 for 18 holes. Carts: $8 per nine holes. Driving range: $2, $1.
PGA pro: Duffy Smith

53 *Egyptian Country Club*

Location: Three miles north of Mounds on U.S. 51
Phone: (618) 745-6412
Membership: Private
Distance: Dual tees, 6,060 yards, par 72
Fees: Weekdays, $10 all day. Weekends and holidays, $12 all day. Non-members must play with a member on weekends.

54 *Rend Lake Golf Course*

This course is recognized annually as one of the top public courses in the Midwest. The 18-hole course is the longest in Southern Illinois. Nine additional holes were opened for play in 1993. The course, which borders the eastern edge of 18,000-acre Rend Lake, features watered fairways and oversized greens.

Location: Six miles north of Benton on I-57, and a fourth-mile west on Illinois 154
Phone: (618) 629-2353
Membership: Public
Distance: 6,814 yards

Fees:	Weekdays, $17 for 18 holes. Weekends and holidays, $21 for 18 holes, with carts and a foursome required before 1 p.m. Senior citizens (55 and older) receive special rates on Mondays. Carts; $6 per person for nine holes, $9 per person for 18 holes. Driving range: $2.75, $3.75 and $4.
PGA pro:	D.W. Davis

🜶55 *Benton Country Club*

Location:	East of Benton on Illinois 14
Phone:	(618) 439-0921
Membership:	Semi-private
Distance:	Nine-hole dual tee layout, 6,300 yards, par 71
Fees:	Weekdays, $8 for nine holes, $11 for 18 holes. Weekends and holidays, $12 all day. Carts: $5 per person, per nine holes, $16 for 18 holes. Driving range: $1.50, $2, $2.50 and $3.
PGA pro:	D.J. Fleetwood

🜶56 *Franklin County Country Club*

Greens fee play is limited and a tee time is a necessity at this fully-watered 18-hole course.

Location:	One mile southwest of West Frankfort on Country Club Road.
Phone:	(618) 932-3144
Membership:	Private
Distance:	6,615, par 71
Fees:	$15 for nine holes, $20 for 18 holes. Carts: $4.25 per person for nine holes, $8.25 per person for 18 holes.
PGA pro:	Gene Carello

⑤⑦ *Green Acres Golf Club*

Location: On Illinois 148, two miles north of Illinois 13 in Energy.

Phone: (618) 942-6816

Membership: Semi-private

Distance: 18 holes, 6,400 yards

Fees: Weekdays, $6 for nine holes, $11 for 18 holes. Weekends and holidays, $7 for nine holes, $13 for 18 holes. Carts: $4 per person for nine holes; $5 for a single rider per nine holes. Driving range: $2, $1.

⑤⑧ *Crab Orchard Golf Club*

Location: One mile west of Carterville on West Grand Avenue.

Phone: (618) 985-2321

Membership: Semi-private

Distance: 6,440 yards, par 70

Fees: Weekdays, weekends and holidays, $8 for nine holes, $15 for 18 holes. Carts: $4.25 for nine holes, $8.50 for 18 holes, $5.25 per single rider per nine holes. Non-members may not make tee times.

PGA pro: Steve Heckel

⑤⑨ *Stardust*

Location: Five miles north of Marion on I-57

Phone: (618) 983-8822

Membership: Semi-private

Distance: 3,156 yards, par 36

Fees: Weekdays, $5 for nine holes, $9 all day. Weekends and holidays, $6 for nine holes, $10 all day. Carts: $4 per person per nine holes.

PGA pro: Jan Jansco Jr.

60 *Fairway Golf Club*

Location: Southeast edge of Marion off Old Creal Springs Rd.
Phone: (618) 997-1140
Membership: Semi-private
Distance: Nine holes, dual tees 5,712 yards, par 72
Fees: Weekdays, $4 for nine holes, $7.50 for 18 holes.
Weekends and holidays, $4.50 for nine holes,
$8.50 for 18 holes. Carts: $5 per nine holes.

61 *Lake of Egypt Country Club*

Location: Ten miles south of Marion at Lake of Egypt Road.
Phone: (618) 995-2661
Membership: Private
Distance: Nine holes, dual tees, par 72

62 *St. Elmo Golf Club*

Location: One mile northwest of St. Elmo; three miles north of
I-70.
Phone: (618) 829-3390
Membership: Semi-private
Distance: Nine holes, 3,250 yards, par 36
Fees: Weekdays, $7 for nine holes, $14 for 18 holes.
Weekends and holidays, $8 for nine holes,
$16 for 18 holes. Carts: $7 per person for 18
holes. Driving range: $2.

63 *Effingham Country Club*

Phone: (217) 347-0424
Membership: Private
Distance: 6,221 yards, par 72
PGA pro: Dave Martin

64 *Jasper County Country Club*

Location: Southwest of Newton off Illinois 33.
Phone: (618) 783-3790
Membership: Semi-private
Distance: Nine hole dual tees, 6,297 yards
Fees: Weekdays, $10 for nine holes, $14 for 18 holes. Weekends and holidays, $16 for 18. Carts: $8 for nine holes, $14 for 18 holes.

65 *Richland Country Club*

Location: 2.5 miles north of Olney on Illinois 130.
Phone: (618) 395-1661
Membership: Semi-private
Distance: Nine holes, dual tees, 6,300 yards, par 35 course. Second nine holes under construction.
Fees: Weekdays, weekends and holidays, (Includes cart) $18 for nine holes, $22.50 for 18 holes.

66 *East Fork Par 3*

Location: Two miles east of Olney on U.S. 50, north two miles, then east one half-mile
Phone: (618) 395-3505
Membership: Public
Distance: 808 yards
Fees: Weekdays, weekends and holidays, $3 for the first round, $2.50 for every round after that. Driving range: $1.75, $1.25.

67 *Lawrence County Country Club*

Location: U.S. 50, west of Lawrenceville.
Phone: (618) 943-2011
Membership: Semi-private

Distance: Nine hole, par 36 dual tee system, plays 3,043 yards the first time and 3,197 yards the second

Fees: Weekdays, weekends and holidays, $7 for nine holes, $12 for 18 holes. Non-members and out-of-county players must play with member on weekends. Carts: $9 per nine holes.

PGA pro: Joe Little, Jr.

68 *Flora Country Club*

Location: Off old U.S. 50 west of Flora.
Phone: (618) 662-2500.
Membership: Semi-private
Distance: 3,022 yards, par 35
Fees: Weekdays, $7 for nine holes, $12 all day. Weekends and holidays: $7 for nine holes, $14 all day. Carts: $4 per person per nine holes .

69 *Fairfield Country Club*

Location: On NW 9th Street in Fairfield.
Phone: (618) 847-7222
Membership: Semi-private
Distance: Dual tees 6,400 yards, par 70
Fees: Weekdays, $6 for nine holes, $10 for 18 holes. Weekends and holidays, $7 for nine holes, $12 for 18 holes. Carts: $10 per nine holes.

70 *Mt. Carmel Municipal Golf Course*

Location: On Park Road, off Illinois 1 and 15 in Mt. Carmel.
Phone: (618) 262-5771
Membership: Public
Distance: 18 holes, 5,907 yards, par 71
Fees: Weekdays , $4.50 for nine holes, $8 for 18 holes. Weekends and holidays, $6.75 for nine holes,

$11.50 for 18 holes. Carts: $9 for nine holes, $16 for 18 holes.

PGA pro: Bruce Bottom

71   ## *McLeansboro Golf Club*

Location: One mile west of McLeansboro on Illinois 142, then south at the sign.
Phone: (618) 643-2400
Membership: Semi-private
Distance: Nine holes, 2,970 yards, par 36
Fees: $7 for nine holes, $12 for 18 holes. Carts: $4 per person per nine holes.

72   ## *Carmi Country Club*

Location: Two miles south of Carmi at the intersection of Illinois 1 and Country Club Road.
Phone: (618) 384-5011
Membership: Semi-private
Distance: Dual tees 5,772 yards, par 71
Fees: Weekdays, $7 for nine holes, $10 for 18 holes. Weekends and holidays, $10 for nine holes, $15 for 18 holes. Carts: $4 per person per nine holes.

73   ## *Saline County Golf & Country Club*

Location: Three miles east of Eldorado on Raleigh Road.
Phone: (618) 273-9002
Membership: Semi-private
Distance: 18 holes, 5,900 yards
Fees: Weekdays, $7 for nine holes, $8 for 18 holes. Weekends and holidays, $8 for nine holes, $9 for 18 holes. Carts: $8 per nine holes.

74 *Shawnee Hills Country Club*

Location: Southeast edge of Harrisburg, near Harrisburg
                  Medical Center.
Phone: (618) 253-7294
Membership: Semi-private
Distance: Nine holes, dual tees 6,198 yards, par 72
Fees: Weekdays, $8 for nine holes, $10 for 18 holes.
                  Weekends and holidays, $7 for nine holes, $9
                  for 18 holes. Carts: $3.75 per person per nine
                  holes.

75 *Hardin County Golf Club*

Location: Half-mile north of Cave-in-Rock on Illinois 1, then
                  left at Rigsby Barnard Quarry.
Phone: (618) 289-4587
Membership: Semi-private
Distance: 2,708 yards, par 35
Fees: Weekdays, weekends and holidays, $6 for nine holes,
                  $9 all day. Carts: $4 per person per nine holes.

76 *Metropolis Country Club*

Location: Four miles north of Metropolis on Country Club
                  Road.
Phone: (618) 524-4414
Membership: Private
Distance: 5,731 yards
Fees: Weekdays , $10 for 18 holes. Weekends and holidays,
                  $15 for 18 holes.

Rock Climbing
& Rapelling

John Payne climbing at Jackson Falls (Photo courtesy of Barbara Payne)

S outhern Illinois is a hotbed for rock climbing enthusiasts. Each weekend climbers from Illinois, Missouri, Kentucky, Tennessee, and Indiana converge on the bluffs in Giant City State Park, Ferne Clyffe State Park, Jackson Hollow, Cedar Bluff, Fountain Bluff, Dixon Springs State Park, Stone Face and Devils Kitchen Lake.

According to Eric Ulner, author of "Vertical Heartland, A Rock Climbers Guide to Southern Illinois," there are about 280 to 300 established climbs at these locations.

The book includes brief outlines of each climb which lists a degree of difficulty for each climb, whether or not technical equipment is required, the size of hand holds and the name of the climber who made the first ascent.

In addition to being blessed with stunning rock formations, Southern Illinois benefits from laws that hold landowners and public agencies blameless in climbing accidents. Although the neighboring areas of Indiana and Missouri feature similar rock formations, restrictive laws bring most climbers to Southern Illinois.

Climbs in Southern Illinois range from the simple to among the most challenging in the country. Climbing is such a popular sport in Southern Illinois that it is included in the newest Shawnee National Forest Plan. The Southern Illinois Climber's Alliance worked with the U.S. Forest Service to see that climbing areas were included in the plan.

The Shawnee Mountaineers are a rock climbing club at Southern Illinois University at Carbondale (SIU-C). They exploit the natural rock formations of Southern Illinois for enjoyment. Some learn to climb using the "climbing wall" and "climbing roof" at the SIU-C Student Recreation Center.

Rapelling is a technique for rapidly descending vertical rock formations. It is extremely popular in Southern Illinois and a great spectator sport. The skills involved in rapelling are very different than those for true rock climbers, the latter being much more challenging. You will commonly see rapellers at Giant City State Park or Garden of the Gods.

River to River
𐃷 *Relay* 𐃷

W hen the River to River Relay began in 1987 it was a curiosity. In a matter of two or three years it was a full-fledged, honest-to-goodness, all-day-long, coast-to-coast (Illinois style) happening.

The race is sponsored by the River to River Runners (who else). Teams are comprised of eight runners, each of whom run three segments of approximately three miles, as the team winds its way from McGee Hill, located near the Mississippi River in Jackson County, to Golconda, a small town on the Ohio River. The first teams leave McGee Hill at about 6 a.m. and the final teams cross the finish line in Golconda somewhere around 7:30 p.m. The first race featured 60 teams.

In just five years the field grew to nearly 200 teams. Although the day is grueling, runners are attracted to the race because it is a team event in an otherwise lonely sport. "Many teams enter primarily just to enjoy it," said Gordon Pitz, one of the race's organizers. "Over half the teams have no serious expectations of winning an award. For some, just finishing the course before sunset is the challenge."

Many teams enter to enjoy the streams and creeks, the flowering dogwoods and the rolling hills of Southern Illinois, but the race is more than an outing in running shoes. Many of the better teams feature former and current collegiate runners. The elite teams finish the roughly 80-mile course in just over seven hours. It has become tradition for teams to cross the finish line *en masse*.

A seat at the finish line in Golconda can produce some light-hearted moments. Many teams pop champagne corks or wave American flags as they cross the finish line. Other teams are more creative. A team of undertakers once carried a casket across the finish line at the courthouse square in Golconda.

The people of Pope County annually turn the square into a carnival for the runners with food, drink and musical entertainment. The runners take advantage of the situation, hanging around for several hours to swap war stories with both teammates and competitors. "It's just a very intense kind of activity, spending eight to 10 hours in close proximity with seven other people," Pitz said. "You get to know them quite well. You're actually only working hard for one-eighth of the time. It's one part working hard and seven parts helping other people and having a good time. That's probably not a bad prescription."

The River to River Relay has gotten so popular that race organizers have to turn away several teams each year. The race is run on the rural roads crisscrossing Southern Illinois. Each team has at least one support vehicle that transports runners to exchange points. The congestion created by the vehicles on the area's rural roads will be the

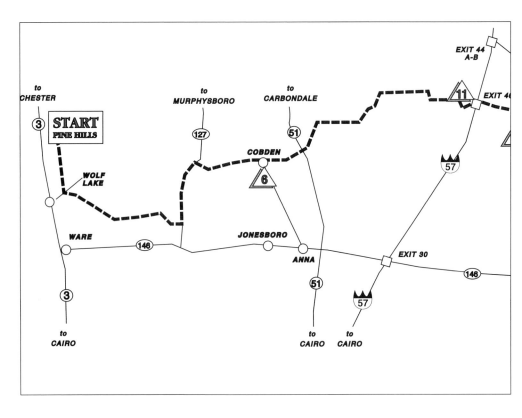

ultimate factor that limits the size of the race. The logistics of moving the runners from one exchange point to another are often as important as actual race strategy. "The race can be very disruptive, particularly if there are local residents who need to drive on the roads against the direction of the race. It can get very tricky," Pitz said.

Although area residents may experience a few inconveniences on race day, several towns along the route have adopted the runners. The Goreville High School band frequently assembles to serenade the runners through town. Cobden residents annually line the streets to cheer the runners through their town. Although Pitz may not know how many teams will enter the race until just before the starter's gun sounds, one thing is certain, the race will be run, rain or shine.

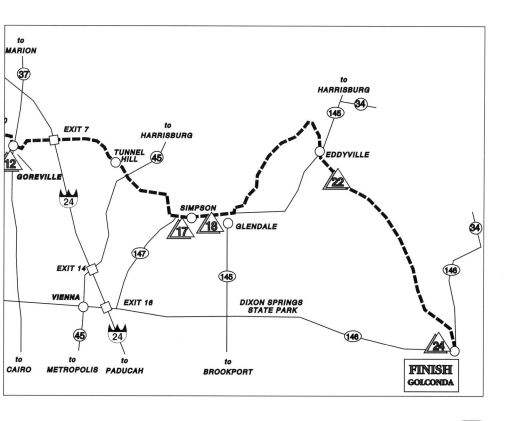

Elevation Maps

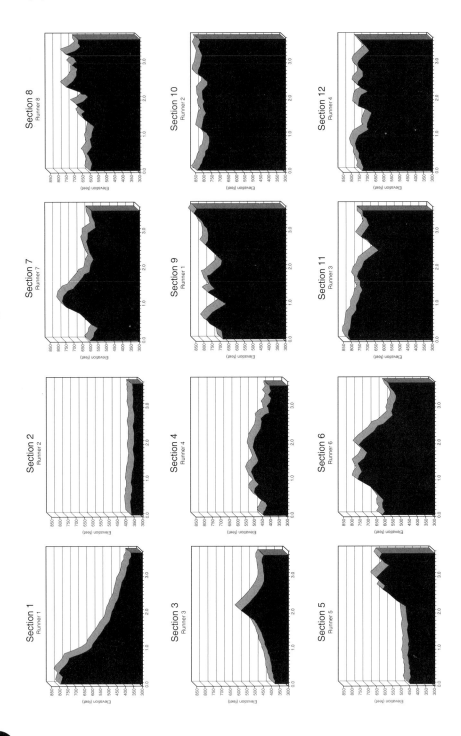

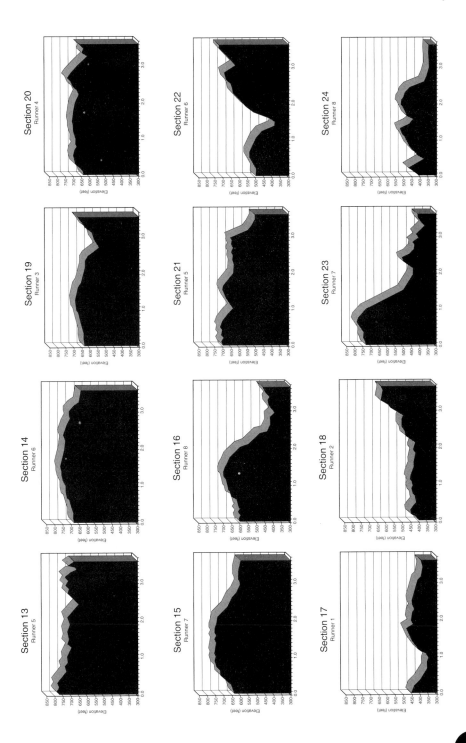

"Everybody will just get wet," said race publicist Judi McHose. "Nothing stops these people. It may ground an airplane, but it doesn't stop a runner. We don't regard it as any big threat."

The scenic course for the River to River Relay is shown in the on pages 386-7. The race avoids most of the larger towns in Southern Illinois by taking side roads. The real story of the course is the ups and downs of the route. Maps on 388-9 show the elevation changes in each segment of the course. A runner may have an easy segment followed by difficult segments or vice versa. Note that there are few relatively flat segments. A good place to view the race is in one of the small towns. Often runners are welcomed by bands or well wishers.

Riverboat Gambling

The riverboat at Metropolis

Blackjack cards fly, roulette wheels spin and slot machines whirr at three riverboat gambling complexes in Illinois. Two of these are floating casinos on the Mississippi in the St. Louis area. The third is on the Ohio River off the state's southern tip.

The southernmost casino is in Metropolis at the tip of the state across the river from Paducah. **The Players Riverboat Casino** features 634 slot and video poker machines over three decks, 28 blackjack tables, two roulette wheels, one Big Six Wheel and four crap tables. Minimum bets fluctuate depending on demand. No limit tables are usually available, while $2 tables are hard to find on weekends. There are bars on every deck and an elegant dockside boat called the **Belle Angeline** houses **Merv Griffin's Bar and Grill** in addition to a buffet (see the Restaurant Section).

A cruise costs from $5 to $12 while a weekend dinner buffet ups the ante to $18. The boat sails every three hours starting at 9 a.m. with the last cruise at 9 p.m. weekdays and midnight on weekends. For more information or reservations call 1-800-935-7700.

The Alton Belle Riverboat Casino is off Illinois 100 in downtown Alton. Signs lead you to the ship. Cruises cost from $3 and $7 and the boat sails at 8:30 a.m. and every three hours thereafter until the last cruise at 11:30 p.m.

For high rollers, there is no betting limit for craps, while slot machines and blackjack tables round out the new gambling boat's games.

Two restaurants are available at the landing where the boat is docked. One of these is a buffet and the other fine dining. Deli sandwiches are available on board and bars are located on every deck. The Riverboat is near a host of tea rooms, antique and other specialty shops in the downtown area. For more information or ticket reservations call 1-800-336-7568.

The newest and biggest of the riverboat casinos is docked across from St. Louis' Arch in East St. Louis. **The Casino Queen** accommodates over 1,500 gamblers on each cruise. Visitors get a great view of the Arch from dock-side. The boat cruises every three hours starting at 9 a.m. with the last cruise at midnight. In addition to the gambling, meals are served with each cruise and cost $4.95 for breakfast, $6.95 for lunch and $14.95 for steak, fish or chicken dinners. Morning cruises are $3, all others $5.

The riverboat is on Front Street and can be reached by exiting I-64 at the 3rd Street Exit. From Missouri take I-55 North to the 4th Street exit. Numerous signs will direct you to the riverboat. For reservations call 1-800-777-0777.

Canoeing &
Kayaking

Canoeing at Lusk Creek (Photo courtesy of the Southern Illinoisan)

C anoeing and its cousin, kayaking, are the undiscovered sports of Southern Illinois. There's great potential in the rivers, creeks and lakes for canoeing and kayaking enthusiasts to explore Southern Illinois. No, it's not the white water paradise of the Rockies, but it is a new and different way to see the area. As Steve Apple, a northern Illinois transplant says, "It's so nice to have all this kayaking in your backyard." Steve's favorite lake is Cedar Lake near Carbondale where he and others take 'full moon' excursions almost every month. They cross the lake and sit on a big rock situated for a perfect view of the full moon. Steve also enjoys the abundant animal life seen along the Big Muddy River.

Steve Apple

The difference between a kayak and a canoe is the number of people that each holds. A canoe sits high in the water and is best paddled by two people while a kayak sits low in the water and is readily maneuvered by one person. The kayak is also hydrodynamic. A kayak can out distance a canoe, going 20 miles or more in as little as three hours.

Launching at rivers and lakes is more difficult for canoers than kayakers. The kayak is made of lightweight material and may weigh as little as 20 pounds and, thus, may be carried by one person. A kayaker has a spray skirt tied around at the waist to prevent water from entering the kayak. It is also easy for a kayaker to right a capsized vessel.

A canoer's paradise is the **Cache River** area. Canoers may explore the swamp and paddle among 1,000-year-old cypress trees and see cypress trees with as many as 22 knees. Swamp canoeing gives the adventurer a wholly different view of Southern Illinois. If you have your own canoe you may access the river at the newly built canoe access at Perks. A canoe outfitter (Cache Core Canoes, phone (618) 845-3817) has recently opened near Ullin. The current on the Cache is mild and the swamp atmosphere unique.

Other prime areas for canoeing/kayaking are Horseshoe Lake in

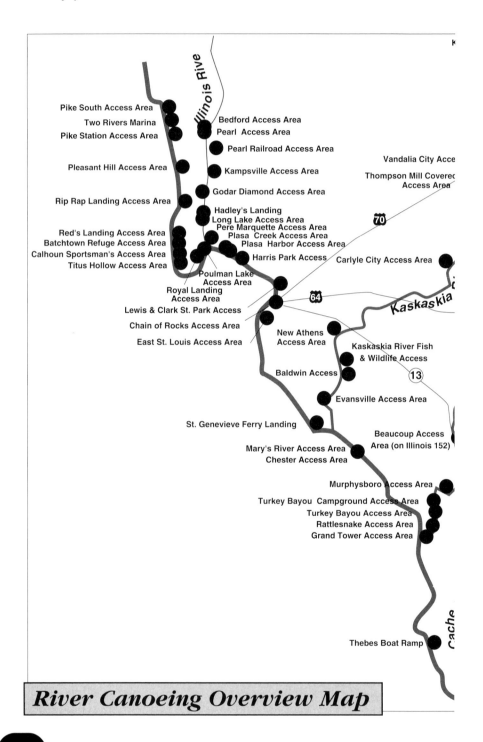

River Canoeing Overview Map

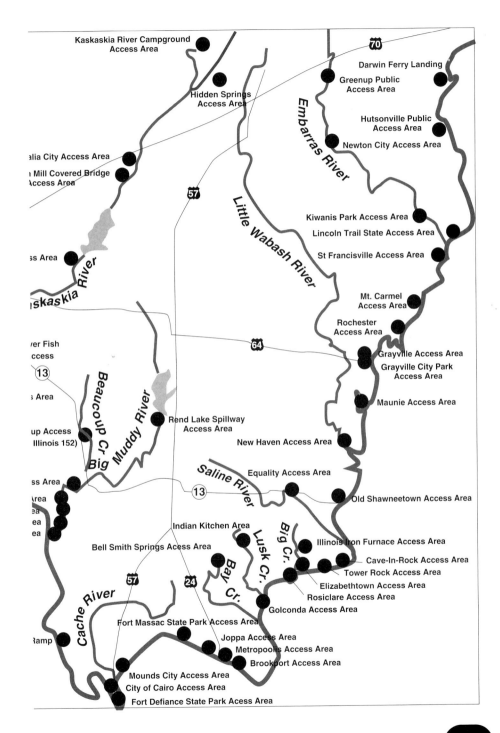

Kaskaskia River Campground Access Area

Darwin Ferry Landing

Greenup Public Access Area

Hidden Springs Access Area

Hutsonville Public Access Area

Newton City Access Area

Embarras River

...alia City Access Area

...n Mill Covered Bridge Access Area

Kiwanis Park Access Area

Lincoln Trail State Access Area

St Francisville Access Area

Little Wabash River

...ss Area

...skaskia River

Mt. Carmel Access Area

Rochester Access Area

...er Fish ...ccess

Grayville Access Area

Grayville City Park Access Area

...s Area

Beaucoup Cr.

Big Muddy River

Maunie Access Area

...up Access (Illinois 152)

Rend Lake Spillway Access Area

New Haven Access Area

...ss Area

Saline River

Equality Access Area

Old Shawneetown Access Area

...rea
...ea
...ea

Indian Kitchen Area

Big Cr.

Illinois Iron Furnace Access Area

Bell Smith Springs Access Area

Lusk Cr.

Bay Cr.

Cave-In-Rock Access Area

Tower Rock Access Area

Elizabethtown Access Area

Rosiclare Access Area

Golconda Access Area

Cache River

Fort Massac State Park Access Area

Joppa Access Area

Metropolis Access Area

Brookport Access Area

...Ramp

Mounds City Access Area

City of Cairo Access Area

Fort Defiance State Park Access Area

deep Southern Illinois, Rend Lake and the Wabash River.

There are many access points on the Ohio and Mississippi rivers. These great rivers and the Wabash provide interesting canoeing and kayaking, but they are filled with danger. All major rivers have hazards such as large floating objects, barges, locks, and very dangerous currents. One local resident of Southern Illinois, Blane Greer, has canoed the entire length of the Mississippi River. His story is filled with adventure from beginning to end.

Canoe rentals are limited in Southern Illinois. Some places to rent canoes are at Little Grassy Lake and Devils Kitchen Lake, at the SIU Student Recreation Center and at Campus Lake at Southern Illinois University.

We have provided maps of Southern Illinois canoeing and kayaking river areas. Access points are indicated. Bear in mind that lakes are also prime areas for participants in this sport. Consult the section on lakes in this book for your options on canoeing and kayaking lakes.

Canoeing on the Cache River (Photo courtesy of the Southern Illinoisan)

W hile talking to some friends the other day, I was surprised to hear they had never canoed the Current or Jacks Fork Rivers in the Missouri Ozarks.

As the conversation continued, we decided a canoe trip was in order this summer.

My wife and I have canoed the Current and Jack's Fork on numerous occasions. The trips have not been without incident, but, on the other hand, our adventures have never led to serious discussions of divorce.

In that regard, we have been more fortunate than some.

Les Winkeler
Sports writer

The Southern Illinoisan, May 21, 1992

Some people may think buying a house or car can be traumatic.

Others may think that guiding your children through the difficult teenage years is the ultimate test of a marriage, but anyone who has spent two days in a canoe with their spouse knows better.

The first bit of advice is no matter what happens, always accept the blame.

Our marriage was tested early on our first canoe trip when the current swept us to the side of the river where our boat became wedged under a fallen tree.

Each time I tried to free the canoe, the current would carry it back to the bank and under the tree. Of course, I knew our predicament was her fault and she was sure I was to blame.

Finally, we were able to free the canoe and resolve our differences. Other couples handle things differently.

After a particularly trying day on the river, one couple found themselves hung up on still another obstruction. The husband got out, freed the canoe and watched helplessly as his wife paddled downstream.

There was nothing he could do, but resort to aquatic hitchhiking.

The second and possibly most valuable piece of advice: find a nice motel.

On one trip, we decided it would be great fun to spend one night camping on the riverbank. The truth is, it would have been fun, if we had thought to bring along a tent, or if it hadn't rained all night.

Four people trying to huddle under two canoes does not make for a good night's sleep.

The rain finally quit near daybreak.

At dawn's first light we were up and ready to get going. One of the people in our party remarkably produced a warm, dry sweatsuit.

She proclaimed that she was not going to get wet all day. We weren't on the river two minutes when her canoe had a head-on collision with a huge stump, sending her careening over the front of the boat.

Seventy-five percent of our group was quite amused.

More good advice: Watch out for idiots.

A lot of people like to scare first-time canoers with horror stories of overturning their canoes.

My wife and I had survived at least five float trips before we capsized. When it finally happened, it wasn't our fault.

We were zipping along smartly when the river narrowed and two stumps formed a gate just wide enough for a canoe to pass through. Rocks protruded from the water on either side of the stumps.

Being experienced outdoors types by this time, we aligned our canoe with the opening between the stumps. We let the current carry us through, only to see a snorkel encased head pop out of the water.

That left us with a difficult decision–decapitate an idiot, or crush the canoe. Unfortunately, we chose the latter.

The impact sent us both hurtling toward the water. Despite being airborne, I was able to yell every obscenity I knew before the water closed in around me.

Final piece of advice: Pack a U-Haul with food.

Looking back on our first canoe trip, the most important consideration was how much beer to bring. Since our cooler was virtually filled with beer and soda, we decided to skimp on food.

Bad idea.

We got off the river, and watched in horror as all our friends began pulling steaks out of their coolers. A bologna sandwich never tasted so cold, never looked so unappetizing.

Cycling

B icycling or simply cycling, is a big sport in Southern Illinois. According to Russ Wright of Carbondale, "Just the beauty of Southern Illinois makes cycling a very attractive recreational activity."

The terrain in Southern Illinois is varied, allowing the cyclist a choice in ride difficulty and scenery desired. Most cyclists prefer the challenge of deep Southern Illinois hills as compared to the flatland common to some of the northern parts of the region. Riding through the Shawnee National Forest with its natural beauty and public use areas can be a wonderful and rewarding experience.

In Southern Illinois, cycling is easily combined with other recreational activities– hiking, swimming or sightseeing. Cyclists develop a healthy appetite as a result of all those calories expended on the ride. Alan Brandenburg, a local cycling enthusiast says "Half the fun is stopping at the local places to eat." Alan's favorite local food pit stops are *The Town & Country* in Elizabethtown, the *Dairy Bar* in Golconda and *Dolly's Place* in Vienna.

Cycling is a great family activity. Cycling is for the very young who have just learned to ride a bike, senior citizens and every age in between. Not to be ignored are the health advantages of cycling. Cycling can be an aerobic sport that will help get you into shape and lose unwanted pounds. It's not uncommon to hear that someone has traded in their stationary bike for one that will get them somewhere.

Cyclists classify their rides as either recreational, touring or racing. *Recreational* riding is usually considered one day or less. Touring involves an overnight stay. Racing may be cross country or on a track designed for the purpose. Bicycles are especially designed for each kind of riding. There are *racing* bikes and *touring* bikes. There are *road* bikes and *mountain* bikes, the latter have sturdy frames and up to 24 gears. Mountain bikes are designed for those who like rough terrain and an off-road experience. There are *hybrid* bikes that combine the features of road and mountain bikes. *Tandem cycles* permit a sharing of the bicycle experience.

Once you have committed yourself to cycling there are a few things that are important to know. Find out if there are local cycling clubs in your area. A few are listed at the end of this chapter. Cyclists are a friendly lot and more than willing to talk cycling and share their experiences. Also, find the nearest bicycle shop. "Bike shops form the hub of our world," cyclist Wright says. You will find the cycling shop the source of most of the information you will need. Upcoming events are usually posted in the local bicycle shop. Shop owners will help the rider select the bicycle suited to them. Shops, their locations and phone numbers are listed at the end of this chapter.

Finally, if cycling appeals to you subscribe to the "bible" of cycling. *Bicycling Magazine* (for subscription information phone 312-726-8185). Cycling safety is always of prime importance. Learn the "Rules of the Road" as published by the Illinois Secretary of State's office. You may obtain a copy at your local driver's examination station. Cyclists should ride with a helmet and gloves, and ride single file when traffic is approaching from either direction.

Sponsored events are important to the cyclist. Generally, the event is hosted by an association such as the Heart Association or Lung Association which provides food, rest stops and t-shirts in return for small entry fees and pledges to the charitable organization. Trips vary in length but are usually 30 to 100 miles. For example, a popular trip through Southern Illinois is known by the acronym BAMMI (**B**icycles **A**cross the **M**agnificent **M**iles of **I**llinois). The Heart Association sponsored trips are eagerly awaited by cyclists. Another sponsored ride, the *Superman* ride begins in Metropolis.

Cycling terminology designates a *century* ride as 100 miles or a *metric century* as 63 miles. Experienced cyclists often exceed 15 miles per hour so a 30 mile trip may only take a couple of hours.

Several popular rides are described on the following pages. They vary in difficulty. It is important to consider physical conditioning before attempting any cycling trek. Generally, rides that are flat and long are less strenuous than shorter hilly rides.

To allow comparison of one ride with another, herein rides are classified from one to five with five being the most difficult:

Difficulty rating **1**: This trail is both short and flat.
Difficulty rating **2**: This trail is short but not flat.
Difficulty rating **3**: This trail is long but only moderately hilly.
Difficulty rating **4**: This trail is both long and hilly.
Difficulty rating **5**: This trail is long and very hilly.

Some of the cycling routes described in the pages that follow have been prepared with assistance of local cycling enthusiasts. Our special thanks to Russ Wright and Alan Brandenburg for helping describe popular cycling routes.

(Photo courtesy of the Southern Illinoisan)

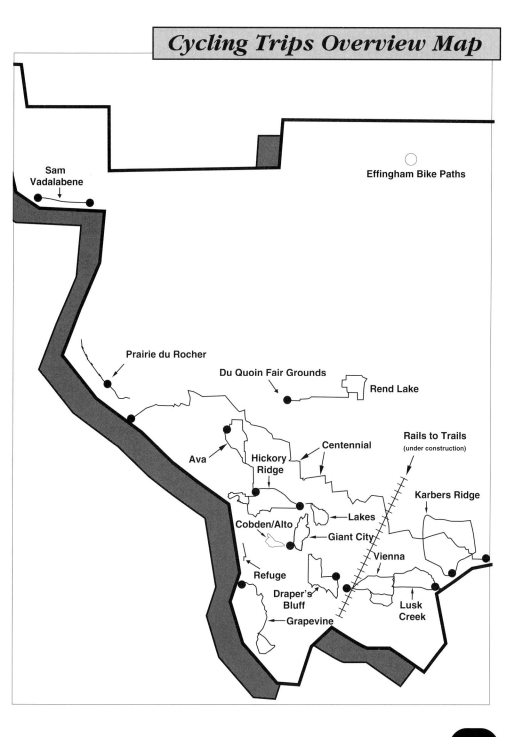

Cycling Trips Overview Map

Effingham Bike Paths

Sam Vadalabene

Prairie du Rocher

Du Quoin Fair Grounds

Rend Lake

Rails to Trails
(under construction)

Centennial

Karbers Ridge

Ava

Hickory Ridge

Lakes

Cobden/Alto

Giant City

Vienna

Refuge

Draper's Bluff

Lusk Creek

Grapevine

The Centennial Route

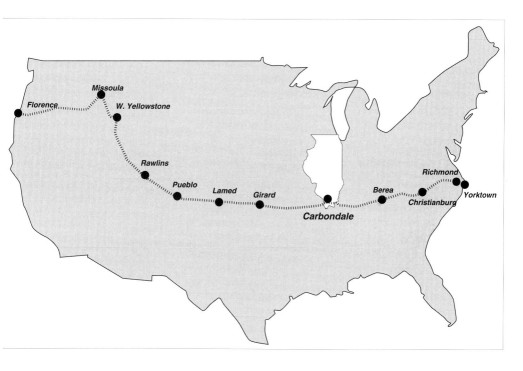

The Centennial Route, formally known as the **TransAmerica Bicycle Trail**, extends from east to west coasts. Southern Illinois enjoys about 140 miles of this 4,200-plus mile trek. Given its length, the TransAmerica Bicycle Trail is for the experienced cyclist. Cyclists can be seen in the spring, summer and fall months, their bicycles loaded with supplies, pedaling their way across Southern Illinois. The scenic Southern Illinois portion of the route is from the Ohio River at Cave-in-Rock to Chester. It presents a moderate to difficult challenge.

Mark Robinson, owner of the Bike Surgeon in Carbondale, has cycled the Southern Illinois portion of the route several times. He enjoys tales of the adventures of transcontinental riders. For eleven years he has operated the Bike Surgeon Hotel–this translates into free

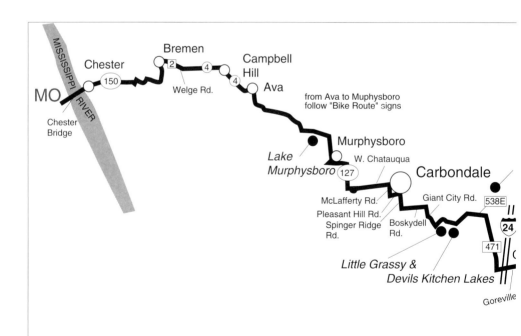

lodging for transcontinental riders. Arrangements for lodging may be made by calling (618) 457-4521.

More detailed maps of the Centennial Route may be obtained from Bikecentennial (P.O. Box 8308, Missoula, MT 59802)

Name: The Centennial Route or TransAmerica Bicycle Trail (in Illinois)
Distance: about 140 miles one way
Difficulty Rating : 4-5

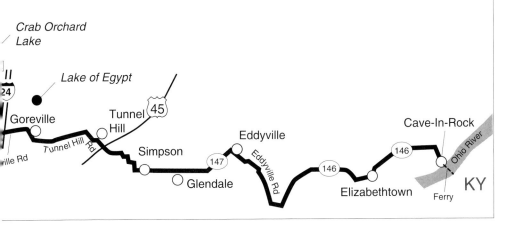

Sam Vadalabene

The Sam Vadalabene Ride is sometimes referred to as the **Great River Road Bike Trail** and is one of the most scenic in Southern Illinois. Virtually every mile of the trail holds views of the Mississippi and the bluffs that line the river on the Missouri side. Riders often see bald eagles, especially in January and February. Break Away Ltd. Bicycle Tours in Granite City often conducts winter cycle tours that travel the Great River Road. If you are without a bicycle, there are numerous bike shops in the Alton area where rentals are available (see listing in this chapter.)

This level trail takes you from Alton to Elsah through Grafton and to Pere Marquette and returns you to Alton. Several turn-arounds are possible to shorten the approximately 32-mile round trip. Crossing the highway is permitted on all breaks in the median. Cyclists are encouraged to stay on the marked bike trails.

Name: The Sam Vadalabene or Great River Road Bike Trail
Distance: About 16 miles one way
Difficulty Rating: 1-2

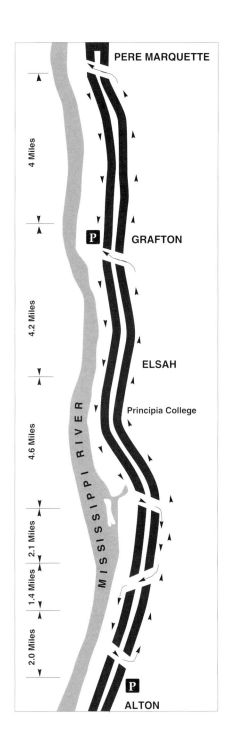

Prairie du Rocher

The Prairie du Rocher Ride is a scenic ride along the bluffs formed by erosion of the Mississippi River. Bikers can take an off-the-road spur to enjoy historic Maeystown but they should be aware that the climb from the river bottoms along Bluff Road to Maeystown is strenuous. Traffic along this route is minimal.

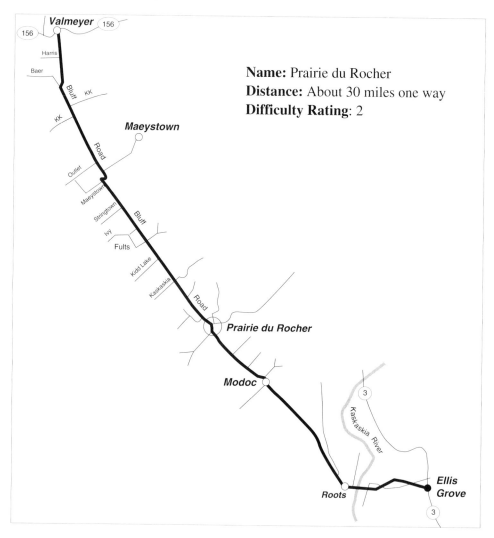

Name: Prairie du Rocher
Distance: About 30 miles one way
Difficulty Rating: 2

Du Quoin State Fairgrounds

This ride is a pleasant, flat trek through and around the fairgrounds at Du Quoin. Although most of the year the fairgrounds are not used for major events, there is often considerable use of the grounds by joggers, walkers and bikers. The map below shows that there are several optional routes to the one indicated.

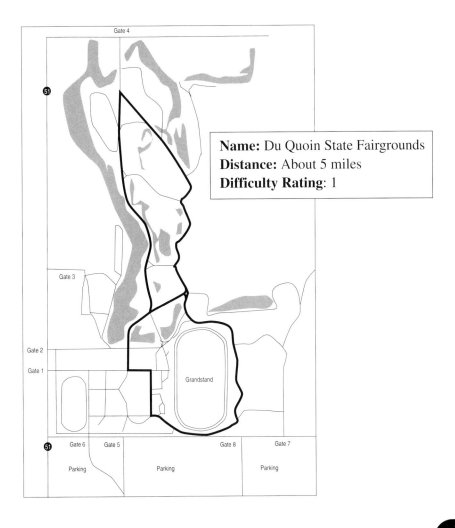

Name: Du Quoin State Fairgrounds
Distance: About 5 miles
Difficulty Rating: 1

Rend Lake

The Rend Lake ride is flat and long. Beginning at Du Quoin, the ride proceeds eastward and traverses scenic backcountry. At the southwestern tip of Rend Lake, the route makes a loop. Before making the loop, check wind conditions. Take the trek across the lake causeway with the wind to your back since strong winds on the lake are common and can make causeway crossing difficult. The loop takes cyclists past Rend Lake Visitors Center and Wayne Fitzgerrell State Park. One option is to take the loop around the lake and omit the trip to Du Quoin.

Name: Rend Lake
Distance: 47-50 miles
Difficulty Rating: 2-3

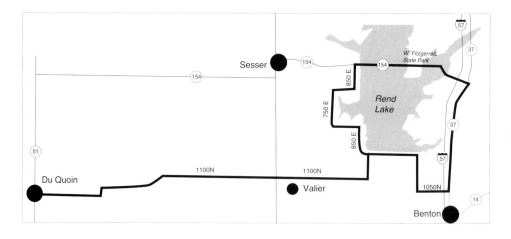

Ava

The Ava ride contains a terminal loop that should be done counterclockwise to obtain full advantage of the view. It combines expanses of agricultural land with some ridgetop climbs. The ride allows good access to Kinkaid Lake. It begins on 23rd Street North in Murphysboro and proceeds north.

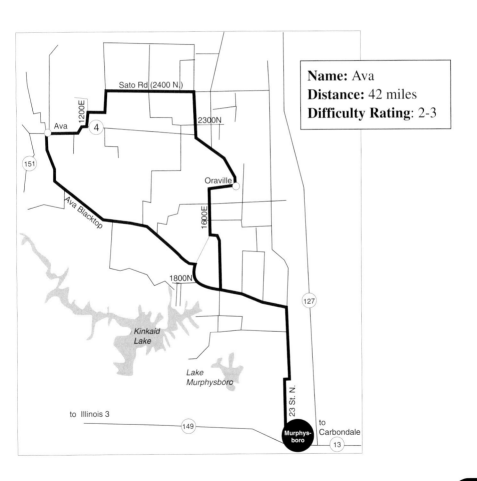

Name: Ava
Distance: 42 miles
Difficulty Rating: 2-3

Hickory Ridge

Hickory Ridge is really two rides referred to as Hickory Ridge 1 and Hickory Ridge 2. The two share a common loop that begins and ends in Carbondale. The westernmost loop is exclusively associated with Hickory Ridge 2. Hickory Ridge 1 traverses two ridges in typical Southern Illinois Shawnee Forest hill country. Hickory Ridge 2 continues through forest and hill country to approach the Big Muddy River. Both Hickory Ridge rides take the biker through Murphysboro.

Name: Hickory Ridge-1 & Hickory Ridge-2
Distance: 25 & 35 miles, respectively
Difficulty Rating: 3-4 & 4, respectively

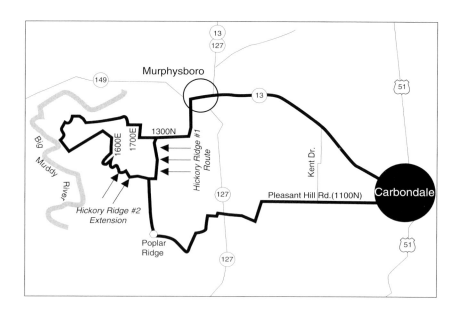

Lakes

One of the most attractive rides in Southern Illinois begins in Carbondale and proceeds southeast passing three major lakes. Along Giant City Blacktop, the ride is semi-residential. An east turnoff takes the rider by Little Grassy and Devils Kitchen lakes. The rider may stop off at Little Grassy Lake where refreshments are available at the concession stand. The Little Grassy Fish Hatchery makes an excellent resting place. On the return loop Crab Orchard Lake is just to the northeast as the rider approaches Carbondale. This ride provides an excellent opportunity for camping along the way.

Name: Lakes
Distance: about 30 miles
Difficulty Rating: 2-3

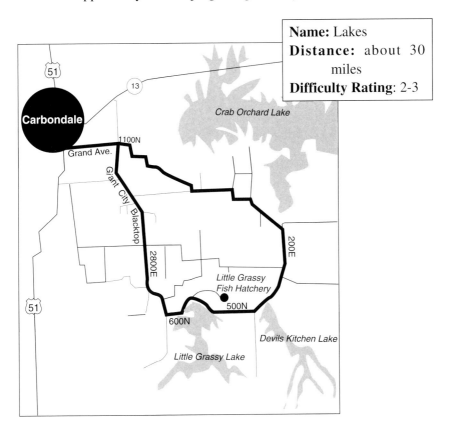

417

Cobden & Alto Pass

This hilly ride traverses some of the small and interesting rural towns of Southern Illinois and provides a nice view of the Shawnee National Forest. Riders may stop at the antique shops in Alto Pass or Cobden or take a side trip to Bald Knob Cross.

Name: Cobden & Alto Pass
Distance: 18 miles
Difficulty Rating: 4

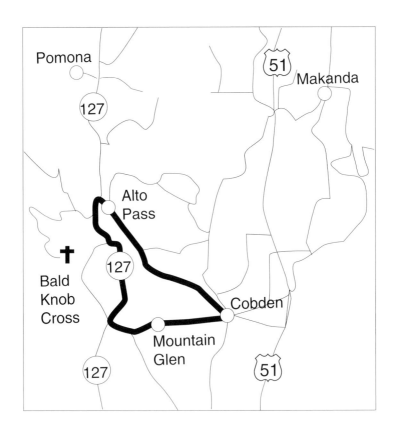

Giant City

Giant City is a loop trail winding through the quaint cities of Makanda and Cobden. While in Giant City State Park, the rider may view and/or utilize as much of the park as desired This includes eating at Giant City Lodge. The Giant City ride is one of the most scenic rides in the Shawnee National Forest.

Name: Giant City
Distance: 40 miles
Difficulty Rating: 4-5

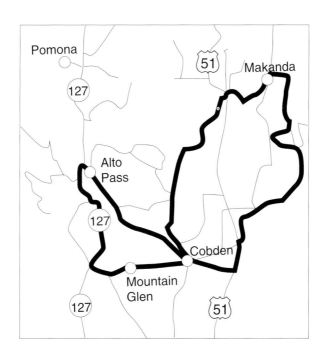

Refuge

The Refuge ride is a short jaunt into the Union County Conservation Area. While a one-way trip is under five miles, the riders may double the distance by retracing the route. Illinois conservation efforts may be viewed at their best at Union County Conservation Area. On this ride, waterfowl are fre- quently seen and riders occasionally catch glimpses of bald eagles in the winter.

Name: Refuge
Distance: under 5 miles
Difficulty Rating: 1

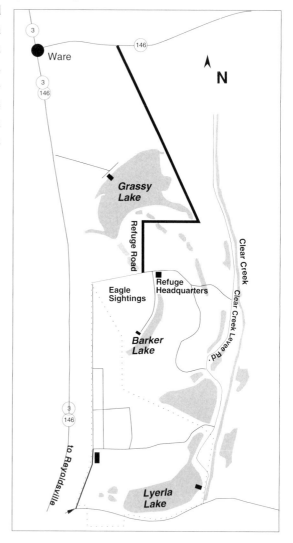

Grapevine

This long trail takes cyclists over one major ridge and the remainder is relatively flat. The ride has variety, crossing both the Shawnee National Forest and agricultural land. On the south loop there are off-the-ride opportunities to explore Horseshoe Lake. The Horseshoe Lake area was under water in the flood of 1993.

Name: Grapevine
Distance: 50 miles
Difficulty Rating: 3

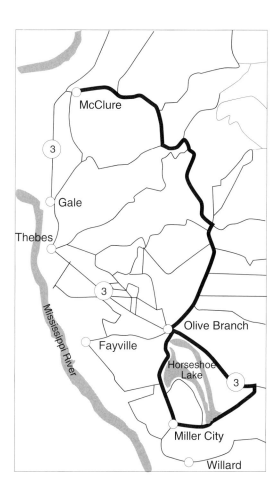

Draper's Bluff

The name of this ride takes its origin from the large bluff that is viewed from much of the southern portion of the ride. The ride passes by Ferne Clyffe State Park, between Devils Kitchen and Little Grassy lakes and through typical Shawnee National Forest land. There are some flat areas in the southern part of this loop ride.

Name: Draper's Bluff
Distance: 45 miles
Difficulty Rating: 4-5

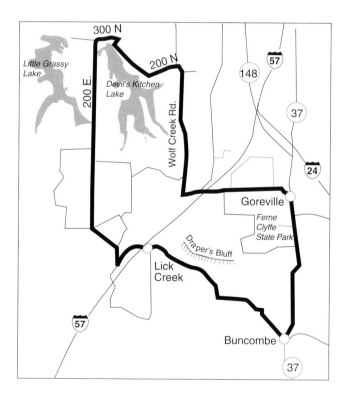

Vienna

The Vienna ride is actually two rides. Both begin and end in Vienna and both take the rider through typical Southern Illinois scenery in the national forest and numerous small towns along the way. The northern route goes by Lake Glendale. Both routes pass Dixon Springs State Park. There are numerous other sites along the way. The biker may choose to make one large loop out of the two smaller loops

Name: Vienna
Distance: upper loop 40 miles; lower loop and return to Vienna 30 miles. Large loop is approximately 50 miles
Difficulty Rating: 3

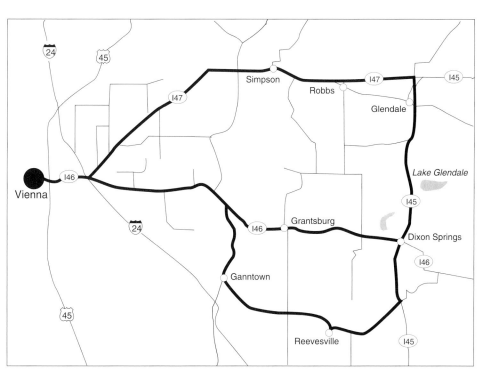

Karbers Ridge

The best of the Shawnee National Forest is seen in the Karbers Ridge ride. The ride is hilly. Camping is available along the way in one of the many recreational areas. The trail passes Garden of the Gods, Pounds Hollow, Rim Rock and Camp Cadiz as well as historic river towns.

Name: Karbers Ridge
Distance: 45 miles
Difficulty Rating: 3-4

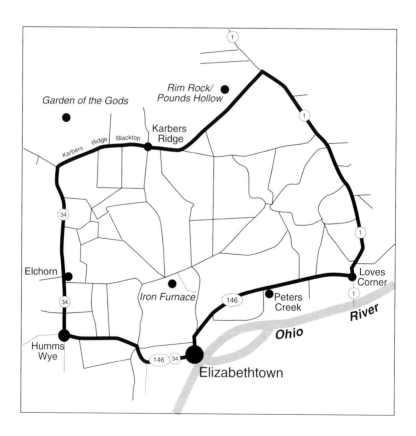

Lusk Creek

There are many interesting features along this route through the Shawnee National Forest circling scenic Lusk Creek. Potential stops include Dixon Springs State Park, Lake Glendale and the river town of Golconda. The hills may be stressful on this loop ride.

Name: Lusk Creek
Distance: 35 miles
Difficulty Rating: 4-5

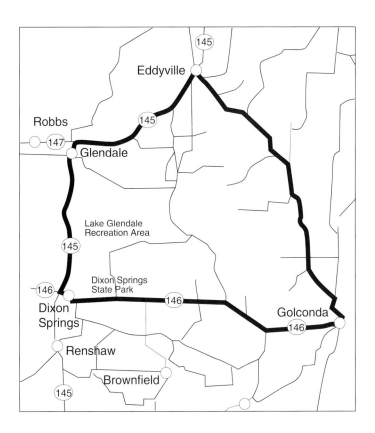

Effingham Bike Paths

The city of Effingham has designated bicycle paths through selected parts of the metropolitan area. Many of the routes are near or cross city recreational facilities. Enjoy a city ride.

Name: Effingham Bike Paths
Distance: Paths of varying lengths
Difficulty Rating: 1

1. Park District Recreational Center
2. Hendelmeyer Park Baseball Diamond
3. Bliss Park
4. Helen Matthes Library
5. Community Park Tennis Courts
6. Community Park Baseball Diamond
7. Community Park Swimming Pool
8. Evergreen Hollow Park Tennis Courts

Rails to Trails

The proposed Rails to Trails is both a hiking and a cycling trail. See the description of Rails to Trails in the hiking section of this book.

Cycling Organizations

Carbondale

Name: The Poplar Camp Touring Club
Contact Person: Marge Hudson
Phone: (618) 529-2891

Name: Southern Illinois University Triathlon Team
Contact Person: Doug McDonald (sponsor) at Phoenix Cycles will put you in touch with current leadership.
Phone: (618) 549-3612

Name: Phoenix SIU Racing Club
Contact Person: Doug McDonald at Phoenix Cycles (sponsor) will put you in touch with current leadership.
Phone: (618) 549-3612

Bicycle Sales, Repair & Rentals

ALTON

A-Z Bike Shop
607 Berkshire Blvd.
(618) 259-5722

Eddie's Bicycle Shop
3320 Fernwood Ave.
(618) 465-6755

Great River Road Bicycle Shop
214 W. 3rd
(618) 465-1204

BELLEVILLE

Bicycle World Inc.
4516 W. Main
(618) 234-0041

Ender's Sales Inc.
3625 W. Main
(618) 233-0378

The Pedal Shop
616 Franklin Ave.
(618) 656-7701

The Touring Cyclist
4632 N. 3rd
(618) 233-8181

BENTON

Wiggs Bicycles
1208 Election
(618) 439-6712

CAIRO

Berbling Tire Co.
1314 Washington
(618) 734-0021

CARBONDALE

Bike Surgeon
302 W. Walnut
(618) 457-4521

Carbondale Cycle Shop
Eastgate Shopping Center
(618) 549-6863

Phoenix Cycles
300 S. Illinois
(618) 549-3612

CENTRALIA

Rick's Bike and Tire
120 W. 16th
(618) 533-2630

COULTERVILLE

Country Peddlin
RR 2
(618) 587-2028

EAST ALTON

The Cyclery
9 East Gate Plaza
(618) 259-5722

EDWARDSVILLE

Edwardsville Cyclery & Sports
244 S. Buchanan
(618) 692-0070

ELDORADO

Lifecycles
2217 Pine
(618) 273-2453

JERSEYVILLE

Medford Schwinn Bicycle and
Sporting Goods
Route 16 E.
(618) 498-5005

MT. VERNON

Mt. Vernon Schwinn Cyclery
1812 Broadway
(618) 244-5632

O'FALLON

Schwinn Pedal In
129 W. First
(618) 632-1442

SALEM

Arnold's Lawnmower and Bike
Shop
803 S. College
(618) 548-0441

SESSER

Gene's Bike Shop
301 W. Young
(618) 625-5808

Cycling Tour Operators

Carbondale

Scenic Cycling Tours
Owners: Sue Teagarden, Marcia Hunt
Address: Route 2 Box 221, Carbondale 62901
Phone: (618) 964-1876
Description: Scenic Cycling Tours is owned and operated by individuals familiar with Southern Illinois. They offer customized one-day tours or weekend tours. The prices vary but are in the range of $15-$25 per person for day tours and $100-$200 for weekend tours. If cyclists do not bring their own bicycles, the tour operators will arrange a rental. The owners prefer that you call them for details.

Granite City

Break Away Tours
Owner: Larry Brinker
Address: P. O. Box ,, Granite City 62040
Phone: (618) 451-8830
Description: Break Away Tours offers a number of tours each year. Most tours are in western Illinois. Tours include The Great River Road Tour of the Eagles, Great River Road/Elsah Spring Tour, Maeystown/Fort De Chartres Summer Special. Many tours start at Elsah. Vacation tours of five or more days are offered. Prices are variable. Contact Break Away Tours for current pricing information. The tour operators will assist in bike rentals, if necessary.

Horseback Riding

Photo courtesy of the Carbondale Convention Bureau

T he southern tip of Illinois is a horseman's paradise. Hundreds of miles of trails crisscross the Shawnee National Forest, and there are numerous campgrounds located throughout the bottom tier of counties that cater to the horseback crowd. Topographic maps that contain horse trails are available at the Shawnee National Forest Headquarters, located on U.S. 45 South in Harrisburg, phone (618) 253-7114. The section on 'Hiking' in this book shows several excellent horse trails in the state parks listed below.

Campground owners joined together to form the Southern Illinois Campground and Ranch Owners Association. While most campgrounds do not allow horses, members of the association cater to the needs of riders. "We're specialty operations," said Frances Land, president of the association. "Basically, our campgrounds are recreation facilitators. We're adjacent to the resource (Shawnee National Forest). We make it possible for the public to conveniently use the National Forest."

Land estimated, conservatively, that the Shawnee National Forest contains about 1,000 miles of trails. She said campground owners try to maintain the Shawnee National Forest trails adjacent to their camps.

The organization sponsors several activities throughout the year. The annual **River to River Ride** is held in early May. The ride begins at High Knob Ranch in the southeastern part of the state and ends at Grand Tower nine days later. This ride travels over part of the 5,000-mile American Discovery Trail.

The **Lake-to-Lake Ride**, from Kinkaid Lake to Horseshoe Lake, is held in mid-June. The four-day ride travels through some of the most interesting sites in Southern Illinois, including La Rue-Pine Hills and the Trail of Tears.

Shawnee Mule Days is a unique event held each August featuring a mule and horse tack sale, mule jumping and a mule marathon.

Finally, the association sponsors the **Illinois Trail of Tears Commemorative Wagon Train** in October. The wagon train follows the Trail of Tears, the route used for the forced removal of the Cherokee Indians in 1838-1839.

The area is also home to the **Nine Day Ride** held in late July and early August. The ride is sponsored by the Southern Illinois Saddle Club Association. For more information on these rides, call (618) 695-2670.

However, this just scratches the surface of annual events in Southern Illinois this year. There are stables and academies that teach English as well as western riding.

Equestrian Trails

Kingsbury Park District

Location: Greenville

Description: Equestrian trails are 1.5 miles north of Greenville in the nature preserve adjoining Governor Bond Lake. There is no camping.

Phone: (618) 664-4949

Pere Marquette State Park

Location: Jersey County north of Alton on Illinois 100

Description: The lower trail and the ski lift area is closed from the day after Labor Day through December 31 and during the spring hunting season. The upper trail, about five miles each way, is open during the fall hunting season, but closed the rest of the year. There is no camping.

Phone: (618) 786-3323

Randolph County Fish and Wildlife Area

Location: Randolph County, five miles north of Chester off County Road DD

Description: Seven miles of wooded trails that may be closed during hunting season. There is no camping.

Phone: (618) 826-2706

Camp Cadiz

Location: Hardin County, southeast of Harrisburg on County Road 7, two miles west of Illinois 1

Description: Access to adjacent Shawnee National Forest Trails. Group campground shared with non-riders. Small corral with hand pump. Pond suitable for watering horses, although access can be difficult. Camping is available with advance notice required.

Phone: (618) 287-2201 or (618) 253-7114

Devil's Backbone Horse Camp

Location: North edge of village of Grand Tower

Description: Unlimited trails along the Mississippi River, along the levee and hills. Can ride to Pine Hills, Trail of Tears State Forest and Shawnee National Forest. Contains fenced horse camp. Nominal fees. Call ahead.

Phone: (618) 565-2196

Ferne Clyffe State Park

Location: South of Goreville off I-57 or Illinois 148 and 37

Description: Eight miles of trails, partially shared with hikers. Access to Shawnee National Forest Trails. Park trails closed during deer season. Camping available, but horses must be tied to hitching rails. State camping fees in effect.

Phone: (618) 995-2411

Giant City State Park

Location: 13 miles south of Carbondale off U.S. 51

Description: Twelve miles of trails, closed during hunting season. Access to Shawnee National Forest trails. Horses cannot be ridden to lodge. Camp contains tie rails. Stable in park has rental horses. Call in advance for camping. State's registration system in effect.

Phone: (618) 457-4836

Newton Lake State Fish and Wildlife Area

Location: Southeast of Effingham in Jasper County off Illinois 33
Description: 11.9 miles of trail along the lake. Trails may be closed during wet weather. No camping available on state property.
Phone: (618) 783-3478

Pyramid State Park

Location: Perry County road west of intersection of Illinois 152 and 13
Description: 16.5 miles of trail, some rugged. Horses may be loaded and unloaded only at the trail entrance and at horse camp area. Horses must be tied to hitch rails provided. Parts of trails shared with hikers. Primitive camping available. State registration system in effect.
Phone: (618) 357-2574

Red Hills State Park

Location: West of Lawrenceville off U.S. 50
Description: 2.5 miles of trails. Water for horses along the trail. There are no camping facilities.
Phone: (618) 936-2469

Saline County State Fish and Wildlife Area

Location: Five miles west of Equality on Illinois 142, follow signs
Description: Five miles of trail that connect with Shawnee National Forest Trails. Primitive camping facilities.
Phone: (618) 276-4405

Sam Parr State Park

Location: Northeast of Newton on Illinois 33
Description: Trail head and equestrian parking located at north end of park. Contains 13 miles of trails with water available along trail. Equestrian camping not available.
Phone: (618) 783-2661

Stephen Forbes State Park

Location: Marion County, off Illinois 37 near Kinmundy

Description: 15 miles of sometimes steep trails around Forbes Lake. Camping area includes pavilion that is a converted barn. Large pond is available for watering horses. State camping fees in effect.

Phone: (618) 547-3381

Trail of Tears State Forest

Location: Northwest of Jonesboro on Illinois 146 and 127

Description: Five separate but connected loops with a combined length of about 18 miles. Could be closed in rainy weather. There are no camping facilities, but picnic facilities, outhouses and hitching racks are located at rest areas.

Phone: (618) 833-4910

Turkey Bluffs State Fish & Wildlife Area

Location: Jackson County, southeast of Chester off Illinois 3

Description: Facility open since 1989. Three miles of horse trails. No camping facilities.

Phone: (618) 826-2706

Wayne Fitzgerrell State Park

Location: West of I-57 on Illinois 154

Description: Nine miles of flat trails. Area closed from September 15-April 15 during hunting season and field trials. Stable with rental horses is open seasonally. State camping registration fees in effect.

Phone: (618) 629-2320

Horse Campgrounds

Most of the campgrounds feature guided rides and most have amenities such as shower rooms and restaurants. Many of the campgrounds also provide guide services for hunting and fishing.

Trail of Tears Sportsman's Club

Route 1, Old Cape Road
Jonesboro, IL 62952
(618) 833-8697

Black Diamond Ranch

Route 3, Box 226
Cobden, IL 62920
(618) 833-7629

Wolf Creek Ranch

Route 1, Box 111
Pomona, IL 62975
(618) 893-4440

Triple T Ranch

Route 3
Vienna, IL 62995
(618) 695-2600

Bay Creek Ranch

Route 1, Box 189
Simpson, IL 62985
(618) 695-2670

Bear Branch Campground

P.O. Box 1
Eddyville, IL 62928
(618) 672-4249

34 Ranch

Route 1
Herod, IL 62930
(618) 264-2141 or 273-9474

High Knob Ranch

Route 2
Equality, IL 62934
(618) 275-4494

Lake Glendale Stable/Outfitters

Route 2 Box 201 A
Golconda, IL 62938
(618) 949-3737 or 949-3375

Horseshoe Bend Campgrounds

Route 1, Box 62
Rosiclare, IL 62982
(618) 285-6953

Stables, Riding Lessons

Rental horses are available at the following locations:

Trail of Tears Sportsman's Club

Jonesboro
(618) 833-8697

Camp Ondessonk

Ozark
(618) 695-2489

Timberline Trails

Wayne Fitzgerrell State Park
(Rend Lake)
(618) 629-2189

Lake Glendale Stable/Outfitters

Golconda (Lake Glendale)
(618)949-3737 or 949-3375

Giant City Stables, Giant City State Park

(618) 529-4110

In addition, several stables in the area feature riding lessons:

Everon

Anna
(618) 833-8704

Rolling Meadows Equestrian Center

De Soto
(618) 549-8001

Houghnhnm School of Horsemanship

Goreville
(618) 995-2431

Silver Star Stables

Carbondale
(618) 985-6214

Le Cheval de Boskydell

Carbondale
(618) 549-4330

Sailing

Photo courtesy of the Southern Illinoisan

I f you prefer quality over quantity, Southern Illinois can be classified as an outstanding destination for sailors. Without question the best sailing location in Southern Illinois is **Carlyle Lake**. With its wide open expanses of water and the flat farmland surrounding it, Carlyle Lake is perfectly suited for sailing. That's not just the opinion of the local chamber of commerce. Each year, from May through September the Carlyle Sailing Association hosts a number of national regattas. The races feature catamarans, Y Flyers, Flying Scots and E Scows among others. Carlyle Lake was selected as a U.S. Olympic Festival sailing location for 1994.

"A lot of people have said it's the best," said Felecia Bamer of the Carlyle Sailing Association. "The group of us that are on the race committee have sailed throughout the Midwest and would say it's the nicest inland lake we have sailed on."

In addition, the Carlyle Yacht Club has a full slate of club races from early May through October. At Carlyle Lake, sailing is a sport well suited to sightseers as well as sailors. The shorelines along South Shore and Eldon Hazlet State Parks offer outstanding vantage points.

The sailboat harbor at Carlyle Lake, located at Eldon Hazlet State Park, features a paved boat parking area, three jib cranes and 400 feet of dock space. In addition, the West Access Marina has sailboat facilities. For more information about sailing on Carlyle Lake, call the Carlyle Sailing Association, (618) 594-3622.

Sailing is also a popular pastime at **Crab Orchard Lake**. The Crab Orchard Sailboat Basin is located on the northwest corner of the lake, adjacent to Playport Marina, just south of Illinois 13. While Crab Orchard does not enjoy the national reputation of Carlyle Lake, it is quite popular with recreational and beginning sailors.

The Southern Illinois University Sailing Club annually offers sailing lessons at the lake on Saturdays and Sundays through the summer. You do not have to be a student or affiliated with the university to take the class.

For more information, call (618) 536-5531.

Rend Lake is the third area lake well-suited for sailing. A nearly 20,000-acre impoundment, Rend Lake would appear to be ideal for sailing, but the lake is crossed by highways, dividing it into segments. However, there are plenty of open spaces for sailors. There is a sailboat harbor located along Illinois 154.

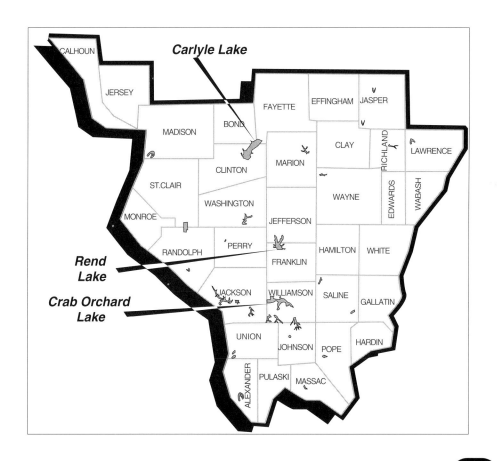

Bird Watching

A yellow-crown night heron (Photo courtesy of Ben Gelman)

Bird watching may be considered by some an odd recreational activity, but when it comes down to it, all of us are bird watchers. Everyone enjoys looking at new, interesting, and beautiful birds. The Illinois state bird, the cardinal, while a fairly common bird, always draws attention. Flocks of geese and the flight of turkey vultures, hawks, and herons are common sights in Southern Illinois, making this a prime area for bird watching. Few experiences can rival seeing a bald eagle up close at sites like the Union County Conservation Area, Horseshoe Lake, or the Elsah area.

Ben Gelman has been a bird watcher for over 60 years and is an authority on the topic. Author of *Bird Watching with Ben* (available from Cache River Press), Ben says Southern Illinois is a great place to watch birds. In his book he compiles a listing of the birds seen in the area. He has participated in the annual Christmas Bird Count at Crab Orchard Lake. This event was started in 1900 by individuals who transferred their energies from hunting birds to watching them. The Christmas Bird Count is held all over the United States. It serves the

Tufted titmouse (Photo courtesy of Ben Gelman)

purpose of monitoring trends in bird populations which, as Gelman says "is a good indicator of the condition of our environment." Gelman also participates in the Annual Spring Migration Bird Count, sponsored by the Illinois Department of Conservation, which monitors populations of birds that are likely to be migratory.

Carbondale is the site of the Southern Illinois Audubon Society. The Audubon Society sponsors the bird watcher's "hot line" that is used to hear and report news of rare bird sightings. Avid bird watchers not only use their eyes but their ears to record the bird population. Bird watching or "birding" is better at some locales than others. The map below shows you the best birding spots.

Ben Gelman

If you want to "privatize" bird watching, set up your own feeder just outside a picture window and watch year around.

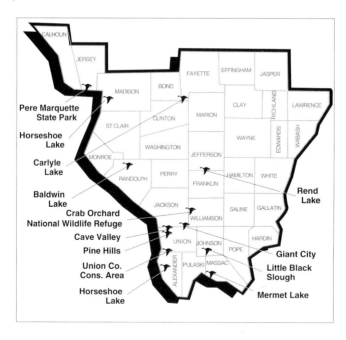

Mushroom Hunting

Professor Walter Sundberg proudly displaying morel mushrooms

S outhern Illinois is a prime region for mushroom hunting. Mushrooms are part of a plant group called fungi that develop among other plants and decaying material. Floras from northern and southern climates mix in Southern Illinois providing a great diversity of mushroom habitats. These habitats support a relatively large number of mushroom species. Mushroom fruiting occurs in spring, summer, and fall in Southern Illinois making the collecting season long.

Dr. Walter Sundberg, a mycologist at Southern Illinois University, is the resident expert for mushroom identification. He has written two books (see below) on the topic suggesting that he knows which mushrooms are good to eat and which are not. "When in doubt, throw it out," Sundberg says when referring to selection of edible mushrooms. Of the 700 species of fungi found in Southern Illinois about 15 to 20 are highly toxic. Edible species found in Southern Illinois include the morel, bear's head (fleshy white tooth fungi), chanterelle, oyster mushroom, sulphur shelf (chicken-of-the-woods), hen-of-the-woods, puff balls, slippery jack, and velvet stem or winter mushroom.

Morels are highly prized mushrooms. Sundberg says that most hunters of this species never divulge their best mushroom locales. Sundberg relates a story of an aging father who, having hunted morels privately for many years, at long-last took his daughter to his secret mushroom hunting spot. The reason–to preserve the secret for the next generation.

The closest place for organized mushroom hunting is the Missouri Mycological Society in St Louis. This organization often plans field trips into Southern Illinois to discover the wonders and diversity of Illinois fungi. Collecting fungi from the Shawnee National Forest is legal.

Bessette, A., Sundberg, W. J. Mushrooms: A quick reference guide to mushrooms of North America. The Macmillan Field Guide Series, 1987, New York, NY

Sundberg, W. J. and Richardson, J. A. Mushrooms and Other Fungi of Land Between the Lakes. 1980 Tennessee Valley Authority

The Performing Arts

Performing Arts Locator Map

I n the early 1980s a local newspaper surveyed Southern Illinois youth about their career plans. Most said they would leave the area to make their way in the wider world. Perhaps that explains why Southern Illinoisans have seen so little of international film star and Benton native, John Malkovich. Though Malkovich may be shy of Southern Illinois, the wider world is not.

Every combination imaginable of performing artists come regularly to the theaters and auditoriums throughout the area. Most performances are found in Metro East, and at or near Southern Illinois University at Carbondale. East of Marion, performing arts become more scarce, but the community college occasionally sponsors a season of fine arts and showcase local music and acting talent. Professional productions include touring opera, play and dance companies, international chamber music and pianists, and superstar rock and country acts.

Community theater survives and thrives in the area with touring community theaters such as The Paradise Alley Players, based in Marion, and other high quality companies with their own roof like the Looking Glass Playhouse in Lebanon. Many local theater groups offer regular dinner theater or, in December, special madrigal dinners, complete with king, court and jester for entertainment. Choral and orchestral performances can be enjoyed at numerous Southern Illinois locations.

Admission prices for performances in Southern Illinois tend to be around half that of comparable performances in St. Louis or Chicago, with the exception of the SIU Arena. The shows are often run by volunteers while local actors, singers and musicians give their performances without pay. Donations from patrons and government subsidies help keep performing arts alive. Costs tend to be low and individual and season ticket prices reflect this fact. At many performances ticket revenue is meant to fund the next production rather than pad an investor's bank account.

The upshot is that tickets for a play rarely exceed $8 and are more commonly $6 or less. Except for the most extravagant madrigal dinner, dinner theater rarely exceeds $15. Professional performing arts is most expensive at Southern Illinois University events, but it is also of the most consistently high quality. Perhaps the best bang for the buck is the Performing Arts Series of the Wabash Valley College in Mt. Carmel, only $6 a show. John A. Logan College in Carterville presents a similar series for only a dollar more.

Most performing groups issue a flier describing the season's shows. These can be obtained by calling or writing the group. Tickets can be booked in a similar fashion. University and junior college box offices tend to be open only two weeks before an in-house production and during business hours. Community theaters often take reservations around the clock with answering machines.

Local performing groups are always eager for an audience, but they are also eager for new talent, both on the production and performing sides of the stage. The phone numbers listed below may be used to inquire into schedules or how to become a part of the production.

McLeod Theater
Southern Illinois University

Hello Dolly at McLeod Theater, Summer Playhouse

•

Location: Communications Building, (1037, west end) Lincoln Drive, Southern Illinois University, Carbondale 62918

Box office: (618) 453-3001

Handicapped access: Yes, signing available for hearing impaired

Major productions: Two fall, two winter-spring, two summer, spring youth theater

Individual tickets: Adults, $8, children and students, $4, seniors (55 and over), $7

•

Of the regular locally-produced theater productions in Southern Illinois, the most professional and elaborate is the McLeod Theater. Produced by students and staff of the Southern Illinois University Department of Theater, the 488-seat auditorium features major contemporary as well as classic plays, musicals and operas.

The first play was staged at the university in the late 19th century as the product of an unseasoned, though enthusiastic, drama club. Since that time players have seen two theaters come and go. In 1966 McLeod and the smaller Laboratory theater were established in the Communications Building. The 1993-1994 season marks the 100th anniversary of play presentations on the SIU campus.

Though it accommodates an orchestra pit, McLeod is not a large theater. While it might justly be said, "There's not a bad seat in the house," the plays are best enjoyed at the center balcony position, section "UA". A McLeod "sponsor," one who has contributed at least $30 over and above the price of season tickets, can also choose front and center on the balcony or center in the stalls below, section "sps". Since back, uncentered rows are far enough away from the stage to make it difficult to discern actors' expressions, and the box office sells tickets on a reserve basis, it is wise to order tickets in advance for a better seat.

The four major productions during the fall and spring semesters are well worth the $8 adult admission fee. Whether a Shakespearean tragedy or Franz Lehar comic opera, costumes and set designs are often requirements for the fulfillment of a master's degree and, as such, do not lack period research, detail or materials. Experienced faculty or professionals from outside the department serve as directors.

The **Summer Playhouse** began as an SIU-sponsored touring company under the original Department of Theater chairman, Archibald McLeod. Today Summer Playhouse presentations are performed in the house named for its founder and draws big crowds during the traditional off season for Southern Illinois' community and university theaters.

Summer Playhouse has drawn national talent to the main stage musicals with orchestral accompaniment, and an audience from all over Southern Illinois and surrounding states. However, the Summer Playhouse faces an uncertain future as spending cuts in higher education have reduced the number of productions from an historic height of five to the present two. If the program survives, fewer and non-musical productions are likely.

For more avant-garde tastes, **original student productions** can be seen in the Laboratory Theater. Also housed in the Communications Building, this smaller theater is completely managed by students and presents everything from one-act plays to improvisational comedies to Greek tragedies. Tickets for fall performances of original master's thesis plays are $3. The Evening of New Plays is generally held in April while more elaborate full-length, original student plays are produced in the summer. The Monday Showcase is free. It features experimental and improvised soap opera spoofs with titles like *The Dumb and the Dying*. Call the McLeod box office to confirm times and dates of all presentations.

–To reach McLeod–

The Communications Building, which contains McLeod Theater (1037) and the Laboratory Theater (1045), is located on the northwest side of the SIU campus on Lincoln Drive. Lincoln Drive makes a semi-circle through the campus, passing by most of the major campus buildings.

The Communications Building can be reached from U.S. 51 driving north: Turn left at the stop light next to McAndrew Stadium onto Lincoln Drive and follow the road for approximately one mile. The Communications Building is on the left.

Shryock Auditorium

●

Location: Southern Illinois University, Old Main Mall, Carbondale
Box office: (618) 453-3379
Handicapped access: Yes
Major productions: Celebrity Series, nine events, October to May; special events, announced during season
Individual tickets: Reserved seating, prices variable, low of $6 to high of $25

●

Shryock Auditorium presents the most extensive series of professional performing arts to be found anywhere in Southern Illinois. Ranging from classical music to broadway musicals and classical ballet to folk theater, Shryock's Celebrity Series represents diversity not found elsewhere in the area. Special events, which generally cost more than regular season shows, bring in more popular recording artists, but these still range from jazz stars like Diane Schuur to rock stars like Joe Walsh. Apart from professional acts, Shryock plays host to recitals from SIU's school of music and to community orchestras.

Built in 1917, Shryock Auditorium is one of the oldest buildings on an old campus. It is also the most majestic, displaying its romanesque sterness and arching dome in the Old Main Mall. The acoustics are exceptional and especially suited to classical music performances. In the theater's balcony is a massive 3,000-pipe, fifty-eight rank, pipe organ built in 1971.

Like most performing arts' series in Southern Illinois, Shryock tries to break even on what it pays for acts and what it earns on ticket sales. Professional shows at Shryock are always less expensive than a similar show in a metropolitan area, sometimes as little as half the price. Tickets are sold for this 1,200 seat auditorium on a reserve basis and the good seats, whether on the balcony or on the main floor, cost $2 extra. Ticket for small plays and chamber music cost around $12 and performances by the Chicago Symphony Orchestra are $25 or more. Ordering tickets in August will save $2 on regular prices. Children's tickets are less.

–To reach Shryock–

Shryock Auditorium is on the SIU campus in the Old Main Mall which is a grassy area north of the student center parking lot. To reach the Student Center from U.S. 51 turn west at the stop lights in front of McAndrew Stadium onto Lincoln Drive. Take the first left into the student center's metered parking lots and walk to Shryock.

Shryock Auditorium on the campus of Southern Illinois University

Southern Illinois University Arena

•

Location: Southern Illinois U.S. 51, Carbondale
Box office: (618) 453-2321
Handicapped access: Yes
Major productions: Six to eight special events from September to April
Individual tickets: Reserved, prices vary

•

For the most popular music groups (including country) and children's extravaganzas, the SIU Arena is the place to go. Elvis Presley, Hank Williams Jr., Bruce Springsteen and the characters from Sesame Street have all entertained under the Arena's massive dome. The Arena books events a few weeks before their appearance so there is no scheduled season. Call the box office periodically during the year for information on events.

Easily the largest venue for performing arts in Southern Illinois, the 10,000-seat arena rarely sells out except for the most popular artists. On the down side, without a ticket bought shortly after they go on sale, a poor seat is a definite risk. Tickets range in price from under $10 for children's shows to over $20 for popular music acts. The good seats cost a bit more.

–To reach SIU Arena–

The SIU Arena is on the south side of Carbondale off U.S. 51. From U.S. 51, turn west onto Pleasant Hill Road and take the first right onto the road leading to the Arena parking lot.

Madrigal Dinner at Southern Illinois University

•

Location: Southern Illinois University, Student Center Ball Rooms, Carbondale
Box office: (618) 453-3493
Handicapped access: Yes
Individual tickets: Non-students, $19.50 or $18, SIU students, $19.50 or $12

•

On three evenings in December the second floor of the university's student center becomes a renaissance banquet hall, complete with king, court and jester. Celebrations prior to the feast include knightly demonstrations of sword play, dancing and tavern songs. When the guests move into the baroque banquet hall, the royal court joins them to amuse with their royal wisdom, foolish antics and rousing melodies. Each course in the feast is announced with a flourish of trumpets and pages dispense the hearty rations as the renaissance entertainment continues. For guests who desire wine, it is recommended that they bring their own since portions served at the banquet are very small. Servers will pour for guests who bring their own wine.

Tickets can be purchased from the SIU Student Center ticket outlet. Lower prices are offered for one of the non-weekend performances.

–To reach the Student Center Ballrooms–

The madrigal dinner and pre-dinner entertainment are held on the second floor of the SIU Student Center. To reach the Student Center from U.S. 51 turn west onto Lincoln Drive at the stoplight in front of McAndrew Stadium and take the first left into the Student Center's metered parking lot.

The Stage Company

●

Location: Corner of East Main and North Washington, Carbondale
Box office: (618) 549-5466
Handicapped access: Yes; Signing available for the hearing impaired
Major productions: Two fall; one winter; one spring
Individual tickets: Reserved seating, $7 Friday and Saturday night;
 $5 Sunday matinee

●

The Stage Company is a community based theater group with the advantage of a symbiotic relationship with the Department of Theater of Southern Illinois University at Carbondale. In addition to a playhouse of its own, The Stage Company benefits from costume and professional expertise from the university, giving the group the ability to perform period pieces with authentic costumes and props in such productions as *The Crucible* by Arthur Miller.

The four annual productions generally include a comedy, a thriller and two dramas. Productions are usually from 20th century playwrights and a play might open its run in the Stage Company as it finishes its first run in a Chicago playhouse.

The plays are competently performed by amateur actors from Carbondale and surrounding towns. Unlike the university's theater program, The Stage Company can cast people who fit the roles they are to play. Instead of a post-adolescent town elder, the town elder in a Stage Company production is more likely to be a town elder in real life.

With only 96 seats in eight rows, The Stage Company auditorium is truly cozy. There are no worries of a poor seat in this theater, but finding one on opening night is another matter. Reservations are recommended.

–To reach the Stage Company–

Carbondale is intersected east-west by Illinois 13 which becomes one-way Main Street running west and one-way Walnut Street running east. The Stage Company is on the northeast corner of East Main and North Washington. It can be reached from U.S. 51 by turning east onto Walnut Street, then north onto Washington Street and crossing the next intersection which is Main Street.

A Stage Company production

Marion Cultural & Civic Center and The Paradise Alley Players

•

Location: Tower Square Plaza, Marion
Box office: (618) 997-4030
Handicapped access: Yes
Major productions: The Patron Series–one fall, one winter, two
    spring; Paradise Alley–two to three
Individual tickets: Prices vary

•

The Marion Cultural & Civic Center, built in the roaring 20s, saw Houdini make fantastic escapes, silent movies wane and the talkies take their place only to succumb to the more hum-drum cinema venues springing up in the 1970s.

The newly-renovated performing arts center now leases out its luxurious facilities to professional dance, drama and musical acts. The 938-seat theater features a 36 ft. x 24 ft. proscenium arch and thrust stage. The tall, majestic walls and ceiling prevent the stage from overpowering the entire theater and allow for a large balcony.

The Patron Series is the Civic Center's professional season of gospel, country, big band and old Hollywood performers. The shows are well attended and often sell out so advanced tickets are recommended.

The **Paradise Alley Players**, Marion's community theater company, calls the Civic Center its home base and performs two to three times a year there. The Players don't confine themselves to the center as they travel throughout Southern Illinois and even to Cape Girardeau, Missouri and Paducah, Kentucky. Dinner theater is a favorite of the Players, and local Holiday Inns often showcase their thespian talents. Tickets range from $5 for a musical to around $15 for a dinner theater presentation. Call Jim Poppy at (618) 997-9031 for schedules and tickets.

–To reach the Marion Civic Center–

The Marion Civic Center is in the southwest corner of the town square. The town square can be reached from I-57 by exiting at Illinois 13 east and turning right/south onto Illinois 37. Take Illinois 37 eight blocks and turn left/east onto Main Street which leads into the square.

The Pyramid Players

•

Location: Rend Lake College Campus, Ina
Box office: (618) 439-9196
Handicapped access: Yes
Major productions: Three per summer, one adult musical, one
    dinner theater, one musical cast with children
Individual tickets: Adults, $6; children, $4

•

The Pyramid Players hail from the Rend Lake area near Benton and showcase that corner of Southern Illinois' acting and directing talent in big musicals like *Brigadoon* and *Oliver*.

Because the Players contain a number of drama, speech and music teachers from the area, they present their main season in the summer. The Players rent the Rend Lake College Theater in Ina for two of their shows and perform in a dinner theater setting at another location for the third.

Community theater is always hard work, but as teachers, many of the key members of the Pyramid Players can devote extra time to the group during the summer. This results in lavish productions like *Barnum* in which jugglers, trapeze artists, a 160-year-old lady and a band belting out 19th century marching tunes make for lively theater.

The college's theater contains a hydraulic pit which might explain the group's penchant for musical spectacles. The theater contains 400 seats and a fan-shaped design with no center aisles. This arrangement makes for a long walk to front row center, but worth it nevertheless.

–To reach Rend Lake Campus–

All non-dinner theater Pyramid Player productions are held at the Rend Lake College theater on the community college's campus. From I-57 take the Ina exit between Mt. Vernon and Benton and follow the signs to the campus.

Alton Little Theater

●

Location: 2450 Henry Street, Alton
Box office: (618) 462-6562
Handicapped access: Yes
Major productions: Five, from October to May
Individual tickets: General admission, $7; students, $4

●

The granddaddy of community theater in Illinois, the Alton Little Theater opened during Franklin D. Roosevelt's first term. It was the brainchild of a couple of college girls, but, in a reflection of the times, its first president was a man. A few years later the Little Theater had lost a fair sum of money and one of those original girls, Dorothy Colonius, bailed the company out. She gave her money (slowly paid back) and her talents to the group until her death in 1979.

Six decades after Dorothy Colonius' dream materialized, the Little Theater produces a five-play mainstage season in its own theater. During the first four mainstage performances the Little Theater aims to please with contemporary favorites like *Steel Magnolias* and Neil Simon works. For the fifth, president Diana Enloe says, "We do it for ourselves." Playgoers might find themselves *Waiting for Godot* along with the actors on stage.

The Little Theater seats 300 with flexible staging including either proscenium or round. It sometimes hosts small musicals, but an evening at the Little Theater will generally meet with a competently produced drama, comedy or mystery.

–To reach the Show Place Theater–
The Show Place Theater is at the corner of Elm and Henry Alton. Turn off Alton's main thoroughfare, State Street, onto Elm and follow the road almost two miles to the theater.

John A. Logan College Plays and Performance Series

•

Location: John A. Logan Community College campus, Carterville
Box office: 1-800-851-4720
Handicapped access: Yes; signing available
Major productions: Five to six professional; five to six in-house
Individual tickets: Reserved performance Series–adults, $7, student/children, $3; In-house–adults, $4; students/children, $3

•

John A. Logan is the biggest of the little colleges in Southern Illinois. It comports itself as such, bringing in five professional performing artists, generally musicians, to augment the quality plays and musicals put on by its theater and music departments.

The Performance Series presents jazz bands, classical pianists and the occasional traveling puppet theater in one of the few performing arts seasons sponsored by a junior college in Southern Illinois. The performers are often the stuff of Chicago's jazz and blues circuit, but the they might also come, in the case of piano virtuoso Yin Cheng-Zong, from China via Carnegie Hall.

The in-house productions showcase young actors. The more experienced hands are department faculty who direct plays. The plays are generally 20th century, ranging from Tennessee Williams to comedy thrillers, though even an adaption of the Arthurian tale, *Sir Gawain and the Green Knight*, appears occasionally on the O'Neil Auditorium Stage. The Christmas presentation is a joint production with the music department and is one of the classic Christmas stories. The music department also presents a musical review to round out the season. A dinner theater is offered with each in-house production and costs $15. Performances are popular and often sell out the 350-seat auditorium. Reservations are recommended for all presentations.

–To reach the Logan O'Neil Auditorium–

The campus is a quarter mile west of the Carterville business district off Illinois 13. Turn north at a stoplight intersection onto Greenbriar Road, go a quarter of a mile, turn right onto campus and take the first right on campus. The main campus building is on the left. The O'Neil Auditorium is in John A. Logan College's main campus building to the right inside the main entrance.

"Blythe Spirit" at John A. Logan's O'Neil Auditorium

Southern Illinois University-Edwardsville

•

Location: Campus of Southern Illinois University, Edwardsville, Communications Building Theater
Box office: (618) 692-2626
Handicapped access: Yes; signing available
Major productions: Arts and Issues–four arts, three lectures, October to May; Season for the Children–three professional; Student Productions–five mainstage, October to May; Summer Program–three student/community
Individual tickets: Arts League Players–general admission; $6 student productions and children's shows–(musicals $1 extra), adults $6, SIU-E affiliate, children, seniors $4.50; Arts and Issues–adult $8, $6 for lectures, student $2, seniors and students, $4.50

•

Southern Illinois' University on the edge of St. Louis, SIU-E, hosts a variety of performing arts, brought in from outside as well as produced within the university itself. The **Arts and Issues** series combines all kinds of performing arts with lectures by important, often political, personalities. The series brings national dance companies like the Stand Rock Indian Ceremonial, traditional repertory theater as well as classical and jazz music to the stage.

University theater productions, directed by faculty and performed by students, are presented in the 397-seat Communications Building Theater. The theater has a balcony that thespians use to stage scenes. Thus, in a theater production a Juliet might be found swooning above as Romeo waxes lyrically in front of the audience. For Christmas, *A Christmas Carol* is a staple at SIU-E. During the summer, community actors team up with students and faculty to present big mainstage musicals and popular comedies.

"The most adventurous theater group in the area," said one St. Louis critic. He is talking about the **Arts League Players** who practice their craft in the Metcalf Student Theater, a separate building and blackbox theater on the SIU-E campus. This tiny, 100-seat theater often sells out when hosting the five yearly performances of alternative theater. Though they perform on the campus, the Players are not affiliated with SIU-E and are angling for an auditorium of their own. The Players present plays with a social message and entertaining spoofs by British playwrights like Tom Stoppard. For schedules and ticket information call (618) 656-1181.

–To reach SIU-Edwardsville–

The campus of Southern Illinois University at Edwardsville is just east of the junction of I-270 and I-255. To enter campus from I-270 take the SIU-E exit. To reach the campus from Edwardsville to the north take Illinois 157 south.

If approaching the campus from I-270, turn north on Illinois 157, follow the signs onto the campus, make a left turn, or "button hook," and take the first right onto Circle Drive. Take the third right which leads to the Communications Building and a parking lot which is just southeast of the Metcalf Student Theater.

If approaching from the north, take Illinois 157 south to the east entrance of the campus, turn right and proceed to the 4-way stop, then turn left following the main road into the campus proper. Turn right on Circle Drive and go two-thirds of a mile to the communications building's service road and turn left.

"Grease" performed at SIU-Edwardsville

Looking Glass Playhouse

•

Location: St Louis Street, Lebanon
Box office: (618) 537-496
Handicapped access: Yes
Major productions: Five, October through May
Individual tickets: $7 musicals; $6 straight plays; senior citizens,
half-price opening night

•

The Looking Glass Playhouse is probably the busiest community theater in Southern Illinois. With five major productions a year and two to four minor ones including June and August shows with children's roles, there is rarely a week in which the playhouse is not in service for rehearsals or performances.

Looking Glass favors big Rodgers and Hammerstein musicals and big sets like the 40-foot drawbridge built for the *Man Of La Mancha*. At a depth of 32 feet, the stage is large enough to accommodate such extravaganzas, and the converted movie house retains superior acoustics for the performances. It is said that on his trip to the United States in 1841, Charles Dickens stopped to browse in Lebanon. Supposedly, Dickens looked at the plains surrounding Lebanon and said it looked like a looking glass. In commemoration of Dickens' visit, the Playhouse presents *A Christmas Carol* every December.

Wabash Valley Arts Council and Community College

•

Location: Wabash Valley College, Brubeck Art Center, Mt. Carmel
Box office: (618) 262-8641, ext. 3212
Handicapped access: Yes
Major productions: Performing Arts Series–five professional, two

local
Individual tickets: General admission, $6

●

One of the few locations for performing arts in Southeastern Illinois, the Wabash Valley College in Mt. Carmel, in co-operation with the Wabash Valley Arts Council, sponsors a seven show season of locally-produced community theater as well as professional jazz, classical music and dance. The Repertory Theatre of America makes an annual appearance performing light comedies at this small community college on the Illinois- Indiana border.

The community theater group puts on a comedy in the fall and a large, well-known musical in the spring in the Brubeck Art Center. These plays are of high caliber and are more likely to sell out the 500-seat, rated theater than are the professional acts.

"A Funny Thing Happened on the Way to the Forum" at
Wabash Valley College Community Theater

–To reach Wabash Valley College–

Wabash Valley College is on the north side of Mt. Carmel, located on College Drive, which is a continuation of the town's main street, Market Street. The college is small and the Brubeck Art Center can be easily found by following campus signs.

Coming to Mt. Carmel from the north, take Illinois 1 south until it intersects Market Street and follow Market Street into College Drive and Wabash Community College on the left. From the south take Illinois 1 north into town until it becomes Market Street and continue to the college. From Indiana to the east take Indiana 64 across the Wabash River to Illinois 15. Continue on Illinois 15 as it becomes Illinois 15/1 and flows into Market Street which leads into College Drive and the college campus.

Cultural Arts Series at Southeastern Illinois College

•

Location: Building B, Illinois 13, east of Harrisburg
Box office: (618) 252-6376
Handicapped access: Yes
Major productions: Six professional
Individual tickets: Adult $6, seniors and youth $5

•

The Cultural Arts Series at Southeastern Illinois College brings in six musical acts each year to play jazz or classical standards. The groups tend to be small and, in the case of *Chopin Lives*, the great composer appears alone to comment on his life and times and to perform his piano music.

College productions can also be seen at Southeastern including an entertaining madrigal dinner in December and a musical in the spring. The shows are directed by faculty, and community actors often make up the cast. Local reviewers give the acting high marks so the $4 admission price ($2 for students) would appear to be worth the price.

–To reach Southeastern Illinois College–
Performances at Southeastern Illinois College take place in the campus theater in Building B on the first floor. The college is six miles east of Harrisburg on Illinois 13. Turn north onto College Drive and park at Building B, one of only three buildings on the campus.

Mitchell Museum

•

Location: Mt. Vernon
Box Office: (618) 242-1236
Handicapped access: Yes
Major productions: Cedarhurst Chamber Music– seven, September to May
Individual tickets: General admission–adults: $12; students, music teachers, orchestra members: $2; dinner performances, $12 to $15

•

The Mitchell Museum in Mt. Vernon hosts a chamber music series of the highest caliber. The musicians come from all over the globe to play at the museum and range from classical to living authors to the Medieval and Renaissance rhythms of the Burgundian Consort. The series began in 1978 and now draws around 200 people to each performance. The acoustics and size of the Mitchell Museum's main art gallery make it perfectly suited to host in chamber music.

The Mitchell Museum sponsors dinner performances of either jazz or small theatrical touring companies. These events are enjoyable evenings and, in the case of theatrical performances, may involve the audience directly in the entertainment.

–To reach Mitchell Museum–

Exit I-57/64 into Mt. Vernon, turn left onto Illinois 15/Broadway and go left/north onto 27th Street. 27th Street runs into Richview Road, go right/east for a block to the museum complex.

Burgundian Consort performance at the Mitchell Museum

Belleville Philharmonic Society

•

Location: Performances at the Scottish Rite, 1267 North 57th Street,
   Belleville
Box office: (618) 235-5600
Handicapped access: Yes
Major productions: Seven per year
Individual tickets: General Admission–adults $7, children free

•

The Belleville Philharmonic is a community orchestra which produces seven classical and pops concerts each year. The most popular
of these is the December production of the *Nutcracker*. These shows
often sell out so the free tickets for children do not apply. For the
three *Nutcracker* performances the orchestra teams up with the
Belleville School of Ballet and professional dancers are imported for
the lead dance rolls. This annual production of the nutcracker is the
only one to be found in Southern Illinois.

Along with most of the Belleville Philharmonic's performances,
the *Nutcracker* is held in the Scottish Rite Valley Bodies of Southern
Illinois, a Masonic lodge. The lodge contains a preceptory which dou-
bles as a luxurious 1,000-seat theater. The seating wraps around the
main floor and stage at a steep angle, insuring that virtually every seat
has an extraordinary view of the performance. The Belleville
Philharmonic also performs at Our Lady of the Snows Shrine near
Belleville and Fisher's Restaurant in Belleville.

–To reach the Scottish Rite–

The Scottish Rite complex is on the northwest side of Belleville
just off Illinois 161 on 57th Street. To reach 57th street from I-64, exit
at Belleville onto Illinois 159 south. Illinois 159 intersects with
Illinois 161 before entering Belleville. Turn right/west and 57th Street
is almost three miles ahead on the left.

Other Performing Arts Centers:

Sesser Opera House (618) 432-7274

This historic building on Sesser's main street hosts two to three professional music acts a year with "hillbilly comedy" included. Tickets are $10 at the door and $8.50 in advance. Local bluegrass groups appear every third Saturday and gospel music can be heard every fourth Sunday with ticket prices $4 to $5.

Masterworks Choral (618) 234-6699

The Belleville–based group is an auditioned adult chorus that performs classical works and Broadway hits with professional musicians from St. Louis. The group performs in area churches and the Quad Cinema in Belleville.

Shawnee Community College (618) 634- 2242

The college stages a Christmas musical which includes community actors and children. In the spring a musical is produced and a dinner theater is included among the performances. The college is in the extreme southern tip of the state near Ullin in Pulaski County off I-57.

McKendree College (618) 537-4481

McKendree College thespians produce straight plays, often Shakespeare or Greek, in the fall and a musical in the spring. The college is at the town of Lebanon off U.S. 50 in St. Clair County.

The Miner's Institute (618) 345-1940

The Miner's Players present three plays a year in The Miner's Institute, a historic Collinsville edifice. Built with money from coal miners in 1917, the institute, and its 1,000-seat theater is at 204 West Main Street.

Sunset Concert Series (618) 536-3393

Every summer Southern Illinois University and the Carbondale Park District bring touring reggae, rock, folk, blues (you name it!) to Carbondale. The steps of Shryock Auditorium in the Old Main Mall on campus and Turley Park are settings for this outdoor evening concert series. The shows are free and very popular.

Centralia Cultural Center (618) 532-2951

The center is a haven for local performing arts including the Centralia Philharmonic Orchestra and Little Theater Players. A giant concert of 300 singing and instrument-playing Centralians get together in December and a madrigal dinner is produced the week before. The Center is at 1250 East Rexford on the east side of town.

The Sesser Opera House

Wineries

I t is debatable whether visiting vineyards is a form of recreation. So we will let you decide. Southern Illinois is not now known for it's wine making activities, although years ago wine making was a very common in certain parts of the area. The soil and weather in Southern Illinois are both suited for growing excellent grapes for wine making.

Recently wine making has sprung up again with three active vineyards and one more in developmental stages. Two are located in the Pamona/Alto Pass area and the other in downtown Waterloo.

Alto Vineyards

Alto Vineyards bottled its first wine in 1988, six years after the first grapes were planted. The first two years of operation were highly successful, with the vintages selling out rapidly. Production has gradually increased to 19,000 bottles to meet heavy demand. About 10 acres of several grape varieties are producing award-winning white and red wines.

Alan Dillard, one of the owners of Alto Vineyards told the story of one of the winery's staff being contacted by a reporter from a prestigious trade magazine. "They asked where we had gone to school to produce such award-winning wines. To their surprise, our response was that, we hadn't."

The grape varieties at Alto Vineyards are French–American hybrids that will tolerate the cold and resist the disease and insects of Southern Illinois. The wines produced from the hybrid grapes range from dry to sweet. Many of the wines are very fruity. A wine tasting area is available at the purchase shop. Only Alto Vineyard wines are available at the shop. A small gift shop is also located on the premises.

Alto Vineyards holds several wine festivals at which time guests may sample and purchase wines and enjoy music of the local area. Contact Alto Vineyards for the dates of upcoming festivals. The vineyards also conducts tours by arrangement.

Location: Alto Vineyards, Ltd, P.O. Box 51 (Illinois 127), Alto Pass, IL 62905
Phone: (618) 893-4898
Hours: April through December, Wed. - Fri.
1 - 6 p.m.; Sat. 10 a.m. - 6 p.m., Sun. 1 - 6 p.m.

Pamona Winery

In mid October 1993, Pamona winery offered its first two wines. Jane Payne and George Majka have the only commercially produced apple wines in Southern Illinois. What's more, they are made from good 'ole Southern Illinois apples. We have not tasted their wines but they stress that they are serious winemakers offering both semi-dry and semi-sweet varieties suitable for table service in an atmosphere of fine dining. We will let you judge for yourselves. They plan to expand to grape wines in the near future.

Location: Pamona; three miles south of Little Grand Canyon on Hickory Ridge Rd.
Phone: (618) 893-2623
Hours: Call ahead; no wine tasting facility as yet

Waterloo Winery

Waterloo Winery is easy to spot as you drive along Illinois 3 through Waterloo. The site of the winery is a homey estate dating back to 1818, established just before Illinois obtained statehood. The site is now a reclaimed strip mine. In this unlikely spot you can find over 35 different wines or varietals; each is made from only one grape variety. The owners do everything from growing the grapes to bottling the wines and marketing them. Most of the grapes are grown in various parts of Southern Illinois and not at the wine tasting facility.

The owners claim they have something for everyone's taste, sweet, fruity and dry and everything in between. Some of the wines are award winners, but none are expensive, ranging in price from $6 to $10 per bottle. Both red and white varieties are available.

Location: 725 N. Market, Waterloo, IL 62905
Phone: (618) 939-8339
Hours: Sun. noon - 5 p.m. from March to Dec.

Unique Restaurants

S ome folks might question whether eating out should be considered recreation. At the very minimum, it is a way to avoid the routine of having to go to the grocery store, fix a meal and clean up afterward. But we're not talking about your average chain restaurant meal. We are talking about the forty-plus best eating establishments in Southern Illinois. We think most will agree that there are some unique and interesting places at which to dine that, if not enjoyable by themselves, will enhance any other recreational pursuits.

Our intent is not to catalogue all the restaurants in Southern Illinois but to feature those which have gained a reputation for being unique either by decor, atmosphere, location or by their menu. We have used our judgment in doing so and fully acknowledge that the eating establishments that we have written about may or may not be on your list of favorites. Please forgive us and write us about your favorite, but nevertheless *bon appetit.*

Pere Marquette Lodge

•

Location: Pere Marquette State Park, Illinois 100, west of Grafton
Phone: (618) 786-2331
Price range: Breakfast, $3.25–6.95; lunch, $4.25– $8.95; dinner,
$5.25–$14.95
Decor: Rustic
Handicapped access: Yes
Hours: Sun.–Thurs. 6:30 a.m. - 9 p.m., Fri.–Sat. to 10 p.m.; Nov.
through March, Sun.–Thurs. 6:30 a.m. - 7 p.m., Fri. – Sat. to
9 p.m.

•

As the early fall leaves turn colors in Southern Illinois, tourists
stream up Illinois 100 north of St. Louis, known as the Great River
Road, towards Pere Marquette State Park in the northwesternmost
corner of Southern
Illinois. In addition to
bluff-top views of the
Illinois River and trails
winding through the
park interior, visitors
find a large, yet rustic,
oak and sandstone lodge
in which they can eat,
drink and be merry after
touring the natural won-
ders outside.

The lodge is of 1930s
vintage and WPA con-
struction. Its origins are
therefore similar to those
of the lodge at Giant

City State Park. In the large anteroom of the lodge is a giant chess set.

Another characteristic which Pere Marquette has in common with its sister lodge farther south is its penchant for serving fried chicken. Fried chicken dinners are the most popular at the lodge, although the Sunday brunches with salads, fruit and carving stations for roast beef also draw crowds.

Reservations are recommended, especially in the fall, to take advantage of the large wine list, steaks, seafoods, breakfast and lunch items at the lodge. Large windows let diners enjoy the scenic beauty of the park while they are eating. Make a reservation for a table with a view of the Illinois River for a perfect finish to a day at the park.

❷ *Fin Inn*

•

Location: Main Street, west end of Grafton (Illinois 100)
Phone: (618) 786-2030
Price range: $6.60 - $10.95
Decor: Rustic, aquatic
Handicapped access: Yes
Hours: 11 a.m. - 8 p.m, daily

•

Fin Inn is the Sea World of Southern Illinois restaurants. But instead of dolphins and tuna, giant aquariums at every table are packed with huge carp, catfish, giant snapping turtles and other underwater

A typical booth featuring an aquarium at the Fin Inn

life from the Mississippi River, on whose banks Grafton is located. Kids, and everybody else, will love to watch the river's teeming life as they wait for similar fare from the Fin Inn's kitchens.

Whole catfish is a favorite dish and buffalo fish is also popular. Turtle is also served, either in soup or fried. This uncommon offering is worth a try as an appetizer. If you don't care for fish, steaks and more commonplace sandwiches are also available.

Not to worry about the fish you see in the aquariums. Unlike lobsters, these are not the animals served for dinner or lunch.

Benjamin's at the Godfrey Mansion

3

•

Location: 6722 Godfrey Rd. (Jct. of Illinois 67 & Illinois 267), Godfrey
Phone: (618) 466-7000
Price range: Lunch, $4.55 - $7.95; dinner, $7.95 - $19.95
Decor: Federal
Handicapped access: Yes
Hours: Tues.–Thurs., 11 a.m. to 9 p.m.; Fri. and Sat., 11 a.m. to 10 p.m.; Sun., 11 a.m. - 8 p.m. (brunch served 11 a.m. - 3 p.m.)

•

A more civilized place for lunch and dinner could hardly be imag-

Diners at Benjamin's

ined. Benjamin's is named for Benjamin Godfrey, the man who bought the mansion in 1834. The gray Greek Revival limestone mansion was built between 1831 and 1833, but Godfrey enlarged the mansion and added the galleries marking the house with a distinct southern influence.

This sandstone and oak mansion furnishes elegant surroundings for the elegant cuisine offered in the restaurant. There are surely few national historic sites where you can enjoy sumptuous steaks, seafood and pasta with a trio of champagne sorbets to finish. On Sundays, a brunch features Belgian waffles and eggs Benedict. One of the most popular lunch dishes is the chicken and broccoli crepes. Reservations are recommended every night.

As his mansion would indicate, Captain Benjamin Godfrey was quite wealthy. Nearby he built a seminary to educate his daughters. Today the seminary is **Lewis and Clark Community College**. The college's architecture remains some of the most beautiful in Illinois which the original name of Monticello Female Seminary (1838) might suggest. Only the best legal services would do for Mr. Godfrey which

Josephine's Tea Room

then, as now, meant the most influential. Thus Abraham Lincoln was Godfrey's personal lawyer and he visited the mansion often in this capacity.

4 *Josephine's Tea Room & Gift Shop*

●

Location: 6109 Godfrey Road (Illinois 67), Godfrey, north of Alton.
Phone: (618) 466-7796
Price range: $3.95 - $5.95
Decor: Country French
Handicapped access: No, but can enter with assistance, bathroom access
Hours: Lunch only, Mon.–Fri., 11 a.m. to 2 p.m.; Sat. 11a.m. to 3 p.m.; closed Sun.

●

Josephine's is another beautiful Godfrey luncheon spot. The tea room and gift shop is in a Victorian house which used to be part of the Monticello Female Seminary.

The tea room's tall windows, extending nearly to the ceiling, sparkle on sunny days and a beautiful view of the garden outside make for a relaxing lunch. The specialty of the house is the Crystal Bowl Salad, which consists of fresh fruit, chunks of white chicken and lettuce with bleu cheese, poppy seeds and salad dressing sprinkled on top. Several other salads are served in ample portions and club sandwiches are also available.

Cane Bottom, My Just Desserts

•

Location: 31 E. Broadway, Alton
Phone: (618) 462-5881
Price range: $1.25 to $4.25
Decor: Country antique
Handicapped access: No
Hours: Lunch only, daily, 10 a.m. - 4 p.m.

•

Among the antique and craft shops in Alton is this restaurant which features light fare and 150 different pies and cobblers. The menu is written on a chalk board and changes nearly every day. This is the only Alton restaurant with a view of the Mississippi River and Riverview park, and it is a lovely view at that.

Diners sit beneath 16-foot-high ceilings. Lunch is served at antique tables and chairs while mirrors date from the Prohibition Era.

Cane Bottom, My Just Desserts, serves "a light lunch and heavy desserts," according to owner Ann Badasch. The favorite is apple praline pie, but this is just one of 150 dessert recipes which rotate during the month. For the main course, Italian salads and chicken salad sandwiches are among the most popular. Reservations are accepted and necessary on Saturdays.

Rusty's

•

Location: 1201 N. Main, Edwardsville

Phone: (618) 656-1113

Price range: $5.50 lunch buffet; $7.75 (ribs) - $40 (Chateaubriand)

Decor: Rooms have different decors, some are rustic, some have art, some emphasize local art

Handicapped access: Yes

Hours: 11 a.m. - 2 p.m. lunch on Mon.–Fri.; 11 a.m. - 2 p.m. Sun brunch; 5 p.m. - 10:30 weekdays and Sun. for dinner. 5 p.m. to midnight on Fri. and Sat.

•

In the heart of the historic commercial area in Edwardsville is Rusty's. The building was built in 1819 and used as a trading post. For over 50 years it has been in operation as a restaurant. To St. Louis residents, Rusty's has become a landmark for good eating "across the river."

According to restaurant personnel the "added extras" draw the crowds at Rusty's. The decor, lighting and music complement the food and the service is superb. The buffet draws a large crowd and the lounge is a popular attraction.

The Inn __again__

•

Location: Heart of the Stockyards in National City, look for
Stockyards signs on Interstate I-55/70 immediately
before the Mississippi River bridge crossing into St.
Louis

Phone: (618) 274-6400

Price range: $5 - $9.50 (lunch)

Decor: Elegant dining atmosphere

Handicapped access: Yes

Hours: 6 a.m. - 2 p.m. on weekdays only; bar is open to 5 p.m. weekdays and to 6 p.m. on Thurs.

•

You enter a unique area in National City when you seek the
Stockyards Inn, described by the management as "Dining fit for a
king." First, you will see a gatekeeper who will let you in to a 120-

year-old operating stockyard. The popular restaurant on the grounds of the stockyards serves only breakfast and lunch but may soon be opening for the evening meal. The Inn <u>again</u> is known for its fine steaks. The staff prides itself on the unique onion soup which is served inside a carved out onion. Desserts are all homemade, the specialty being bread pudding made with whiskey. Breakfast is served cafeteria style.

Although some people refer to this restaurant as the Stockyards Inn, the proper name is The Inn <u>again</u>. The original inn burned down in 1986 and another was rebuilt in 1987. A vice president of the organization owning the restaurant sought advice from her secretary for a new name. Her secretary said, "Just call it The Inn again." They did.

The Inn <u>again</u> is a two story brick building decorated elegantly with stained glass windows and carved wood. It seats up to 250 people and has banquet facilities.

⑧ *Michael's Restaurant*

•

Location: 415 Broadway, Highland
Phone: (618) 654-8646
Price range: Lunch $5 - $8; Dinner $10 - $20
Decor: Swiss
Handicapped access: Yes
Hours: Lunch 11 a.m. - 2 p.m.; Dinner weekdays 5 p.m. - 9 p.m.; Sun. 5 p.m. - 10 p.m.; Sat. 5 p.m. - 11 p.m.

•

In the Swiss-German town of Highland, there is an eye-catching Swiss chalet complex consisting of a restaurant and lodging facility. The dimly-lit, but well-decorated restaurant has been around since the early 1940s, serving as a landmark for Highland.

Michael's Swiss Inn features fresh fish, prime rib and veal in a cozy atmosphere. Loca residents and St. Louis guests testify to the good food.

The Swiss Inn hosts Oktoberfest and Mayfest celebrations with entertainment and German food cooked outdoors.

Michael's Swiss Inn

⑨ *Trenton House Restaurant & Inn*

•

Location: 2 E. Broadway, Trenton
Phone: (618) 224-9331
Price range: $2.50 - $15.95; buffet weekdays $5.50, weekends; break-
        fast is served for $6.95.
Decor: Country
Handicapped access: Yes
Hours: Weekdays 6 a.m. – 10 p.m.; weekends 6 a.m. - 11 p.m.

•

The stamped tin ceiling is all that reveals the age of this 150-year old building that has been a restaurant for 100 years. The Trenton House draws guests all the way from St. Louis.

Guests have a choice of menu selections or a buffet. Good 'ole Southern Illinois fried chicken is featured on the buffet. Take our word for it, the chicken is delicious. Fried chicken is also a staple on weekends. Skip the chain restaurants when you're in the area and try the Trenton House.

The Trenton House as it appeared years ago

Diamond Mineral Springs

•

Location: #1 Pocahontas Rd; located one block west off Illinois
      160 N. off I-70 (west of Grantfork)
Phone: (618) 675-2655
Price range: $7.95 - 9.95
Decor: Country, family style
Handicapped access: Yes
Hours: 5 p.m.-9 p.m. Wed.-Fri; 4 p.m. to 10 p.m. on Sat.; and 11 a.m.-
      9 p.m. on Sun.

•

Q. What do you do when you build a hotel complex with the central attraction being a mineral spring, and the spring dries up? **A.** You convert to a restaurant.

That's just what happened at Diamond Mineral Springs. The building was constructed about 100 years ago as a hotel with natural springs to draw customers from St. Louis. The long-gone mineral springs helped build the town of Grantfork. The only indication of a town now is a road sign.

To enter Diamond Mineral Springs is to step back in time. Hundreds are treated to a family style atmosphere. There is also an outdoor seating area.

The menu is simple and posted on the wall. The management says that you will enjoy their chicken and homemade sausage.

Fin & Feather

•

Location: 2100 N. Emerald Rd. one mile south of Keyesport and 4.5
    miles east of Illinois 127
Phone: (618) 749-5330
Price range: $6 (chicken), $17.50 (beef tenderloin)
Decor: Ski lodge
Handicapped access: No
Hours: 4 p.m. - 10 p.m. Mon.–Fri.; 12p.m - 10 p.m. on Sat.

•

Way out in the country near Carlyle Lake you'll be surprised by the presence of a restaurant, the Fin & Feather. It's a relatively new, being in operation since 1986.

How does such a restaurant survive with no passing traffic? According to the owner, Dave Gaudette, the restaurant draws from major cities in Illinois and nearby states. Most of the guests have made reservations well in advance.

Dave attributes his success to a restaurant concept which includes his commitment to quality food, service, cleanliness, hospitality and value. If you find he satisfies these criteria let us and/or Dave know. He is committed to making the concept work.

Yes, there is a comprehensive menu, but the restaurant boasts nightly specials, examples being steak and lobster ($22), stuffed trout, New York strip with crab ($18), and steak and swordfish ($18).

Yes, the rumors are true. The Fin & Feather has been known to serve caribou, elk, alligator, frog legs, turtle and even giraffe, but don't expect these to be on the menu.

The decor is pleasing and relaxing. This restaurant truly qualifies as recreational.

Centralia House

•

Location: 111 N. Oak, Centralia (near the railroad tracks), ten miles
       from Centralia exit off I-64 or I-57
Phone: (618) 523-9754
Price range: Lunch $5 - $9; dinner $15 - $23
Decor: Victorian or has been described as "early brothel"
Handicapped access: No
Hours: Mon.–Fri. 11 a.m. - 10 p.m.; Sat. 5 p.m. - 10 p.m.; closed Sun.

•

    The Centralia House was originally built about 1854 as a saloon
and gambling house. It was the social center of the city until 1918 and
was restored in 1969 by the current owners. The restoration preserved
the original flavor of the saloon. The magnificent original oak bar and
stamped tin ceiling draw your attention. Ask the management about
the original iron front to the building.

The decor is a fraction of what you will enjoy at the Centralia House. The cuisine is equally pleasing. The style of cooking is generally Cajun and Continental French. The house specialty is the Centralia House Shrimp. If you order the special, you will be provided with a bib and napkin. The wine list consists of up to 70 wines.

Jim Brady, shot in the attempted assassination of former President Ronald Reagan, is a native of Centralia. He visits Centralia several times a year to to enjoy the shrimp at Centralia House. Civil War generals Grant, McClellan and Sherman are known to have eaten at the inn.

Here's an idea for those living near Carbondale who yearn for a new and interesting experience. Take the Amtrak from Carbondale to arrive in Centralia about 5 p.m. Walk across the street to the Centralia House, dine leisurely, and return to Carbondale on the train that evening.

Original Mineral Springs Hotel & Restaurant

•

Location: 506 Hanover, Okawville
Phone: (618) 243-5458
Price range: $1.50 - $19; breakfast is served
Decor: Eclectic
Handicapped access: No
Hours: Weekdays 7 a.m. - 10 p.m.; Weekends 7 a.m. - 11 p.m.

•

The restaurant associated with the Mineral Springs Hotel has a reputation for serving fine food. On Friday nights the restaurant hosts a seafood buffet for $9.95. A variety of prime rib cuts are featured on Saturdays. On Sundays, the restaurant reverts to the old Southern Illinois standby, fried chicken and also includes shrimp in buffet style.

Most of the time guests eat in the lounge area. There is a large dining area for groups.

Farmer's Inn

•

Location: Between Millstadt and Columbia on Illinois 158
Phone: (618) 476-3433
Price range: Dinner only is served $5 - $11.50
Decor: Country
Handicapped access: Yes
Hours: Wed.-Sun. 4 - 9:30 p.m.; closed Mon. and Tues.

•

The owners claim the "best fried chicken in Southern Illinois." That's a tough claim to substantiate since chicken is the specialty throughout Southern Illinois. We'll let you make up your own mind.

All-you-can-eat dinners are featured on the weekends and chicken and dumplings featured on Sunday. Homemade pies and a salad bar are also offered. We found the innkeepers to be very friendly and the customers seemed to be enjoying themselves.

No one is exactly certain when the Inn was built. The records show that taxes were first paid on the building in 1896, but records indicate the building was present in 1862 when it was a saloon.

One of two original jail houses behind Wartburg Inn

15

Wartburg Inn

•

Location: In Wartburg southwest of Waterloo
Phone: (618) 939 - 8981
Price range: $5.95 - $11.50
Decor: Rustic, antique with weapons, implements and all kinds of paraphernalia
Handicapped access: Yes
Hours: Mon - Fri. 4 - 10.30 p.m.; Sat. noon - 10 p.m., Sun. noon - 9 p.m .

•

Traveling between Waterloo and Maeystown you will go through Wartburg. As the saying says, "Don't blink your eyes or you will miss

The outside front of the Wartburg Inn

it." If not attentive, you may also miss the Wartburg Inn. Look for what appears to be a combination of an antique store and a junk yard on the west side of the road–that's the Wartburg Inn. The closer you get the more you will find the Inn interesting. There is a myriad of antique license plates on the front of the building. Now, you know you have found the right place.

If you are an antique lover, the interior will delight you. The walls are jam-packed with antiques that will keep you fascinated for hours. Look around; the owners appreciate your interest.

The Inn was built as a post office and grocery store over 100 years ago. It was also a filling station at one point. It has been the Wartburg Inn since 1976.

The decor is just part of the Wartburg experience. The Inn features a variety of menu items. The specialty is cod, baked or fried. It is the home of the "Wartburger", a 1/3 pound burger recommended by the proprietors. The Inn is also famous for its garnished, baked potato dishes, with potatoes exceeding one pound. Don't miss it.

The dining area at the Westerfield House

The Westerfield House

•

Location 8059 Jefferson Rd., Freeburg
Phone: (618) 539 - 5643
Price range: $38.50 per person
Decor: Antique Colonial
Handicapped access: Yes
Hours: Dinners on weekends; hours variable, call for specifics

•

The Westerfield House is an elegant restaurant, not far from St. Louis' metropolitan center, but set in a distinctly rural corner of Southern Illinois. A seven course dinner is prepared with meticulous care while the authentic Colonial decor presents patrons with a feast for the eyes. A 'unique dining experience' is a cliche, but in this case it's appropriate.

Most of the furniture in the house dates to the 18th century, although the 100-candle light (modified) chandelier is said to be from a 17th century Massachusetts church. Waiters also dress in Colonial garb.

Herb luncheons are served between April and October and a guided tour of the herb garden (with more than a hundred kinds of herbs) is given before lunch. Reservations are required for lunch or dinner and may be necessary a year in advance for the Christmas holiday dinners, when this bed and breakfast sparkles with ribbons and festive lights.

Directions: From St. Louis: travel over the Poplar Street Bridge to I-64 East to I-255 South to Illinois 15 east. From North County: over the Chain of Rocks Bridge (I-270 East) to I-255 South to Illinois 115 East. From South County go over the Jefferson Barracks Bridge to I-255 North to Illinois 15 East.

You will come to an intersection on Illinois 15 with Eckert's

Country Store on your left. You are one mile from Jefferson Road (Jefferson Road is approximately 12 miles from the Illinois 15 exit). At Jefferson Road, the only road with a left turn lane, there is a green S.A.V.E. sign on the right side of Illinois 15, and a large American Legion Freedom Farm on the left. You can only turn left. Go approximately two miles to the "Westerfield House."

 # *Hoefft's Village Inn*

•

Location: Mill & Main, Maeystown
Phone: (618) 458-6425
Price range: $3.75 - $9.00
Decor: Country
Handicapped access: Yes
Hours: Mondays 5 a.m. - 3 .p.m.; serving three meals a day Tues.
through Sun. 5 a. m. - 9 p.m.

•

Maeystown is a must to visit. While there visit Hoefft's Village Inn. Upstairs you will find a tavern with a few tables and downstairs is a restaurant that seats up to 250. You'll be eating in a restaurant that was built in the 1890s as a tavern. Historical records indicate that at one time the building was repossessed for $200.

There are daily specials which generally include a meat, potatoes and a vegetable. Remember you are in a village with a strong German heritage.

Take the opportunity to stroll from the restaurant to the historic sites in Maeystown.

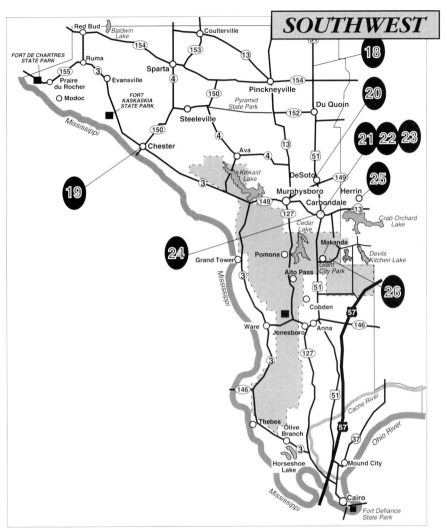

Traveler's Cafe

●

Location: U.S. 51, 15 miles north of Du Quoin
Phone: (618) 787-2301
Price range: $6 (chicken) - $22 (lobster)
Decor: Casual
Handicapped access: Yes
Hours: Wed.–Thur. 4:30 p.m. - 9 p.m.; closed Mon. and Tues.

●

If not the oldest, the Traveler's Cave is one of the oldest continually operating dining establishments in Southern Illinois. It has served Southern Illinoisans for almost 70 years. Prior to the early 1920s the restaurant was a farmhouse.

The specialty of the house is country ribs and onion rings. So what? Well, we are told by customers that they prefer the ribs without sauce. In other words, the ribs are cooked so well that sauce detracts from the taste. The onion rings are unique, made from scratch by a special recipe. Enough description, you'll just have to see for yourself why customers like the Traveler's Cafe specialities.

Reids' Harvest House Smorgasbord

•

Location: 2440 State St., two miles east on Illinois 150, Chester
Phone: (618) 826-4933
Price range: Mon. - Thur. lunch $4.50; Mon. - Thur. dinner $5.45; Friday seafood buffet - $11.95; Sat. buffet $5.45; Sun. buffet $5.75; breakfast is served
Decor: Country
Handicapped access: Yes
Hours: Sun.–Thur. 7 a.m. - 9 p.m.; Fri and Sat. 7 a.m. - 10 p.m.

•

The Reids family puts on a feast known throughout Southern Illinois and into St. Louis. In 1982 this restaurant started on a big scale, seating approximately 300 and believing that "if we build it, they will come." And they did, making this venture every business person's dream.

Reids' Harvest House is famous for its Friday night seafood buffet, the Seafood Lover's Dream. Southern Illinoisans travel from miles around to eat crab legs, stuffed crab, frog legs, fried oysters, chilled and fried shrimp, baked cod, fried scallops, fried clams, fried catfish and much more.

At a typical Saturday dinner smorgasbord you can expect to find fried chicken, barbecued roast pork, fried catfish, spaghetti or lasagna, meat loaf, bunches of vegetables and a large salad bar.

And, it's all you can eat!

Tom's Place

●

Location: U.S. 51, just north of De Soto
Phone: (618) 867–3033
Price range: $8.95 - $26.95
Decor: Mounted large animals, secluded booths
Handicapped access: Yes, but not to code
Hours: Tues.–Sat.: 5 - 9 p.m. (last seating)

●

Tom's is a former speakeasy and road house. The layout of the restaurant reflects its romantic and historic past. Several dining rooms that seat two to 10 people are available upon request. Although the restaurant has been recently remodeled, it retains its classic menu of steaks, seafood and wild game. Both venison and lobster are available at Tom's though the most popular dish is the prime rib. Tom's often has advertised two-for-the-price-of-one prime rib specials. An added delicacy is the escargot, rarely found in area restaurants.

An ample wine list composed of California, French and German varieties complements the culinary delights to be found in one of Southern Illinois' premiere fine dining experiences.

Although Tom's is located in a country setting, reservations are recommended and a necessity to secure one of the private dining rooms.

21

Tres Hombres

●

Location: 119 N. Washington, Carbondale
Phone: (618) 457-3308
Price range: $5 - $8
Decor: Stained wooden interior
Handicapped access: Yes, but not the bathrooms
Hours: Sun.–Thur. 11 a.m. - 10 p.m; Fri. and Sat. to 11 p.m.

●

"Authentic Mexican cuisine, casual dining atmosphere, lovely hostesses and great margaritas by the pitcher," is how co-owner Gary Robinson sums up one of the most popular restaurants in deep Southern Illinois.

"Tres," as it is known by locals, is a popular eating and watering hole and features live music in the bar on Thursday nights. Reservations are essential Thursday through Saturday nights and a good idea any other evening. In addition to popular fajita and nacho dishes, the restaurant serves south of the border favorites like steak and chicken burritos and chimichangas.

Located in Carbondale, the restaurant is near the largest university in Southern Illinois and right down the street from The Stage Company.

Mary Lou's

•

Location: 114 S. Illinois Avenue, Carbondale
Phone: (618) 457-5084
Price range: $2 - $5
Decor: American diner and local photographs
Handicapped access: Yes
Hours: Tues. - Sat. 7 a.m. - 2 p.m.

•

On November 17, 1987, the governor of Illinois proclaimed Mary Lou Trammel Day and all her customers were urged to give her a kiss. Whether Mary Lou received more kisses that day than usual is not recorded, but her diner remains as testimony to one of Southern Illinois' enduring institu-

*The counter at
Mary Lou's*

tions. The restaurant is now run by Mary Lou's daughter, Marilyn, and her husband Robert who have continued the tradition of banter and fried food started by Mary Lou in 1962.

A long bar and booth seating in the back is framed by walls covered with numerous historical photographs of Carbondale. The food served includes sandwiches such as hamburgers, tenderloin and sausage and eggs as well as plate lunch specials like meatloaf and tuna casseroles. Several types of pie are available for dessert, but the biggest seller is the homemade biscuits and gravy on Saturday when university students and townspeople pile in for breakfast.

 23

The Mississippi Flyway

●

Location: Murdale Shopping Center, West Main Street, Carbondale
Phone: (618) 529-9363
Price range: $2.50 - $8.50
Decor: Hunting themes with numerous stuffed animals on the walls
Handicapped access: Yes

●

You'll find ducks and geese, mallards and crappie; largemouth bass and turkey–all this in the Mississippi Flyway–the restaurant, that is, not the migratory path for geese.

Midway between Lake Kinkaid and Crab Orchard Wildlife Refuge, the restaurant is a favorite with Southern Illinoisans. Offered in this family pub are the popular catfish sandwiches as well as Italian beef and steaks. Reservations are not accepted, but the restaurant is quite large so there is only an occasional waiting list on Friday nights.

Restaurant Tokyo

•

Location: 218 N. Illinois Avenue, Carbondale
Phone: (618) 529-2580
Price range:$4 - $20 (reduced lunch prices)
Decor: Modern, oriental
Handicapped access: Yes
Hours: Lunch 11:30 a.m. - 2 p.m.; dinner 5 p.m - 10 p.m.;
       Sun. noon - 9 p.m.

•

You won't find another one of these in Southern Illinois outside the St. Louis metropolitan area. It's a Japanese restaurant, complete with sushi and other authentic Japanese foods served with sake and beer. Since the owner is Korean there are several items on the menu that are Korean delights.

It is a tastefully decorated restaurant and on most Fridays and weekends a musician plays old favorites, light classical or sometimes jazz on a grand piano, adding to the elegant atmosphere of the establishment.

Sushi must be served very fresh and cannot be frozen, so the restaurant imports the fish from either coast in inert gas packs which keep it fresh, but not frozen.

Restaurant Tokyo's most popular dish is the lightly battered (and less jarring) tempura seafood. But don't be bashful, try the sushi and you'll probably find that, while the idea may be unappealing, raw fish is not so bad after all.

25

Mary's

•

Location: 509 S. Park, Herrin
Phone: (618) 942-2742
Price range: $14 - $40
Decor: Classic American
Handicapped access: Yes
Hours for reservations: Lunch: Tues. through Fri. 11:00 a..m. to 1:30 p.m.; Dinner on weekdays from 7:30 p.m.; Sat., 5:30 p.m. - 8:30 p.m.

•

Seafood is flown in daily from Florida's gulf coast. The weekend rotating menu includes game birds like quail and duck. Small, separate dining rooms accommodate four to 30 patrons among the plush curtains, small lamps perched on inn tables and cushioned armchairs.

This is Mary's, Southern Illinois' finest and most luxurious restaurant. Everything is made from scratch in the small kitchen of this Victorian-style, peach and white trimmed house. The popular seafood dishes include salmon, swordfish and tuna steaks.

Mary's is not a restaurant to visit if you are in a hurry. Patrons often spend three hours over lunch and drinks and 90 minutes over dinner. However, the management may require that your lunch stay be much shorter. The atmosphere and the food warrant the description, "dining experience." In order to experience Mary's, reservations, especially on Saturdays, are recommended.

Giant City Lodge

•

Location: Giant City State Park, east of Makanda
Phone: (618) 457-4921
Price range: Breakfast $2 - $4.25; lunch, $2 - $6; dinner, $5 - $13
Decor: Rustic country lodge
Handicapped access: Yes
Hours: Mon.–Sat, 8 a.m. - 8:30 p.m.; Sun. 8 a.m. - 8 p.m.

•

"The lodge," as it's known to area residents, is a Southern Illinois original. Sitting among the woods of Giant City State Park, the restaurant is a popular destination for a weekend's entertainment so reservations are recommended Friday night through Sunday. The lodge specializes in a family style chicken dinner with all the "fixins," which is served exclusively on Sundays.

There is also a wide variety of steaks (including prime rib) and seafood to

The anteroom at Giant City Lodge

choose from for lunch as well. The breakfast menu includes omelets.

The views from the huge windows in the dining room remind patrons that this restaurant is in the country. The architecture of the entire lodge lends to the effect. It was built in the 1930s in the Depression Era by the Civilian Conservation Corps and constructed of sandstone, white oak and pine. A high ceiling and a giant fireplace dominate one of the largest and most attractive restaurant waiting rooms anywhere. A small gift shop is located here. Leading out of the anteroom is a bar area serving as the entrance to the large dining rooms. Giant City Lodge is the ultimate in relaxation and country enjoyment.

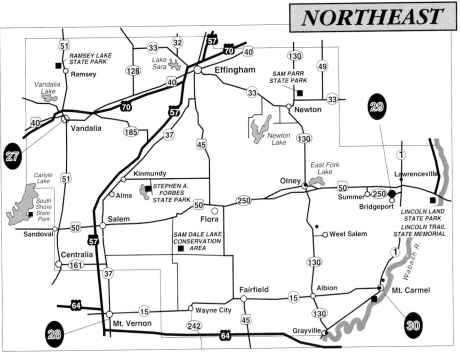

NORTHEAST

Cuppy's Old Fashioned Soda Fountain & Kitchen

•

Location: 402 W. Gallatin Street, across from the Old State Capitol,
    Vandalia
Phone: (618) 283-0054
Price range: $1.50 - $3.95
Decor: Antique Drug Store
Handicapped access: Yes
Hours: Daily 7:30 a.m. - 5:30 p.m.; closed Sun.

•

Across from one of the foremost historic sites in Southern Illinois, the Old State Capitol, is one of the most historically decorated eating establishments. Cuppy's, as it is known around town, has converted its interior into an old-fashioned soda fountain and drugstore, with the authentic decor transported from a 1924 Springfield establishment.

Its gray marble bar and oak cabinets with lighted stained glass will send you back to a simpler time, complemented by the simple fare of sundaes, chicken salad and tuna salad sandwiches. The cabinets, once used to store pharmaceutical items now display memorabilia, mainly from the early part of the century. The decor was brought from Watts Drugstore in Springfield, and visitors to Vandalia can now enjoy it with a light breakfast or lunch at Cuppy's. Reservations for large groups are requested.

King Barbacoa (Duke's)

Location: 918 Gilbert, Mt. Vernon
Phone: (618) 242-2264
Price range: $2 - 6
Decor: Minimal; go for the barbecue not the decor
Handicapped access: No
Hours: 10 a.m. - 6 p.m.

Better known as Duke's, King Barbacoa has been in business for many years and serves what most folks in Mt. Vernon rate as the best barbecue. A barbecue sandwich goes for $2.50 and a slab of ribs $14. The customer has a choice of mild or hot sauces on pork or beef. Unlike barbecue served throughout much of the area, the sauce does not overwhelm the taste of the meat. There are only a few tables in King Barbacoa so many orders are "to go."

King Barbacoa is owned by Duke and Mary Bowman. Their daughter, Nada Bowman often works the friendly, but somewhat isolated, restaurant. To reach King Barbacoa, head south on South 10th Street until reaching Gilbert Street.

Nada Bowman ready to help you at King Barbacoa

Gray's

•

Location: 955 E. State St., Bridgeport (near Lawrenceville)
Phone: (618) 945-9501
Price range: $ 5 - $12
Decor: Lacking; go for the friendly atmosphere
Handicapped access: No
Hours: 8a.m. - midnight. Food service until 10:30 p.m.

•

There is a scarcity of notable restaurants in the northeast portion of Southern Illinois. Fast food restaurants have taken over. The residents of the area lament the closing of many of their favorite eating places. However, if pressed, most folks in Lawrenceville will recommend Gray's in Bridgeport. Although Gray's is a tavern, it is better known for its food and is primarily a family restaurant, seating about 120 individuals.

Catfish and steaks are the specialties at Gray's. Even on a week night the five cooks at Gray's are busy pushing out one plate after another to serve the large crowd.

Guy Hadley's

•

Location: 416 Market St., Mt. Carmel
Phone: (618) 262-4849
Price range: $2 - $7
Decor: Nostalgic 50's fountain style
Handicapped access: Yes

•

Guy Hadley's is one restaurant in Southern Illinois that has survived the years. Others have come and gone. Guy Hadley, the original owner, is quoted as saying "I opened this place way back in 1917, and since then I've seen it change from a confectionery to a lunch counter and candy store to a popular full service cafe."

In trying to survive, where many local-owned, non-chain, restaurants have succumbed to the fast-food restaurants, Guy Hadley's has renovated in recent years to take on a 1950's soda fountain motif. A Wurlitzer jukebox sits near the entrance. Old books are shelved at each booth and 1950's memorabilia adorn the walls.

Sandwiches are popular at Guy Hadley's, the most popular being the breaded tenderloin for $2.45. A soda fountain lets you choose some of those sinful ice cream desserts and pies that are also popular.

Guy Hadley's is currently owned by Terry Beckerman.

Jukebox at Guy Hadley's

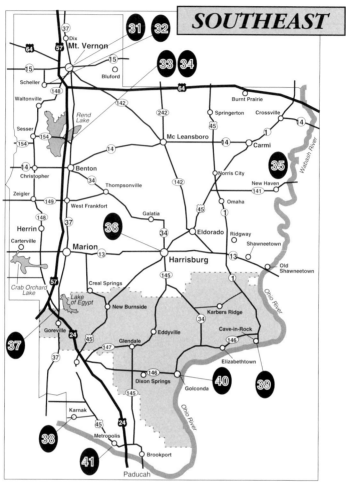

Opal's Smorgasbord

•

Location: 912 S. 10th (Illinois 37 south of Mt. Vernon city center)
Phone: (618) 242-9897
Price range: $4.29 for smorgasbord
Decor: Family restaurant atmosphere
Handicapped access: Yes
Hours: 11 a.m. - 7 p.m. seven days a week

•

Opal Justice loves to cook. Her favorite hobby turned into a business in 1962. The business flourished and has become known throughout Southern Illinois as a good place to eat. In recent years Opal could

Opal's buffet

not handle the volume, so she sold the restaurant. Nevertheless, Opal's continues to serve the chicken buffet that made it famous. We hear through the grapevine that Opal, who is in her 80s, still likes to cook and frequently calls people up and invites them over for dinner.

Opal's Smorgasbord is the best bargain in Southern Illinois for the hungry individual on a limited budget. Until recently the price for the 40-item smorgasbord was $3.99. There has recently been a small increase in the price. Remember, it's all you can eat.

Author's note: Within minutes of opening at 11 a.m. on Saturday, I counted over 50 people eating the smorgasbord. The sample of chicken I received told me to go back again when I'm hungry.

Scheller Playhouse

•

Location: Scheller Playhouse
Phone: (618) 279-7887
Price range: $9 - $12.95
Decor: Rustic
Handicapped access: Yes
Hours: Mon.–Thurs. 8 a.m. to 10 p.m. (lounge till 1: a.m.); Fri. - Sat. 8 a.m. to 12 midnight (lounge till 1 a. m.)

•

There are ample proportions, both of space and food, in this former general store dating back to the last century. Scheller Playhouse is famous for its seafood and especially its seafood buffet, served twice monthly and every Friday during Lent (of course). Steaks and pasta mingle with crab legs, frog legs and the ever popular cod sandwiches on the menu.

Reservations are taken, but rarely necessary, as a great dining hall can be opened up to accommodate hundreds. A big pot-bellied stove groans away in the kitchen heating up the "fixins." Patrons can have a drink from the bar while they are waiting or can even hang around until 1 a.m. if the fancy strikes them. Leave your signature on a signature post or at the chimney stretching up from the bar out of the building. Scheller Playhouse isn't far from Mt. Vernon and its elegant Mitchell Museum. For an entertaining dinner, nothing in Mt. Vernon can match it.

Burton's Cafe

•

Location: Illinois 37, Whittington, six miles north of Benton
Phone: (618) 629-2515
Price range: $1.45 - $4.75
Decor: Traditional diner
Handicapped access: Yes
Hours: Tues. - Thurs. 7 a.m. - 7 p.m.; Fri. and Sat. until 8 p.m.

•

"Home of the famous white pie," it's called and deservedly so. Burton's Cafe in Whittington, just down the road from Rend Lake, has been serving breakfast, lunch and dinner since it was opened by the Burton family in 1935. Three owners later, Bob Jones, is the second generation of his family to run the establishment, serving hot cakes, omelets, veal sandwiches, chili, fish, tenderloins and chicken and dumplings just to name a few of the dishes.

But don't forget the pies. They're made fresh early in the morning and include cream, peanut butter, chocolate, cherry, coconut and rhubarb.

The cafe is dressed up for holidays, but is a pretty standard design. As Bob Jones said, "We just try to make everybody comfortable, we don't put on a lot of airs."

Windows

•

Location: Wayne Fitzgerrell State Park, three miles west of Whittington
Phone: (618) 629-2454
Price range: Breakfast, $1 - $4.50; lunch $1 - $6; Dinner $3 - $14
Decor: Modern
Handicapped access: Yes
Hours: Nov.–April: Sun.–Thurs., 8 a.m. - 8 p.m., Fri. and Sat. until 9 p.m.; May–Oct., Sun. - Thurs. 8 a.m. - 9 p.m., Fri. and Sat. until 10 p.m.

•

Windows is aptly named. Sitting dockside on Rend Lake, the restaurant offers fine dining in a lakeside setting which is, despite the abundance of lakes in the area, rare for Southern Illinois. The interior of the restaurant is tastefully decorated and patrons can dine on the terrace in good weather.

A large menu features everything made from scratch, including the restaurant's own cuts of meat. Steak Duncan, a charbroiled New York strip steak with sauteed mushrooms and green chilies is a favorite. Catfish, shrimp, scampi and orange roughy should satisfy the seafood lover. Pies made from scratch, complete the dinner.

Windows also serves breakfast and lunch and is equipped with a fully-stocked bar and adjoining lounge. Entertainment during the summer includes folk singers on the deck.

Two Tony's

•

Location: 1015 E. Main Street, (Illinois 1) Carmi
Phone: (618) 382-8555
Price Range: $4.75 - $6.25
Decor: Antique country
Handicapped access: Yes
Hours: Wed. - Sun. 11 a.m. to 8 p.m., closed Mon. and Tues.

•

The smorgasbord to end all smorgasbords is found in the little town of Carmi on the eastern side of Southern Illinois. Lined up on a 60 foot-long buffet is a 100 pound joint of roast beef, chicken and dumplings, green beans, yams, corn, salads, and fresh fruits, just to name a few. All of the food is made from scratch and it changes a little bit every day.

Ruth Ann Smith, the owner with her husband Ted, summed it up: "We have great food." It's an all-you-can-eat buffet costing a little more for dinner than for lunch.

Matching its expansive smorgasbord, Two Tony's displays an enormous collection of hats. Nearly 2,000 are arranged on the walls, both ladies' and men's, caps and bonnets. In addition to hats, antique farm implements of every description plus cow and horse bells decorate the interior. There is still room for 500 diners. Reservations are necessary only for large groups.

Johnson's Southern Style Bar-B-Q

•

Location: 700 E. Walnut, Harrisburg
Phone: (618) 252-0477
Price range: $1.95 - $12
Hours: Mon.–Sat. 9:30 a.m. - 8:00 p.m.; Sun. 10 a.m. - 7 p.m.

•

Through its barbecue sauce, Johnson's is probably the best-known barbecue restaurant in a region full of barbecues. Indeed, a more modest shell for such a renowned establishment could hardly be imagined. It rates a shop barely larger than a drive-through in Harrisburg.

The sandwiches come in hot and not-so-hot varieties. Whole chickens or sides of barbecue pork, barbecued mutton and beef are available for take out. Johnson's is a quick, easy stop on the way to any number of destinations in the Shawnee National Forest, including Garden of the Gods, which lies about 20 miles southeast of Harrisburg.

Longhorn Restaurant

•

Location: Three miles north of Goreville on Illinois 37
Phone: (618) 995-9575
Price range: $4 - $8
Decor: Country ranch and rodeo
Handicapped access: Yes

•

Diners may be familiar with choosing their own lobster before dinner, but choosing their own cow is beyond the experience of most. The Longhorn Restaurant, near the Lake of Egypt, is as close to this experience as you are likely to find.

Above the restaurant is an arena where spectators can witness the cattle, pig, goat and horse auctions. Cattle, hogs and goats are for sale every Monday night and no admission ticket is required. Horse auctions are held the second Friday of every month. Tickets, which cost $2, can be reserved by calling (618) 995-2114.

Downstairs, the restaurant serves up most of what's on auction above. Friday and Saturday night is steak night, while other days might feature roast beef or meatloaf. But one thing you can be sure of according to manager Cheryl Douglas, everything is made from scratch and that includes the desserts. "We're famous for our pies," she said, and then rattles off a list: "apple, cherry, pecan, blackberry cobbler, rhubarb, lemon ... anything that you could possibly imagine, we'll make a pie out of."

That's what they'll rustle up for you at the Longhorn.

38 *Our Place*

●

Location: 107 Washington St. (Illinois 169), Karnak
Phone: (618) 634-2224
Price range: $2.19 - $11.95
Decor: Antique Victorian motif
Handicapped access: Yes, not the rest rooms
Hours: Lunch, Mon.–through Fri. 10:30 a.m. - 1:30 p.m; Dinner Mon.–Thurs. 4 - 9 p.m.; Fri. and Sat. until 10 p.m.

●

"I'd recommend the president eat there," said an enthusiastic patron of Our Place, although it is unlikely the president will be passing through tiny Karnak in Pulaski County, anyone visiting swampy Heron Pond a few miles away could do worse than to stop by this pleasant cafe.

The interior decor is dominated by a giant stained antique cabinet filled with a collection of clown figurines; an old muscle-powered sewing machine stands, somehow fittingly, in the window. The explanation for the clowns is co-owner Chad Wilson was a clown during his college career and still bears an affection for them.

The restaurant serves a variety of sandwiches, one of the most popular is the Tin Lizzy, a turkey, bacon and cheddar combination. Pizza is also served and at a very reasonable price ($11.95 for a 16" pizza with the works.) A specialty of the house is the Italian Avanti bread which is also used for pizza crust. Freshly baked cakes and pies with ice creams and yogurts are offered for dessert.

Our Place and owner Peggy Wilson

39

Cave-In-Rock Restaurant

●

Location: Illinois 1, Cave-In-Rock State Park near Golconda
Phone: (618) 289-4545
Price range: $2.50 - $10.95
Decor: Rustic
Handicapped access: Yes
Hours: 8 a.m. - 7 p.m.; closed Dec. to Feb.

●

The majestic meandering of a big river through the countryside is an impressive sight. As they enjoy the scenery through big windows in the restaurant or outside on the patio, patrons of Cave-In-Rock Restaurant will find gastronomic delights to complement the beauty of the Ohio River. Diners enjoy catfish dinners, grilled tenderloins, steaks and made-from-scratch rolls and desserts.

Terry Clark, the concessionaire with his wife Mary, calls the view of the river and Kentucky countryside, "spectacular." The sandstone and stained cedar restaurant is a rustic structure, blending well with the park and its scenery. The restaurant does not take reservations and alcohol is not served.

The Mansion at Golconda

●

Location: Columbus Street (a block south of Main street), Golconda
Phone: (618) 683-4400
Price range: $8 - $20
Decor: Elegantly decorated Victorian Mansion
Handicapped access: No, but assistance is available.
Hours: Daily for lunch, 11 a.m. - 2 p.m.; Mon.–Sat. for dinner, 5 p.m. - 9 p.m.; closed Sunday night

●

The Mansion is Victorian, the food exquisite and the place is Golconda. Golconda where? A more unlikely location for an elegant restaurant could hardly be imagined. But there sits The Mansion in the center of a tiny Ohio River town, miles from a major population center. It is, however, near Cave-In-Rock State Park and several Shawnee National Forest sites including the popular Garden of the Gods.

Since 1986 patrons have enjoyed quail, duck, chicken, steaks, seafood and chops, while dining beneath crystal chandeliers and among the elaborately carved woodwork, marble facings and antiques. The mansion was built by a Victorian merchant in 1894. A tour of the mansion will take you through a 19th-century version of conspicuous consumption and is a worthwhile experience in and of itself.

In the dining room, patrons can take part in their own conspicuous consumption by sampling the amazingly varied menu. Prime rib is a favorite on Saturday nights (the only time it is served), but the menu ranges from lobster tail to rack of lamb. "I honestly don't think there's another restaurant that comes close to what we do," said Marilyn Kunz, half of the husband and wife team that owns and manages the restaurant. Reservations are required on Saturday nights and recommended the rest of the time.

The Kunz's themselves are an interesting pair. Having given up the rat race in Chicago (she was an accountant and he was a plant manager), they have opened a restaurant/bed and breakfast in the more relaxed atmosphere of Golconda. Now they work day and night to maintain their own business.

Merv's Bar & Grill & The Celebrity Buffet

•

Location: Metropolis, Ohio Riverfront
Phone: Individual, 1-800-935-7700; Group, 1-800-935-1111, reservations are recommended
Price range: $3.95 - $13.95
Decor: Late Victorian
Handicapped access: Yes
Hours: Buffet 8 a.m. - 8 p.m.; Bar and Grill, 11 a.m. - 11 p.m.

•

If lunch in a floating restaurant on the Ohio River sounds like an enticing idea, how about breakfast and dinner, too. It is all possible at Merv Griffin's Landing in Metropolis. Merv Griffin has given his name and about 150 photos of himself schmoozing with celebrities to this floating restaurant, the dock for **Players International Riverboat Casino** (see Riverboat Section).

A breakfast buffet is open until 11 a.m. when the ship's Belgian chef, Raymond VanBerel, directs the transition to the lunch and dinner selections. "Our cooking is French cooking with German and Italian influence," said the European trained chef. VanBerel prepares a diced beef, onion and mustard stew called Beef a la Flamande. In addition, pork a la orange and more traditional American dishes such as catfish and roast beef are available for passengers waiting for the adjoining riverboat casino to sail and the dice to roll.

You don't have to buy a ticket for the casino riverboat to eat at the buffet, and that goes for Merv's Bar and Grill as well. Reservations, however, are recommended for the Bar and Grill where a set menu of burgers, prime rib, shish kabobs, oysters and salads await visitors. On the third floor a banquet hall seats about 150 for weddings, meetings or other events.

The buffet line at Merv's Bar & Grill

The decor on the restaurant ship is a collection of bits and pieces, mostly from 19th-century buildings. A St. Louis company built the ship and used this unorthodox technique with the result that every ceiling is different. Some are ornate copper designs, another is composed of doors painted uniformly white. The bar and grill area is especially handsome with green marble pillars over which ornate copper trimming serves as a backdrop for the bartenders. Also in the bar and grill as well as downstairs at the ticket and gift shop area are old historic photos of Metropolis, a collection any local museum would be proud to display.

Bed & Breakfasts, Guest Houses, & Country Inns

Looking down the river from the deck at Tara Point Inn

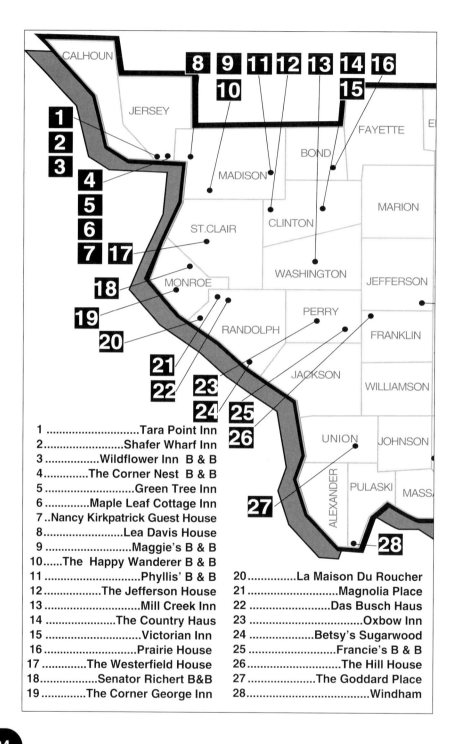

1 ....Tara Point Inn
2.......................Shafer Wharf Inn
3 ....Wildflower Inn B & B
4..............The Corner Nest B & B
5 ....Green Tree Inn
6 ....Maple Leaf Cottage Inn
7 ..Nancy Kirkpatrick Guest House
8.........................Lea Davis House
9 ....Maggie's B & B
10......The Happy Wanderer B & B
11 ....Phyllis' B & B
12 ....The Jefferson House
13 ....Mill Creek Inn
14 ....The Country Haus
15 ....Victorian Inn
16 ....Prairie House
17 ....The Westerfield House
18..................Senator Richert B&B
19 ....The Corner George Inn

20...............La Maison Du Roucher
21 ....Magnolia Place
22 ....Das Busch Haus
23 ....Oxbow Inn
24 ....Betsy's Sugarwood
25 ....Francie's B & B
26............................The Hill House
27 ....The Goddard Place
28...Windham

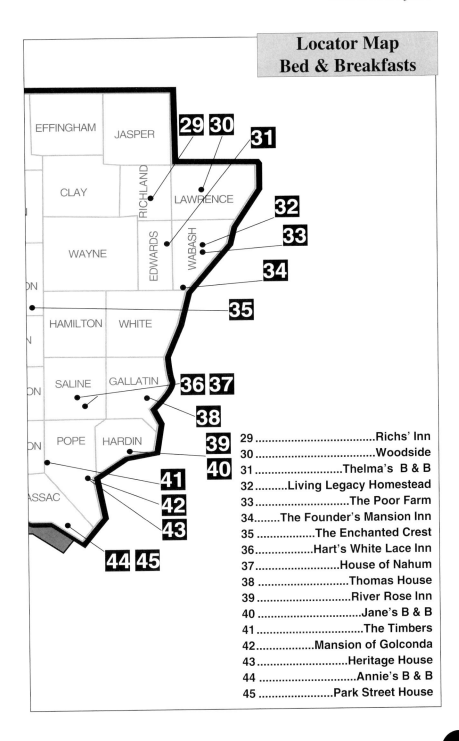

B ed and breakfasts and country inns provide the coziness of a home atmosphere and a close interaction with people of varied backgrounds and interests. The New Englanders, and eastcoasters, in general, successfully pioneered the industry, and this type of recreation has been slow in reaching Southern Illinois. Southern Illinois' bed and breakfast industry is, however, now in a growth phase with several new bed and breakfasts and inns on the drawing board. Few of the Southern Illinois bed and breakfasts were started prior to the mid 1980s.

The authors were not able to visit every bed and breakfast, but over 90 percent were visited. In almost every instance, we found the proprietors friendly and proud of their bed and breakfast, its history and its offerings. We were astonished by the variety of bed and breakfasts in Southern Illinois. They ranged from historic river town mansions with antique furnishings, to modern prairie and ranch settings, with almost every combination in between. Each bed and breakfast is distinctive, having its own atmosphere and appeal.

State and local laws govern what may be called a bed and breakfast and what may be called a guest house or a country inn. Bed and breakfasts are owner/manager occupied and have up to five guest rooms. Breakfast only is served. Country inns may have more than five guest rooms and generally serve meals other than breakfast. Less stringent rules apply to bed and breakfasts than to establishments with more than five guest rooms. Most proprietors hold the number of guest rooms to under five to meet the standards for a bed and breakfast. Most establishments listed belong to the Illinois Association of Bed and Breakfasts.

The bed and breakfasts and inns provide a refreshing get away from the routine, and we highly suggest that you give them a try. Southern Illinois bed and breakfasts are located in a general way on the map at the beginning of this section. More specific regional maps follow to help pinpoint their locations. As you can see, many of the bed and breakfasts are situated along the Ohio or Mississippi rivers and take advantage of the views and recreation along these waterways.

1   *Tara Point Inn*

•

Location: #1 Tara Point Estates, Grafton, IL 62037
Phone: (618) 786-3555
Manager/Owner: Larry & Margaret Wright
Number of rooms and baths: Four guest rooms with two shared baths
Room rate: $117 full river-view room ($95 weekdays); and $107 for hill side rooms ($85 weekdays)
Meals: Continental breakfast
Air conditioning: Central air
Smoking policy: No smoking in rooms or bathrooms
Credit cards: No credit cards; checks and travelers checks accepted
Handicapped access: Limited (small step up entrance)

•

The owners of Tara Point Inn designed and built the house originally as a private retirement home in 1990. In 1991, they felt the home was so ideally situated that the west wing was opened as a bed and breakfast. The view from the inn is magnificent. Their brochure makes the claim that "most visitors tell us that our view is the most spectacular in the Midwest." We agree that it is absolutely spectacular. One may look up and down the Mississippi and Illinois Rivers from the bluff-top vantage point where the inn is situated. In addition, a wrap-around veranda is conducive to sitting and relaxing while taking in the view. The inn is only a short distance from St. Louis, Missouri (40-45 min. travel). Inside, a spacious game room offers numerous activities including pool, darts, television, shuffleboard and more. Complimentary snacks and a wet bar are available. Numerous sites, including Pere Marquette State Park, may be seen in the Grafton area while at Tara Point Inn.

Above: The innkeeper, Larry Wright, is shown enjoying the river view.
Below: Aerial view of Tara Point Inn.

2   *Shafer Wharf Inn*

●

Location: 220 W. Main (P. O. Box 453), Grafton, IL 62037
Phone: (618) 374-2821
Manager/Owner: Mary Ann Pitchford
Number of rooms and baths: Two bedrooms with private baths
Room rate: $75 double occupancy
Meals: Hearty country breakfast included
Air conditioning: Central air
Smoking policy: No smoking
Handicapped access: None

●

Shafer Wharf Inn in Grafton

Grafton was the site of the largest fresh water fishing port between the Great Lakes and New Orleans. Built in approximately 1874, Shafer Wharf Inn was moved to the Shafer Wharf Historic District overlooking the Mississippi and Illinois rivers. The inn was placed in operation as a bed and breakfast in 1989. The inn's balcony provides an excellent view of the district's historic architecture dating from the mid and late 1800s. The inn's decorations reflect the country French influence in the Grafton area. Bicycles are included in the room rate and may be used to travel the 25-mile trail linking Alton and Pere Marquette State Park.

3 *Wildflower Inn Bed and Breakfast*

•

Location: Box 31, Mason Hollow Rd., Grafton, IL 62037
Phone: (618) 465-3719
Manager/Owner: Tom and Dave Thompson
Number of rooms and baths: Two guest rooms with private baths
Room rate: $59 double occupancy
Meals: Full country breakfast and tea in evening
Air conditioning: Central air
Smoking policy: No smoking in rooms; smoking in solarium
Credit cards: Master Card and Visa or personal check
Handicapped access: None

•

This secluded Cape Cod Saltbox house is nestled in a ravine on 40 acres. Guests may hike over trails on the scenic 40 acres. One acre of display gardens is available for guests to stroll. A spring-fed creek is located on the property. A gift basket is presented and English tea (Earl Grey) is served upon arrival. The inn boasts a quiet environment, large bedrooms, and a sitting area in each room. The inn is located one-half mile off the Great River Road (Illinois 100) in the historic and scenic Grafton area. Request detailed directions from the innkeeper.

The Wildflower Inn Bed and Breakfast is associated with the Wildflower Farm, which sells wild flowers, herbs, perennials and dried flowers. In the near future the innkeepers plan tours and herbal lunches. A recently restored log cabin has been moved to the property. The small cabin dates from 1837 and is reported to have belonged to Daniel Boone's nephew.

The Wildflower Inn

Corner Nest Bed & Breakfast

•

Location: 3 Elm St., P. O. Box 220, Elsah, IL 62028
Phone: (618) 374-1892
Manager/Owner: Bob and Judy Doerr
Number of rooms and baths: Four, three with private baths
Room rate: $60-70 double occupancy, weekday discount to $55-65
Meals: Full breakfast included on weekends; continental breakfast on weekdays
Air conditioning: Central air
Smoking policy: Smoking permitted
Credit cards: Visa, Master Card, Discover Card
Handicapped access: Inquire

•

The Corner Nest Bed and Breakfast was constructed in 1883 and the inn's balconies overlook the Mississippi River which is just a half block away. The scenery in the Elsah area is described as the "best of the Mississippi." Breakfast is served on the screened-in porch when weather permits. The bed and breakfast is newly redecorated. It is close to numerous activities including riverboat gambling, a water theme park and a bike trail. A cozy and private atmosphere is provided by the Innkeepers. The Corner Nest has in-room televisions.

The welcome sign

5   *The Green Tree Inn*

•

Location: P. O. Box 96, 15 Mill Street, Elsah, IL 62028
Phone: (618) 374-2821
Manager/Owner: Mary Ann Pitchford
Number of rooms and baths: Nine guest rooms with private baths
Room rate: $65-90 double occupancy
Meals: Complimentary gourmet breakfast
Air conditioning: Yes
Smoking policy: No smoking
Credit cards: Visa and Master Cards
Handicapped access: Yes

•

Elsah is ranked first in the state of Illinois for the 19th Century Village Concept. The Green Tree Inn is situated ideally to appreciate the historic appeal of this town. Constructed in the mid 1850s this country style inn includes a general store with the style and decor of the mid 1800s. All rooms have balconies and offer panoramic views. The price of lodging includes a gourmet breakfast, free use of bicycles and a gift certificate of $5 for the gift shop. Non-alcoholic wine is served upon arrival; cocktails are provided at the fireside. Bald eagles are abundant in the area January through March. River charters, a riverside bike trail and antiquing are nearby. The Green Tree Inn has been featured in several national magazines. Historical lectures and talks on herb gardening are occasionally offered.

The Green Tree Inn

6 *Maple Leaf Cottage Inn*

•

Location: 12 Selma, 38, 40, 42, 44 La Salle, P. O. Box 156, Elsah, IL
    62028
Phone: (618) 374-1684
Manager/Owner: Katrina Hess, Patty and Jerry Taetz
Number of rooms and baths: Four cottages, each with private bath
Room rate: $75 double occupancy
Meals: 4-5 course breakfast
Air conditioning: Central air and individual units
Smoking policy: No smoking
Credit cards: Master Card, Visa
Handicapped access: One room semi-accessible

•

Welcome sign at Maple Leaf Cottage Inn

Those who love a touch of privacy will enjoy the Maple Leaf Cottage Inn. Some of the buildings on the grounds date back into the 1800s and have been extensively remodeled. An inn was established in 1949 but the operation of the facility as a bed and breakfast was not begun until more recently. This grouping of buildings offers meals in addition to breakfast and lodging. Cranapple Frappe is the breakfast specialty. The authors can attest to its unique appeal. The recipe is given to each guest upon request.

The four cottages are connected by winding brick pathways embraced by wildflower gardens and shade trees in the English style. The guest rooms are decorated superbly. The Maple Leaf Cottage Inn is available for dining for small groups by reservation. A small (limited) gift shop is in the Cottage House. The inn is situated in the historic Elsah area which offers many recreational opportunities.

Maple Leaf Cottage Inn

7

Nancy Kirkpatrick Guest House

●

Location: Shafer Wharf District, P.O. Box 96, Elsah, IL. 62028
Phone: (618) 374-2821
Manager/Owner: Mary Ann Pitchford
Number of rooms and baths: Two bed rooms with two private baths
Room rate: $65 double occupancy
Meals: Includes full breakfast
Air conditioning: Yes
Smoking policy: No smoking
Credit cards: Master Card and Visa

●

Grafton is an excellent example of one of the Mississippi River towns established by fishermen and French fur traders. The Nancy Kirkpatrick Guest House captures the beauty of the riverfront scenery as fur traders saw it first in 1673. The Cape Cod style guest house was built in the 1860s and was only recently restored. The Guest House opened in 1988. It offers a wrap-around porch that provides views of the Illinois and Mississippi Rivers. The rate includes free use of bicycles.

In 1993 the town of Grafton was flooded. Call to determine if this bed and breakfast is open.

8 *Lea Davis House*

•

Location: 519 State St., Alton IL 62002
Phone: (618) 463-1103
Manager/Owner: Fred Derk and Greg Leavey
Number of rooms and baths: Two guest rooms and shared bath
    (only one room rented at a time)
Room rate: $65-75 double occupancy
Meals: Continental breakfast
Smoking policy: Inquire
Credit cards: None; personal checks accepted
Handicapped access: None

•

The Lea Davis Guest House is one of the newest bed and break-fasts in Southern Illinois. The house is situated just three blocks from riverboat gambling in Alton. It is a center chimney house dating from 1840 furnished with country antiques.

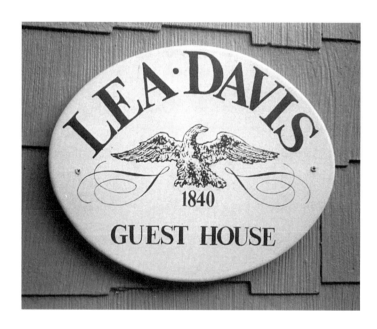

9

Maggie's Bed & Breakfast

•

Location: 2102 N. Keebler Rd., Collinsville, IL 62234

Phone: (618) 344-8283

Manager/Owner: Maggie Leyda

Number of rooms and baths: Five guest rooms, some with private bath

Room rate: $25 single; $35 double occupancy; $50 double occupancy for private bath

Meals: Full breakfast with homemade jellies and jams

Air conditioning: Room air conditioners

Smoking policy: Smoking permitted

Credit cards: Inquire

Handicapped access: One room

•

This late 1800s boarding house is situated on a hill on the north side of town. Maggie, the innkeeper, has been operating the house as a bed and breakfast for seven years. Maggie is a veteran hostess with many stories and artifacts to bear witness to her world travels. Maggie treats guests to her own special recipes. A hot tub is located in the basement reading room. Contact Maggie for a detailed map to this bed and breakfast.

Entryway at Maggie's Bed & Breakfast

Guest Room at Phyllis' Bed & Breakfast

10   *The Happy Wanderer*

•

Location: 309 Collinsville Ave, Collinsville, IL 62234
Phone: (618) 344-0477
Manager/Owner: Yvonne Holst
Number of rooms and baths: Four rooms with a shared bath
Room rate: $50 double occupancy; $35 single occupancy
Meals: Hearty continental breakfast
Smoking policy: Smoking on porches only
Credit cards: Inquire
Handicapped access: None

•

This 1889 home opened as a bed and breakfast in 1991. The Happy Wanderer Bed and Breakfast prides itself on making the guest feel like they are in a home atmosphere. Guests may read in the common room or obtain beverages from the refrigerator or stroll in the back yard. Board games are available to the guests. Numerous knick-knacks are located throughout the house and many are for sale.

11   *Phyllis' Bed & Breakfast*

•

Location: 801 Ninth St., Highland, IL 62249
Phone: (618) 654-4619
Manager/Owner: Bob and Phyllis Bible
Number of rooms and baths: Four rooms each with private bath
Room rate: $50 double occupancy; $45 single occupancy
Meals: Complimentary expanded continental breakfast
Air conditioning: Central air
Smoking policy: None
Handicapped access: No

•

553

Highland is known as New Switzerland. The town's Swiss-German heritage is evident in the businesses, homes and festivals. The Inn was constructed in the late 1800s and has been kept up through the years. There is a newly-constructed porch in the rear of the residence where guests may relax. The bathrooms are ultraclean and spacious. Breakfasts include homemade blueberry muffins. The gift shop contains items from the local area.

12 *The Jefferson House*

•

Location: 305 W. Broadway, Trenton, IL 62293
Phone: (618) 224-9733
Manager/Owner: Sharon Hardin
Number of rooms and baths: Three rooms, shared baths
Room rate: $45 double occupancy; $42.50 single occupancy
Meals: Full breakfast, requests taken
Air conditioning: Central air
Smoking policy: No smoking in guest rooms
Credit cards: No
Handicapped access: No

•

The Jefferson House was built in 1924 and up until its purchase by Sharon Hardin was a one-owner home. Bed and breakfast operation began in January 1990. Cozy and comfortable decorations are seen throughout the house and down comforters cover all double beds. A VCR and two televisions are available for guest use. The living room has a fireplace. The backyard is available for guests to relax.

13

Mill Creek Inn

•

Location: 504 N. Mill (Illinois 127), Nashville, IL 62263
Phone: (618) 327-8424 or 327-8718
Manager/Owner: Bill and Barb Garlich
Number of rooms and baths: Two guest rooms;two private baths
Room rate: $42-45 single occupancy; $52-55 double occupancy
Meals: Full breakfast
Air conditioning: Room air conditioning
Smoking policy: Smoking permitted
Credit cards: Master Card, Visa
Handicapped access: None

•

The Mill Creek Inn fronts Illinois 127 but contains an expansive tree-filled back yard that overlooks Mill Pond. The back yard offers a wonderful place for strolling and relaxing. The inn, built in 1856, was originally a home. It boasts many antique features including 58 shutters, constructed with wooden pegs and thought to be original. A city swimming pool and a golf course are nearby.

Mill Creek Inn

14   *The Country Haus*

•

Location: 1191 Franklin (at U.S. 50 & Route 127), Carlyle, IL 62231
Phone: (618) 594-8313
Manager/Owner: Ron and Vickie Cook
Number of rooms and baths: Four rooms all with private baths
Room rate: $45-55 double occupancy, singles & business discounts
Meals: Full breakfast, juice and sodas complimentary; evening snack
Air conditioning: Yes
Smoking policy: No smoking
Credit cards: Visa, Master Card and American Express
Handicapped access: None

•

The Country Haus is one of two bed and breakfasts in Carlyle that

Country Haus

serve the expanding recreational activity associated with Carlyle Lake. Located at the main crossroad in Carlyle, the Country Haus is a turn-of-the-century restoration of one of the private homes in the area. Although the bedrooms are not large, there is a library and television for relaxing and talking with other guests. Ron and Vickie Cook, the young and vivacious owners, are very personable and have run this bed and breakfast since 1989. The Country Haus boasts a jacuzzi and a gift shop.

15   *The Victorian Inn*

•

Location: 1111 Franklin Street, Carlyle, IL 62231
Phone: (618) 594-8506
Manager/Owner: Mary and Dennis Mincks
Number of rooms and baths: Three guest rooms with shared bath
Room rate: $55 double occupancy; singles discount
Meals: Hearty country style continental breakfast complimentary
Air conditioning: Yes
Smoking policy: No smoking except in kitchen
Credit cards: Visa, Master Card
Handicapped access: None

•

The Victorian Inn, a Historical Society Landmark, is a prime example of the grand style of late 1800s Victorian architecture. This spacious bed and breakfast is exceptionally clean and well decorated. The inn is especially conducive to relaxation in the foyer while simultaneously admiring its architectural grandeur. A special children's room is available. Guests are provided with robes and slippers. Picnic lunches are available upon request and afternoon tea is complimentary. Guests frequently enjoy many of the recreational opportunities of Carlyle Lake and the area.

16   *Prairie House*

•

Location: Seven miles South of Greenville, IL 62246 (signs direct guests at turnoff)

Phone: (618) 664-3003 or 664-1492

Manager/Owner: Bob Funderburk

Number of rooms and baths: Five guest rooms and loft; one room has private bath

Room rate: $35-55 double occupancy; $25 single occupancy

Meals: Complimentary breakfast or tickets to a local restaurant

Air conditioning: Yes

Smoking policy: No smoking

Credit cards: Visa and Master Cards accepted

Handicapped access: None

•

For those inclined to enjoy an out-of the-way bed and breakfast, the Prairie House offers a ranch setting well off the main road. The Prairie House is one of three bed and breakfasts situated close to the popular fishing and sailing haven at Carlyle Lake. Started in 1989 as a bed and breakfast, the housing complex first was a sales office for log homes. The interior of the bed and breakfast and restaurant are all pine and handsomely constructed. The restaurant will seat 100 and is commonly used for banquets, weddings and other special occasions. Guests may stroll the 30-acre grounds, fish in the pond and rent horses by reservation. A hot tub is a new addition for the enjoyment of guests.

---

next page–Lounging area at the Prairie House (above)
next page–Inside the dining building at the Prairie House (below)

17 *The Westerfield House*

•

Location: RR 2, Box 34, Freeburg, IL 62243
Phone: (618) 539-5643
Manager/Owner: Jim and Marilyn (and Jessie) Westerfield
Number of rooms and baths: Three guest rooms with private baths
Room rate: $169.79 double occupancy
Meals: Includes dinner and breakfast
Air conditioning: Central air
Smoking policy: Smoking permitted
Credit cards: Visa and Master Card
Handicapped access: Yes

•

The Westerfields founded one of the pioneer bed and breakfasts in the Midwest. The Westerfield House, originally the home of the owners, was opened in 1983 as a bed and breakfast. This log house, made of pine, is elegantly furnished with authentic colonial furniture. An herb garden containing 140 varieties (40 varieties of mint alone) is conspicuous at the entrance of the inn. The house prides itself on its gourmet dining, especially its evening meal. Herbal lunches are also

served on specific dates. The innkeepers and staff dress in colonial attire. The inn serves many St. Louis visitors and has been featured in several national magazines. Obtain directions and a calendar of gourmet events from the owner.

The herb garden at the Westerfield House

18 *The Senator Richert Residence*

•

Location: 216 E. Third St., Waterloo, IL 62298
Phone: (618) 939-8242
Manager/Owner: Ed and Kathi Weilbacher
Number of rooms and baths: One suite with private bath (14 ft. by 19 ft.) with large bath
Room rate: $75 double occupancy
Meals: Full breakfast (spinach and sausage strata is Kathi's specialty)
Air conditioning: Central air
Smoking policy: No smoking
Credit cards: Visa and Discover
Handicapped access: None

•

One of Southern Illinois' newest bed and breakfasts, the Senator Richert Residence is located in the historic district of Waterloo. The residence was built in approximately 1866 and takes its name from the senator who enlarged the home to its present size. The only guest room is a spacious suite containing antiques from Mrs. Richert's father. The suite opens into another spacious and well decorated room, the sitting room. Here a television and phone are available for guest use. The third room, the private bath is also spacious and includes a footed tub.

The Senator Richert Residence as it appeared years ago

19 *The Corner George Inn*

•

Location: Corner of Main & Mill, Maeystown, IL 62256
Phone: (618) 458-6660
Managers: David and Marcia Braswell
Number of rooms and baths: Five guest rooms with private baths
Room rate: $65-95 double occupancy
Meals: Full breakfast provided
Air conditioning: Central air
Smoking policy: No smoking
Credit cards: Master Card, Visa
Handicapped access: One room

•

The Corner George Inn, built in 1884, is centrally situated in historic Maeystown, a quaint and relatively unspoiled German settlement dating back to the 1850s (see Historic Sites Section). The inn is a restored "frontier" Victorian hotel.

Within just a few blocks of the Inn and an easy walk, there are numerous examples of the original architecture of the period. The owners have gone out of their way to restore the old hotel into a bed and breakfast. The rooms are spacious as are the sitting rooms on both floors. One sitting room is especially large. It was formerly the old ballroom of the hotel, and is especially cozy.

The owners are antique lovers and have amply furnished the inn with antiques, including claw-footed bathtubs and pedestal sinks for each bathroom. The unusual name of the inn has its roots in the home's colorful history. The friendly innkeepers will be pleased to tell you the story.

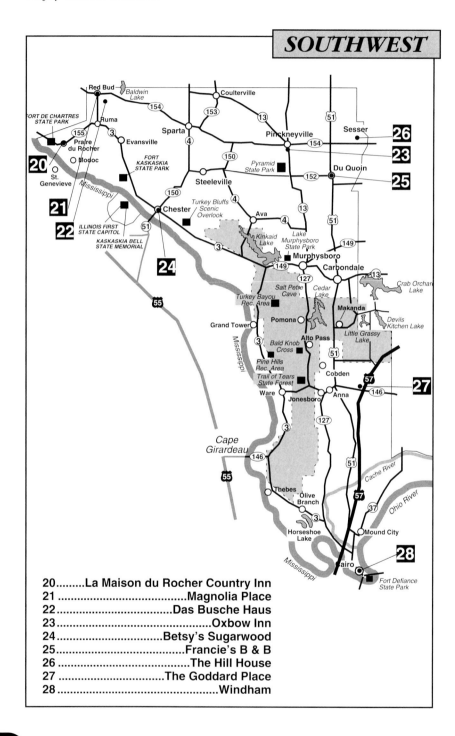

SOUTHWEST

20 *La Maison du Rocher Country Inn at Prairie du Rocher*

•

Location: #2 Duclos and Main, Prairie du Rocher, IL 62277
Phone: (618) 284-3463
Manager/Owner: Jan Kennedy
Number of rooms and baths: Two rooms, each with private bath
Room rate: $55-85 double occupancy
Meals: Full country style breakfast
Air conditioning: Central air
Smoking policy: No smoking in rooms; designated smoking area
Credit cards: Visa and Master Card
Handicapped access: None

•

La Maison du Rocher (House of Rock) Country Inn is situated in the French settlement area on the Mississippi River bottoms. Prairie du Rocher is the oldest settlement in Southern Illinois. The old two story limestone rock building that serves as the inn was constructed in 1885. Originally the building was a hotel. In 1986 it was restored to include a kitchen and banquet room with the first floor used primarily as a dining room and kitchen. The decor is French Victorian. As the name implies the setting is country. The inn boasts home-style cooking and homemade breads. Alcohol is served. A solarium filled with plants provides a comfortable place to relax. Private luncheons, banquets and celebration dinners are held on request. The inn is centered in an historic area with numerous sites to visit. Jan Kennedy is a knowledgeable and personable hostess with a unique ability to make you enjoy listening.

| 21 |

Magnolia Place

•

Location: 317 S. Main, Red Bud, IL 62278
Phone: (618) 282-4141
B&B Manager/Owner: Dolly Krallman
Number of rooms and baths: Four rooms, two with shared bath; the
   suite has a whirlpool
Room rate: $60-140
Meals: Full breakfast in dining room or gazebo
Air conditioning: Yes
Smoking policy: Smoking in selected areas
Credit cards: Visa, Master Card
Handicapped access: None

•

Among the newest of the bed and breakfasts is Red Bud's
Magnolia Place, not to be confused with Magnolia Manor in Cairo.
The stately circa 1856 building is centrally located on Main Street in
the historic area of Red Bud. The decoration is 18th century English
with fine antiques located throughout the house. The house and guest
rooms are spacious and elegant.

Equally appealing is the yard area which boasts a 200-year-old
sweet gum tree, a sitting area and a gazebo. The landscaping provides
a private atmosphere although Main Street is just yards away. Guests
may elect to have breakfast outside in the gazebo.

Above:on opposite page: Dining room at La Maison du Rocher
Below: Oxbow B & B from the road (see pages ahead)

22   *Das Busche Haus*

•

Location: Route 2, Box 242, Red Bud, IL 62278
Phone: (618) 282-2181
Manager/Owner: Ed and Bonnie Piel
Number of rooms and baths: Four guest rooms, one with private
    bath
Room rate: $45 double occupancy
Meals: Continental breakfast provided
Air conditioning: Unknown
Smoking policy: No smoking inside
Credit cards: Inquire
Handicapped access: No

•

Das Busche Haus was built in 1873 and is located in the country east of Red Bud. This small renovated house was inherited by the current owners who live next door. They have decorated this guest house in an early 20th century, American country style. Numerous antiques are located throughout the house. The decorations provide a warm atmosphere for guests. The owners also have an antique shop in what was formerly a chicken house. The air is clean and the view is typical prairie. Inquire of the owners for directions.

23   *Oxbow Bed and Breakfast*

●

Location: Route 1, Box 47, Pinckneyville, IL 62247
Phone: (618) 357-9839
Manager/Owner: Doc Doughty
Number of rooms and baths: Five guests rooms with private baths
Room rate: $50 double occupancy
Meals: Large country breakfast
Air conditioning: Central air
Smoking policy: No smoking inside
Credit cards: Visa, Master Card
Handicapped access: None

●

Built over a two year period starting in 1929 by a wealthy businessman, this bed and breakfast is newly opened. Although the Oxbow Bed and Breakfast is situated on Illinois 127 at the southern outskirts of Pinckneyville, it provides the feeling of a secluded hideaway. From the highway, the mature trees partially obscure the view of the large house and the ranch that lies behind. A spacious lawn is available for guests to roam and view the Arabian horses that are raised by the owner. The guest rooms are decorated in the style of the Civil War era and named for battles and people of the times.

Photo on page 566

24　Betsy's Sugarwood

•

Location: Box 3, 217 E. Buena Vista, Chester, IL 62233
Phone: (618) 826-2555
Manager/Owner: Betty Barnes-Hihn
Number of rooms and baths: Four guest rooms with private baths
Room rate: $50-75; $5 credit for single occupancy
Meals: Complimentary four course breakfast
Air conditioning: Central air
Smoking policy: Restricted; no smoking in sleeping room
Credit cards: Visa, Master Card
Handicapped access: No

•

Betsy's Sugarwood is named for the numerous hard maple trees on the property. The large two and a half story building is located on a bluff overlooking the Mississippi River. All rooms are on the second floor and each boasts a tremendous view of the river. The bed and breakfast is furnished with antiques. Refreshments are served upon arrival and late arriving guests may find a snack in their rooms.

Guests may walk the short distance to the Mississippi River and the historic inns and taverns nearby, and may take advantage of the numerous activities in the Chester area. Betty Hihn also operates an antique shop next door.

25   *Francie's Bed and Breakfast Inn*

•

Location 104 S. Line St., Du Quoin, IL 62831

Phone: (618) 542-6686

Manager/Owner: Francie Morgan

Number of rooms and baths: Three with private baths; two share a bath

Room rate: $50-80 double occupancy

Meals: Full breakfast included in bed, on the balcony or tea room

Air conditioning: Central air

Smoking policy: Restricted smoking areas

Credit cards: Visa, Master Card

Handicapped access: None

•

The Victorian style building now known as Francie's was constructed in 1908 as one of three children's homes by the Children's Home and Aid Society of Illinois which housed hundreds of homeless children for 39 years. Like many older homes that showed the wear and tear of time, it was eventually abandoned. The current owner realized its potential and purchased it in 1986.

A native of the area, Francie Morgan often played with the children housed in the home. She took pride in restoring the home to its original state. Francie has a display of photographs in the inn that capture scenes from the Children's Home's past. Francie boasts that this B & B is a short bicycle ride from Du Quoin State Fairgrounds and near numerous golf courses. Lawn games are available on the premises. Bicycles are frequently loaned to guests to explore the local area. A small gift shop features arts and crafts from the Southern Illinois area. The main dining area is the tea room which seats 60 people. It is used not only to serve guests breakfast but for local club and organizational meetings. Francie's has a liquor license for meals. A special brunch is served on Valentine's Day, Easter, Mother's Day and

St. Patrick's Day. Guests find that the muffins, which are prepared daily by the English cook, are excellent.

Francie's B& B

Dining area at Francie's B & B

26 # The Hill House

•

Location: 503 S. Locust, Sesser, IL 62884
Phone: (618) 625-6064
Manager/Owner: Gwen and Dewey Nussbaum
Number of rooms and baths: Three guest rooms with private baths
Room rate: $45-55 double occupancy
Meals: Expanded continental
Air conditioning: Central air
Smoking policy: No smoking
Credit cards: Visa and Master Cards
Handicapped access: None

•

This is one of the newer bed and breakfasts in Southern Illinois, open since the fall of 1991. The Hill House was built in 1914 by James Hill, also the builder of the Sesser Opera House, an impressive architectural structure on the National Historic Register. The current owners, only the third in the history of the house, pride themselves on their recent renovation of the home. Antiques are seen throughout the home and the china constitutes a decorative theme in the kitchen. Many guests enjoy the recreational opportunities of nearby Rend Lake.

Gwen Nussbaum in one of the guest rooms

| 27 | *The Goddard Place* |

•

Location: Route 2, Box 445G, Anna, IL 62906
Phone: (618) 833-6256
Manager/Owner: Jim & Edna Goddard
Number of rooms and baths: Three rooms with shared bath
Room rate: $40 double occupancy; $30 single occupancy
Meals: Full breakfast; evening snack
Air conditioning: Central air
Smoking policy: No smoking in rooms
Credit cards: Visa and Master Card
Handicapped access: Yes

•

The Goddards built their country ranch-style home east of Anna as a bed and breakfast in 1989. They entertained their first guests just two months after the home was completed. This bed and breakfast is for the individual seeking a pleasant relief from city life. The home is decorated with a modern country flair. The bedrooms are well decorated and the entire house is exceptionally clean. Wood and stone are themes in the home. The Goddards own 70 acres that guests may enjoy. A large fishing pond lies behind the house and is visible from the full-length deck at the rear of the house. Guests may fish, bicycle, hike or simply relax and enjoy the scenery and the cozy atmosphere. Please ask the Goddards for specific directions to the Goddard Place.

28 *Windham Bed and Breakfast*

•

Location: 2606 Washington Ave, Cairo, IL 62914
Phone: (618) 734-3247
Manager/Owner: Helen Bishoff
Number of rooms and baths: Three guest rooms, one with private bath
Room rate: $65-80
Meals: Full breakfast (elegant) in the formal dining room
Air conditioning: Central air
Smoking policy: No smoking in guest rooms
Credit cards: No; personal checks accepted
Handicapped access: No

•

For those who love 19th century architecture, antiques and historical detail, this is clearly the most impressive bed and breakfast in Southern Illinois. Windham is listed on the National Register of Historic Places. The magnificent 1876 Italianate style mansion was built by Thomas Halliday, once mayor of Cairo and Illinois state senator. He lived in the mansion with his wife and ten children. The home is located on "Millionaire's Row" where numerous other homes of fine quality are found. Next door is even more impressive Magnolia Manor, a home restored by the Cairo Historical Society (See Historic Sites section). Windham's bedrooms are named after the four daughters of the main families owning the mansion. The lawn is spacious, dotted with large old trees that provide ample shade. The entire bed and breakfast is amply decorated with fine antiques. Bishoff delights in telling guests the history of the neighborhood and Cairo area. If you are a bed and breakfast addict, Windham is a must.

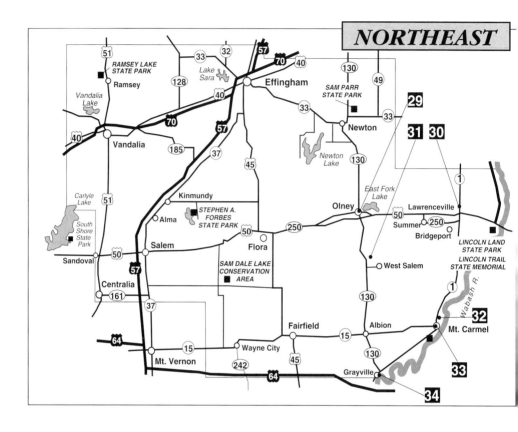

29

Richs' Inn

●

Location: 328 S. Morgan, Box 581, Olney, IL 62450
Phone: (618) 392-3821
Manager/Owner: Max and June Rich
Number of rooms and baths: Three guests rooms, one with a private
    bath
Room rate: $35-45
Meals: Full "hearty" breakfast
Air conditioning: Window units
Smoking policy: Restricted
Credit cards: Master Card, Visa
Handicapped access: None

●

Richs' Inn is one of the newer bed and breakfasts in Southern
Illinois. The three story inn is a 12-room Victorian home built in the
Civil War Era. Since it was constructed, ownership has changed many
times and the building fell into disrepair. In the 1930s the home was
restored by a Kentucky owner. The Richs' purchased the home in
1971 and continued to make improvements. The home features an
elegant black walnut staircase and 11-foot ceilings. Many of the original features of the home have been preserved. Guests may enjoy the
large porches in the front and rear of the residence, the formal dining
room, reading rooms, antique furnishings and are welcome to use the
piano in the parlor. There are numerous attractions in the Olney
region which guests may enjoy while staying at Richs' Inn. Most of
all, guests should see the famous protected white squirrels that inhabit
Olney.

30   *Woodside*

●

Location: Box 101, Locust Lane, Lawrenceville, IL 62439
Phone: (618) 943-2147
Manager/Owner: Gretchen and Walt Wisnewski
Number of rooms and baths: A guest loft overlooking living room
Room rate: $40 double occupancy
Meals: Evening snack and full complimentary breakfast
Air conditioning: Central air
Smoking policy: No smoking inside
Credit cards: No; personal checks accepted
Handicapped access: No

●

This modern home in a suburban area boasts a guest room loft that overlooks a chalet-style living room and has a view into the wooded back yard. There is a swimming pool and deck in the back yard for guest use. Robes, thongs and bath accessories are provided for guest use. The home is mostly furnished with family antiques. Lawrenceville is located just across the Wabash River from historic Vincennes, Indiana. Ask the Wisnewski's for directions.

The loft at Woodside

31 *Thelma's Bed and Breakfast*

•

Location: 201 S. Broadway, West Salem, IL 62476
Phone: (618) 456-8401
Manager/Owner: Thelma Lodwig
Number of rooms and baths: Five guest rooms with shared baths
Room rate: $15 single, $30 double, $75 per person per week
Meals: Full breakfast
Air conditioning: Yes
Smoking policy: No smoking
Credit cards: No; takes personal checks
Handicapped access: None

•

Large two-story (plus attic) prairie style brick house that serves as Thelma's Bed and Breakfast was built in 1919. The home was four square, a design inspired by Frank Lloyd Wright and has oak woodwork. Guests are free to use the living room, dining room and den. There is a spacious yard.

▪32▪ *Living Legacy Homestead*

•

Location: Route 146A, RR #2, Mt. Carmel, IL 62863

Phone: (618) 298-2476

Manager/Owner: Edna Anderson

Number of rooms and baths: Three guest rooms; one with private bath and the others with shared baths

Room rate: $35 single occupancy; $45-55 double occupancy; children extra; seniors discount

Meals: Full country breakfast

Air conditioning: Central air on first floor; fans upstairs

Smoking policy: No smoking

Credit cards: No

Handicapped access: Yes

•

The Living Legacy Homestead is unique in Southern Illinois in that it is the only restored log cabin homestead. The home dates back into the 1870s and is furnished with antiques and period furniture. The logs of the original home are apparent from the inside. This newly-restored home features an exposed loft where a gift shop is located. Tours are conducted of the home and surrounding ten acres. Several interesting original farm buildings are located on the site. The Living Legacy Homestead may be reserved for group meeting or gatherings. Guests often enjoy the nearby state parks. Please contact Edna Anderson for detailed directions.

33   *The Poor Farm*

•

Location: RR #3, Box 31A, Mt. Carmel, IL 62863
Phone: (618) 262-4663
Manager/Owner: John and Liz Stelzer
Number of rooms and baths: Currently under expansion
Room rate: $40-50 double occupancy
Meals: Full country breakfast
Air conditioning: Room air
Smoking policy: Designated smoking areas
Credit cards: Visa and Master Card
Handicapped access: Yes

•

At the time of our visit to The Poor Farm this bed and breakfast was not open. One of the future managers was hard at work restoring

The Poor Farm under renovation

what was a home for destitute individuals prior to, during and after the Depression Era.

Built in 1915, this large rural brick structure once housed up to 25 individuals, who, if they were able-bodied, worked on the adjoining farm. More recently it was used as a dormitory, but thereafter fell into disrepair. The grandmother of the present owner ran the county-owned poor farm.

Many antiques were in place when we visited and the owners hope to make the site a repository for history of the local area. The kitchen has an antique country flair. Inquire about directions from the managers.

Liz Stelzer in the newly decorated dining area

34   *Founder's Mansion Inn*

●

Location: 119 N. Court, Grayville, IL 62844
Phone: (618) 375-3291
Manager/Owner: Jan Bowen
Number of rooms and baths: Five guest rooms with private baths
Room rate: $55-75 double occupancy
Meals: English style breakfast complimentary
Air conditioning: Room air conditioner
Smoking policy: Smoking allowed
Credit cards: Visa, Master Card
Handicapped access: None

●

The Founder's Mansion Inn stands out as a unique architectural landmark in the central region of Grayville. Built in 1886, this Queen Anne style inn is magnificent to view and tour. The current owner is only the third. The previous owners were the town fathers and thus the name "Founders" Mansion Inn.

You will greatly appreciate the inn's decorations. Many antiques from throughout the world are seen in this spacious home. Upon restoration, the current owners found writing dating back to the 1800s on the wall. From this came the idea to leave selected walls with uncovered plaster showing so that guests may sign the walls and add a small message or drawing.

Photo on page 584

Founder's Mansion Inn

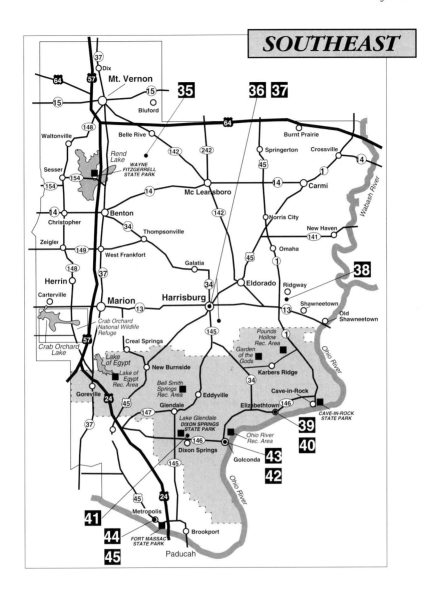

35   *The Enchanted Crest*

●

Location: Route 1, Box 216, Belle Rive, IL 62810
Phone: (618) 736-2647
Manager/Owner: Lloyd and Carolyn Blackwell
Number of rooms and baths: Two guest rooms with shared bath
Room rate: $45 double occupancy
Meals: Full breakfast and an evening snack
Air conditioning: Room Air conditioning
Smoking policy: Smoking allowed
Credit cards: Visa, Master Card
Handicapped access: No

●

This grand 18-room Victorian brick mansion was constructed in 1881 out of solid brick in the countryside south of Belle Rive. It has been placed on the National Register of Historic Places and truly stands out along with the more modern, though still old, magnificent farm buildings on the grounds. The old barn has a large loft that guests may visit and where the owner gives basket-making classes. There is a genuine farm atmosphere which may be enjoyed on the 10 acres of lawns surrounding the mansion. Guests are welcome to stroll the grounds and visit the small creek south of the house and the orchard at the side. The owners are proud of the hundreds of varieties of herbs planted in numerous herb gardens. Gourmet lunches and dinners and country Victorian tea are available upon request. Carolyn Blackwell displays numerous quilts in the gift shop. For those who love horses, bale and board is available. Several national magazines have featured the Enchanted Crest.

The Enchanted Crest

36   *Hart's White Lace Inn*

•

Location: 400 E. Church St. (one block from intersection of Route 45 and Route 13), Harrisburg, IL 62946
Phone: (618) 252-7599
Manager/Owner: Betty Cusie
Number of rooms and baths: Five guest rooms with four baths
Room rate: $45-65
Meals: Continental breakfast gratis
Air conditioning: Central air
Smoking policy: No smoking
Credit cards: Visa and Master Card
Handicapped access: None

•

The Hart's White Lace Inn in Harrisburg was originally the home of the late B. E. Hart who owned the largest department store in Southern Illinois. The cozy Queen Anne style of the home is exaggerated by lace curtains and two fireplaces. The home and the guest rooms are exceptionally clean and well decorated. There is a television in the common room. Guests may use the washer and dryer. The owners cater small parties on the patio on special occasions.

37   *House of Nahum*

•

Location: One mile off Illinois 34 to Rudement, 10 miles south of
    Harrisburg, 90 Sally Holla Lane, Harrisburg 62946
Phone: (618) 252-1414
Manager/Owner: Sona Thomas
Number of rooms and baths: Three guest rooms with private baths
Room rate: $48 (single); $60 (double)
Meals: Bountiful homemade breakfast, custom designed
Air conditioning: Yes
Smoking policy: Smoking on porch only
Credit cards: Visa and Master Card
Handicapped access: None

•

The House of Nahum is located in a country setting near many of
Southern Illinois' outdoor attractions. It's a new two story house built

The House of Nahum

in 1991 and located on a wooded five acres literally bordering the Shawnee National Forest. The house has a veranda that wraps fully around the house. The veranda has a swing for relaxing and just pondering nature. Incidentally, the word Nahum means comfort and consoling.

The House of Nahum is decorated with antiques. No pets or children are allowed. In appropriate weather, breakfasts are served on the back deck. A creek is at the rear of the house. In the fall, the House of Nahum is often frequented by hunters.

38

The Thomas House Bed & Breakfast

•

Location: RR #1, Junction, IL 62954
Phone: 1-800-866-6716; also (618) 272-7046
Manager/Owner: Jane Thomas
Number of rooms and baths: One with private bath; two share a bath
Room rate: $40-55 double occupancy
Meals: "Bountiful breakfast" in gourmet style or by arrangement
Air conditioning: Central air
Smoking policy: Inquire
Credit cards: Master Card and Visa
Handicapped access: No

•

The Thomas House Bed & Breakfast is situated in the wide open agricultural space north and west of Junction. Guests have the use of the modern modified salt box style house. A pool table and satellite TV are available. Breakfast may be served outside in the screened-in porch. The innkeeper prides herself on both the quality and quantity of her breakfast. She accepts families with small children and babies. The Thomas House is located one mile north of the intersection of Illinois 1 and 13 on the east side of the road. The bed and breakfast is twenty minutes from Garden of the Gods and Shawnee National Forest.

39 *River Rose Inn*

•

Location: #1 Main St., P.O. Box 78, Elizabethtown, IL 62931
Phone: (618) 287-8811
Manager/Owner: Elizabeth and Don Phillips
Number of rooms and baths: Four guest rooms with private baths and a honeymoon suite cottage (private bath)
Room rate: $50-85; single rate is $45; honors state rates
Meals: Gourmet breakfast served
Air conditioning: Room air
Smoking policy: Smoking in designated areas
Credit cards: Master Card and Visa
Handicapped access: None

•

Elizabethtown is a quaint river town on the Ohio with numerous antique shops and small restaurants. The River Rose Inn overlooks the Ohio River and provides a lazy atmosphere. The house is a Greek

Gothic mansion. Antique Empire furnishings are seen throughout this bed and breakfast, and all rooms have river views. A swimming pool and jacuzzi in the back yard are for guest use. Soft drinks and condiments are provided. Built in 1914, history tells us that the bricks used to build this mansion were transported from Pittsburgh, Pennsylvania to Elizabethtown.

40 *Jane's Bed and Breakfast at Williams Village Inn*

●

Location: Box 44, Elizabethtown, IL 62931
Phone: (618) 287-7088
Manager/Owner: Jane Williams
Number of rooms and baths: Three rooms and shared bath
Room rate: $30 double occupancy
Meals: Continental breakfast
Air conditioning: Room air
Smoking policy: Smoking allowed
Credit cards: No
Handicapped access: None

●

This turn-of-the-century home was opened as a bed and breakfast in 1988. It features a common room with television. Coffee is available 24 hours a day. This bed and breakfast is popular with hunters during deer season.

593

41   *The Timbers*

●

Location: Dixon Springs, IL (write Box 339, Golconda, IL 62938)
Phone: (618) 683-4400
Manager/Owner: Marilyn and Don Kunz
Number of rooms and baths: Three guest rooms, some with private baths
Room rate: $60-100 double occupancy
Meals: Complimentary breakfast provided
Air conditioning: Central air
Smoking policy: No smoking in sleeping rooms
Credit cards: Visa, Master Card, Discover Card
Handicapped access: Inquire

●

This contemporary bed and breakfast has a country setting. The house sits at a high point on 37 acres with a stocked pond. There is an open design to the lower level giving the guest a feeling of spaciousness. This bed and breakfast is located in the Shawnee National Forest which boasts many natural and scenic spots for visitors to enjoy. The Mansion at Golconda (see next page) will handle reservations.

42   *The Mansion at Golconda*

•

Phone: (618) 683-4400
Location: 519 Columbus Ave., Golconda, IL 62938
Manager/Owner: Marilyn and Don Kunz
Number of rooms and baths: Three guest rooms with private baths; one room has a Jacuzzi
Room rate: $75-90 April through December; January through March discounts are available
Meals: Full breakfast; bar service
Air conditioning: Central air
Smoking policy: Smoking only in bath rooms; restricted smoking in dining rooms
Credit cards: Visa, Master Card, Dinner's and Discover Cards
Handicapped access: None

•

The Mansion at Golconda sits along the Ohio River. Unfortunately, a large levee prevents a superb view of the river. However, this is the only drawback as The Mansion and grounds are worthy of touring. The Mansion is listed on the National Register of Historic Places. Once the private home of the mayor of Golconda, it served as a hotel since 1928. An extensive renovation was undertaken in 1981 that now provides The Mansion's Victorian atmosphere. The Mansion is also an elegant restaurant that will seat 60 for formal dining and serve breakfast on a sunlit porch for up to 30. A cozy lounge is present. The Mansion is abundantly furnished with fine antiques and each room is tastefully decorated.

43 *Heritage Haus*

Location: Main and Columbus, Box 562 Golconda, Il 62938
Phone: (618) 683-3883
Manager/Owner: Jim and Jean Banks
Number of rooms and baths: Four guest rooms, one with private bath
Room rate: $25 per bed
Meals: Continental breakfast
Air conditioning: Yes
Smoking policy: Allowed
Handicapped access: None

Hunters, fishermen, and businessmen find this a convenient place to stay. Located in downtown Golconda it is close to city conveniences. One bedroom has a Paul Bunyan bed and another a brass bed. Some rooms have refrigerators and there is a patio downstairs for guest use.

Annie's

44   *Annie's*

•

Location: 403 E. 2nd St., Metropolis, IL 62960
Phone: (618) 524-7980
Manager/Owner: Annie Jackson
Number of rooms and baths: Five guest rooms, one with private bath
Room rate: $65-75
Meals: Flexible–guests may request favorite
Number of rooms and baths: Yes, central air
Smoking policy: None
Credit cards: Visa, Master Card
Handicapped access: None

•

This federal style home was constructed prior to the Civil War and is located one block from the Ohio River. At one time William McBane, one of the founders of Metropolis owned the home. In 1882 the house was severely damaged. For about 100 years the home went through a series of owners and a period of increasing dilapidation. In 1978 Joe and Annie Jackson purchased the home, and over the next 10 years Annie took charge of renovations, including the addition of modern conveniences. The bed and breakfast will open when renovations are complete. Call for further information.

45   *The Park Street House*

At press time the authors became aware of a new bed and breakfast opening in Metropolis. For information call (618) 524-5966.

Campgrounds & Cabins

C amping is almost universally enjoyed. However, some say the ground gets harder as they get older; so they turn to camping in recreational vehicles. Whatever your pleasure, Southern Illinois is loaded with camping facilities of all kinds. They are both public and private.

The following list was compiled by various state and tourism sources. We have organized the listing by counties so that the site can be found readily on a locator map. Once you have found the location, then find the site under the listed county.

Happy campfires to you!

The "Rent-A-Tent" program

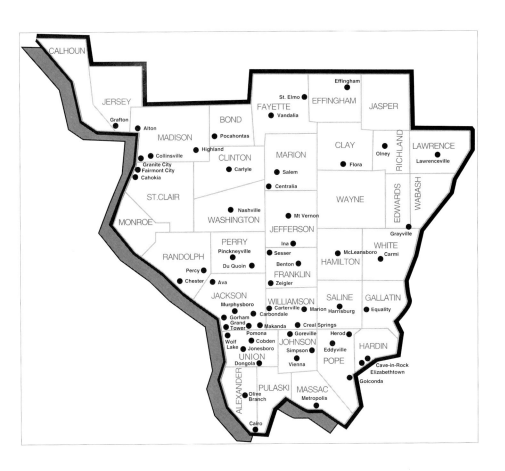

Legend

E—electrical hookups
W—water hookups
S—sewer hookups

ALEXANDER CO.

• *CAIRO*

Garden Inn Trailer Park
(618) 734-2711.
Level, shaded RV spaces behind a motel.
From junction take Illinois 3 and U.S. 51

and I-57: go one-eighth mile north on
U.S. 51.
Facilities: 37 sites, seven full hookups, 10
water and electric (30 amp receptacles),
flush toilets, hot showers, public phone,
ice.
Recreation: Outdoor pool.
1992 rates $10 per vehicle.
Open all year

• *OLIVE BRANCH*

Horseshoe Lake Conservation Area State Park
(618) 776-5689.
Wood flatlands.
From south end of town, southeast two
miles on Illinois 3. Good paved interior

roads.

Facilities: 153 gravel, 50 ft. average site width, 15 day max. stay, 78 E (30 amps), restrooms only, dump, limited groceries, BBQ.

Recreation: Horseshoe Lake – pan fishing, boating, ramp, dock, rental, playground.

1992 rates $4 - $9.

Open: March to November

BOND COUNTY

• *POCAHONTAS*

Tomahawk Campground, (Private)

(618) 669-2781.

Grassy flatlands.

From junction of I-70 and Illinois 143 Pierron Exit 30, east six miles on Illinois 143 to County Road 600E/Jamestown Road, south 1 mile. Good gravel interior roads.

Facilities: 135 sites: 14 gravel, 16 grass, some shaded, 22 pull-thrus 30x60, 30 W, 30 E (20/30 amps), a/c (charge), electric heat (charge), restrooms, showers (charge), dump, mobile sewer service, security, public phone, limited groceries, ice, RV supplies, LP gas.

Recreation: Pond, bass fishing, tackle, swimming, boat rental, horseshoes, rec hall, game room, planned activities, playground, rec field.

1992 rates $9 -$13.50.

CLAY

• *FLORA*

Charley Brown Park, (Public)

(618) 662-8202.

Wooded flatlands.

From junction of U.S. 50 and U.S. 45, west 1 mile. Good gravel interior roads.

Facilities: 125 gravel, 72 E (30 amps), restrooms and shower, dump, lake, fishing, swimming pool, playground.

1992 rates $6. No reservations.

Open: May 15 to November 1.

Odd Fellows

Illinois 1, Box 256, Clay City, IL 62864.

(618) 689-3465.

10 miles east on U. S. 50 (Clay City) then three miles north on County Road then

1.5 miles east (follow signs).

Facilities: 50 sites (50 E, 50 W, 50 S, two drive-thrus), dump, flush toilets, showers, store, snack bar.

Recreation: Rec. hall, boating, fishing.

Open: April 1 - November 1.

CLINTON COUNTY

• *CARLYLE*

Boulder Access Area, (Public Corps)

(618) 226-3586.

Grassy flatlands.

From town east seven miles on U.S. 50 to Boulder Road, north six miles (L). Good paved interior roads.

Facilities: 77 paved, some shaded, 14 day max stay, 77 E (30 amps), restrooms and showers, dump, public phone, laundry, LP bottles only, BBQ.

Recreation: Carlyle Lake: bass fishing, playground.

1992 rates $8.

Open: April 1 to Sept. 30.

Coles Creek Recreation Area, (Public Corps)

(618) 226-3211.

Grassy flatlands.

From town, east seven miles on U.S. 50 to Boulder-Ferrin Road, north four miles, follow signs (L). Good paved interior roads.

Facilities: 148 paved, some shaded, 14 day max stay, 148 E (30 amps), restrooms and showers, dump, public phone, laundry, BBQ.

Recreation: Carlyle Lake – bass fishing, swimming, playground.

1992 rates $8. No reservations.

Open: May 1 - November 1.

Dam West Recreation Area, (Carlyle Lake , Corps of Engineers)

(618) 594-4410.

From junction U.S. 50 and Illinois 127: go one-half mile north on Illinois 127, then one-half mile east.

Facilities: 113 sites, 21 ft. max. RV length, 113 electric, flush toilets, hot showers, sewage disposal, laundry, public phone, tables, fire rings, grills.

Recreation: Lake swimming, boating, ramp, dock, lake fishing, playground, hiking trails.

Open April 1 - November 30.

Eldon Hazlet State Park
(618) 594-3015.
From junction U.S. 50 and Illinois 127: go two miles north on Illinois 127.
Facilities: 372 sites, 336 electric, flush/pit toilets, hot showers, handicapped accessible restroom facilities, sewage disposal, limited grocery store, tables.
Recreation: Boating, ramp, dock, lake fishing, playground, hiking trails.
Open all year.

McNair Campgrounds, (Carlyle Lake , Corps of Engineers)
(618) 594-2484.
From Illinois 127 and U.S. 50: go 1 mile east on U.S. 50.
Facilities: 25 sites, 25 water and electric, flush toilets, hot showers, fire rings, grills.
Recreation: Lake swimming, lake fishing, playground.
Open: April 1 - October 31.

South Shore State Park
(618) 594-3015.
From junction Illinois 127 and U.S. 50: go five miles east on U.S. 50.
Facilities: 33 sites, 35 ft. max RV length, 33 no hookups, pit toilets, sewage disposal, tables, fire rings.
Recreation: Boating, ramp, lake fishing, playground.
Recreation open to the public.
Open all year.

EDWARDS COUNTY

• *GRAYVILLE*

Hilltop Campground, (Public)
(618) 375-3671.
Suburban, wooded hills. From junction of I-64 and Illinois 1, Exit 130, north 1.5 miles on Illinois 1 to North St., east four blocks to Water St., south a quarter mile to Walnut St., east 1 block to Oxford St., south 0.25 miles. Good gravel interior roads.
Facilities: 25 gravel, mostly shaded, 14 day max stay, 15 W, 15 E (15 amps), restrooms and showers, dump.
Recreation: Wabash River-fishing, boat ramp, pool, playground.

1992 rates $5. No reservations.
April 1 - November 1.

EFFINGHAM CO.

• *EFFINGHAM*

Camp Lakewood
(217)342-6233.
Level, shady sites overlooking river.
From junction I-70/I-57, Exit 160 and Illinois 32/33: go one-fourth mile north on Illinois 32/33, then one-fourth mile east on Ford Avenue, then one-fourth mile north on Raney St., then one-half mile west on Rickelman Avenue.
Facilities: 110 sites, 12 full hookups, 48 water and electric (30 & 50 amp receptacles), 50 no hookups, 25 pull-thrus, a/c allowed (charge), heater allowed (charge), cable TV, tents available, group sites for tents/RVs, flush toilets, hot showers, sewage disposal, laundry, public phone, limited grocery store, RV supplies, ice, tables, fire rings, wood.
Recreation: Recreation room, coin games, indoor heated swimming pool (charge), boating, 10 horsepower limit, ramp, fishing, playground, sports field, horseshoes, volleyball.
Recreation open to the public. Open all year.
1992 rates $13.50 - $17.50 for two persons.
Credit Cards Accepted: MC, VS.

Lake Sara Campgrounds
(217) 868-2964.
Rolling lakeside location with shade and grass.
From junction I-70, Exit 160 and Illinois 32: go three and one-half miles northwest on Illinois 32; then three-fourths mile south on Lake Sara Road, then 1.25 miles west on Moccasin Road, then one-half mile south on Beach Road, then one-fourth mile west on a county road.
Facilities: 315 sites, 50 full hookups, 200 water and electric (20 & 30 amp receptacles), 65 no hookups, season sites, 10 pull-thrus, a/c allowed (charge), heater allowed (charge), tenting available, RV storage, flush toilets, hot showers, sewage disposal, laundry, public phone, limited grocery store, RV supplies, ice,

tables, wood, church service.

Recreation: Recreation room, equipped pavilion, coin games, boating, canoeing, dock, water skiing, lake fishing, basketball hoop, playground.

Open April 1 - November 1.

1992 rates $10 - $13.50 for four persons. No refunds.

Timber Trails Campground

(618) 326-8264.

Private wooded flatlands.

From junction of I-70 and Mulberry Grove/Maple St., Exit 52, north 0.7 miles on Maple St., to Illinois 140, west 1 mile. Good gravel interior roads.

Facilities: 122–57 gravel, 65 grass, some shaded, 20 pull-thrus (30x70), 122 W, 37 S, 122 E (20/30 amps), a/c (charge), electric heat (charge), restrooms and showers, dump, security, private phone, limited groceries, ice, snacks, RV supplies, LP gas.

Recreation: Pond, bass fishing, tackle, swimming, horseshoes, rec. hall, planned activities, playground, rec field.

1992 rates $7.50 - $12.50.

FAYETTE COUNTY

• *VANDALIA*

KOA-Vandalia, (Private)

(618) 427-5140.

Wooded flatlands. From junction of I-70 & U.S. 40 Exit 68, north one-quarter mile on U.S. 40 to frontage road, west 1 block. Good gravel interior roads.

Facilities: 52 sites total, 34 gravel, 18 grass, mostly shaded, 24 pull-thrus, 28x55, 49 W, 18 S, 52 E (20/30 amps), a/c (charge), electric heat (charge), restrooms and showers, dump, security, public phone, laundry, limited groceries, ice, RV supplies, LP gas, BBQ.

Recreation: Pond, bass fishing, tackle, boat rental, pool, adult room, rec hall, game room, playground, rec field.

1992 rates $13 - $18.50.

Credit Cards Accepted: MC, VS.

Open: April 1 to October 31.

Ramsey Lake State Park

I-70 Exit 63, then 13 miles north on U.S. 51 then 1 mile west on PR.

Facilities: 210 sites (150 E), dump, flush

toilets, showers.

Recreation: Swimming,, boating, fishing, riding.

Handicapped accessible.

Open all year.

• *ST. ELMO*

Bail's Timberline Lake Campground, (Private)

(618) 829-3383.

Wooded flatlands. Good gravel access road.

From junction of I-70 & Interstate Drive Exit 76, north one-quarter mile on Interstate Drive to U.S. 40, east one-quarter mile to Elm St., north 1.2 miles to County Road 2070N, west one-half mile. Good gravel interior roads.

Facilities: 50 grass, mostly shaded, 22 pull-thrus, 30x40, 50 W, 26 S, 50 E (20/30 amps), AC (charge), electric heat (charge), dump, mobile sewer service, security, private phone, ice, BBQ.

Recreation: Timberline Lake: bass fishing, tackle, boating, ramp, dock, rental, playground.

1992 rates $8 - $12.

Open: April 1 - November 1.

FRANKLIN COUNTY

Gun Creek Recreation Area, (Corps of Engineers-Rend Lake)

(618) 724-2493.

Fromjunction I-57, Exit 77 & Illinois 154: go one-fourth mile west on Illinois 154, then one-half mile south, then west.

Facilities: 100 sites, 100 no hookups, pit toilets, public phone, tables, fire rings, grills.

Recreation: Boating, ramp, lake fishing, playground, planned group activities. Recreation open to the public.

Open April 1 through October 31. Facilities fully operational May 16 - Sept. 16.

North Sandusky Creek Recreation Area, (Corps of Engineers-Rend Lake)

(618) 724-2493.

From junction I-57, Exit 77 and Illinois 154: go six miles west on Illinois 154, then 1.5 miles south on Rend City Road.

Facilities: 121 sites, 121 electric, flush toilets, hot showers, handicapped accessible restroom facilities, sewage disposal, public phone, tables, fire rings, grills.

Recreation: Lake swimming, boating, ramp, lake fishing, playground, planned group activities. Recreation open to public.

Open April 1- October 31. Facilities fully operational May 16 - September 16.

South Marcum Recreation Area, (Corps of Engineers-Rend Lake)
(618) 724-2493.

From junction Illinois 37 and Illinois 14: go one-half mile north on Illinois 37, then three-fourths mile west on Petroff Road, then three miles north and west, then north to east end of main dam.

Facilities: 157 sites, 133 electric, 14 no hookups, pit toilets, handicapped restroom facilities, sewage disposal, tables, fire rings, grills.

Recreation: Lake/pond swimming, boating, ramp, lake/pond fishing, playground, planned group activities, tennis court, sports field, hiking trails.

Recreation open to the public. Open May 1 - September 30. Facilities fully operational May 16 - September 16.

South Sandusky Creek Recreation Area, (Corps of Engineers-Rend Lake)
(618) 724-2493.

From junction I-57, Exit 77 and Illinois 154: go six miles west on Illinois 154, then 3.5 miles south on Rend City Road.

Facilities: 121 sites, 111 electric, 10 no hookups, flush toilets, hot showers, handicapped accessible restroom facilities, sewage disposal, public phone, tables, fire rings, grills.

Recreation: Lake swimming, boating, ramp, lake fishing, playground, planned group activities.

Recreation open to the public. Open April 1 - October 31. Facilities fully operational May 16 - September 16.

• *SESSER*

Coy & Wilma's Camping
Turn off I-57, Exit 77 at 154. Drive across lake to first blacktop road to the left. Follow blacktop to stop sign. Coy and Wilma's on the right.

(618) 525-2101.

Camping rates: $10 by the day; $60 by the week; $150 by the month.

Facilities: Camping sites, grocery store on the grounds, fishing supplies, two completely furnished apartments (for reservations and information on the apartments phone or inquire at the store), bottle gas for your campers, check-out time 5 p.m., completely furnished laundromat.

Wayne Fitzgerrell State Park
(618) 629-2320.

From Sesser: go six miles east on Illinois 154.

Facilities: 285 sites, 35 ft. max RV length, 245 electric, 40 no hookups, flush/pit toilets, hot showers, handicapped accessible restroom facilities, sewage disposal, public phone, limited grocery store, ice, tables, fire rings, grills.

Recreation: Boating, ramp, lake fishing, playground, sports field, horseshoes, hiking trails.

Open all year. Facilities fully operational April - November

GALLATIN COUNTY

• *EQUALITY*

High Knob Ranch
(618) 275-4494.

Two miles north of Karber's Ridge, Hardin County.

Ride to scenic Garden of the Gods, wooded camp sites, RV sites, water, electric, dump station, toilets, concession stand, gift shop. Bring your horses, trails available.

HAMILTON COUNTY

• *McLEANSBORO*

Hamilton County State Conservation Area
(618) 773-4340.

From McLeansboro: go 14 miles east on Illinois 14, then 1 mile south on entrance road.

Facilities: 61 sites, 61 electric, flush/pit toilets, sewage disposal, public phone, limited grocery store, ice, tables, fire rings, grills.

Recreation: Boating, 10 horsepower limit, canoeing, ramp, dock, 18 rowing/four pedal boat rentals, fishing, hiking trails.
Open all year.

HARDIN COUNTY

• *CAVE-IN-ROCK*

Cave-In-Rock State Park
(618) 289-4325.
From junction Illinois 146 and Illinois 1: go two miles south on Illinois 1.
Facilities: 60 sites, 35 ft. max RV length, 35 electric, 25 no hookups, Pit/marine toilets, handicapped accessible restroom facilities, sewage disposal, laundry, public phone, limited grocery store, ice, tables, grills, wood.
Recreation: River swimming, boating, ramp river/pond fishing, playground, hiking trails.
Open all year.

Shawnee National Forest, (Tower Rock Campground)
(618) 287-2201.
From junction Illinois 1 and Illinois 146: go four miles west on Illinois 146, then 1 mile south on county road 101.
Facilities: 35 sites, 22 ft. max RV length, 35 no hookups, tenting available, pit toilets, tables, fire rings.
Recreation: Boating, ramp, river fishing, hiking trails.
Recreation open to the public. Open May 1 - December 15.

• *CENTRALIA*

Raccoon Lake City Park
2.5 miles east on Illinois 161 then one-half mile north on Moonglow Road.
Facilities: 50 sites (6 E, 5 W), dump, flush toilets.
Recreation: Boating, fishing.
Open: June 1 - October 1.

• *ELIZABETHTOWN*

Shawnee National Forest (Camp Cadiz)
10 miles north of Elizabethtown county road then two miles west on County Road 4.
Facilities: 25 sites.
Recreation: Fishing.

Open: May 15 - September 6.

Garden of the Gods (Shawnee National Forest)
Six miles west of Elizabethtown on Illinois 146 then eight miles north on Illinois 34 then two miles northwest and three miles north on county road.
Facilities: 12 sites, flush toilets.
Open: April 15 - October 15.

Shawnee National Forest, (Pounds Hollow Recreation Area)
Six miles west on Illinois 146 then eight miles north on Illinois 34 then five miles east on county road to Karbers Ridge then 5.5 miles north on county road 17.
Facilities: 76 sites.
Open: April 15 - December 15.

Rosiclare City Park
Three miles west on Illinois 146 then three miles south on Illinois 34.
Facilities: 25 (25 E), flush toilets.
Recreation: Swimming, boating, fishing.
Open: April 1 - November 1.

JACKSON COUNTY

• *AVA*

Shawnee National Forest, (Johnson Creek Campground)
Go four miles south of Ava on Illinois 151.
(618) 687-1731.
Facilities: 77 sites, 77 no hookups, tenting available, flush/pit toilets, sewage disposal, tables, grills.
Recreation: Lake swimming, boating, canoeing, ramp, lake fishing, hiking trails. Recreation open to the public.
Open early April through mid December Facilities fully operational Open: May 1 - October 15. No water in cold weather.

• *CARBONDALE*

Crab Orchard Lake
(618) 985-4983.
Box 229.
I-57 Exit 54 B, then 8.5 miles west on Illinois 13.
Facilities: 315 sites (150 E), dump, flush toilets, showers, store, snack bar.
Recreation: Rec. hall, swimming, boating,

fishing.
Open all year.

Giant City State Park
Nine miles south of Carbondale on Illinois 51 then four miles east on county Road.
Facilities: 161 sites (117 E), dump, flush toilets, showers, snack bar.
Recreation: Boating, fishing, riding.
Handicapped accessible.
Open all year.

• GORHAM

Turkey Bayou (Shawnee National Forest)
(618) 687-1731.
Wooded flatlands. Southeast one-half mile on County Road TR913 to Illinois 3, south two miles to county road 786, east four miles to county road-786A, north 0.7 miles.
Facilities: 13 dirt, 32 ft. max RV length, 14 day max stay, toilets, BBQ.
Recreation: Lake, fishing.
1992 rates $4. No reservations.
Open: April 1 - December 15.

• GRAND TOWER

Devils Backbone
(618) 565-8380.
Public wooded hills.
From town, west one mile on Illinois 3 to Park Road, north one-quarter mile. Good paved interior roads.
Facilities: 52 total, 24 gravel, 14 grass, 14 dirt, 25 ft. average, shaded, 14 pull-thrus, 52 W, 52 E (30 amps), restrooms and showers, dump, public phone, BBQ.
Recreation: Mississippi River, fishing, swimming, boat ramp, horseshoes, playground, rec. field.
1992 rates $7. No reservations.
Open: March - December

• MAKANDA

Giant City State Park
Box 70 (618) 457-4921.
Wooded hills.
From junction of U.S. 51 and Makanda Road, east 2.5 miles on Makanda Road. Good paved interior roads.
Facilities: 125 gravel, 50 ft. average. site width, some shaded, 14 day max stay,

125 E (15 amps), restrooms and showers, dump, BBQ.
Recreation: Lake: bass fishing, boat ramp, rec. hall, playground.
1992 rates $9. No reservations.

• MURPHYSBORO

Lake Murphysboro State Park
(618) 684-2867.
Wooded hills.
From junction of Illinois 149 and Illinois 127, west 3.5 miles on Illinois 149. Fair paved interior roads.
Facilities: 54 gravel, 25 ft. average site width, 40 ft. max RV length, some shaded, 18 pull-thrus, 14 day max stay, 54 E (30/50 amps), restrooms and showers, dump, public phone, limited groceries, ice.
Recreation: Lake Murphysboro: fishing, tackle, boating, ramp, rental, playground.
1992 rates $8. No reservations.

JEFFERSON COUNTY

• BENTON

Benton KOA
(618) 439-4860.
A grassy campground with open or shaded sites on rolling terrain beside the interstate.
From junction I-57, Exit 71 & Illinois 14: go one-eighth mile east on Illinois 14, then one mile north on Du Quoin St.
Facilities: 73 sites, 33 full hookups, 23 water and electric, three electric (20, 30 & 50 amp receptacles), 14 no hookups, 18 pull-thrus, a/c allowed (charge), heater allowed (charge), tenting available, group tent sites, flush toilets, hot showers, sewage disposal, laundry, public phone, grocery store, RV supplies, LP gas, ice, tables, grills.
Recreation: Rec. room, coin games, swimming pool, basketball hoop, playground, sports field, horseshoes.
1992 rates $12.50 - $15.50 for two persons.
Open all year.
Discount: KOA 10% value card discount.
Credit Cards Accepted: MC, VS.

• INA

Sherwood Camping Resort
I-64 Exit 80 • I-57 Exit 83, Ina, IL
(618) 437-5530. Box 98.
(Near Rend Lake and nine miles south of
Mt. Vernon).
Facilities: Swimming, fishing, paddle-
boats, golf and tennis nearby, pavilion,
game room, shady sites, full hookups,
long pull thrus, camping cottages.

• MT. VERNON

Archway Trailer Parkway, (Private)
(618) 244-0399.
Grassy flatlands. Gravel access road.
From junction of I-57 and Illinois 15, Exit
95, west three-quarters mile on Illinois
15 (R). Good gravel interior roads.
Facilities: 44 sites total, 24 gravel, 20
grass, 30 ft. average site width, mostly
shaded, 44 pull-thrus, 44 W, 38 S, 44 E
(20/30 amps), a/c (charge), electric heat
(charge), restrooms, showers, dump,
security, phone, laundry, ice.
Recreation: Pond, bass fishing.
1992 rates $13.
Credit Cards Accepted: MC, VS.

JERSEY COUNTY

• GRAFTON

Pere Marquette State Park
(618) 786-3323.
From junction Illinois 100 and U.S. 67, go
25 miles west on Illinois 100.
Facilities: 157 sites, 82 electric, 75 no
hookups, flush/pit toilets, hot showers,
sewage disposal, public phone, tables.
Recreation: Boating, ramp, dock, row
boat rentals, fishing, playground, hiking
trails.
Open all year.

JOHNSON COUNTY

• GOREVILLE

Ferne Clyffe State Park
(618) 995-2411.
From town: go one-fourth mile south on
Illinois 37.
Facilities: 109 sites, 64 water and electric,
45 no hookups, flush toilets, hot show-
ers, handicapped accesibles restroom
facilities, sewage disposal, public phone,
tables, fire rings, grills, wood.
Recreation: Lake fishing, playground,
hiking trails.
Recreation open to the public.
Open all year. Facilities fully operational
March - September

• near SIMPSON

Bay Creek Ranch
Box 189. (618) 695-2670.
One mile north of Glendale, Illinois 145
and 147, one mile north on Cedar Grove
Church Road, Pope County.
Facilities: Family camping, wooded RV
and tent sites, water, electric, dump station, showers and restrooms, weekend
mini rides, guides and meals, special
activities in season, hunters welcome,
bring your horse, direct access to
Shawnee trails.

Triple T Cedar Lake Ranch
(618) 695-2600.
A campground with grass and shade on
rolling terrain.
From junction I-24, Exit 14 and U.S. 45:
go six miles north on U.S. 45, then two
miles east on a county road.
Facilities: 200 sites, 175 water and electric
(15 & 30 amp receptacles), 25 no
hookups, seasonal sites, tenting available, flush/pit toilets, hot showers,
sewage disposal, public phone, ice,
tables, wood.
Recreation: Recreation room, pavilion,
lake swimming (charge), boating, seven
horsepower limit, lake fishing, hiking.
Recreation open to the pubic. Open all
year.
1992 rates $9 per family.

LAWRENCE COUNTY

• LAWRENCEVILLE

Red Hills State Park
Nine miles west of Lawrenceville on U. S.
50.
Facilities: 119 sites (119 E), dump, flush
toilets, showers, snack bar.
Recreation: Boating, fishing, riding.
Handicappped accessible.
Open all year.

MADISON COUNTY

• *COLLINSVILLE*

Amerigas Collinsville
(618) 344-6000.
From junction of I-55 north bound, and Illinois 159 east one block on Illinois 159 to fronting road, north two blocks.

• *GRANITE CITY*

Greater Saint Louis KOA
(618) 931-5160.
Private suburban grassy flatlands. Good gravel access road.
From junction of I-270 and Illinois 3, Exit 3A, south one block on Illinois 3 to Chain of Rocks Road, east one-half mile (R). Good gravel interior roads.
Facilities: 81 gravel, some shaded, 72 pull-thrus 25x60, 81 W, 57 S, 81 E (30 amps), a/c (charge), electric heat (charge), restrooms and showers, dump, security, phone, laundry, limited groceries, ice, RV supplies, LP bottles only.
Recreation: Pool, horseshoes, game room, playground.
1992 rates $12 to $18.
Credit Cards Accepted: MC, VS.
March 1 - November 15.

Horseshoe Lake State Park
(618) 931-0270.
From junction I-270 and Illinois 111, go four miles south on Illinois 111.
Facilities: 48 sites, 35 ft. max RV length, 48 no hookups, pit toilets, sewage disposal, public phone, limited grocery store, tables, fire rings.
Recreation: Boating, 25 horsepower limit, ramp, row/sail boat rentals, lake fishing, playground, hiking trails.
Open all year.

Trail's End
(618) 931-5041. 3225 W. Chain of Rocks Road, Granite City, IL 62040.
I-270 exit 3A, then one block south on Illinois 3 then one block east on south frontage road.
Facilities: 45 sites (45 E, 45 W, 45 S, two drive-thrus), dump, flush toilets, showers, laundry.
Open all year.

• *HIGHLAND*

Mick's Lake and Recreational Campground
(618) 644-5855.
A rural location on grassy rolling terrain.
From junction of I-70, Exit 21 and Illinois 4: go three miles south on Illinois 4, then two miles east on U.S. 40, then one-half mile north on county road 2800 east, then one-fourth mile west on county road 530 north.
Facilities: 190 sites, 150 water and electric (20/30 amp receptacles), 40 no hookups, seasonal sites, a/c allowed (charge), heater allowed (charge), tenting available, group sites for tents/RVs, RV storage, flush/pit toilets, hot showers (charge), sewage disposal, LP gas refill by weight, ice, tables, wood.
Recreation: Pavilion, lake swimming (charge), boating, electric motors only, canoeing, five row boat rentals, lake fishing (charge), basketball hoop, playground, horseshoes, hiking trails, volleyball. Recreation open to the public.
1992 rates $8 - $10 for four persons.
Open all year. Facilities fully operational April 1 - November 1.

MARION COUNTY

• *SALEM*

Stephen A. Forbes State Park
(618) 547-3381.
Wooded hills.
From junction of I-57 and U.S. -50 Salem Exit, east seven miles on U.S. 50 to Omega Lake Road, north seven miles, follow signs. Good paved interior roads.
Facilities: 115 gravel, 75 ft. average site width, mostly shaded, four pull-thrus, 14 day max stay, 115 E (30 amps), restrooms and showers, dump, public phone, limited groceries, ice, snacks, RV supplies, BBQ.
Recreation: Forbes Lake: fishing, tackle, swimming, boating, ramp, dock, marina, rental, horseshoes, playground.
1992 rates $8 - $9. No reservations.

607

MASSAC COUNTY

• *METROPOLIS*

Fort Massac State Park
(618) 524-4712.
From junction I-24 & U.S. 45, go 2.5 miles west on U.S. 45.
Facilities: 58 sites, 35 ft. max RV length, 48 electric, 10 no hookups, flush/pit toilets, handicapped accessible restroom facilities, sewage disposal, public phone, tables, fire rings, grills.
Recreation: Boating, ramp, river fishing, playground, hiking trails.
Open all year.

PERRY COUNTY

• *DU QUOIN*

Du Quoin State Fairgrounds
U.S. 51 South. (618) 542-9373.
Facilities: Campgrounds approx. 30 sites with full hookups, $10 per night, unlimited primitive camping, hot showers, flush toilets, dump station, beautiful grounds surrounded by several lakes, ideal for groups and rallies.

• *PINCKNEYVILLE*

Pyramid State Park
(618) 357-2574.
Wooded flatlands.
From junction of Illinois 154 and Illinois 13, south six miles on Illinois 13 to county road, west 2.75 miles. Fair gravel interior roads.
Facilities: 54 gravel, 35 ft. average site width, 14 day max stay, toilets, dump, public phones, BBQ.
Recreation: Boulder Lake and 23 other lakes: fishing, boat ramp, planned activities.
1992 rates $4. No reservations.

• *PERCY*

Community Lake
Illinois 4 South Percy, IL 62272.
(618) 497-2942.
Illinois 150 then 4.5 miles south on Illinois 4.
Facilities: 110 sites (110 E, 110 W, 15

drive-thrus), dump, flush toilets, showers, laundry.
Recreation: Rec hall, shuffleboard, swimming, boating, fishing, motorbikes permitted.
Open: April 1 - November 1.

POPE COUNTY

• *EDDYVILLE*

Bear Branch Campground
P.O. Box 1 (618) 672-4249.
Two miles north of Eddyville, Illinois 145, Pope County.
Facilities: The Log Cabin Restaurant sets the theme for this lovely hilltop campground overlooking the Shawnee National Forest, 80 RV and tent sites, water, electric, dump station, showers and restrooms. Campers to rent, fishing pond, bring your horses, trails available, hunters welcome. Open year round.

• *GOLCONDA*

Barren Creek Cottages
Illinois 3, Box 136. (618) 683-4004.
Two cabins; two-three bedrooms, two bedroom - $50 (two people); $10 per add'l person (two bedroom will sleep up to seven people); three bedroom - $60 (two people) (three bedroom will sleep up to 8); $10 per add'l person.
Facilities: Heating/air conditioning, color TV, private boat docks, public boat ramp nearby.

Deer Run Campground
Two miles South on blacktop road from Golconda. P.O. Box 839. (618) 683-8410.
Facilities: 22 campsites with electric, water and sewage at each site, showerhouse and air conditioned country rooms, drive-thru hook-ups, quick access to the beautiful Golconda Marina & Smithland Pool on the Ohio River with excellent fishing, ice, soda, etc., beautiful country sites.
Campground open seven days a week March - November.

Dixon Springs State Park
(618) 949-3394.
Wooded hills.

From junction of I-24 and Illinois 146, Exit 16, east 12 miles on Illinois 146. Good paved interior roads.

Facilities: 40 gravel, 30 ft. average. site width, no slide-outs, 35 ft. max RV length, some shaded, 14 day max stay, 40 E (30 amps), toilets, dump, public phone, ice, snacks, BBQ.

Recreation: Stream, swimming, pool, playground.

1992 rates $8. No reservations.

Lake Glendale Stables/Outfitters

Box 201 A.

Stables (618) 949-3737 • Home (618) 949-3375.

Located in the Lake Glendale Recreation Area, two miles north of Illinois 146/145 intersection in Pope County.

Facilities: Horse rentals, one hour to overnight pack trips, great horses for the experienced or not, horses broutgh to your location. Deer and turkey hunt camps, guides, licensed outfitters for Lusk Creek Wilderness Area. Open all year.

Lusk Creek Lodge

Box 225. West of Golconda

(502) 898-3892 for reservations.

Two units. $15 per person.

Facilities: Complete kitchen, living room with color TV, boat ramp next to units, restaurants and convenience store nearby.

• *HEROD*

34 Ranch

Campground (618) 264-2141 • Home (618) 273-9474.

Four miles south of Herod on Illinois 34, Pope County.

Facilities: Family camping, RV and tent sites, electric, water, dump station, showers and restrooms, party barn and arena available for events, shows, rodeos. Home of Keyhole Stables, rental horses, outfitting, overnight trips, guides by reservation only. Fishing ponds, hunters welcome. Home of One Horse Gap Trail Ride held second week in June and October.

• near *VIENNA*

Shawnee National Forest, (Lake Glendale-Bailey Place)

(618) 658-2111.

From Vienna: go 12 miles east on Illinois 146, then two miles north on Illinois 145.

Facilities: 50 sites, 50 no hookups, tenting available, pit toilets, public phone, tables, patios, grills, wood.

Recreation: Lake swimming.

Open all year.

Shawnee National Forest, (Lake Glendale-Oak Point)

Campground (618) 658-2111.

From Vienna: go 12 miles east on Illinois 146, then two miles north on Illinois 145.

Facilities: 74 sites, 32 ft. max RV length, 74 no hookups, tenting available, flush toilets, hot showers, handicapped accessible restroom facilities, sewage disposal, public phone, tables, grills, wood.

Recreation: Lake swimming, boating, ramp, lake fishing, hiking trails.

Recreation open to the public.

Open all year.

Shawnee National Forest, (Lake of Egypt-Buck Ridge)

Campground.

From town: go seven miles northwest on I-24, then three miles east on Tunnel Hill Blacktop. Follow signs.

Facilities: 41 sites, 32 ft. max RV length, 41 no hookups, tenting available, pit toilets, handicapped accessible restroom facilities, tables, grills.

Recreation: Lake swimming, lake fishing.

Open March 15 - October 31

RANDOLPH COUNTY

• *CHESTER*

Fort Kaskaskia, (State Historical Site)

(618) 859-3741.

From junction Illinois 3 and Illinois 150: go two miles west on Ft. Kaskaskia Road.

Facilities: 75 sites, 75 no hookups, pit toilets, handicapped accessible restroom facilities, sewage disposal, tables.

Recreation: Fishing, playground, hiking trails.

Open all year.

Randolph County Conservation Area

(618) 826-2706.

From junction Illinois 3 and Illinois 150, go six miles northeast on Illinois 150 to County Road DD.

Facilities: 90 sites, 35 ft. max RV length, 90 no hookups, flush/pit toilets, handicapped accessible restroom facilities, sewage disposal, public phone, limited grocery store, tables, fire rings, grills.

Recreation: Boating, 10 horsepower limit, ramp, dock, row boat rentals, lake fishing, hiking trails.

Open all year.

RICHLAND COUNTY

• *OLNEY*

Lakeside RV Park

(618) 393-4351.

Level shaded campground across the highway from a lake.

From junction U.S. 50 and Illinois 130: go three miles north on Illinois 130, then three-fourths mile east and one-fourth mile north on county roads.

Facilities: 65 sites, 60 water and electric (20 & 30 amp receptacles), five no hookups, seasonal sites, 10 pull-thrus, tenting available, flush/chemical toilets, hot showers, sewage, disposal, public phone, LP gas refill by weight/by meter, ice, tables.

Recreation: Pavilion, lake swimming, boating, dock, three motor boat rentals, lake fishing, playground, badminton, sports field, horseshoes, volleyball.

Open April 1 - October 15.

1992 rates $10 - $12 for two persons.

SALINE COUNTY

• *HARRISBURG*

Redbud (Shawnee National Forest)

From Harrisburg: 16 miles south on Illinois 145 then 3.5 miles west on county road 447 then one and three-fourths miles south on county road 848.

Facilities: 20 sites.

Open: May 20 - September 8

Teal Pond (Shawnee National Forest)

16 miles south on Illinois 145 then 3.5 miles west on forest service road 447.

Facilities: Nine sites.

Recreation: Swimming, boating, fishing.

May 20 - September 6.

Saline County Conservation Area

(618) 276-4405.

From junction Illinois 13 and Illinois 142: go one mile southeast on Illinois 142, then four miles south on blacktop road.

Facilities: 45 sites, 35 ft. max RV length, 45 no hookups, flush/pit toilets, handicapped accessible restroom facilities, sewage disposal, public phone, limited grocery store, ice tables, fire rings, grills, wood.

Recreation: Lake swimming, boating, 10 horsepower limit, canoeing, ramp, dock, lake fishing (charge), playground, horseshoes, hiking trails, volleyball.

Open all year. Facilities fully operational April - September

ST. CLAIR COUNTY

• *FAIRMONT CITY*

Safari RV Park

(618) 271-0955.

Private suburban, grassy flatlands.

From junction of I-70 and Illinois 111, Exit 6, south 0.2 miles on Illinois 111 to Collinsville Road, (first light,) west 0.2 mile (L). Good gravel interior roads.

Facilities: No tents, 22 gravel, 18 ft. average. site width, 22 full hookups (30/50 amps), a/c (charge), electric heat (charge), security, private phone.

1992 rates $15.

• *CAHOKIA*

Cahokia RV Parque

(618) 332-7700.

Private suburban grassy flatlands.

From junction of I-255 and Illinois 157, Exit 13 west 2.5 miles on Illinois 157 to Illinois 3, north 500 ft. (L). Good gravel interior roads.

Facilities: 119 gravel, 21 pull-thrus 25x100, 119 W, 76 S, 119E (30/50 amps), restrooms and showers, dump, security, public phone, laundry, ice, LP gas.

Recreation: Pool, adult room, game room.
1992 rates $18 - $22.
Credit Cards Accepted: MC, VS.

UNION COUNTY

• *COBDEN*

Black Diamond Ranch
South of Alto Pass on Illinois 127.
(618) 833-7629 for reservations and questions.
Facilities: Camping, six rooms, one bunkhouse, barn, lodge building, horseback and hiking trails, hunters welcome, meals on request. Horsemen bring your current Coggins papers.
Open all year.

• *DONGOLA*

Crooked Arrow Ranch
Box 18.
(618) 827-4100.
Facilities: Come see the lilac colored out building, enjoy primitive camping and have picnic on the ground, Controlled horseback riding, day camp, parties and hiking trails.
Group rates, handicapped and general public welcome.
Call for details.

• *JONESBORO*

Trail of Tears Sports Resort
Old Cape Road.
(618) 833-8697.
Eight miles south of Jonesboro in Union County.
Facilities: Ride the southern branch of the Trail of Tears, see historic landmarks, bring your horse or rental horses and guides are available, spring and autumn trail rides, restaurant, A/C lodge with sleeping facilities, camp sites, showers, restrooms, hunters welcome, outfitters, excellent deer, turkey, waterfowl hunting and fishing nearby, upland game preserve, 3-D archery, sporting clays, pistol and rifle ranges, miniature golf, summer youth camp.

• *PAMONA*

Wolf Creek Ranch
Box 111. (618) 893-4440.
Six miles northwest of Alto Pass, IL (Illinois 127) in Jackson County.
Facilities: Enjoy wilderness camping at its best. Immediate access to Shawnee National Forest Trails. Graveled RV sites, tent sites, shade, groups welcome, guides available upon request. Bring your horse, plenty of water for horses. Occasional bluegrass and country music.

• *WOLF LAKE*

Pine Hills (Shawnee National Forest)
(618) 833-8576.
Wooded hills.
North one mile on county road 13 to county road-336, north one-half mile.
Facilities: 12 dirt, 22 ft. max RV, length, 14 day max stay, toilets, BBQ.
Recreation: Stream.
1992 rates $4. No reservations.
Open: April 1 to December 15.

WASHINGTON CO.

• *NASHVILLE*

Washington County Conservation Area State Park
(618) 327-3137.
Wooded flatlands.
From junction of I-64 and Illinois 127 Exit 50, south four miles on Illinois 127, follow signs. Good paved interior roads.
Facilities: 150 gravel, 40 ft. average site width, mostly shaded, 14 day max stay, 50 E (30 amps), restrooms and showers, dump, public, phone, limited groceries, ice, snacks, BBQ.
Recreation: Washington County State Lake: fishing, tackle, boating, ramp, dock, rental, playground.
1992 rates $4 - $9. No reservations.

WAYNE COUNTY

Sam Dale Lake State Park
Eight miles on Illinois 50 then eight miles south on County Road then 3.5 miles east on county road.

Facilities: 118 sites, (68 E), dump, flush toilets, snack bar.
Recreation: Boating, fishing.
Open all year.

WHITE COUNTY

• *CARMI*

Burrells Park Campground, (City Park)
(618) 382-2693.
From junction Illinois 14 and Illinois 1: go north on Third St., then two miles north on Stewart St.
Facilities: 25 sites, 20 full hookups, (30 amp receptacles), five no hookups, flush toilets, hot showers, sewage disposal, tables.
Recreation: Lake fishing, playground, volleyball.
Open April 15 - October 15.

WILLIAMSON CO.

• *CREAL SPRINGS*

Buck Ridge- Shawnee National Forest
(618) 658-2111.
Wooded hills.
From town, south three miles on Illinois 2 to county road-870, west 1.75 miles to county road-871, northwest 0.4 miles to frontage road-871A, west 1.2 miles.
Facilities: 41 dirt, 32 ft. max RV length, 14 day max stay, toilets, BBQ, lake fishing.
1992 rates $5. No reservations.
Open: March 15 to December 31.

• *MARION*

Devils Kitchen Boat Dock & Campground
(618) 457-5004.

Box 187, Carbondale, IL 62901.
I-57 Exit Marion, then 3.5 miles west on Illinois 13 then six miles south on Illinois 148 then four miles west on Grassy Road then follow signs.
Facilities: 52 sites (30 E, 30 W, 25 drive-thrus), dump, flush toilets, showers, stove, snack bar, restaurant.
Recreation: Boating, fishing.
March 1 - December 15.

Motel Marion Campground
(618) 993-2101.
RV spaces behind a motel.
From junction I-57, Exit 53 and Main St. go one-fourth mile east on Main St.
Facilities: 25 sites, 25 water and electric (20 amp receptacles), tenting available, flush toilets, hot showers, sewage disposal, public phone, ice.
Recreation: Swimming pool.
Open all year.
1992 rates $8.50 per vehicle.
Credit Cards Accepted: MC, VS.

Little Grassy Campground & Boat Dock, (Public)
(618) 457-6655.
Wooded hills.
Fromjunction of I-57 and Illinois 13, west three miles on Illinois 13 to Illinois 148, south 4.5 miles to Grassy road, west six miles, follow signs. Good paved interior roads.
Facilities: 68 sites total, 11 paved, 57 gravel, 30 ft. average site width, mostly shaded, 68 W, 14 S, 68 E (20/30 amps), restrooms and showers, dump, public phone, limited groceries, ice, snacks, BBQ.
Recreation: Little Grassy Lake: fishing, tackle, swimming, boating, ramp, dock, rental.
1992 rates $8 - $11.
March 1 - November 30.

Lodging

A compendium of recreation cannot ignore lodging. Ideally, there is lodging for everyone of the right type, location, and price.

In the process of compiling a listing of lodging available in Southern Illinois, we have attempted to contact each by mail to verify the accuracy of our information. Since we were successful in about half of our attempts, some prices or data may vary from that listed. Those lodgings that have responded to recent inquiries for information are underlined. If there is any concern about the information provided, contact the listed source for the most updated information.

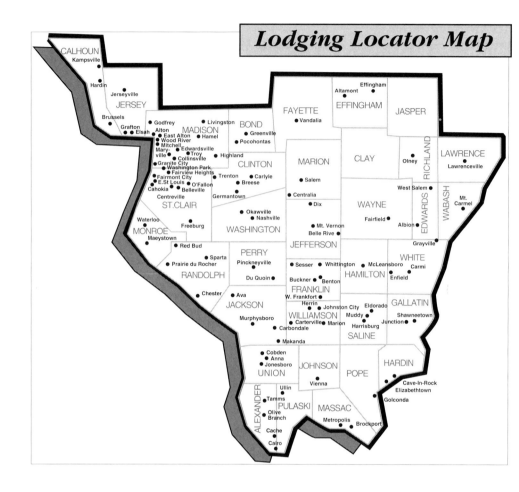

Lodging Locator Map

ALEXANDER CO.

• *CACHE (62913)*

Melton's Fishing Camp, RR1, East side
   Dr. on Horseshoe lake
(618) 776-5504
Nine rooms. $15-$30
Facilities: Lounge
Discounts: Seniors (inquire)

Southernaire Motel, R. R., Box 72.
   Located on the banks of Horseshoe
   Lake
(618) 734-2908

Nine rooms. Call for rates.
Discounts: Weekly rates.
Facilities: Boat rental available, kitch-
   enettes
Rooms are not handicapped accessible.
Credit cards are not accepted.

• *CAIRO (62914)*

Belvedere Motel, 3901 Sycamore.
   Highway 51, Exit #1 from I-57
(618) 734-4020
12 rooms. S–$20.; D–$25.
Discounts: Senior citizens, weekly rates.
Rooms are not handicapped accessible.
Credit cards accepted: MC, VS, AE

Best Way Inn, I-57, exit 1.
(618) 734-0215
38 rooms. S–$26.50; D–$38.84
Discounts: 10% for senior citizens, truck
    drivers, commercial.
Facilities: Dining, lounge, swimming (out-
    door).
Two handicapped accessible rooms avail-
    able.
Credit cards accepted: MC, VS, AE, DS

Lakeside Lodge, RR1, P.O. Box 250
(618) 776-5609
8 rooms
No credit cards accepted
No discounts available

City Motel, 214 Washington, U. S. 51
(618) 734-0285
Non-US operated
21 rooms. Would not release pricing
    information
Discounts: Unknown
Credit cards accepted: Unknown

Garden Inn Motel, Campground &
    Mobile Home Park, U.S. 51.
(618) 734-2711
14 rooms. S–$25; D–$30; S–$125/week;
    D–$140/ week
Facilities: Dining (nearby),
Rooms are handicapped accessible.
Credit cards accepted: MC, VS

Plaza Motel, 3705 Sycamore.
(618) 734-2101
22 rooms. Call for rates.
Facilities: pets accepted

Windham Bed & Breakfast, 2606
    Washington Ave.
(618) 734-3247
3 rooms. $65-$80.
Discounts: Local businesses.
Facilities: Meeting room, breakfast for
    guests, laundromat by arrangement.
Rooms are not handicapped accessible.
Credit cards accepted: None

Worthington Courts, RR 1
(618) 776-5333
14 rooms

• *OLIVE BRANCH (62969)*

Horseshoe Lake Motel, Route 3 S.
(618) 776-5201
22 rooms. Summer rates: 2 people, 1
    bed–$24; Up to 4 people, 2
    beds–$27.50. Fall hunting season rates:
    $36-$44.50.
No discounts available.
Facilities: Dining (nearby), office safe for
    valuables.
Handicapped accessible rooms.
Credit cards not accepted.

• *TAMMS (62988)*

Fayne's Motel, Highway 127 S.
(618) 747-2895
10 rooms
Facilities: Dining, entertainment

BOND COUNTY

• *GREENVILLE (62246)*

2 Acres Motel, I-70 & Illinois127, S. 40.
(618) 664-3131
20 rooms. $28.50-$38
Discounts: AARP (in winter).
Facilities: Dining.
Rooms are not handicapped accessible.
Credit cards accepted: MC, VS, Dis

Best Western Country View Inn,
I-70 & Illinois 127.
(618) 664-3030
60 rooms. $32-$45
Discounts: Senior citizens, AAA, military,
    government, trucker, corporate.
Facilities: Meeting/convention services,
    dining, lounge, swimming (outdoor).
Handicapped accessible rooms.
Credit cards accepted: MC, VS, AE, DC,
    DS, AM, DC/CB

Budget Host Inn, I-70 & Illinois 127.
(618) 664-1950 or 1-800-BUD-HOST
31 rooms. $31–$43. $3 per extra person.
Facilities: Meeting/convention services,
    lounge, heated swimming (outdoor),
    whirlpool, kitchenette available, conti-
    nental breakfast.
Handicapped accessible rooms.
Credit cards accepted: MC, VS, DC, CB,
    AE, DS

Prairie House, RR 4, Box 47AA
(618) 664-3003
5 rooms. $35–$45
Credit cards accepted: MC, VS

Uptown Motel, 323 S. Third St., Illinois
127
(618) 664-3121
Facilities: Pets accepted

• *POCAHONTAS (62275)*

Powhatan Motel, I-70, Exit 36
(618) 669-2271
12 rooms. inquire about price
Facilities: Pets accepted, dining, lounge,
handicapped accessible rooms
Discounts: None
Credit cards accepted: MC, VS, AE

Tahoe Motel, I-70, Exit 36; I-70 &
Illinois 40
(618) 669-2404

12 rooms. $30–$40
Facilities: Pets accepted, handicapped
accessible rooms
Credit cards accepted: Yes, inquire

Wikiup Motel, Corner of Plant &
Johnson.
(618) 669-2293
21 rooms. Winter rates: S–$23–$40, $4
for extra persons
No discounts available.
Rooms are not handicapped accessible.
Credit cards accepted: MC, VS, DS

CALHOUN COUNTY

• *BRUSSELS (62013)*

Wittmond Hotel, 108 Main Street.
(618) 883-2345.
6 rooms $30–$40
Facilities: 1847 restored inn. Dining
(family-style meals), lounge.

Rooms are not handicapped accessible.
No credit cards accepted.

• *HARDIN (62047)*

Hardin Hotel, Box 456.
(618) 576-9003.
12 rooms. $21.20.
Facilities: Dining (nearby).
Rooms are not handicapped accessible.
Credit cards accepted: MC, VS

• *KAMPSVILLE (62053)*

Kampsville Inn, Second & Joliet.
(618) 653-4413
5 rooms. $20
Facilities: Dining (seats 150 people),
    lounge.
No discounts.
Rooms are not handicapped accessible.
No credit cards accepted.

CLINTON COUNTY

• *BREESE (62230)*

Knotty Pine Motel, 215 N. 4th, I-270 &
    I-57
(618) 650-3000
10 rooms. $28 - $47
Facilities: Dining, meeting, convention,
    pets
Discounts: Seniors
Rooms are not handicapped accessible
Credit cards accepted: MC, VS

• *CARLYLE (62231)*

Carlyle Lane Restaurant & Motel, 1220
    12th
(618) 594-2474
26 rooms. $28–$40
Facilities: dining, meeting/convention,
    spa, outdoor swimming, pets accepted
Discounts: senior, corporate
Credit cards accepted: MC, VS, AE, DS

Country Haus Bed & Breakfast, 1191
    Franklyn St.
(618) 549-8313
4 rooms. $45–$55
Credit cards accepted: MC, VS, AE

Motel Carlyle, Illinois 127 & Fairfax St.
(618) 594-8100

19 rooms. $24–$30
Discounts: commercial
Facilities: Dining (nearby), lounge, enter-
    tainment, swimming (outdoor), laun-
    dromat, kitchenettes & safe deposit box
    available.
Rooms are not handicapped accessible.
All major credit cards accepted.

Riddel's Court, 1951 Franklin

Sunset Motel, 1631 Franklin
(618) 594-4838
Facilities:12 rooms, pets accepted

The Victorian Inn Bed & Breakfast,
1111 Franklyn St.
(618) 594-8506
$55
Credit cards accepted: MC, VS.

• *GERMANTOWN (62245)*

Starlite Motel, 1311 Lake Park Dr.,
    Illinois 161
(618) 523-4313
10 rooms. $26–$30
Rooms have limited handicapped accessi-
    bility.
Facilities: Dining
Credit cards accepted: MC, VS

• *TRENTON (62293)*

Jefferson House Bed & Breakfast, 305
    W. Broadway
(618) 224-9733
2 rooms

EDWARDS COUNTY

• *ALBION (62806)*

Albion Motel, Illinois 15 W. Albion
(618) 445-2311
10 rooms. S–$21.25, D–$21.50, $2 addi-
    tional persons
Facilities: Direct dial phones & cable TV
Credit cards accepted: VS, MC

• *WEST SALEM (62476)*

Thelma's Bed & Breakfast, 201 S.
    Broadway, Box 185
(618) 456-8401
Five rooms. $20–$80 per week.

Facilities: Shared bath, spacious living & dining areas, adapted for long-stay guests. Full breakfast served daily.
No credit cards accepted

EFFINGHAM COUNTY

• *ALTAMONT*

Aloha Inn, Southside of I-70, Exit 82
(618) 483-6300.
25 rooms. $26–$33.
Facilities: Dining, laundromat, truck parking, playgrounds.
Rooms are not handicapped accessible.
Credit cards accepted: MC, VS

Altamont Motel, U. S. 40 & Main, 0.5 mile N. of I-70 at Exit 82.
(618) 483-6143
17 rooms. $20 & up
Facilities: dining (nearby), color cable TV, free HBO, kitchenette available, non-smoking rooms available
Credit cards accepted: MC, VS, AE, DS.

Stuckey's Carriage Inn, I-70 at Exit 82
(618) 483-6101
38 rooms. $28–$42
Facilities: Swimming (outdoor), restaurant,lounge, meeting room, golf course nearby
Rooms are not handicapped accessible
Credit cards accepted: VS, MC, AE, DS, DC/CB

• *EFFINGHAM (62401)*

Abe Lincoln Motel, Junction I-70 & 57 at exit 159; second red light turn right
(217) 342-4717
18 rooms. $21.95 & up
Facilities: Dining nearby, pets accepted, handicapped rooms
Credit cards accepted: MC, VS, Dis, AE

Anthony Acres Resort, RR 2
(217) 868-2950
24 rooms
Facilities: Meeting/Convention, golf outdoor pool, pets accepted
Handicapped accessible rooms.

Best Inns of America, 1209 North Keller Dr.
(217) 347-5141 or 1-800-237-8466

83 rooms. S–$34.88. $6 extra per person
Facilities: Outdoor pool, pets accepted, handicapped rooms ,truck parking

Best Western Raintree Inn, I-57 & I-70, Exit 159
(217) 342-4121
65 rooms. $28–$45
Discounts: AAA, AARP, government, military, trucker.
Facilities: Dining, lounge, nightclub, entertainment, swimming, cable TV, free breakfast
Handicapped accessible rooms.
Credit cards accepted: All major credit cards accepted

Lincoln Lodge Motel, I-70/I-57 & U.S. 45
(217) 342-4133
25 rooms. $26–$33
Facilities: Dining (nearby)
Discounts: AARP, trucker

Budgetel, 1103 Ave. of Mid-America, Exit 160 off I-57 & I-70
(217) 342-2525
Discounts: Group rates, corporate, children 18 & under stay free with parents
Facilities: Conference rooms, suites
Credit cards accepted: AE, DS, MC, VS, DC/CB

Cloverleaf Motel, Illinois 33 & 40 East.
(217) 342-4655
17 rooms. $15.95–$21.95
No discounts available.
Facilities: Dining (nearby), laundromat (nearby).
Handicapped accessible rooms.
Credit cards accepted: VS

Days Inn Effingham, West Fayette Rd
(217) 342-9271 or 1-800-325-2525
122 rooms. $36.88–$45.88 ($5 per person beyond 2 persons)
Facilities: pets accepted, handicapped accessible rooms, pool (outdoor), dining (nearby), free popcorn, meeting rooms, free shuttle to airport & area attractions.
Credit cards accepted: All major credit cards
Discounts Available: travel agents, employees, AAA, AARP, group

Effingham Econo Lodge, 1205 Keller
(217) 347-7131
74 rooms. $29.95–$44.95
Handicapped accessible rooms.
Discounts: Senior, AAA, military
Facilities: Meeting rooms, Spa/Sauna,
 indoor pool, pets accepted, handicapped
 rooms
Credit cards accepted: MC, VS, DC, Din.
 Cb.

Effingham Motel, 702 E. Fayette Ave
(217) 342-3991
16 rooms
Facilities: pets accepted

Hampton Inn, I-57 & I-70, Exit 160
(217) 342-4499
62 rooms. $44–$55
Facilities: Dining (nearby), meeting
 rooms, pool (indoor), free breakfast in
 room, jacuzzis available, health and fitness center.

Holiday Inn, 1600 W. Fayette
(217) 342-4161
136 rooms. $36–$60
Discounts: AARP, Quest, Priority Club,
 AAA.
Facilities: Meeting/convention services,
 dining, lounge, entertainment, swim-
 ming (outdoor).
Handicapped accessible rooms.
Credit cards accepted: MC, VS, AE, DC,
 DS, DC/CB

**Keller Ramada Inn & Convention
 Center**,
Junction of I-57 & 70, Illinois 32-33.
(217) 342-2131, 1-800-535-0546
169 rooms; 8 condos $49–$99
Facilities: Meeting/convention services,
 dining, lounge, entertainment, swimming (indoor/outdoor), health club, spa,
 sauna, video games, rides, children's
 pool, free cable & HBO.
Designated rooms are handicapped accessible.
Discounts: AARP, corporate, AAA.
Credit cards accepted: AE, VS, MC, DC,
 DS

Paradise Inn Motel, 1000 W. Fayette
 Ave.
(217)342-2165.
33 rooms. S–$25; D–$35

Discounts: AAA (guaranteed per AAA
 book), seniors.
Facilities: Dining (nearby), lounge
 (nearby), laundromat (nearby), pets
 accepted.
Rooms are not handicapped accessible.
Credit cards accepted: MC, VS, AE, DS

Super 8, 1400 Thelma Keller Dr.
(217) 342-6888
49 rooms
Handicapped accessible rooms.
Discounts available

U.S. Inn, 1606 W. Fayette Ave
(217) 342-4667
55 rooms
Facilities: pets accepted, handicapped
 rooms

FAYETTE COUNTY

• *VANDALIA (62471)*

Days Inn Vandalia, Illinois 40 West.
(618) 283-4400; 1-800-359-5881
61 rooms. $38–$79
Discounts: Days Inn National Discount;
 Clubs
Facilities: Meeting/convention services,
 dining, swimming (outdoor), safe
 deposit box, sand volleyball court.
Handicapped accessible rooms.
Credit cards accepted: MC, VS, AE, DS,
 DC

Jay's Inn, Illinois 185N, I-70 & U.S. 51
 on Illinois 185 N.
(618) 283-1200
31 rooms. S–$25; D–$30
Facilities: Outdoor pool, dining, lounge
Credit cards accepted: MC, VS, AE, D.C.
 DS

Mabry Court Motel, 1502 N. 8th
(618) 283-9840

Markham Inn, I-70 & Illinois 51 N, Exit
 63
(618) 283-4400
91 rooms. $35–$39
Facilities: Handicapped accessible rooms,
 pets accepted (small), outdoor pool,
 dining
Credit cards accepted: MC, VS, AE, DS,
 DC, CD

Discounts: AAA, AARP, military, government.

Robbins Motel & Restaurant, I-70 & U.S. 51 North
(618) 283-2363

Vandalia Travelodge, 1500 N. Sixth Street.
(618) 283-2363; (618) 283-3050
48 rooms. S–(one person)–$29.; S–(two persons)–$33; D–(two persons)–$38; Family Rate–$35
Discounts: Senior citizens (15%).
Facilities: Dining/lounge (nearby), swimming (outdoor), playground, pets accepted
Handicapped accessible rooms.
Credit cards accepted: MC, VS, AE, DS, CB, DC

FRANKLIN COUNTY

• *BENTON (62812)*

Benton Gray Plaza Motel, 706 W. Main. E. off of I-57 (exit, 71)
(618) 439-3113
31 rooms. S(1)–$24; D (4)–$37
No discounts available.
Facilities: Located three minutes from Rend Lake, pets accepted(one room).
Discounts: Seniors, AARP
No handicapped accessible rooms.
Credit cards accepted: MC, VS, AE, DC, CB

Motel Benton, 407 N. Main. Illinois 37 (618) 435-3105 (3205)
20 rooms. S–$22–$28; D–$30–$34; Weekly rates (double), $120–$140
Discounts: Senior citizens, military
Facilities: outdoor grills, picnic tables, free local calls.
Rooms are limited handicapped accessible.
Credit cards accepted: MC, VS, AX, Disc, DC, CB

Days Inn, 711 W. Main. Exit 71 off I-57
(618) 439-3183
114 rooms. $33.88 & up
Discounts: AAA & AARP.
Facilities: Meeting/convention services, dining, lounge, entertainment, swimming (outdoor), laundromat (nearby),

pets accepted
Handicapped accessible rooms.
Discounts: AAA, AARP
Credit cards accepted: MC, VS, AE, DS, DC

• *BUCKNER*

Buckner–Rend Lake Motel, Illinois 14
(618) 724-4122

• *SESSER (62884)*

Coy & Wilma's One-Stop, Illinois 1. (618) 625-2101(or 5267)
Two apartments above store. $30 per night for two people.
Facilities: Store on site; close to Rend Lake.

The Hill House, RR 1, Box 759
(618) 625-6064
3 rooms. $45–$55
Credit cards accepted: MC, VS

• *WEST FRANKFORT (62896)*

HoJo Inn, 1001 Factory Outlet Dr., I-57 to Illinois 149, Exit 65 W.
(618) 932-2171
43 rooms. $30–$60
Facilities: 24 hr. free coffee, suites with jacuzzis, VCR, refrigerator, microwaves, cable TV.

Gray Plaza Motel, 1010 W. Main. (618) 932-3116
50 rooms. $24–$36.50
AARP & other discounts available.
Rooms are handicapped accessible.
Facilities: 24 hr. restaurant across street
Credit cards accepted: MC, VS, DS, AE, DC

Motel 37, Illinois 37 North
(618) 932-3461

• *WHITTINGTON (62897)*

Rend Lake Resort & Restaurant
(618) 242-8849
42 Rooms including cabins. $58 & up
Facilities: Dining, meeting rooms, lounge, tennis, outdoor pool.
Rooms are not handicapped accessible.
Discounts: seniors, government

Credit cards: All major

GALLATIN COUNTY

- *JUNCTION (68984)*

Crossroads Motor Inn, Illinois 1 & 13.
(618) 272-3461
25 rooms. S–$21.80; D–$26.80; three or
    more–$31.80
Discounts: Available for more than one
    night's lodging.
Facilities: Meeting/convention services,
    dining, swimming (outdoor).
Rooms are not handicapped accessible.
Credit cards accepted: MC, VS

Thomas House, RR 1
(618) 272-7046 or 1-800-866-6716
3 rooms. $40–$55
Credit cards accepted: MC, VS

- *SHAWNEETOWN (62984)*

Shawnee Chief Motel, Shawnee Avenue.
(618) 269-3193
25 rooms. S–$22.50; D–(1 bed)–$24.50;
    D–(2 beds)–$30 + tax
Discounts available.
Rooms are not handicapped accessible.
Credit cards: MC, VS, AE

HAMILTON COUNTY

- *McLEANSBORO (62859)*

Sleepy Grove Motel, RR 3
(618) 643-2747

HARDIN COUNTY

- *CAVE-IN-ROCK (62919)*

Cave-In-Rock Motel, Illinois 1, Box 25.
    One mile north of Ohio River.
(618) 289-3296
Seven rooms. $26 & up
Discounts available.
Rooms are not handicapped accessible.
Credit cards not accepted.

**Cave-In-Rock State Park Lodge &
    Cabins.**
(618) 289-4545
Four cabins, eight rooms. $49–$62
Discounts: Weekly rates, government &
state rates
Facilities: Dining, camping, concessions.
    Cabins overlook the Ohio River.
Handicapped accessible cabin available.
Credit cards accepted: MC, VS

- *ELIZABETHTOWN*

River Rose Inn Bed & Breakfast, 1
    Main St.
(618) 287-8811
Five rooms
Facilities: Swimming pool and jacuzzi,
    gourmet breakfast provided

William's Village Inn, Main Street (618)
    287-7088
Three rooms. $27.50, $5 per additional
    person
Continental breakfast provided.

JACKSON COUNTY

- *AVA (62907)*

Red Brick Guest House, Ava
(618) 426-3941

- *CARBONDALE (62901)*

Bel-Aire Motel, 905 East Main.
(618) 549-2151
17 rooms. $16.55–$23; $58.50 weekly
Facilities: Dining (nearby), pets accepted
Handicapped accessible rooms.
Credit cards are not accepted.

Best Inns of America–Carbondale, 1345
    E. Main.
(618) 529-4801, 1-800-237-8466
86 rooms. $35.88–$49.88
Discounts: Group rates, senior citizens,
    AARP, AAA.
Facilities: Meeting/convention services,
    pets accepted, dining, lounge, entertain-
    ment, swimming (outdoor), safe deposit
    box.
Handicapped accessible rooms.
Credit cards accepted: MC, VS, AE, DS,
    DC, DS

Days Inn, 801 E. Main.
(618) 457-3347
70 rooms. $32–$55.
Discounts: seniors, AARP
Facilities: Lounge, swimming (outdoor),

laundromat (nearby), dining (nearby).
Limited handicapped access.
Credit cards accepted: MC, VS, AE, DS,
DC, CB

Heritage Motel, 1209 W. Main.
(618) 457-4142
15 rooms. $25–$45
No discounts available.
Facilities: Laundromat.
Rooms are not handicapped accessible.
Credit cards accepted: MC, VS

Knights Inn, 3000 W. Main.
(618) 529-2424
60 rooms. $30–$50
Discounts: Group rates, AAA, SIU,
AARP, government, Sam's Club.
Facilities: Meeting/convention services,
dining, lounge, entertainment, sauna,
swimming (indoor), in-house laundry,
safe deposit box, pets accepted
Handicapped accessible rooms.
Credit cards accepted: all major credit
cards accepted

Relax Inn, 700 E. Main
(618) 549-0889
28 rooms. $30–$50
Facilities: Laundromat & lounge nearby
Credit cards accepted: yes, but not specified
Discounts: AARP, Senior

Sunset Motel, 825 E. Main.
(618) 457-5115
22 rooms. S–$15.95, D–$20.95 plus
$2/person; $60 per week; $240 per
month
Facilities: Restaurant (nearby).
Credit cards accepted: MC, VS, Dis, DC,
AX

Super 8 Motel, 1180 E. Main.
(618) 457-8822
63 rooms. S–(1 person)–$35; S–(2 per-
sons)–$41.88; D–(2 persons)–$42.88;
D–(3 persons)–$47.88; D–(4 per-
sons)–$52.88.
Discounts: Senior citizens, federal/state
government, military, trucker, travel
agent, AARP.
Handicapped accessible rooms.
Credit cards accepted: MC, VS, AE, DS,
DC, CB

Touch of Nature Environmental Center
Southern Illinois University
(618) 453-1121
38 lodge rooms & cabins. $31–$50
Discounts: SIU alumni
Facilities: Meeting/convention services;
dining; lounge; schedule social events;
swimming (outdoor at Little Grassy
Lake w/beach); volleyball, horseshoes,
canoes; pontoon boat; safe available.
Handicapped accessible rooms.
Credit cards accepted: MC, VS, DS

Uptown Motel, 309 E. Main.
(618) 457-4156
13 rooms. S–$25; D–$35
No discounts available.
Rooms are not handicapped accessible.
Credit cards accepted: MC, VS, AE, DS

• *MAKANDA (62958)*

Giant City Lodge, Illinois 1, Box 70
(618) 457-4921
34 cabins. $40, $50, $75 per night (two
persons, $5 extra person).
No discounts available.
Facilities: Meeting/convention services,
dining, lounge, outdoor pool, horseback
riding May–Nov, hiking.
Handicapped accessible rooms.
Credit cards accepted: MC, VS, DC.

• *MURPHYSBORO (62966)*

Motel Murphysboro & Appledome,
Junction of Illinois 13, 127 & 149.
(618) 687-2345 or 1-800-626-4356
31 rooms. $38.50–$42.50
Discounts: AARP, senior citizens, savers
club, AAA Encore, special group rates.
Facilities: Dining (nearby), lounge
(nearby), entertainment (nearby),
spa/sauna, fitness center, swimming
(indoor), pets accepted, laundromat,
limousine service to facility.
Handicapped accessible rooms.
Credit cards accepted: MC, VS, AE, DS,
DC, CB

Riverside Inn(to become Days Inn),
Illinois 13, Box 429. (618) 687-2244
(prices & facilities will change in the
near future—inquire.)
39 rooms. S–(1 person)–$29.88; S–(2 per-

sons)–$36.88; D–(2 persons)–$36.88; D–(3 persons)–$43.88; D–(4 persons)–$50.88; King (1 person)–$35.88; King (2 persons)–$42.88.

Discounts: AARP, 10% discount for cash sales.

Facilities: Miniature golf, go-carts, driving range, batting cages.

Handicapped accessible rooms.

Credit cards accepted: MC, VS, AE, DS

JEFFERSON COUNTY

• *BELLE RIVE (62810)*

Belle Rive, RR 1, Box 216 (618) 736-2647

Two guest rooms. $45

Check & credit cards accepted

• *DIX (62830)*

Scottish Inns, 1-57 & Texico Rd, exit #103

(618) 266-7254

24 rooms. $19.99–$45

Facilities: Indoor pool, pets accepted,

Credit cards accepted: MC, VS, AE, DS

• *MT. VERNON (62864)*

Best Inns of America, Frontage Rd. of I-57 & Illinois 15.

(618) 244-4343

155 rooms. $29.88–$38.88

Discounts: AARP, AAA, military.

Facilities: Swimming (outdoor). Free continental breakfast.

Handicapped accessible rooms.

All major credit cards accepted.

Best Western Inn I-57 at I-64.

(618) 242-6370 or 1-800-528-1234

109 rooms. $37–$60; suites available; up to two children free with two paying adults

Discounts: AARP, AAA,senior, Allstate Motor Club, commercial, military, government, entertainment card.

Facilities: Meeting/convention services, dining, banquet, lounge, swimming (outdoor), coffee makers.

Rooms are not handicapped accessible.

All major credit cards accepted.

Daystop––Days Inn, 750 10th

(618) 244-3224/ 1-800-325-2525

36 rooms. $29.50–$37

Facilities: Outdoor pool, pets accepted, handicapped accessible rooms

Discounts: Senior, AARP, AAA

Credit cards accepted: unknown

Drury Inn, I-57 & 64 at Illinois 15.

(618) 244-4550 or 1-800-325-8300

80 rooms. $43–$62 w/"Quickstart Breakfast"

Discounts: Senior citizens, corporate, AAA, AARP, government, Sam's.

Facilities: Meeting/conference rooms, swimming (outdoor), pets accepted

Handicapped accessible rooms.

All major credit cards accepted.

Holiday Inn, Illinois 15 at I-57 & 64

(618) 244-3670 or 1-800-752-4874

188 rooms. $45–$58

Discounts: AARP, AAA, military, corporate, group.

Facilities: Meeting/convention services, dining, lounge, entertainment, spa/sauna facilities, swimming (indoor), ping pong, video games, safe deposit box, van service to motel.

Handicapped accessible rooms.

All major credit cards accepted.

Economy Inn, 1319 Salem Rd.

(618) 242-4700

39 rooms. $20–$35

Discounts: AARP, AAA, military.

Facilities: Dining, lounge, free coffee in AM.

Rooms are not handicapped accessible.

All major credit cards accepted.

Motel Mt. Vernon, 800 Main

(618) 242-3551

Ramada Hotel, 222 Potomac Blvd

(618) 244-7100 or 1-800-2-RAMADA

236 rooms. $44–$50 and up

Discounts: AAA, AARP, government, corporate, executive preferred, military, tour bus, super saver weekend, Ramada Business Card.

Facilities: Meeting/convention services, dining, lounge, entertainment, spa/sauna facilities, sundeck, fitness center, swimming (indoor), safe deposit box.

Handicapped accessible rooms.
All major credit cards accepted.

Motel 6, 333 S. 44th
(618) 244-2383 or 1-800-851-8888
80 rooms. $28 & up, $6 per extra person
Discounts: AARP, AAA, military, trucker.
Facilities: Swimming (outdoor).
Handicapped accessible rooms.
All major credit cards accepted.

Super 8 Motel, I-57 at I-64 at Illinois 15
(618) 242-8800
63 rooms. $29.88–$36.88
Discounts: AARP, AAA, military, trucker.
Handicapped accessible rooms.
All major credit cards accepted.

Thrifty Inn, I-57 & 64 at Illinois 15
(618) 244-7750
41 rooms. $35.88–$39.88
Discounts: AARP, AAA, military.
Handicapped accessible rooms.
All major credit cards accepted.

Travel Inn, 750 S. 10th
(618) 244-3224
39 rooms. $23.88–$32.88
Discounts: AARP, AAA.
Facilities: Swimming (outdoor).
Rooms are not handicapped accessible.
All major credit cards accepted.

JERSEY COUNTY

• *ELSAH (62028)*

Corner Nest Bed & Breakfast, 3 Elm, P.
  O. Box 220
(618) 374-1892
4 rooms. $67–$70
Discounts available.
Bike trails, walking trails, boating, antique
  shopping all nearby. Adjacent to
  Mississippi River.
Two handicapped accessible rooms avail-
  able.
Credit cards accepted: MC, VS,
AE, DS

Green Tree Inn, 15 Mill Street
(618) 374-2821
Nine rooms. $65–$90 (includes breakfast
  & chilled cocktails fireside)
No discounts available.

Facilities: Meeting/convention services,
  dining, lounge, limousine service to
  facilities. Located in historic village
  known as the "New England of the
  Midwest." Adjacent to bike trails, 60
  antique shops, boating, sailing, special-
  ity shops & marina.
Handicapped accessible rooms.
Credit cards accepted: MC, VS

Historic Maple Leaf Cottage Inn,
12 Selma/ #s38, 40, 42 & 44 LaSalle
(618) 374-1684
Four rooms. $75 (includes breakfast).
No discounts available.
Facilities: Dining (full gourmet breakfast),
  air conditioning, television, one handi-
  capped accessible room.
Credit cards accepted: MC, VS
Discounts: repeat guests

• *GRAFTON (62037)*

Jersey Hollow Motel, Box 1C
(618) 786-3834
Five rooms. Call for rates.
No discounts available.
Handicapped accessible rooms.
No credit cards accepted.

Nancy Kirkpatrick Guest House, 210
  W. Main
(618) 374-2821
Two rooms. $65 per couple (includes
  breakfast).
No discounts available.
Facilities: Meeting/convention services,
  limousine services to facility. 1860
  Cape Cod located in a historic district
  overlooking Mississippi River. Boating,
  biking, horseback riding, apple picking
  and bald eagle watching nearby.
Rooms are not handicapped accessible.
Credit cards accepted: MC, VS

**Pere Marquette Lodge & Conference
  Center**, P. O. Box 75.
(618) 786-2331
Guest houses–22 rooms; Lodge–50
  rooms.
$60 two adults.
No discounts available.
Facilities: Dining, lounge, video games,
  indoor swimming pool,
tenis courts, sauna, gift shop.

Handicapped accessible rooms.
Credit cards accepted: MC, VS, AE, DC, CB, DS

Shafer Wharf Inn, 220 W. Main.
(618) 374-2821
3 rooms. $75per couple (includes breakfast).
No discounts available.
Facilities: Meeting/convention services, limousine services to facility. 1874 Country French located in a historic district overlooking Mississippi River. Boating, biking, antiquing, museums, apple picking bald eagle watching nearby.
Rooms are not handicapped accessible.
Credit cards accepted: MC, VS

Wildflower Farm & Inn, mason Hollow Rd.
(618) 465-3719
2 rooms. $59
Facilities: solarium, herb garden, hiking trails
Credit cards accepted: MC, VS

• *JERSEYVILLE (62052)*

Lorton's Colonial Inn Hotel, 114 W. Arch.
(618) 498-6833
Three rooms. $30–$45
Facilities: Dining, hot tub, cable, lounge
Credit cards accepted: MC, VS

Frontier Lodge, 730 S. State Street.
(618) 498-6886
20 rooms. $31–$35
Facilities: Dining (nearby).
Rooms are handicapped accessible
Credit card accepted: MC, VS, AE, DS

JOHNSON COUNTY

• *VIENNA (62995)*

Budget Inn (Motel & Restaurant), I–24 at Illinois 146.
(618) 658-2802
16 rooms. S–$29.95; D–$32.95
Discounts: With six night stay, seventh night is free.
Facilities: Meeting facilities, dining.
Rooms are not handicapped accessible.
Credit cards accepted: MC, VS, DC

Dixon Motel, near junction of U.S. 45 & Illinois 146
(618) 658-3831

LAWRENCE COUNTY

• *LAWRENCEVILLE (62439)*

Gas Lite Motel, One mile South on Illinois 1.
(618) 943-2374
20 rooms. S–$25–$30; D–$35; T–$40
No discounts available.
Facilities: Dining (nearby).
Handicapped accessible rooms.
Credit cards accepted: MC, VS, AE, DC

Woodside Bed & Breakfast, PO Box 101
(618) 943-2147
One room. $40
No credit cards accepted.

MADISON COUNTY

• *ALTON (62002)*

College Crest Motel, 1809 Bunting Dr. Homer Adams Parkway & Illinois 140
(618) 465-3212
Nine rooms. Call for rates.
Discounts available. Weekly rates available.
Handicapped accessible rooms.
Credit cards are not accepted.

Holidome Indoor Recreation Center, 3800 Homer Adams Parkway.
(618) 462-1220
138 rooms. $58-$73
Discounts: Great Rates (weekend special)
Facilities: Meeting/convention services, dining, lounge, entertainment, spa/sauna facilities, swimming (indoor), safe deposit box, limousine service to facility.
Handicapped accessible rooms.
Credit cards accepted: MC, VS, AE, DS, DC
Lea Davis Guest House, 519 State St.
(618) 463-1103

Lewis & Clark Motor Lodge, 530 Lewis & Clark Blvd.
(618) 254-3831
28 rooms. $25–$45

Facilities: dining, entertainment
Discounts available. AARP
Credit cards accepted: MC, VS, AE, DS, DC, ISC, DC

Ramada Inn, 1900 Homer Adams Parkway.
(618) 463-0800
123 rooms. $56–$62 plus $6 per person for more than two adults
Discounts: Based on availability & date, please inquire
Facilities: Meeting/convention services, dining, lounge, entertainment, swimming (outdoor), safe deposit box, golf (nearby).
Handicapped accessible rooms.
Credit cards accepted: All major credit cards.

Stratford Motor Hotel, 229 Market, corner of 3rd & Market
(618) 465-8821
50 rooms. $37–$65 Children under 12 stay free
Facilities: Meeting/convention services, dining, lounge, safe deposit box, pets accepted, laundromat.
Handicapped accessible rooms.
Discounts: Yes, inquire
Credit cards accepted: MC, VS, DS, CB/DC

Super 8 Motel of Alton, 1800 Homer Adams Parkway.
(618) 465-8885
63 rooms. Inquire for rates. Children under 12 stay free.
Discounts–Senior citizens (10%); truckers (10%), AARP, etc. Free coffee.
Handicapped accessible rooms.
Credit cards accepted: MC, VS, DS, AE, DC/CB

Travel Inn, 717 E. Broadway.
(618) 462-1011
62 rooms. Call for rates.
Discounts available. Free coffee.
Facilities: Small conference room, swimming (outdoor), safe deposit box.
Handicapped accessible rooms.
Credit cards accepted: MC, VS, AE, DC

• *COLLINSVILLE (62234)*

Beck's Lodge & Apartments, 1105 St

Louis Rd.
(618) 344-9763

Best Western Bo-Jon Inn, I-55/70 & Illinois 159
(618) 345-5720
40 rooms, $38–$49
Facilities: pets accepted, handicapped accessible rooms, outdoor pool
Discounts: AARP
Credit cards: MC, VS, DS, DC, AE

Best Western Heritage Inn, 2003 Mall Rd.
(618) 345-5660
80 rooms.
Discounts: AARP, senior citizens, AAA, military, corporate, trucker & group rates & others.
Facilities: Meeting/convention services, swimming (outdoor), laundromat.
Some rooms are handicapped accessible.
Credit cards accepted: MC, VS, DS, AE, DC/CB

Camelot Inn, 295 N. Bluff Rd.
(618) 345-2100
89 rooms. S–$28.80; D–$38; T–$43; Q–$45 incl. tax
Discounts: AARP, AAA, military, corporate, senior citizens, trucker, group.
Facilities: Swimming (outdoor), dining (nearby), laundry, HBO.
Handicapped accessible rooms.
Credit cards accepted: MC, VS, AE, DS

Days Inn, 1803 Ramada Blvd.
(618) 345-8100
60 rooms. S–$37–$44; D–$42–$65, $5 per additional person
Discounts: AARP, corporate, group rates, senior citizens.
Facilities: Dining, lounge, swimming (outdoor), 10 min. from casino
Handicapped accessible rooms.
Credit cards accepted: MC, VS, AE, DS, DC

Drury Inn, 602 N. Bluff Rd.
(618) 345-7700
123 rooms. S–$50–$60
Discounts: AAA, AARP (senior citizens) & government rates.
Facilities: Free "Quickstart Breakfast". Meeting rooms, swimming (indoor), health club passes available, safe

deposit box.

Two handicapped accessible rooms.

Credit cards accepted: MC, VS, AE, DS, CB, DC/CB

Happy Wanderer Inn Bed & Breakfast, 309 Collinsville Ave.

(618) 344-0477

4 rooms. $25–$50

Holiday Inn, 1000 Eastport Plaza Dr.

(618) 345-2800

230 rooms. S–$67; D–$74; T–$80; Q–$86

Discounts: AARP, senior citizens, group rates.

Facilities: Meeting/convention services, dining, lounge, spa/ sauna facilities, swimming (indoor), laundromat, safe deposit box.

Handicapped accessible rooms.

Credit cards accepted: MC, VS, AE, DS

HOJO, 301 N. Bluff Rd.

(618) 345-1530, 1-800-654-2000

89 rooms. S–$25–$60, $5 per additional person.

Discounts: AAA, senior citizen, state & group rates.

Facilities: Dining, lounge, swimming (outdoor), laundromat, safe deposit box, 10 min. from riverboat casino.

Rooms are not handicapped accessible.

Credit cards accepted: MC, VS, AE, DS

Maggie's Bed & Breakfast, 2102 Keebler Rd

(618) 344-8283

Five guest rooms. $35–$50

Handicapped accessible rooms

Motel 6, 295-A North Bluff Road

(618) 345-2100,

87 rooms. $28–$33, $6 per additional adult

Facilities: Outdoor pool, pets accepted

Rooms are not handicapped accessible

Super 8, 2 Gateway Dr.

(618) 345-8008

63 rooms.

Discounts: AARP, AAA, Super 8 V.I.P., state, federal, group rates, military.

Handicapped accessible rooms.

Credit cards accepted: MC, VS, AE, DS

Pear Tree Inn, 552 Ramada Blvd.

(618) 345-9500

105 rooms. $38–$44, summer rates higher

Discounts: Senior citizen, group rates.

Facilities: Swimming (outdoor), safe deposit box.

Handicapped accessible rooms.

Credit cards accepted: MC, VS, AE, DS

Quality Inn, I-55 & I-70, 475 N. Bluff Rd.

(618) 344-7171, 1-800-221-2222

175 rooms. $40–$65

Facilities: Indoor pool, dining, sauna, fishing, golf & tennis nearby handicapped accessible rooms, riverboat gambling nearby

Credit cards accepted: inquire for specifics

• *EAST ALTON (62024)*

Lewis & Clark Motor Lodge, 1060 Lewis & Clark Blvd.

(618) 254-3831

28 rooms. $25.50–$45.25

Discounts: Weekly rates.

Facilities: Swimming (outdoor), safe deposit box.

Rooms are not handicapped accessible.

Credit cards accepted: MC, VS, AE

• *EDWARDSVILLE (62025)*

University Inn, I-270 & Illinois 157.

(618) 656-3000

147 rooms. S–$28; D–$44

Discounts: AARP, AAA, Incredible, corporate, state/federal, U.S.A., travel agent, airline, Quest, Sept. Days.

Facilities: Meeting/convention services, dining, lounge, entertainment, spa/sauna facilities, swimming (indoor/outdoor), jacuzzi, playground, safe deposit box.

Handicapped accessible rooms.

Credit cards accepted: MC, VS, AE, DS, DC, ER

• *GODFREY (62035)*

HI-WAY House Motor Inn, 3023 Godfrey Rd., Illinois 67

(618) 466-6676

62 rooms. $31–$36

Discounts: AARP, senior, corporate, military, government

Facilities: dining, non-smoking rooms,

HBO, lounge, meeting room.

Redwood Motel, 5609 Godfrey Road.
(618) 466-3715
12 rooms. Call for rates & details.

• *GRANITE CITY (62040)*

Apple Valley Motel, 709 E. Chain of
   Rocks Rd.
(618) 931-6085
19 rooms

Best Western Camelot Inn, 1240 E.
   Chain of Rocks Rd.
(618) 931-2262
54 rooms. S–$29; D–$36+ tax.
Discounts: AARP, military, senior citizen,
   trucker.
Facilities: Meeting/convention services,
   dining (nearby), lounge (nearby), swim-
   ming (outdoor), laundromat.
Handicapped accessible rooms.
Credit cards accepted: MC, VS, AE, DS,
   DC, motel card.

Canal Motel, R. R. 1.
(618) 931-0744
11 rooms. Call for rates.

Chain of Rocks Motel, 3228 W. Chain of
   Rocks Rd.
(618) 931-6600
37 rooms. S–(1)–$23.50; S–(2)–$25;
   D–(2)–$29; $2 per additional person.
No discounts available.
Facilities: Swimming (outdoor), game
   room, Landshire sandwiches, laundro-
   mat.
Rooms are not handicapped accessible.
Credit cards accepted: MC, VS, AE, DS,
   DC

Granite City Lodge, 1200 19th St.
(618) 876-2600
44 rooms. S–$25; D–$32; $2 per addi-
   tional person.
Facilities: Swimming (outdoor), laundro-
   mat (nearby), dining (nearby).
Discounts: Military.
Handicapped accessible rooms.
Credit cards accepted: MC, VS, AE
Greenway Motel, 701 E. Chain of Rocks
   Rd.
(618) 931-0292

Illini Motel, 1100 Niedringhaus Ave.
(618) 877-7100
37 rooms. $24–$32 + tax.
Discounts: Senior citizens, military.
Rooms are not handicapped accessible.
All major credit cards accepted

Land of Lincoln Motel, 3220 W. Chain
   of Rocks Rd. 270 & Illinois 3 S.
(618) 931-1414
34 rooms. S–(1)–$22.50; Queen–$25.60;
   D–(2)–$29.85; $2 per additional
   person.
Weekly special rates. No other discounts
   apply.
Credit cards accepted: MC, VS, DC,AE,
   DS, Corporate Card

Midwest Motel, 912 Thorngate Dr.,
I-270 & 203 N, exit old Alton Rd.
(618) 797-2400
14 rooms. $20–$28
Facilities: microwaves & refrigerators in
   all rooms, cable & free HBO
Credit cards accepted: MC, VS

Sun Motel, 619 West Chain of Rocks
   Road.
(618) 931-1366
Call for rates & facilities.

• *HAMEL (62046)*

Innkeeper Motel & Restaurant, I-55 @
   Illinois 140.
(618) 633-2551
26 rooms. S–$25; D–35; $4 per additional
   person, weekly and monthly rates
Discounts: Senior citizens, military, commercial.
Facilities: Meeting/convention services,
   dining, lounge, transportation to motel
   available. Features include nearby lake
   and guest fishing. pets accepted welcome. Motor home spaces available.
   Ample truck parking.
Handicapped accessible rooms.
Credit cards accepted: MC, VS

• *HIGHLAND (62249)*

Cardinal Inn, Walnut & Illinois 143.
(618) 654-4433
11 rooms. $32–$48
Discounts available: weekly rates
   $135–$165.

Credit cards accepted: MC, VS, AE, DS

Country Inn, I-55 @ Exit 37.
(618) 637-2600
20 rooms. S–$26.30; D–$31.70
Discounts available: weekly rates.
Facilities: Cafe open 24 hours. Ample,
    well-lighted parking. pets accepted.
    Adjacent to 24-hour gas station.
Handicapped accessible rooms.
Credit cards accepted: MC, VS, AE, DC

Michael's Swiss Inn, 425 Broadway
(618) 654-8646
20 rooms. $54–$64
Facilities: Dining, meeting rooms, spa,
    outdoor pool, lounge, handicapped
    rooms, occasional entertainment
Discounts: none
Credit cards accepted: MC, VS, AE, D.C.,
    DS

Phyllis's Bed & Breakfast, 801 9th St.
(618) 654-4619
4 rooms. $40–$55
Facilities: Breakfast served
Credit cards accepted: MC, VS

• *LIVINGSTON (62058)*

Country Inn Motel, I-55, Exit 37
(618) 637-2600
20 rooms
Facilities: Dining, pets

• *MARYVILLE (62062)*

Best Western Bo-Jon Inn, I-70, I-55 &
    Illinois159.
(618) 345-5720
40 rooms. Call for rates.
Discounts: Senior citizens, AAA, truckers,
    corporate, military.
Facilities: Swimming (outdoor).
Handicapped accessible rooms.
Credit cards accepted: MC, VS, DS, CB,
    DC, AE, Amoco Multi-Card

Best Western Heritage Inn, Illinois 157
(618) 345-5660

Pear Tree Inn, 1-55-70 & 157
(618) 345-9500

• *MITCHELL (62040)*

Apple Valley Motel, 709 E. Chain of
    Rocks Rd.
(618) 931-6085
19 rooms. Call for rates.
Facilities: Dining (nearby).
Discounts available.
Rooms are not handicapped accessible.
Credit cards accepted: MC, VS

Best Western Camelot, 1240 E. Chain of
    Rocks Rd.
(618) 931-2262

• *TROY (62294)*

Carol House Inn, Illinois 162 & I-55,
    909 Edwardsville Rd.
(618) 667-9916
95 rooms. $30–$33, $5 per additional
    person
Facilities: Outdoor pool, pets accepted,
    handicapped rooms
Major credit cards accepted

Roadhouse Inn, Junction I-55 & I-70 &
    Illinois 162, 700 Edwardsville Rd.
(618) 667-9911
18 rooms. S–$26; D–$30
Discounts: Senior citizen.
Facilities: Dining (nearby)
Rooms are not handicapped accessible.
Credit cards accepted: MC, VS, AE

• *WASHINGTON PARK (62204)*

Econo Inn, 5307 Bunkum Rd, I-64 &
    Kingshighway (Illinois 111)
(618) 271-1455
25 rooms. S–$28; D–$32, $5 per extra
    person
Rooms are not handicapped accessible.
Credit cards accepted: MC, VS

• *WOOD RIVER (62095)*

Bel-Air Motel, 542 W. Ferguson Ave;
    Illinois 3 &143
(618) 254-0683
10 rooms. S–$23.75; D–$28.45
Discounts: Senior citizen.
Facilities: Lounge (nearby), entertainment
    (nearby), limousine service to facility
    available.

Rooms are not handicapped accessible.
Credit cards accepted: MC, VS, AE, DC

MARION COUNTY

• *CENTRALIA (62801)*

Bell Tower Inn, 200 E. Noleman.
(618) 533-1300
57 rooms. S–$35; D–$40; King–$40;
Suites available.
Discounts: Senior citizens, AAA
Facilities: Meeting/convention services,
swimming (indoor), complimentary
continental breakfast daily.
Handicapped accessible rooms.
Credit cards accepted: MC, VS, AE, DS,
DC, CB

Holiday Motel, 404 N. Poplar.
(618) 532-1841
25 rooms. $20 and up
Discounts: Free night's lodging with
seven night stay.
Facilities: Dining.
Handicapped accessible rooms.
Major credit cards accepted.

Motel Centralia, 215 S. Poplar. U.S. 51
just S. of 2nd St.
(618) 532-7357
57 rooms. S–$28.50; D–$37
Discounts: Senior citizen.
Credit cards accepted: MC, VS, AE, DS,
DC

Home Motel, 326 W. Noleman
(618) 532-5633
13 rooms. $24–$30
Facilities: Dining (nearby), HBO
Credit cards accepted: MC,VS, DC,AE

Langenfeld Hotel, 104 W. Broadway
(618) 532-7315

Queen City Motel, 402 N. Elm.
(618) 532-1881
21 rooms. $21& up
Discounts available.
Handicapped accessible rooms.
Credit cards accepted: MC, VS, DC, AE

• *SALEM (62881)*

Continental Motel, U.S. 50 East. (618)
548-3090

25 rooms. S–$18.99; D–$22.99; $3per
extra person.
Discounts: AARP, repeat guests.
Facilities: Meeting room accommodating
up to 20 people; picnic table/grill.
Ground floor rooms are handicapped
accessible.
Credit cards accepted: MC, VS, DS, AE,
DC, CB

Days Inn, 1812 W. Main.
(618) 548-4212
100 rooms. S–$30–$42
Discounts: AARP, Days Inn Discount
cards.
Facilities: Meeting services, dining,
lounge, swimming (outdoor), laundromat, safe deposit box, van service.
Handicapped accessible rooms.
Credit cards accepted: MC, VS, AE, DS,
DC/CB

Grand Motel, 1234 W. Main Street. I-57,
Exit 116
(618) 548-1548
21 rooms. S–$22.95
Discounts: AARP ($1 off room rate),
truckers
Facilities: pets accepted, dining
Credit cards accepted: MC, VS, CC, AE.

Lakewood Motel, 1500 E. Main (U.S.
50E).
(618) 548-2785
19 rooms. S–$18; (2)–$20; D (2 beds, 2
people)–$22; $2 each additional person.
Facilities: Playground, near city park and
pool.
All major credit cards accepted.

Restwell Motel, 700 W. Main Street.
(618) 548-2040
12 rooms. $16-$22 weekly rates for some
rooms
pets acceptedacceptable
No discounts available.
No credit cards accepted

Starlite Motel, 2039 W. Main
(618) 548-4422

Salem Super 8, I-57 & US 50, Exit 116
(618) 548-5882
58 rooms
Facilities: Meeting rooms, pets accepted,
handicapped rooms, free continental

breakfast
Credit cards accepted

MASSAC COUNTY

• *BROOKPORT (62910)*

Lawrence Motel, U.S. 45 North.
(618) 564-2414
12 rooms. $17-$30,
No discounts available.
No credit cards accepted.

• *METROPOLIS (62960)*

American Inn Motel, 1502 W. 10th St.
On U.S. 45
(618) 524-7431
20 rooms. S–$18; D–$25 and up.
Facilities: Lounge
Discounts: Senior citizen, trucker.
Rooms are not handicapped accessible.
Credit cards accepted: MC, VS

Asford Motel, 1531 E 5th
(618) 524-4600

Best Inns of America, 2055 5th St. I-24
& U.S. 45
616-524-8200 or 1-800-237-8466
63 rooms. $44.88–$51.88
Facilities: Pool (outdoor), dining (nearby),
meeting rooms, FAX
Discounts: AAA, seniors, Sunday night
stay gives fee voucher for river boat.
Credit cards: VS, MC, DS, AX, DC, CB

Metropolis Inn, I-24 & Illinois45.
(618) 524-3723; FAX 618-524-3802
52 rooms. $38 and up
Discounts: Senior citizen, trucker.
Facilities: Meeting services, indoor pool in
1994
Handicapped accessible rooms available.
Discounts: none
Credit cards accepted: MC, VS

Days Inn, U.S. 45 East, Next to Kentucky
Fried Chicken
(618) 524-9341
46 rooms. S–$31
Discounts: Senior citizen, trucker.
Facilities: Meeting/convention services,
dining, lounge, swimming (outdoor),
laundromat. Bowling alley, pizza house
with recreation room and state park

nearby.
Handicapped accessible rooms.
Discounts: most standard discounts
offered, seniors, AARP
Credit cards accepted: MC, VS, AE, DC,
Dis

MONROE COUNTY

• *MAEYSTOWN (62256)*

**The Corner George Inn Bed &
Breakfast**, Main & Mill.
1-800-458-6020
Seven roomsand guest cottage. $65–$95.
Dining in ballroom. No smoking.
Restored 1880's elegance in historic 19th-
century German village,horse drawn
carriage rides, shops, bakery, restaurant.
Credit cards accepted: MC, VS
Facilities: one handicapped room

• *WATERLOO (62298)*

Senator Richert Residence, 216 E.
Third.
(618) 939-8242
One suite. $75
Bed & Breakfast accommodations. 1867
Victorian Mansion.
Credit cards accepted: MC, VS

Sunset Motel, 206 S. Market Street.
(618) 939-7503
6 rooms. S–$25
Facilities: Laundromat.
Rooms are not handicapped accessible.
Credit cards are accepted.

PERRY COUNTY

• *DU QUOIN (62832)*

Francie's Bed & Breakfast Inn, 104 S.
Line St.
(618) 542-6686
Five rooms. $50–$80
Discounts: 5th night of 5-night stay free
Facilities: Meeting room, lunch and tea
room, arts and crafts shop.
Entertainment available for special occa-
sions. Yard games, bicycling on site;
public swimming pool, tennis courts,
fairgrounds nearby.
Rooms are not handicapped accessible.
Credit cards accepted: MC, VS

Hub Motel, 423 W. Main Street.
(618) 542-2108
26 rooms. S–$24; D–$32
Discounts: none
Facilities: Laundromat (nearby).
Rooms are not handicapped accessible.
Credit cards accepted: MC, VS, AE, DS

Motel Du Quoin, U.S. 51 S.
(618) 542-2181
23 rooms

Realm Motel, 617 N. Hickory
(618) 542-4297

Royal Inn, 1010 S. Jefferson; Illinois
U.S.51
(618) 542-4335
38 rooms. inquire about price

St. Nicholas Hotel & Lounge, 12 S. Oak
St.
(618) 542-2183
40 rooms. $20 & up.
No discounts available.
Facilities: Dining (nearby), guest laundry.
Rooms are not handicapped accessible.
Credit cards accepted: VS

• *PINCKNEYVILLE (62274)*

Fountain Motel, 112 S. Main St.; Illinois
127
(618) 357-2128
26 rooms. $24–$36
Discounts: senior citizens.
Facilities: Meeting room for 100, pets
accepted
Handicapped accessible rooms.
Credit cards accepted: MC, VS, AE, DC,
Dis

Oxbow Bed & Breakfast, Illinois 13/127,
Box 47.
(618) 357-9839
Six rooms. $50-$55.
No discounts available.
Facilities: Breakfast, lounge, fitness
center, library, rec. room.
Rooms are not handicapped accessible.
Credit cards accepted: MC, VS

POPE COUNTY

• *GOLCONDA (62938)*

Barren Creek Cottages
(618) 683-4004
Seven rooms

Daisy's on the Bluff, Box 152.
(618) 683-3565
One room. $25–$40
Facilities: Private bath, coffee & fruit provided, kitchen privileges.

The Getaway, Box 217.
(618) 683-4101 or 8751
One cabin–two bedrooms. D–$50
Discounts: Weekly rates.
Facilities: Complete kitchen, boat dock,
fishing.
Cabin is not handicapped accessible.
No credit cards accepted.

Heritage Haus, Main & Columbus.
(618) 683-3883
Four rooms. $25 each
Facilities: BBQ grill, central air, electric
hook-ups, private & shared baths, continental breakfast.

The Mansion of Golconda, 515
Columbus.
(618) 683-4400
Four rooms. $75–$85
No discounts available.
Facilities: Meeting facilities, dining,
lounge.
Rooms are not handicapped accessible.
Credit cards accepted: MC, VS, AE

**Marilee's Guest House Bed &
Breakfast**, Corner of Washington &
Monroe.
(618) 683-2751
Three rooms. S–$25; D–$45(includes
breakfast)
No discounts available.
Facilities: Laundromat (nearby).
Rooms are not handicapped accessible.
No credit cards accepted.

Michael's Motel, Adams St.
(618) 683-2424
12 rooms. S–$30; $3 per additional adult.
Discounts: Weekly rates.
Handicapped accessible rooms.
Credit cards accepted: MC, VS

Rainbow Inn, PO Box 68

(618) 683-7673
Five rooms
Facilities: pets accepted

Up-the-Creek Cabin, RR 2.
(618) 683-7725
One cabin. $15 per person.
No discounts available.
Facilities: Kitchen, television, VCR, boat
   dock with electric hookup.
Rooms are not handicapped accessible.
No credit cards accepted.

PULASKI COUNTY

• *ULLIN (62992)*

Best Western Cheekwood Inn,
I-57, exit 18.
(618) 845-3700
40 rooms. S–$34 and up
Discounts: AAA, senior citizen, govern-
   ment, corporate.
Facilities: Dining, swimming (indoor),
   laundromat, pets accepted, spa.
Handicapped accessible rooms.
Credit cards accepted: MC, VS, AE, DS,
   CB, DSDC, JCB, En Illinois

RANDOLPH COUNTY

• *CHESTER (62233)*

Betsy's Sugarwood, 217 E. Buena Vista,
   Box 3.
(618) 826-2555
34 rooms. $45-70 (discount for single
   occupancy)
No discounts available.
Rooms are not handicapped accessible.
Credit cards accepted: MC, VS

Floyd's, Highway 3
(618) 826-9888

Hi-3 Motel, R. R. 2, Box 322.
(618) 826-4415
Eight rooms (renovations planned this
   year will increase the number of rooms
   to 25 or more & expand available facilities). S–$20.90; D–$28.30; 3
   people–$32.50; 4 people–$36.70; 5
   people–$46.60 tax included.
Facilities: Dining (nearby), swimming
   (nearby).

Rooms are not handicapped accessible.
Credit cards accepted: MC, VS, AE

Royal Motor Lodge, 1012 State (IL
   Illinois 150).
(618) 826-2341
30 rooms. $21–$37
Facilities: Restaurant & lounge (adjacent),
   pets accepted
No discounts available.
Credit cards accepted: MC, VS

• *PRAIRIE DU ROCHER (62277)*

La Maison du Rocher Country Inn,
#2 Duclos & Main, Box 163.
(618) 284-3463
Two rooms, one cottage. $55 & $85
No discounts available.
Facilities: Dining (full menu), banquet &
   meeting facilities, laundry (nearby).
Rooms are not handicapped accessible;
   dining area is handicapped accessible.
Discounts: Seniors
Credit cards accepted: MC, VS

• *RED BUD (62278)*

**Das Busche Haus Guest House Bed &
   Breakfast**, Box 242
Three rooms. $45
Credit cards accepted: MC, VS

Magnolia Place, 317 S. Main
(618) 282-4141
4 rooms. $60–$140
1850s renovated home now a bed &
   breakfast.
Facilities: breakfast served, elaborate
   garden area
Credit cards accepted: MC, VS

Red Bud Motel, 1103 S. Main.
(618) 282-2123
14 rooms. S–$25; D–$30
No discounts available.
Facilities: Dining (nearby).
Rooms are not handicapped accessible.
Credit Card accepted: MC, VS

• *SPARTA (62286)*

Mac's Sparta Motel, 700 S. St. Louis;
   Illinois 4
(618) 443-3614
29 rooms. $18.50–$32

633

No discounts available.
Facilities: Dining (nearby), pets accepted
Handicapped accessible rooms.
Credit cards accepted: MC, VS, AE

Poolside Motel, 402 E. Broadway.
(618) 443-3187 or 3731
46 rooms. S–$15–$32; Suites
    (S)–$33–$38
Discounts: Military.
Facilities: Meeting services, swimming
    (outdoor), large BBQ grills, poolside
    patios, laundry service, safe deposit box
    available, limousine service to facility
    available.
Handicapped accessible rooms.
Credit cards accepted: MC, VS, AE, DS

RICHLAND COUNTY

• *OLNEY (62450)*

Rich's Inn, 328 S. Morgan, P.O. Box 581
(618) 392-3821
Three rooms $35–$45
Credit cards accepted: MC, VS

Royal Valley Inn, 1001 W. Main
(618) 395-2121
Discounts: on weekly rates.
Rooms are not handicapped accessible
Credit cards accepted: MC, VS, AE.

The Holiday, 1300 S. West/ Junction of
    U.S. 50 & U.S. 130.
(618) 395-2121; Fax: (618) 395-2121
92 rooms. $34–$49
Discounts: AARP, corporate, trucker.
Facilities: Meeting/convention services,
    dining, spa/sauna facilities, fitness
    center, swimming (indoor), safe deposit
    box available, limousine service from
    airport available.
Handicapped accessible rooms.
Credit cards accepted: MC, VS, AE,
    DC/CB

SALINE COUNTY

• *ELDORADO (62930)*

Neal Motel Inc., U.S. 45.
(618) 273-8146
Six rooms. S–$25; D–$30
No discounts available.

Facilities: Dining (nearby), lounge
    (nearby), entertainment (nearby).
Handicapped accessible rooms available
    on ground floor.
Credit cards accepted: MC, VS

Star Motel, U.S. 45 Eldorado
(618) 273-8017

• *MUDDY (62965)*

Days Inn, U.S. 45, Box 3.
(618) 252-6354
81 rooms. $39–$51
Discounts: AARP, seniors, corporate,
    group.
Facilities: Meeting/convention services,
    dining, lounge (nearby), entertainment,
    swimming (outdoor), laundromat.
Rooms are not handicapped accessible.
Credit cards accepted: MD, VS, DS, DC

• *HARRISBURG (62946)*

Plaza Motel, 411 East Poplar on Illinois
    13.
(618) 253-7651
45 rooms. S–(1 person–standard room)
    –$27.12; S –(2 people–
standard room) –$33.02; S –(king room–1
    person) –$33.21;
S–(2 people-king room) –$39.15
Discounts: Frequent stay discount (10th
    night free), seniors (62 & up).
Facilities: Dining (nearby), laundromat
    (nearby), spa/sauna, pets accepted, fit-
    ness center.
Rooms are not handicapped accessible.
Credit cards accepted: MC, VS, AE, DS,
    DC

Uptown Motel, 605 E. Poplar.
(618) 253-7022
11 rooms. $22.31–$30.81
Discounts: Sr. citizens.
Rooms are not handicapped accessible.
Credit cards accepted: MC, VS, AE

White Lace Bed & Breakfast, 400 E.
    Church
(618) 252-7599
5 rooms. $45–$65
Facilities: Breakfast provided

ST. CLAIR COUNTY

• *BELLEVILLE (62220-62223)*

Belleville Motel, 931 S. Belt West
  (62220)
(618) 233-4551
14 rooms

Cinderella Motel, 1438 Centreville Ave.
  (62220)
(618) 233-7410
16 rooms. $25.50–$31.95
Facilities: pets accepted, dining & lounge
  nearby
No handicapped accessible rooms
Credit cards accepted: MC, VS, AE

EJ Motel, 8230 Highway 15
(618) 538-5181
Facilities: pets accepted, handicapped
  accessible rooms

Executive Inn Motel, 1234 Centreville
  Ave.
(618) 233-1234
S–$36.84; D–$44.26; $5 per additional
  person.
Discounts: AARP, military, corporate,
  government, groups.
Facilities: Meeting/convention services,
  dining, lounge, fitness center, swim-
  ming (indoor & outdoor), safe deposit
  box
Rooms are not handicapped accessible.
Credit cards accepted: MC, VS, AE, DS,
  DC, CB

Hyatt Lodge, 2120 W. Main St. (62223).
(618) 234-9400; 1-800-62-HYATT for
  reservations.
80 rooms. S –$38; D–$44 Suites–$42 and
  up; $6 per additional adult.
No discounts available.
Facilities: Meeting services (15-20
  people), dining (adjacent), lounge (adjacent), swimming (outdoor), safe deposit
  box, cable television, free HBO, video
  rental.
Handicapped accessible rooms (1).
Discounts: Seniors
Credit cards accepted: MC, VS, AE, DS,
  DC, CB

Imperial Inn, 600 E. Main (62221)
(618) 234-0177
42 rooms. $26–$50

Facilities: pets accepted, laundromat
Discounts: Seniors, military, AARP, AAA
Credit cards accepted: AE, DC, MC, VS

King's House, 700 N. 66th St
(618) 297-0584
64 rooms.
Facilities: meeting facilities

Pilgrim's Inn Motel, 9500 W. Illinois
  (618) 397-1162
78 rooms
Facilities: Dining, meeting/convention
Handicapped accessible rooms

Scott Lodge, RR 2 Belleville (62221)
(618) 744-1244
21 rooms,
Facilities: Pets

Shaw's Motel, 1019 S. 59th
234-0784

Sleepy Hollow Motel, 602 S. Belt West
  (62220).
(618) 233-8680
26 rooms. S–$25; D–$32 & up.
No discounts available.
Facilities: Dining (nearby), lounge
  (nearby).
Rooms are not handicapped accessible.
All major credit cards accepted.

Terrace Motel, 747 S. Belt West;
  Junction of Illinois 15 &158
(618) 234-1505; 1-800-301-1505 (234-
  1505)
12 rooms. $25–$35
Facilities: pets accepted, kitchenettes,
  laundromat
Credit cards accepted: MC, VS

Town House Motel, 400 S. Illinois
  (62220)
(618) 233-7881
55 rooms.
Facilities: Dining, meeting/convention,
  entertainment, spa/sauna fitness center,
  indoor pool

• *CAHOKIA (62206)*

Trails End Motel, 600 Water St.
(618) 337-2010
14 rooms. $24–$30
Rooms are not handicapped accessible

635

Credit card accepted: MC, VS

• CASEYVILLE (62232)

Caseyville Best Inns, 2423 Old Country Inn Rd.
(618) 397-3300 or 1-800-237-8466
84 rooms. $41.88-$49.88
Facilities: Outdoor pool, handicapped rooms
Discounts: Seniors, AAA
Credit cards accepted: MC, VS, AE, DS, DC, CB, DN

American Motel, 1-57 & Trucker Dr.
(618) 398-5010
50 rooms. $31.90–$85
Discounts: Senior citizen, corporate.
Facilities: Dining (nearby), lounge (nearby), swimming (outdoor), limousine service to facility.
Handicapped accessible rooms (two).
Credit cards accepted: MC, VS, AE, DS, DC, CB

• CENTREVILLE

Economy Inn, 7109 Old Missouri Rd., Illinois 157/13 & 163 Junction.
(618) 337-1337
20 rooms. $30–$35
Facilities: In- room radio
Discounts: Group rates, seniors
Credit cards accepted: MC,VS

• EAST ST. LOUIS ((62220-5)

Blackmon's Motel, 1301 Baugh Ave. (62205)
(618) 874-5337

Hillcrest Motel, 9th & Exchange (62201)
(618) 482-2949
20 rooms
Facilities: Meeting/convention

• FAIRMONT CITY (61841)

Indian Mound Motel, 4700 Collinsville Rd
(618) 271-9570
29 rooms. $20–$24
Facilities: Dining
Discounts: Senior
Rooms are not handicapped accessible

Credit cards accepted: MC, VS, AE, DC

Rainbo Court Motel, 5280 Collinsville Rd.
(618) 875-2000
35 rooms
Facilities: Pets accepted

US 40 Motel, 6016 Collinsville Rd.
(618) 874-4451
23 rooms

• FAIRVIEW HEIGHTS (62208)

Drury Inn, #12 Ludwig Drive.
(618) 398-8530
107 rooms. S–$46–$52
Discounts: AAA, AARP (senior citizen), government rates.
Facilities: Free "Quickstart Breakfast", meeting rooms, satellite television, swimming (outdoor), game room, health club passes available, safe deposit box.
Four handicapped accessible rooms.
Credit cards accepted: MC, VS, AE, DS, CB, DC

French Village Motel, 1344 N. 94th
(618) 397-7943
31 rooms

Ramada Inn, I-64 & Illinois 159
(618) 632-4747
160 rooms. $42–$59
Facilities: Dining, meeting rooms, entertainment, outdoor pool, lounge, laundromat
Handicapped accessible rooms
Discounts: Seniors, government, corporate
Credit cards accepted: MC, VS, AE, DS, CB, DC, DS.

Super 8 Motel, 2 Ludwig Dr.
(618) 398-8338 or 1-800-800-8000
81 rooms.
Facilities: Meeting rooms, pets accepted, dining (nearby)
Handicapped accessible rooms.
Discounts: Seniors
Credit cards accepted: MC, VS, AE, DS, DC/CB

Trailway Motel, 10039 Lincoln Trail.
(618) 397-5757

30 rooms. S–$22 –$28; D –$26 –$30; $5 add. person.
Discounts: Senior citizen (10%).
Rooms are not handicapped accessible.
Credit cards accepted: not specified

- *FREEBURG (62243)*

Gabriel Motel, 600 N. State St.
(618) 539-5588
20 rooms. $25 & up.
No discounts available.
Handicapped accessible rooms.
Credit cards accepted: MC, VS

- *O'FALLON (62269)*

Comfort Inn, 1100 S. Eastgate Dr., Exit 19B off I-64
(618) 624-6060
96 rooms. $42–$50 and up; $6 per additional person.
Discounts: AARP, AAA, military, corporate, family rates.
Facilities: Meeting services (up to 25 persons), dining (nearby), lounge (nearby), 10-person spa, swimming (outdoor), safe available, satelliteTV.
Handicapped accessible rooms.
Credit cards accepted: MC, VS, AE, DS, DC

UNION COUNTY

- *ANNA (62906)*

Anna Plaza Motel, Illinois 146.
(618) 833-5215(4232)
16 rooms. S–$18; D–$22
Discounts: Available for long stays.
Facilities: Dining (nearby), cable TV.
Rooms are not handicapped accessible.
Credit cards accepted: MC, VS, AE

- *COBDEN (62920)*

Black Diamond Ranch, Illinois 3; 6 miles S. Alto Pass on Illinois 127
(618) 833-7629
Six rooms. $33–$40
Facilities: pets

- **JONESBORO (62952)**

Lincoln Motel, 601 E. Broad.

(618) 833-2181
20 rooms. S (1)–$18.90; S (2)–$21; D–$28.
Rooms are not handicapped accessible.
Discounts: AARP, senior, commercial rate,military
Credit cards accepted: MC, VS, AE, DS

The Goddard Place Bed & Breakfast, RR 2, Box 445G
(618) 833-6256
Three rooms. $45
Credit cards accepted: Yes, inquire

Trail of Tears Sportsman's Club, RR 1, Old Cape Road.
(618) 833-8697
Rustic bunkrooms-sleep four people.
$15 per person nightly.
Discounts available.
Facilities: Kitchen, dining, lounge, hunting, fishing, outfitting & certified guide services, stables, trail rides, game dressing & storage, special hunts & field trials, sporting clay range, hay rides & cookouts, hunting & fishing licenses, riding/fishing/shooting lessons.
Credit cards accepted: MC, VS

WABASH COUNTY

- *MT. CARMEL (62863)*

Living Legacy Homestead, Box 146A, RR 2
(618) 298-2467
3 guest rooms. $35–$65
Credit cards accepted: MC, VS, AE

Manor Motel, 1816 N. Cherry
(618) 262-8131

The Poor Farm Bed & Breakfast, RR3, Box 31A
(618) 262-HOME
5 rooms. $35–$70

Shamrock Motel, 1303 N. Cherry Street.
(618) 262-4169
15 rooms. S–$29.75–$36
Rooms are not handicapped accessible.
Credit cards accepted: VS, MC.

Town & Country Motel, Illinois 1 South.
(618) 262-4171

S–$21; Q–$24; D–$28 + tax.
Facilities: Swimming (outdoor).
Credit cards are accepted.

Uptown Motel, 511 Market Street.
(618) 262-4146
S–$18; D–$20.; Twin–$22; Waterbed-$25
Credit cards are accepted.

WAYNE COUNTY

• *FAIRFIELD (62837)*

Crown Motel & Restaurant, Illinois 15
    W.
(618) 842-2695
30 rooms. $25
Facilities: Dining, pets accepted, handi-
    capped rooms

Fairfield Uptown Motel, 201 South First;
    Illinois 15 & U.S. 45
(618) 842-2191
35 rooms. S–$22; S (2 people)–$24;
    D–$26; 3 beds (3 people)–$40
    Discounts available.
Facilities: Meeting services, dining, bowl-
    ing alley (nearby), tennis courts
    (nearby), racquet club (nearby), small
    pets accepted, limousine service to
    facility available.
Some rooms are handicapped accessible.
Discounts: Seniors
Credit cards accepted: MC, VS, AE, DS,
    DC

WASHINGTON CO.

• *NASHVILLE (62263)*

Mill Creek Inn Bed & Breakfast, 560 N.
    Mill,. Illinois 127
(618) 327-8424 or 327-8718
2 rooms. S–$42-45; D–$52-$55
Facilities: Meeting services, limousine
    service to facility, breakfast included.
Rooms are not handicapped accessible.
Credit cards accepted: MC, VS

Nashville Motel, Illinois 15 & 127.
(618) 327-4472
12 rooms. S–$23; D–$28
Discounts: Senior citizen.
Facilities: Dining (nearby), entertainment
    (nearby), laundromat (nearby).

Handicapped accessible rooms.
Credit cards accepted: MC, VS, AE, DS

U.S. Inn, I-64 & Illinois 127, Exit 50
(618) 478-5341
52 rooms. $31.79-$40.59
Facilities: Meeting rooms, spa, pets
    accepted, handicapped rooms, jacuzzi,
    dining, non smoking rooms, free coffee
Credit cards accepted: inquire

• *OKAWVILLE (62271)*

**Original Mineral Springs Hotel &
    Bathhouse, Inc**. 506 Hanover St.
(618) 243-5458
50 rooms. $30-$75
Discounts: Tour agencies, senior,
    AARP,AAA, military, government.
Facilities: Meeting/convention services,
    dining, lounge, spa/sauna, swimming
    (indoor & outdoor), game room
Handicapped accessible rooms.
Credit cards accepted: MC, VS, AE, DC

Super 8 Motel, I-64 & 177, Exit 41.
(618) 243-6525
40 rooms.
Discounts: AARP, senior citizen, trucker,
    travel agent.
Facilities: Whirlpool tubs in suites, safe
    deposit box.
Handicapped accessible rooms.
Credit cards accepted: MC, VS, AE, DS,
    DC

WHITE COUNTY

• *CARMI (62821)*

Carmi Motel, 1008 W Main
(618) 382-4121,
30 rooms, $22-$25
Facilities: HBO, pets
Credit cards accepted: MC, VS, AE,
    DC/CB

Midwest Motel, 1707 Highway 14
    (Illinois 14) W.
(618) 382-2313
11 rooms. $30-$50
Rooms are not handicapped accessible
Credit cards accepted: MC, VS, AE, DS

• *ENFIELD (62835)*

Ecko Motel, RR 2, U.S. 45 & IL 14
(618) 963-2861
25 rooms. $20-$30
Rooms are not handicapped accessible
Credit cards accepted: MC, VS

• *GRAYVILLE (62844)*

Best Western Windsor Oaks Inn,
2200 S. Court St.
(618) 375-7930
60 rooms. S–$46.-$80; $5 per additional
   person.
Discounts: AARP, AAA, military, corporate, government, student, trucker,
   group & extended stay rates.
Facilities: Meeting/convention services,
   dining, lounge, swimming (indoor),
   laundry services, safe available, fishing
   and boating nearby.
Handicapped accessible rooms.
Credit cards accepted: MC, VS, AE, DS,
   DC

Founder's Mansion Inn, 119 N. Court
   Illinois 1 North near I-64
(618) 375-3291
Five rooms. $55-$75
Credit cards accepted: MC, VS

WILLIAMSON CO.

• *CARTERVILLE (62918)*

Pin Oak Motel, Illinois 13.
(618) 985-4834
20 rooms. S (1)–$23.75; S (2)–$25.90
No discounts available.
Facilities: Dining, lounge, swimming (out-
   door), laundromat.
Rooms are not handicapped accessible.
No credit cards accepted.

• *HERRIN (62948)*

Park Avenue Motel, 912 N. Park Ave.
(618) 942-3159
20 rooms. S (1)–$24; S (2)–$27; D–$29;
   $2 per additional person.
Rooms are not handicapped accessible.
Credit cards accepted: MC, VS

• *JOHNSTON CITY (62951)*

Farris Motel, Illinois 37 S.
(618) 983-8086
15 rooms. S–$20; D–$28
No discounts available.
Facilities: Dining (nearby).
No credit cards accepted:

Stone Motel, Illinois 37 N.
(618) 983-7121
11 rooms. S–$18 & up
Discounts: Senior citizen (5%).
Handicapped accessible rooms.
No credit cards accepted.

• *MARION (62959)*

Best Western Airport Inn, New Illinois
   13 W.
(618) 993-3222.
34 rooms. $37-$72
Facilities: Pets accepted,
Free continental breakfast, whirlpool
   available with room, outdoor pool
Discounts: AARP, AAA, government,
   military
Credit cards accepted: MC, VS, AE, DC,
   DS, Amoco Multi

Best Inns of America, New Illinois 13
   W.
(618) 997-9421 or 1-800-237-8466
104 Rooms. S–$33.88; D–$41.88 (2
   people); King–$44.88
Discounts: Senior citizen (10% over 55),
   VIP Club, AAA.
Facilities: Dining (nearby), swimming
   (outdoor).
Handicapped accessible rooms.
Credit cards accepted: MC, VS, AE, DC,
   DS, CB

Comfort Inn, 2600 W. Main.
(618) 993-6221 or 1-800-221-2222
122 Rooms. $40-$65
Discounts: AARP, corporate, senior citizen.
Facilities: Meeting/convention services,
   dining (nearby), swimming (outdoor),
   laundromat (nearby), safe deposit box,
   limousine service to facility.
Handicapped accessible rooms.
All major credit cards accepted.

Gray Plaza Motel, New Illinois 13 W.
(618) 993-2174
30 rooms. S–$25; D–$30 + tax
No discounts available.
Facilities: Pets accepted
Rooms are not handicapped accessible.
Credit cards accepted: All major

Holiday Inn, Holidome, New Illinois 13
W.
(618) 997-2326 or 1-800-648-4667
200 rooms. S–$58, D–$72
Discounts: Senior citizen (10%),AARP,
AAA, Amoco rate, government,
Priority Club, Great Rates.
Facilities: Meeting/convention services,
dining, lounge, entertainment, spa facil-
ities, swimming (indoor & outdoor),
laundromat, safe deposit box, airport
pick up service to facility, game room,
tennis courts.
Handicapped accessible rooms.
Credit cards accepted: MC, VS, AE, DS,
DC,CB, JCB.

Marion Courts Motel, 110 S. Court.
(618) 993-8131 or 8132
45 rooms. S (1)–$18; D(4)–$26; $3 per
additional person. Weekly rate $75
Discounts: None
Facilities: Dining (nearby)
Rooms are not handicapped accessible.
Credit cards accepted: MC, VS, AE, DS

Motel Marion & Restaurant, 2100 W.
Main.
(618) 993-2101
S–$22.50; D–$24.50
Discounts: None
Facilities: Cable television, swimming
(outdoor), restaurant (nearby), campground with water and electricity, dump
station.

Motel 6 (Regal 8 Inn), New Illinois 13
W. (618) 993-2631 or 1-800-851-8888
79 rooms. S (1)–$28 and up
Discounts: none specified
Facilities: Swimming (outdoor), play-

ground.
Some rooms are handicapped accessible.
Credit cards accepted: MC, VS, AE, DS,
DC

Red Lion Inn, New Illinois 13 East. of I-
57, exit 54a
(618) 997-1351
90 rooms. S–$21.50; D–$29.62
Discounts: Senior citizen, corporate.
Facilities: Meeting/convention services,
dining (nearby), lounge, entertainment,
swimming (outdoor), laundromat.
No handicapped accessible rooms.
Credit cards accepted: MC, VS, AE, DS,
DC, CB

Shoney's Inn, 1806 Bittle Place Rd.
(618) 997-7900 or 1-800-222-2222
115 rooms. $46-$63
Discounts: Seniors, corporate, state, federal
Facilities: Meeting/convention services,
dining, spa/sauna, fitness, swimming
(indoor & outdoor), free shuttle; taxi
service to Inn ($5).
Handicapped accessible rooms.
Credit cards accepted: MC, VS, AE, DS,
DC, DS

Super 8 Motel, New Illinois13 W..
(618) 993-5577 or 1-800-800-8000
63 rooms. $28.88-$35.88
Discounts: AAA, AARP, government,
corporate, member card
All major credit cards are accepted.

Toupal's Country Inn, RR (Lake of
Egypt & I-57)
(618) 995-2074
17 rooms. 36.99-$46.99
Facilities: Pets accepted, handicapped
rooms, near Lake of Egypt, parking for
boats and RVs.
Discounts: None
Credit cards Acceptable: VS, MC, DS

Uptown Motel, 110 W. College
(618) 993-6221

Appendix 1: *Tourism Councils, Tourism Information & Welcome Centers*

State of Illinois Tourism
Phone: 1-800-ABE-0121

Southern Illinois Tourism Council
Address: P.O. Box 40, Whittington, IL. 62897 (near Rend Lake)
Phone: (618) 629-2506

Carbondale Convention & Tourism Bureau
Phone: (618) 529-4451 or 1-800-526-1500

Collinsville Convention & Visitors Bureau
Phone: (618) 345-4999 or 1-800-289-2388

Greater Alton/Twin Rivers Convention & Visitor's Bureau
Phone: (618) 465-6677 or 1-800-258-6645

Mt. Vernon Convention & Visitor's Bureau
Phone: (618) 242-3151 or 1-800-252-5464

Southernmost Tourism Bureau
Address: P. O. Box 278, Ullin IL 62992 Exit 18 off I-57
Phone: (618) 845-3777 or 1-800-248-4373

Southwestern Illinois Tourism & Convention Bureau
Phone: (618) 654-3556 or 1-800-782-9587

Williamson County Tourism Bureau
Phone: (618) 997-3690 or 1-800-433-7399

Trail of Tears Welcome Center
Location: Union County I-57 (northbound), Anna, IL
Phone: (618) 833-3811

Rend Lake Welcome Center
Location: Franklin County, I-57 (Northbound), Whittington, IL
Phone: (618) 438-2310

Silver Lake Welcome Center
Location: Madison County, I-70 (Eastbound), Highland, IL
Phone: (618) 654-6220

Cumberland Rd. Welcome Center
Location: Clark County, I-70 (Westbound), Metropolis, IL
Phone: (217) 826-5822

Fort Massac Welcome Center
Location: Massac County, I-24 (Westbound), New Baden, IL
Phone: (618) 524-3466

Gateway Welcome Center
Location: St. Clair County, I-64 (Eastbound), New Baden, IL
Phone: (618) 566-2487

Index